Indian Drama in English

Some Perspectives

Indian Drama in English

Some Perspectives

Edited by

Abha Shukla Kaushik

ATLANTIC

PUBLISHERS & DISTRIBUTORS (P) LTD

Published by

ATLANTIC

PUBLISHERS & DISTRIBUTORS (P) LTD

7/22, Ansari Road, Darya Ganj,
New Delhi-110002
Phones : +91-11-40775252, 23273880, 23275880, 23280451
Fax : +91-11-23285873
Web : www.atlanticbooks.com
E-mail : orders@atlanticbooks.com

Branch Office
5, Nallathambi Street, Wallajah Road,
Chennai-600002
Phones : +91-44-64611085, 32413319
E-mail : chennai@atlanticbooks.com

ISBN 978-81-269-1772-3

Printed in India at Nice Printing Press, A-33/3A, Site-IV,
Industrial Area, Sahibabad, Ghaziabad, U.P.

Preface

Drama in India is as old as its customs, starting right from the Vedic era. The distinct style of Indian dramaturgy evolved as an illustration of the rich mores of Indian traditions, rituals, customs and ethnicity from Bharat Muni's *Natya Shastra* which is also known as the fifth veda. It is said to have taken recitation from Rig Veda, imitation from Yajur Veda, melody from Sama Veda, and aesthetics from Atharva Veda as a means to subtly communicate significant experiences. With the passage of time, Indian drama moved from being narratives of heroes who were either royal or celestial, to being realistic representation of Indian society. Drama flourished in ancient India but with the decline of Sanskrit language it slipped into oblivion. However, the folk tradition continued unhampered in its various regional forms for a long time and kept the dramatic tradition alive.

After the British came to India, a new awakening came over and the modern theatre was established by the British for their entertainment. Watching and reading the plays of western dramatists such as Shakespeare and Ibsen inspired the Indian writers to revive the Indian theatre and the dormant impulse of drama got strengthened once again.

In the pre-Independence era, playwrights like Rabindranath Tagore, Sri Aurobindo and Harindranath Chattopadhyaya contributed significantly to the growth of Indian English drama. The works of these three dramatists are notable for poetical excellence, thematic variety, symbolism and morality. With time, the nature of English drama changed once again, from being a depiction of the European lifestyle, to showcasing Indian culture and traditions and propagating ideas of freedom, and after Independence to being a broader representation of the social political and economic life of the country. In the meanwhile, drama in regional languages also started to emerge as an important genre. Writers like Dharamvir Bharati, Badal Sircar, Mohan Rakesh, Vijay Tendulkar and Girish Karnad began to experiment and use remarkable innovations in themes, treatment and technique. Eminent theatre personalities like Habib Tanvir, Girish Karnad, Vijay Tendulkar, Mahesh Dattani, Manjula Padmanabhan and many others are responsible for the movement of English drama in India towards maturity, making it stand apart as a distinct art form which is both serious and dignified. English drama which began in India in the era of British imperialism as an illustration of British mistreatment has now flowered into a showcase of the rich Indian tradition, folklore, customs, rituals, conventions and rites alongside the innovativeness of English drama.

Drama today has emerged as a powerful resurgent medium to project the problematic of the social, cultural, political, traditional and historical changes that the Indian society faces besides the issues related to gender, class, caste and communities.

Present anthology contains twenty-seven scholarly papers looking at Indian English drama from a variety of critical positions providing useful insights. Girish Karnad is an eminent dramatist who writes in both Kannada and English. He employs the devices of myth, folklore and history in order to create a new consciousness about the absurdities of human life and conflicts. His plays are rooted in the cultural and political situations of the present times. He uses myth, folklore and history deftly to raise very contemporary questions. There are a number of papers on Karnad in this collection. The paper by Shobha Diwakar explores how myth and folklore have been used by Karnad to convey the mechanisms of human nature. G.A. Ghanshyam's paper discusses how the mores of cultural ethos that represent the underlying values and principles of life have been delineated by Karnad in his plays. Shivaji Shankar Kamble has provided a close study of new morality in Karnad's famous play *Tughlaq*, while Nidhi Mehta studies the representation of deceit, atrocities and politics in the same play. The paper by Krishna Singh traces the evolution of themes in

Karnad's plays. Dramatic technique has come to occupy an important place in critical discussions. The paper by Shahewar Syed and AparaTiwari attempts to study how the traditional and the contemporary have been blended by Karnad in *Naga-Mandala*. My own paper is about the need to rewrite history in the postcolonial context so as to restore the unsung heroes of the past to their rightful places with reference to Karnad's *The Dreams of Tipu Sultan*.

Vijay Tendulkar has changed the form and pattern of Indian drama by developing flexible, carefully crafted form demolishing the constraints imposed by the three-act play format. His plays raise pertinent questions about love, sex, marriage and moral values exposing the hollowness of social value system. T.R. Muralikrishnan's paper on Tendulkar's play *Silence! The Court is in Session* exposes the double standards of the society when dealing with issues related to women. R. Manjushree and Ashok Saini have discussed the themes of Tendulkar's plays in their papers. The paper by Shukla Chatterjee and Sukla Basu offers a peep into a lesser known play by Tendulkar *A Friend's Story*.

In recent years, Indian English drama has found a new life in the works of Mahesh Dattani who has brought the apparently ugly, mean and unhappy facets of life to the forefront. His plays address the comparatively unexplored, contemporary issues like the expression and repression of human sexuality, alternate sexual preferences, socially unacceptable or questionable attitudes and codes and their consequences for the individual. Quite a few papers in this anthology are devoted to analysing his plays from different perspectives. Saptarshi Mallick and Dibyabibha Roy have studied the concepts of patriarchy and deviance and the hypocrisy surrounding the institutions of family and marriage in Dattani's plays. T. Sasikanth Reddy has analysed two of Dattani's plays *Tara* and *Seven Steps Around the Fire* from the feminist perspective. Abin Chakraborty has studied the play *Final Solutions* as being testimony to the possibility of a new India beyond the binaries of communal conflicts. Alpana Saini has compared Satish Alekar's *The Terrorist* and Dattani's *Brief Candle* against a similar background. Vivekanand Jha, Sanchita Das and Raichel M.

Sylus have studied various aspects of the very popular and famous play *Tara* by Dattani in their respective papers. N. Ankanna's scholorly paper discusses Dattani's technique in *Dance Like a Man.*

Besides these, this anthology also includes papers on writers like Rabindranath Tagore, Habib Tanvir, Gurcharan Das, Satish Vyas, and Badal Sircar who are stalwarts of Indian English drama in their own right. Tagore's *Chitra* has been analysed by Usha Kishore whereas R.T. Bedre and K.U. Gangarde attempt to assess Tanvir's *The Living Tale of Hirma*. Basavraj Naikar's paper provides a close analysis of Gurcharan Das's *Larins Sahib* which deals with the colonial encounter between the native Indians and the Imperial British. Indira Nrityanandam's article throws light on Satish Vyas's *Trilogy of Two Act Plays*, and Nirban Manna has studied Badal Sircar's *That Other History* as an existential text. Pinaki Roy has traced a brief history of Indian drama in his paper.

I would like to take this opportunity to thank all the contributors for their well-researched papers which have enriched this anthology. My sincere thanks to Atlantic Publishers and Distributors (P) Limited for bringing out the book. The collection will certainly prove to be useful to students, research scholars, teachers and others with interest in English Literature, especially drama.

Abha Shukla Kaushik

Contents

Contributors

Shobha Diwakar, Retd. Head Dept. of English, C.P. Mahila Mahavidyalaya, Jabalpur, Madhya Pradesh.

Usha Kishore, an internationally published writer, poet, critic and translator, Isle of Man, UK.

G.A. Ghanshyam, Professor of English, Govt. M.L. Shukla College, Seepat, Bilaspur, Chhattisgarh.

Shivaji Shankar Kamble, Associate Professor of English, Padmabhushan Vasantraodala Patil Mahvidyalaya, Kavathe Mahankal, Dist Sangli, Maharashtra.

Indira Nityanandam, Smt. S.R. Mehta Arts College, Ahmedabad, Gujarat.

Abha Shukla Kaushik, Associate Professor of English, AKPG College, Hapur, Panchsheel Nagar, Uttar Pradesh.

R.T. Bedre, Assistant Professor of English, ACS College, Gangkahed, Maharashtra.

K.U. Gangarde, Project Fellow, ACS College, Gangkahed, Madhya Pradesh.

Basavaraj Naikar, Professor of English, Karnataka University, Dharwad, Karnataka.

Saptarshi Mallick, Dept. of English, University of Calcutta, Kolkata, West Bengal.

Dibyabibha Roy, Dept. of English, University of Calcutta, Kolkata, West Bengal.

Vivekanand Jha, Poet, Editor, Translator and Research Scholar, L.N. Mithila University, Darbhanga, Bihar.

Raichel M. Sylus, Asst. Professor (SS), Dept. of English, Avinashilingam University for Women, Coimbatore, Tamil Nadu.

Saurabh Mishra, Asst. Professor of English, Rajiv Gandhi Institute of Petroleum Technology, Rae Bareli, Uttar Pradesh.

T. Sasikanth Reddy, Academic Consultant in English, YSR Engineering College of Yogi Vemana University, Proddatur Town, YSR Dist., Andhra Pradesh.

Krishna Singh, Assistant Professor of English, Govt. College, Shahdol, Madhya Pradesh.

Abin Chakraborty, Guest Lecturer, Presidency College, Kolkata, West Bengal.

T.R. Muralikrishnan, Dept. of English, MES College Marampally, Aluva, Kerala

Nirban Manna, Research Scholar, Dept. of English, Banaras Hindu University, Varanasi, Uttar Pradesh.

N. Ankanna, Asst. Professor of English, Yogi Vemana University, Kadapa, YSR Dist., Andhra Pradesh.

Shukla Chatterjee, Lecturer of Communicative English, Dr. B.C. Roy College of Pharmacy and AHS, Durgapur, West Bengal.

Sukla Basu (Sen), Professor of English, Dept. of English and Other Modern European Languages, Visva Bharati, Kolkata, West Bengal.

Alpna Saini, Assistant Professor, Centre for Comparative Literature, Central University of Punjab, Bathinda, Punjab.

Pinaki Roy, Assistant Professor of English, Malda College, Malda, West Bengal.

Sanchita Das, Lecturer in English, Surya Sen Mahavidyalaya, Siliguri, West Bengal.

Ashok K. Saini, Faculty, Dept. of English Language, State Council of Educational Research & Training, Narendranagar, Tehri Garhwal, Uttarakhand.

Shahewar Syed, Assistant Professor of English, Hawabagh Women's College, Jabalpur, Madhya Pradesh.

Apara Tiwari, Professor of English, Government College, Sihora, Jabalpur, Madhya Pradesh.

R. Manjushree, Assistant Professor of English, Alva's College, Moodbidri, Dakshina Kannada, Karnataka.

Lipipuspa Nayak, Lecturer of English, Senior Academic Translator and Critic of Indian Language Literature, Bhubneswar, Orissa.

1 Flowering Tributary of Indian English Drama Girish Karnad: A Study of *Naga-Mandala*

Shobha Diwakar

> The art of the pen is to rouse the inward vision, instead of laboring with a drop-scene brush as if it were to the eye because our flying minds cannot contain a protracted description.
>
> —*Meredith*

Drama or the performing art appeals to the eye because it has the power to create an image, which insulates the mind and interconnects it with the body to help visualize the multiple characters portrayed in all their complexities and collective reactions upon the stage. This participating activity stimulates the reader's own reactions in such a manner that the co-existing cultural frame into which the characters are cast condition her/his thinking. Essentially speaking drama or 'natak' is not new to India as it already existed in the form of folk or 'Jatara', however, the drama in the real sense was closely associated with the Brahamanic idealistic view, which restricted its growth. Encompassed within the strings of religion, castes and orthodoxy, the characters were strung up as puppets and individuality was denied. Stereotyped and inelegant, Indian drama greatly differed from the Greek drama, which the Athenians seriously enjoyed and on which Aristotle modeled his *Poetics*.

It is believed by critics like Horrwitz that Hindu drama originated out of the 'Divine Thought' from which 'sprang the Natya Veda', that is, the Veda of the Theatre—out of the four Vedas—dance from the Rig, song from the Sama, mimicry from Yajur and passion from Atharva. Brahma commanded the celestial architect, Vishvakarma to build a stage in Indra's heaven while Bharatmuni 'was appointed Theatrical manager' and conductor of the heavenly performances' (http:// www.theatre) history.com/asian/horrwitz02.html). This is considered to be the first ideal of the beginnings of early drama in India, which later flowered into the Sanskrit drama and commenced with the writings of Asvaghosa, followed by Bhasa, Bhavabhuti, later on by Kalidasa's works produced around the fifth century. Indian English drama developed between the years 1901-47 in the hands of Madhusudan Dutta, Sri Aurobindo, T.P. Kailasaram, Vasudeva Rao, Rabindra Nath Tagore, besides, a host of others. After post-independence, between the years 1947-2005, other playwrights like Pratap Sharma, Asif Currimbhoy, Guru Charan Das, Shiva K. Kumar, Girish Karnad, Vijay Tendulkar and Mahesh Dattani, to name a few, rose like meteors in the sky with their versatile writings. These playwrights have explored every dramatic machinery to draw upon historical, mythical sources; from folktales to puranic characters to the current depressive, incongruous happenings of the modern and the post-modern world caught in the throes of social, religious and cultural conflicts, intellectual awareness and political upheavals even as the neglected woman of yesterday, today and tomorrow awaits redemption and resurrection from socio-cultural traumas. Karnad's *Naga-Mandala* portrays the picture of the emerging New Assertive woman armed with an independent mind of her own (like Nora, in *The Doll's House*). The social realism depicted in the play is packed with emotional intensity and charm.

Karnad's use of a folktale in the play highlights the futile gesture of man to throttle the inherent desires and urges of the human body to defeat the power of regeneration and to use the wedded wife as chattel. In his whim to dominate man forgets that even God fulfils the desire of the earth and helps to fertilize it with rain and shower, failing which the earth cracks open and restrains production. Rani, the initially feeble minded woman, a captive in her own house, lives a solitary life till the arrival of Kurudavva who gives her the roots to conquer her love but, which is consumed by the Naga who falls in love with her and teaches her the meaning of conjugal love. In this way the Naga becomes what Dewey says is the "connecting link between artist and audience", and which, is related to the "Qualities of sense...(and) has esthetic quality" (107 and 120). Besides, "Hinduism also recognizes the romance of married love" as Mookerji observes, and "does not believe in individuality... that spiritually and socially husband and wife are incomplete, each without the other..." (131). However, in *Naga-Mandala*, Appanna the man discards all these beliefs, tortures his lawfully wedded wife and enjoys the company of his concubine. It is on this theme that Karnad focuses his attention and rescues Rani from a loveless marriage through the goodness of Kurudavva and the entry of the Naga.

The action of the play begins in Act II with the wooing of Rani, which is clothed in the rich and sensuous imagery of Shringara Rasa or erotic love and Shringar Viyoga. The last few lines of Act I set the plot in motion and the reader is made aware of the fact that something strange is about to happen. This message is conveyed by story: "As you know, a cobra can assume any form it likes. That night, it entered the house through the bathroom drain and took the shape of—(the Cobra takes the shape of Appanna) (*NM*, 18). The tenderness with which the Naga addresses Rani takes her by surprise and the dramatic manner in which it coaxes and caresses Rani, casts a spell of thrill in the otherwise dull and miserable life of the lovelorn girl so ruthlessly chucked aside by her own husband in favour of his concubine. Rani's womanliness, her innocence, her coyness, her fright, her resistance and occasional doubt as to the Naga's identity (when she beholds its image in the mirror), are mists and shadows through which she emerges as the evolutionary agent and though there is conflict and fear, her actions remain decisive.

This young and pretty heroine of the play, trapped into a hopeless marriage is gradually enamoured and does away with her initial resistance even as the Naga visits her every night and indulges in sexual love. Nevertheless, the mornings are a real trial in her life as the real Appanna threatens her with vile words. The irony of this is revealed when Rani says: "You talk so nicely at night. But during the day I only have to open my mouth and you hiss like a...stupid snake" (Act II, 22). The wooing, none the less, continues till Rani becomes pregnant, hearing which the Naga advises her to keep it a secret, and from here the story again undergoes a change as Appanna loses temper and beats her for having found a lover calls her a 'harlot' and a 'slut' (Act II, 33). Rani is nonplussed as she remains innocently unaware of the Naga's presence in her life, even as she is overcome by maternal instincts and is somewhat bewildered by the accusation.

The play highlights the need for love, the fulfillment of sexual desires amidst the endless trials, which a woman has to endure and through which she has to emerge before she attains victory over her male counterpart. Karnad's social awareness of these problems that exist in society is commendable as it is a protest against male hegemony. Woman is not a bird to be caged with her wings clipped off; she is life, pulsating with sentiments, thoughts and feelings. If she is neglected and dishonored, the family suffers as is written in the Hindu scriptures because she is regarded as Devi and is worshipped as such, yet this makes no difference to Appanna. Kurudavva is the ray of hope and Naga, the Life-Force, taut and intense in his purpose to propagate and fulfill the demands of the flesh denied by the husband. Mookerji writes, "...the cosmic process is itself conceived as the union of the Divine Prakriti (Nature) with Divine Purusha (Spirit), in man this union is attained in the mystery of conjugal love [which] becomes the social sacrament (131). Zimmer says "Life-Force is expressed in terms of massiveness and bulk, with a thoroughly respectable realism..." (57). Since Rani is denied this bliss, the need is fulfilled by the Naga, assuming the form of Appanna, even as she is compelled to live isolated from human company by her jealous and villainous husband; locked up in her marital house. The entry of the Naga thus creates an invigorating dramatic effect and becomes the agent of social protest, sinister though it sounds. Yet, snakes do have the power to change into human form and is considered to be Shiva's garland, It is believed "The Naga is Shiva's garland, and has the power to assume human form and deceive wives in the guise of their husbands" (qtd. in Diwakar, 77). This stabbing reality forces the reader to sit up and think about the goodness of human life with courage and perseverance rather than to turn back like a coward. Keeping this innate goodness of human nature in mind, Karnad redeems Rani while he relentlessly thwarts and defeats her petty husband.

It is interesting to note that while Karnad confers the name of Rani, which means a Queen to the woman character he does not give the man any name but calls him Appanna, which means any man. The words are written in capitals to convey the significance of this reality to the reader. As per her name, Rani finally rules the house but the man is given no identity. The purpose behind this denial is to reveal the basic animal nature inherent in man, his vindictive attitude and his meanness for which he is rightly punished in the end along with his concubine and condemned to live as Rani's slaves. Since beggars cannot be choosers, they happily accept their fate just as the Naga had promised Rani. "Naga: ...Don't worry. Your husband will become your slave tomorrow. You will get all you have ever wanted" (Act II, 35). The words of the Naga hail as prophecy. Rani lives like a Queen while Karnad crushes the man and the woman for their vanity, lust and their passionate pride. It is believed "Nagas are genii superior to man", as Zimmer writes and since they are also "door guardian" (dvarapala) (63), the Naga protects Rani. While writing these subtle truths of life Karnad exposes the duality of human nature and through the Naga seeks to assert that "Shiva, [is] the force supreme of the universe", the "creator and destroyer of the universe" (129).

Karnad handles this myth of Shiva/Naga in a highly artistic manner and a style distinguished for its simplicity, lucidity and its texture. Symbols like 'stone image' 'tender bud' (*NM*, 19 and 22), are enchanting figures of speech while sentences such as "Frogs croaking in pelting rain", "When the flame of forest blossoms into a fountain of red..." (*NM*, 25), and the farcical manner in which the Naga impersonates Appanna, are all dealt with in a style, which is simple yet, which highlights the eroticism of the scene. This is shown when Rani says, "I didn't know you were such a bad man.... Had I known, I would never have agreed to marry you. What will Father and Mother say if they come to know?" (*NM*, 25). The lines reveal Rani's girlish innocence, which has been conveyed brilliantly by the dramatist in a simple language; a language that tells how ignorant Rani really is. This gulling therefore produces a cathartic effect upon the reader and eases the tension built up in the previous act. The dialogues reverberate with social criticism while Rani's sentiments are clothed in virgin sentimentality. The rich imagery unveiled in Act II transcends the powers of creativity, even as Rani and the Naga unite in love. It is later when she becomes pregnant and the village folks put her on trial on her husband's plea that reality dawns upon her about the Naga's ministrations in her life. After protecting Rani from the fury of the villagers and her husband it is ultimately the Naga who finally withdraws from the human world so his beloved can live happily with her husband and her child...with the tiny snake (later) buried in her hair as a mark of her 'wedded bliss' (*NM*, 45). Karnad portrays Kurudavva as fate and the Naga as a human entity both of whom redeem Rani from Appanna, who lives in self-deception.

In depicting the character of Appanna, a ruthless man, Karnad voices the view about "the law of Karma", which states that "each individual will get the return according to the energy he puts forth" (Radhakrishnan, 219). Hence, Appanna pays for his Karma. In *Naga-Mandala*, it is the purpose of the dramatist to bring home these simple moral truths and stimulate the reader's thought process. However, Karnad does not preach. It is left for the reader to decipher the truth. Karnad is a creative artist whose aim is to bring about a social awareness through his art and expose the hollowness of ancient, rigid and obsolete incongruous ideas imposed on women, under the shadow of religious impositions deeply imbedded in the male psyche. Aroosha Rana states "when talking about art for social change, one must look deeper at the roots of the artist's human experience and the breadth of the artist's intention to create a conscious action to the art work". It is obvious that "tangible human experiences, an artist's surroundings, his thoughts and his emotions, all influence his work" (1). Karnad's penetrating eyes look deep into these social issues and presents before the reader the character of Rani, which acts as an enzyme on the mind of the reader. It is in this context that an artist's vision is enlarged and helps to stimulate the reasoning faculties of the reader. The deplorable human condition of women like Rani who are oppressed and ill-treated, seek redress through the artistic vision of dramatists like Karnad who have unbiased power to peep deeply into these tyrannical offences committed by man in the name of religious taboos and male hegemony inherited through patriarchy. It is through the intervention of the Naga that Karnad seeks to illustrate this reality and the futility of such an outlook. The symbol of the Naga is an ironical satire on society and its obsolete traditions in which the cultural mould is cast.

Contextually, it may be said that Karnad comes close to Arthur Adamov in presenting the "strictures imposed on the individual by society", as Wellworth writes (27). Like Adamov, Karnad artistically raises his voice to shell out the falseness of such constrictions. With a flow of rhythmic movement experienced by the reader in Act II with the arrival of the Naga in human form, the dramatist captures the attention of the reader and excites her/him with the suspense that is gradually unfolded in soft overtones of eroticism. This mysterious wooing matches the emotional maturity of Rani who till then had been asleep in the pursuit of her drudgery. The conjugal happiness of married life that exists in the male and the female is gently revealed as the essence of human existence. It is this reality that Karnad focuses his attention upon and makes the reader aware of the loss which Rani has suffered from. By transforming the Naga into a human being, Karnad brings harmony into Rani's life; nevertheless, the Naga's basic nature remains that of a serpent who fights against all odds and obstacles that come between him and Rani. So he fights against the dog and the mongoose (Act II, 29), and finally conquers Rani's love after her initial coy resistance. Loaded with beautiful and picturesque imagery, the poetic beauty and the emotional strength of Act II, gives expression to the reader's own deep felt verdict. This conforms to Dewey's view that "The emotion of the author and that aroused in us are occasioned by scenes in the world and they blend with the subject matter...." Because, "We are reconciled to the conclusion...we feel it is inherent in the movement of the subject matter portrayed" (68). The entry of the Naga, thus imparts form, variety and rhythm to the movement of the plot and theme of the play until its sad exit, ultimately lifting the veil off Rani's delusion but leaving Appanna with many unanswered questions.

Through *Naga-Mandala*, Karnad expresses Dewey's view that "Morals are assigned a special compartment in theory and practice.... Wherever social divisions exist, practices and ideas that correspond to them fix metes and bounds, so that liberal action is placed under restraint...." "What is true of the individual is true of the whole system of morals in thought and action" (348-49). Karnad subtly highlights these issues in the play and also conforms to what Bharat states in his *Natya Shastra*: "Drama becomes instructive to all through the action that it images and through the sentiments arising out of them" (qtd. in Kantak, 69). Thus, *Naga-Mandala* penetrates deeply into the evils that are rampant in society in some form or the other against the fair sex and the dilemma in which she is placed. In the words of Sandra Schneiders "...women have become aware of their inferior status and actual oppression in family, society, and Church, they have also become aware that the gender of God, God's assumed masculinity, has functioned as the ultimate religious legitimation of the unjust social structures which victimize women" (5). She further writes "Marital fidelity was never absolutely required of men whereas a woman's infidelity was considered an offence against her husband's property rights.... A husband who had been betrayed by his wife would at least have divorced her if he had not had her executed. A wife who had been betrayed would be expected, nevertheless, to be faithful and loving" (33). Whether it is in India or anywhere else in the world, these statements assert the inferior position in which society places women (down the ladder), in the name of religion.

Feminists like Simone de Beauvoir also write "...marriage normally subordinates wife to husband.... The paradox of marriage lies in the fact that it has at once an erotic and a social function: .... He is a demigod endued with virile prestige and destined to replace her father: protector, provider, teacher, guide; the wife's existence is to unfold in his shadow; he is the custodian of values, the sponsor of truth, the ethical vindication of the couple" (480). These views also condition the mind of the Indian male; in fact, the entire male community of the whole world. Beauvoir is not wrong when she writes "Marriage incites man to a capricious imperialism: the temptation to dominate is the most truly universal, the most irresistible one there is; to surrender the child to the mother, the wife to the husband, is to promote tyranny in the world" (483). A close reading of *Naga-Mandala* clearly throws light on the truth of what Beauvoir states. Not only this, she also asserts how a husband issues commands and 'plays the lord and master' and the 'commands' he issues are in tones of severity 'He not only shouts but also this farce (becomes) a daily reality for his wife'. Whenever the wife tries to show a sign of independence he considers her as a 'rebellion' (484). Appanna's attitude towards Rani is well described in this statement. In Act I there are many incidents when Rani is ordered, slapped, pushed aside and thrown on the floor. For example, when she goes out of the house and pours the curry into the ant hill and enters the house Appanna yells authoritatively: "Rani, where have you been?" When he does not receive an answer he yells back, "I said, where have you been? Rani, answer me!" Since Rani does not reply he lets her enter the house. But the moment she steps in he slaps her hard so that 'she collapses on the floor'. Even as Rani lies fallen Appanna locks the door from outside and walks out with 'Just cold contempt' (*NM*, 17). Karnad makes it very obvious that men treat women as the dirt of their feet and not only disrespect her but also use her abusively to satisfy their whim and sadistic animalism inherent in their nature. The right to control and dominate is age old and Schneider says it is related to "Patriarchy a social system based on the *patria potestas,* i.e. the absolute and unaccountable power over wives and concubines.... In classical Greek and Roman societies this authority of ownership extended even to the power of life and death. Children, especially girls, were often deemed valueless to the father and left to die..." (11). Karnad's artistic vision brings home these truths in *Naga-Mandala*.

Anyone who looks deeply into this world wide problem and makes an effort to understand the reason will realize that besides being ingrained in religious texts and the social foundation of patriarchy, this view is instilled in the minds of the growing boy child that he is superior to the female and is treated as such. This system has its roots on the sexual power of the male to create. The Indian legends claim Shiva to be the creator and the destroyer and worship him in the form of 'lingam' or the phallus, which represents the male sex organ. Zimmer writes that it is believed that Shiva gave origin to Brahma and Vishnu from the 'lingam'. "Thus Shiva appears augmented in the lingam... as the all-comprising, basic element" (129-30). This power of creating life exerts authority in all forms of family life which makes the woman 'powerless' and dependant upon the male. Schneider also believes patriarchy to be the cause of "racism, ageism, classism, colonialism, and clericalism as well as of sexism" (12 and 13).

Contextually, the Hindu Dharma Shastras regard the "wedded woman", says Prabhu, to be "the source of Dharma, Artha and Kama;...and also the source of Moksha". He quotes "No man even when he is in a temper should ever do anything that is disagreeable to his wife. For happiness, joy, virtue—all depend upon the wife." In the same context Prabhu quotes the scriptures and writes that since the husband's authority over his wife remains unchallenged "he must not consider this in isolation and must never get cross with her even though she may happen to do so" (227). Even a casual reading of the play reveals that Appanna does not fulfill any of these demands towards his wife as is stated in the *Griha Sutras*, according to which the 'pati' or 'bhartri', must always protect his wife (Prabhu, 227). Karnad draws the character of Appanna as an inhuman being, an animal in human existence who not only lacks 'samskaras', which are a part of 'Varna Dharma', but also does not abide by the laws of 'Saptapadi, or the holy fire around which the husband and wife go around seven times. Perhaps

Appanna rejects these demands because "Manu and other Smritis demand the wife to remain faithful to the husband not only till he is alive but even after his death" and that he must be "worshipped as a deity even though he happens to be a man of bad character and has no good quality in him" (qtd. in Prabhu, 231). In this way whether it is Manu, Vyas, Vatsayana, the *Mahabharat* or the *Ramayana* or any other scripture, all lay emphasis on the authority of the man and the dedication and submissiveness of the woman. Prabhu quotes from the *Ramayana* "Women who love their husbands—whether he treats them well or ill...attain high status; and the husband, whether wicked or lustful, is highest God to the wife of good morals" (234).

The foregoing statements centre round the Hindu conception of the duties assigned to a wife and her responsibilities, however, it willfully ignores the foulness of man and portrays him to be a God or 'pati parmeshwar', as the husband is generally addressed as. When Karnad peers deeply into these false social ideals and seriously contemplates upon the vices and virtues religiously prescribed for a woman, his conscience stifles him and so he weaves the character of a badly used woman, Rani and helps her to redeem herself from the prison in which she is caged and in this way breaks down the barriers and the web of social and religious taboos and liberates her so she too can enjoy her individuality and free herself from these self-proclaimed customary evils. By liberating Rani, Karnad not only supports feminists but also agrees with what Varahmira, the ancient astronomer wrote in favour of women. Prabhu quotes "...Women have been driven into misdeeds by men shamelessly, ...but women are superior in virtues" (275). By raising Rani to the pedestal of a Devi, Karnad endorses the view. Although Manu lays stress on the superiority of the male he also states that men owe their existence to women hence they should not slander them because they will never gain happiness by doing so. He goes a little further and says 'if a faithless man seeks to be purified of his sin' he has to 'wear the donkey's skin with the hair outside' and 'beg alms for six months' and announce "I have been faithless to my wife; please give me alms" (276).

Unfortunately Appanna is not made to wear the 'donkey's skin' and 'beg alms' but is punished to be a slave to his wife forever along with his concubine.

As one of India's foremost Indian English Dramatists in whose hands the concept of modern drama has grown and matured Karnad remains unparallel. The cool manner in which he delves into this cultural and social pattern of conflicting values and the manner in which he exposes the hollowness of such ideals makes him a great contemporary artist. His postmodern ideas related towards the emancipation of women are indeed wholesome and though Indian society has not completely broken out of its cultural mould or lost its religious identity, new concepts of behaviour and emerging relationships between the sexes have definitely ushered a sense of freedom in the modern woman. The Indian outlook on marriage and morals are undergoing fundamental changes and with globalization, values and precepts have also changed drastically. The decay set in society in the name of religion and false beliefs needs to be dealt with stringent laws. Also much can be achieved through education and social upliftment, which will bring enlightenment. The feeling of inferiority ingrained in a woman since childhood must be curbed. Radhakrishnan calls man 'a pathological creature' who is 'capable of sublime goodness and intense evil...and of ruthlessness which inflicts pain' Man is aware of evil but he enjoys to indulge in it and so practices it (151). In *Naga-Mandala*, Karnad, the master craftsman, sympathetically views the situation and imparts to it a symbolic significance by exploring the potentials of Indian folktales and myths in drama, the visual art, to convey the mechanisms of human nature and the fact that man and woman are interdependent and that the whole universe is conceived because of the union of *Purusha* and *Prakriti*. The myth of the Naga justifies this truth.

WORKS CITED

Beauvoir, Simone de. "The Married Woman", *The Second Sex*, Trans. & Ed. A.M. Parshley, Great Britain: Penguin Books, Rep. 1975.

Dewey, John. "Substance and Form", *Art as Experience*. New York: Capricorn Books, 1958.

——. "The Act of Expression", Capricorn Books, 1958.

——. "Art and Civilization", Capricorn Books, 1958.

Diwakar, Shobha. "Rani and the Rhythm of Life", *Indian Drama in English: A Kaleidoscopic View*. Ed. P. Gopichand and P. Nagasuseela. New Delhi: Sarup Book Publ. Pvt. Ltd., 2010.

Horrwitz, E.P. "The Origin of the Hindu Drama", *The Indian Theatre: A Brief History of Sanskrit Drama*. London: Blackie & Son Ltd., 1912.

Kantak, V.Y. "Bharat and the Western Concept of Dharma", *Indian Poetics and Western Thought*. Ed. M.S. Kushwaha, Lucknow: Argo Publishing House, 1998.

Karnad, Girish. *Naga-Mandala Play with a Cobra*. New York: OUP, 1990. All textual quotations are from this edition.

Meredith, George. "Appeals to the Imagination" qtd. Worsfold W. Basil, *Judgment in Literature*. London: J.M. Dent & Sons Ltd., 1951.

Mookerji, Kumud Radha. "Outline of Indian Thought", *Glimpses of Ancient India*, Gen Eds. K.M. Munshi and R.R. Diwakar, Bombay: Bhartiya Vidya Bhavan, 1961.

Prabhu, Nath Pandri. "The Family", *The Hindu Social Organization: A Study in Socio Psychological and Ideological Foundations*. Bombay: Popular Prakashan Pvt. Ltd., 1995.

Radhakrishnan. "Human Personality and its Destiny", *An Idealistic View of Life*. London: Unwin Books, 1967.

Rana, Aroosha. "What is Art for Social Change?", *Art for Social Change: Exploring Trends in the Spectrum*. American Center Bulletin: Mumbai, June 2006.

Schneider, Sandra M. "The Dilemma for Women", *Women and the World*. New York: Paulist Press, 1986.

Wellwarth, George. "Arthur Adamov The Way Out of the Void", *The Theatre of Protest and Paradox: Development in the Avant-Garde Drama*. New York: University Press, 1975.

Zimmer, Heinrich. "Maya in Indian Art", *Myths and Symbols in Indian Art*. Ed. Joseph Campbell. New York: Pantheon Books, 1946.

——. "The Guardians of Life", Pantheon Books, 1946.

——. "The Cosmic Delight of Shiva", Pantheon Books, 1946.

2 Rabindranath Tagore's *Chitra*: A Feminist Reading

Usha Kishore

Rabindranath Tagore's *Chitra* has been described as "a lyrical feast", and "loveliest drama" by Edward Thompson (Rao, 1980) in the 20th century and "a dramatic sermon on the theme of true love" and "a dream of flawless beauty in an awakened state" by Reshu Shukla (149) at the beginning of the 21st century. This legendary play continues to enthral audiences around the world even at the present time. It has been interpreted and staged in numerous languages and in numerous performance genres including drama, performance poetry, dance drama and pure dance forms, in India and abroad. The most recent performance, in Trinidad and Tobago in November 2011, in the Manipuri dance repertoire was part of the 150th birth anniversary celebrations of the Indian Nobel Laureate (*Daily Pioneer,* Dec. 2011). This journey of *Chitra* through the century subscribes to the internationalism that Tagore had envisioned. However, Chitra is not merely a lyrical play that binds languages, cultures and nations together; it brings to the forefront, a major feminist discourse that was born in British India.

Like other Tagore plays, viz., *The King and Queen* and *Sacrifice, Chitra* too features revolutionary feminist themes. In *The King and Queen,* Queen Sumitra unconventionally assumes a political role, while in *Sacrifice,* Gunavati defies royal decree to perform an animal sacrifice to Goddess Kali. Chitra's strong feminist theme is reflected in the eponymous title; she is a warrior princess, who protects her nation and unabashedly declares her love for Arjuna. Existing beyond textual boundaries, Tagore's female protagonists are rooted in his desire for equality and justice for women; in creating them, the playwright goes against the grain of a tradition that advocated child marriage, ostracised widows, denied education to women and condemned equality among the sexes. Tagore's championship of women can be identified with the gendered poetic yearnings for a Motherland, *Bharat Mata*. This championship stems from the writings of Raja Ram Mohun Roy and Bankim Chandra Chatterjee and parallels Mahatma Gandhi's call for the emancipation of women.

Bankim Chandra Chatterjee was one of the first Indian writers, who sanctified nationalism, identifying it with the Hindu worship of the female goddesses. In his novel, *Ananda Math*, patriotism takes lyrical expression in the song, *Vande Mataram*. Chatterjee rejuvenated the Indian tradition of mother goddess and gave to the ailing nation, the vision of Motherhood. This intellectual idea of the motherland infused with religious fervour acted as a great driving force. Freedom in the abstract was then visualised in religious terms, which brought more concreteness to the Indian minds. The Motherland was made more meaningful than a geographical stretch or a group of individuals, constituting a nation. Tagore was certainly influenced by this ideology of the sanctification of the nationalist cause. Tagore's women were equally influenced by Raja Ram Mohun Roy's reformist strategies against outrageous Hindu practices like *sati*, child-marriage and widow ostracisation. Tagore, like Sarojini Naidu, uses the concept of the ideological "Mother India", in order to protest against the victimisation of women and to awaken the masses at a historic juncture. There is diversity in Tagore's portrayal of womanhood: woman is portrayed as mother, lover and life-force or *Jiban Debta* and symbolically venerated as Motherland. The poet has attempted to give an equal stance to womanhood in order to generate a gender representation challenging patriarchal authority in British India. Tagore's nonconformist championship of women was not only instrumental in creating self-awareness among women during and after the Indian Independence struggle, but also has visionary significance in the fact that it anticipates the postcolonial concerns for the subaltern. Perhaps, this championship of women made Tagore a well-received voice in Pre-Independent India and the West, especially within the context of the suffragette movement.

Tagore's non-conformism reaches its radical zenith in *Chitra,* where he challenges the social entrapment of women. The tragic state of Indian women in Pre-Independent India, especially in Tagore's native Bengal is highlighted through the protagonist Chitra, who subverts her subaltern status in a patriarchal Hindu society. Tagore takes his feminism one step further by highlighting female sexuality. Although earlier critics like K.R.S. Iyengar (Iyengar, 136-38) do not approve of the reading of the sexual element in *Chitra,* one has to acknowledge the sexual innuendoes. Chitra's exposition of sexuality generates key feminist debates within the play.

It is well-known that *Chitra* is based on the Indian epic *Mahabharata* and narrates the story of Chitrangadha, one of the wives of Arjuna. Chitra is the warrior-princess of Manipur, whom Arjuna meets during his ascetic wanderings. Taking into consideration, the context of production, the play was first published in 1914, when Indian women led protected and almost cloistered lives, the character of Chitra is anachronistic and visionary as she is a warrior princess, donning a masculine mailshirt and nurturing the ambition of challenging the illustrious Kuru warrior, Arjuna to battle. On meeting him however, she falls in love, discards her masculine mailshirt and dons female garb to seduce Arjuna out of his celibacy. In the first instance, Arjuna is unimpressed and rejects her. Subsequently, Chitra implores Madana and Vasanta to teach her the art of wooing and to bless her with seductive beauty. In the closing lines of the play, the eponymous heroine Chitra reveals her true identity to Arjuna and demands equality.

Chitra is an epitome of the exotic woman, expressing her sexuality. This is illustrated in Scene I, at the very opening of the play; Chitra expresses her sexuality by discarding her warrior outfit and appealing to Madana, the God of Love to grant her feminine wiles of seduction:

> ...O Love, god Love...

> Now, teach me thy lessons; give me the power of the weak and the weapon of the unarmed hand. (*Chitra*, 8) and to Vasantha (Spring) to give her the ultimate sensual, feminine form: ...Vasantha, youthful Lord of the Seasons, take from my young body. This primal injustice, an unattractive plainness. For a single day make me superbly beautiful, even as beautiful as was the sudden blooming of love in my heart. Give me but one day of perfect beauty. (*Chitra*, 9-10)

These lines evoke the mood of the play and fore-shadow the rising action within the drama, dominated by a central female character, going against the grain of Indian Literary conventions of male protagonists. The opening lines of the play also succeed in the exposition of the characters, Madana, who describes himself as "the first born in the heart of the Creator", binding "in bonds of pain and bliss in the lives of men and women" (*Chitra*, 1) and Vasanta, The King of Seasons, who is "Eternal Youth" personified. Tagore personifies Spring through Vasanta and love and passion through Madana. Both Madana and Vasanta are effective symbols of beauty, youth and passion used to portray Chitra's sensuality. The Vasanta element can be called the progeny of Kalidasa's *Ritusamhara*, while Madana, the Indian Cupid is based on myth; Madana and Vasanta are considered co-conspirators of romance.

In the opening scene, through *analepsis*, Chitra narrates her tale of woe to Madana and Vasanta, describing her meeting with Arjuna, who almost ridicules her "boyish countenance", while she feels the pangs of love: ...for the first time in my life I felt myself a woman, and knew that a man was before me (*Chitra*, 4-5).

In these lines, Chitra realises her femininity as she has been a warrior princess, brought up to defend the nation rather than being primed in the art of *shringara*. Tagore probes into the female psyche and successfully brings out the inner most female desires, effectively chronicling the *bildungsroman* of the female psyche.

Scene II portrays a seduction ritual, an ultimate expression of female sexuality, where Chitra becomes a sensuously beautiful woman with the blessing of Madana and Vasanta. Arjuna engages in soliloquy and poetises Chitra's beauty in a besotted dreamlike fashion. Chitra's narcissistic admiration, in the waters of the lake, is narrated by Arjuna in *analepsis*:

Methought the vague veiling of her body should melt in ecstasy into air as the golden mist of dawn melts from off the snowy peak of the eastern hill (*Chitra*, 11).

The visual images, the pathetic fallacy and nature metaphors, all serve to project Chitra's newfound beauty and Arjuna seems clearly intrigued: "She bared her bosom and looked at her arms, so flawlessly modelled..." (*Chitra*, 12).

He praises her blossoming youth and the tender bloom and blush of her skin. The entrance and exit of Chitra by the lakeside takes a diurnal rhythm as the entrance is compared to dawn, unveiling her beauty and the exit to dusk, Chitra walking away like a beauteous evening fading into night. The whole soliloquy is reminiscent of the Ovidian accounts of Actaeon, who unwittingly observes Diana bathing in a forest spring. The analogy of Chitra to the goddess of Dawn is another allusion to Indian myth, with Tagore indulging in the feminisation of myth.

The dramatic irony here is effective as Arjuna falls in love with Chitra's borrowed beauty, not realising that she is the same woman, he had spurned earlier. The meeting between Arjuna and Chitra in Scene II, sets the rising action of the One Act play and foreshadows their union as Arjuna declares himself the "love hungered guest" at Chitra's door. Here Chitra taunts Arjuna:

> Oh Shame upon you! What have you seen in me that makes you false to yourself?
> ...Surely this cannot be love, this is not man's highest homage to woman.
> ...Arjuna, the fame of your heroic manhood is false. (*Chitra*, 18)

Yet, lovelorn Arjuna forgets and foregoes his vow of celibacy which "is dissolved as the moon dissolves the night's vow of obscurity" and affirms:

> You alone are perfect; you are the wealth of the world, ...the goal of all efforts, the one woman! (*Chitra*, 18)

Chitra, in a final state of dilemma, pleads with Arjuna to go away and not, to woo "the deceit of a god". Chitra's moral conflict is illustrated here as the warrior princess encounters her womanly desires. Chitra's constant sense of shame and guilt at the deceitful wooing of Arjuna recurs throughout the play.

Scene III is the pivotal scene. It narrates the union of the protagonist with her heart's desire and the fulfilment of her love, although marred by her sense of guilt at her deceitful wooing. Once more in *analepsis*, Chitra narrates her sexual encounter with Arjuna to Madana and Vasanta. Pathetic fallacy is evoked again to bring out a spring time ritual of love and passion with overwhelming sensual images of the air redolent with perfume, the chirping of crickets, the languorous reflections of trees, hanging motionless in the lake and Arjuna's intense look touching Chitra's body like tapering fingers of flame. Here nature becomes the metaphor of female sexuality. There is no explicit description of the union, only Tagore's intelligent manipulation of metaphor, imagery, symbolism and innuendo. These literary devices mask an explicit union and exercise great sensitivity towards the moral sensibility of the Indian and possibly Edwardian readers of the time:

> And I stretched out my arms to him. The moon set behind the trees. One curtain of darkness covered all. Heaven and earth, time and space, pleasure and pain, death and life merged together in unbearable ecstasy.... (*Chitra*, 24)

Albeit the masking of the sexual encounter in nature imagery and other poetic devices, Chitra's confessions are a clear expression of female sexuality, making her *en par* with passionate Greek heroines like Helen, Antigone and Jocasta. Chitra is often compared to *Kalidasa's Shakuntala* (Iyengar, 136) as she indulges in passionate longing in the initial stages of the play, evolving into an empowered woman towards the closure.

Scene VIII, sets the falling action of the play; dramatic irony is used again when Arjuna tries to imagine what the real Princess Chitra would be like. The disguised Chitra paradoxically convinces him that the princess does not have her sensuous form. But the roving mind of Arjuna envisions Princess Chitra, the warrior:

> I seem to see her in my mind's eye, riding on a white horse, ...like the Goddess of Victory dispensing glad hope all around her. (*Chitra*, 44)

Arjuna seems jaded with the intoxicating languor of his current relationship; he seeks more than physical passion. Arjuna's voice is that of the playwright himself, demanding an empowered womanhood beyond sexuality. In Chitra, one glimpses Nike, the Greek winged goddess of victory or Durga, the slayer of Mahishasura. Like Bankim Chandra Chatterjee, Tagore evokes the tradition of the Mother Goddess in order to portray the warrior princess.

The climatic, closing Scene IX constitutes of *anagnorisis* when Arjuna realises that the golden goddess who satiated his desires is none other than princess Chitra. The protagonist shamefully confesses to Arjuna that she had borrowed the beauty of heaven in order to woo him. Finally, with true heroic valour, Chitra declares:

> I am Chitra. No goddess to be worshipped, nor yet the object of common pity to be brushed aside like a moth with indifference. (*Chitra*, 57)
>
> Thus revealing herself, Chitra demands equality: ...If you deign to keep me by your side in the path of danger and daring, if you allow me to share the great duties of your life, then you will know my true self. (*Chitra*, 57)

The falling action of the play is sustained in Arjuna's yearning for the original Chitra and his final acceptance: "Beloved, my life is full" (*Chitra*, 58). Arjuna, the famed Kuru archer, is not only a role model for the warrior princess but also becomes the man of her heart.

The play conforms to the genre of Pastoral Comedy with vibrant nature imagery, dramatic irony, romance, symbolism, deception and disguise, but with an unsterotypical female protagonist, a warrior princess. The play chronicles the coming of age of Chitra, her moral conflict and her rise to the status of a woman, beyond sexuality. In declaring herself as not a goddess to be worshipped or a moth to be brushed aside with indifference, Chitra challenges the self-contradictory traditions of deifying and defying womanhood by patriarchal authority. Chitra's words are those of an empowered Indian woman and a synecdoche of the Indian nation in the making. Here nation and narration meet in Chitra as the coming of age of Chitra is an allegory of the coming of age of the Indian nation and its yearning for independence.

Tagore's Chitra cannot be fixed in a mythical world; she is the portrayal of the Indian woman in Pre-Independent India, struggling for self expression and gender equality. Chitra is subjected to the continuous play of history, culture and gender. In her mythical world, she raises questions of otherness and challenges the position of women in a man's world. The setting of the play is Epic India, where most of the warriors were men. In this context, Chitra is a lone female crusader, crossing boundaries, breaking stereotypes and coming out of her mythical self to challenge gender inequality. The emergence of Chitra as an empowered woman can be paralleled with the emergence of the emancipated Indian woman, who was partnering her male counterparts in the Indian independence struggle.

In the creation of the character Chitra, Tagore seems to foresee the feminist thought processes of Irigaray and Cixous who emphasise that "women have been historically prevented to express their sexuality and if they are able to do so, a new site of *difference* would be created" (Jones, 359). In Irigaray's view (335), the female consciousness and sexuality have been misrepresented in male discourse. Anticipating this thought process, Chitra's female consciousness and sexuality are explored by Tagore, a male Indian writer in colonial times. Chitra is certainly caught in a man-centred world, but she goes against the grain and dons the warrior garb to protect her country, in the absence of a male heir. But upon meeting Arjuna, Chitra briefly discards her masculine mailshirt to assume a sensuous feminine form. Contrary to the Irigaray theory and that of Cixous (Jones, 359), who believes that 'feminine gesture is not culturally but libidinally brought about', Tagore's Chitra expresses her sexuality within cultural parameters. However, Chitra conforms (in anticipation) to the Cixous (335) dogma of a woman in her inevitable struggle against conventional man; she is a universal woman subject who brings women to their meaning in history.

Tagore's Chitra is not repressed; she expresses herself, in a highly articulate manner and takes the form of subversive thought, at a time when Indian women were doubly colonised by the male patriarchy and the British Raj. New socio-political and cultural structures are constructed through Chitra. Through Chitra, Tagore breaks the male parameters that conceptualise female sexuality. The sexual opposition between Chitra and Arjuna both in love and war is also highlighted. The Arjuna-Chitra relationship in the play is a highly complex one. Initially, Chitra is the anti-thesis of the masculine stereotype of feminine beauty and sexuality. She dons the mailshirt of the warrior and harbours an ambition to challenge Arjuna to battle; but when Chitra meets Arjuna, she seduces him with her borrowed beauty. Hence, Chitra obligingly caters to Arjuna's fantasies by metamorphosing into the sensual woman. Here, Tagore visualises a feminist Chitra, whose desire "speaks the same language as man's" (Irigaray, 355).

Tagore creates an oriental woman, who expresses her desire; he thus foresees and at the same time refutes Western feminist theorists, like Irigaray, who is of the opinion that "woman's desire has doubtless been submerged by the logic that has dominated (the West) since the time of the Greeks" (Irigaray, 356). Chitra's sexuality is not violated by Arjuna; she willingly succumbs to his desires; she contests for a denied feminine sexuality. Chitra re-discovers her womanhood that had been castrated by her mailshirt, which again defines socio-cultural norms for the male warrior. She does not submit to a culture that oppresses her but chooses to radically liberate herself.

Chitra is a diversion to the monotony of sameness used in the Western portrayal of the Eastern woman. In analysing the character of Chitra, contemporary Western feminist thought has to be brought into the framework of Eastern womanhood. Chitra is no stereotypical "average third world woman" (Mohanty, 172). Who is sexually constrained but she is an empowered female force, who has control over her body and sexuality. Mohanty's distinction of Western feminist representation of the Eastern women seems to have been pre-challenged in the portrayal of Chitra. Tagore has re-thought the assumptions made about Indian women at home and abroad, in the creation of this female protagonist.

Tagore projects the social and spiritual context of Indian women through Chitra. In his orthodox world, Tagore creates a new entity that is Chitra, a woman demanding equality. He re-interprets Hindu mythology and at the same time, challenges patriarchy and cultural stereotypes. Chitra goes way beyond women as the dominated species, women as universal dependants and women as subordinates in familial/religious systems. Tagore's Chitra is not only an exotic, erotic entity but an empowered female force. Chitra can be interpreted as the manifestation of the Hindu concept of *Shakti*. Like Urvashi, another of Tagore's heroines, Chitra breaks the codes of convention that negate her. Her characterisation brings about harrowing explosions as "a man writes woman" as opposed to the Cixous ideology of "woman writing woman".

Chitra like the other women in Tagore's works is not a cultural and ideological composite third world woman as differentiated by Mohanty (173). She is not a product of hegemonic discourses, but created by a man, championing womanhood in colonial India. Tagorean women cannot be homogenized either; they possess an innate tendency to express themselves in challenging circumstances. Tagore's women resist patriarchal authority within their cultural framework and regardless of class, ethnic or racial location, empower themselves, breaking western stereotypes of the eastern other. In retrospect, they challenge contemporary western feminist theories and assumptions made about eastern women. Their sexuality is not controlled and they are not universal dependants. They do not correspond to the images of "the veiled woman, the chaste virgin and the obedient wife" (Mohanty, 191), stemming from colonialist discourse. They are not even a paradigmatic mediation between the stereotypical eastern subdued and the Western independent woman. They are in fact radicals, crossing the limits of the socio-cultural norms. Considering the time and place of Tagore's works, his women characters are the imaginings of a playwright's mind that craved for women's rights.

PRIMARY SOURCE

Tagore, Rabindranath. *Chitra,* London: Macmillan. 1953.

WORKS CITED

Cixous, Hélène. "The Laugh of the Medusa", *Feminisms.* Ed. Herndl, Price, Diane, and Robyn. R. Warhol. New Jersey: Rutgers University, 1996, 334-49.

Irigaray, Luce. "This Sex which is not one", *Feminisms.* 350-356.

Iyengar, K.R.S. "Tagore the Playwright", *Indian Writing in English,* Ed. Iyengar and Prema Nandakumar, Fifth Edition. New Delhi: Sterling. 1985. 122-44.

Jones, Rosalind Ann, "Writing the Body—towards an understanding of l'écriture feminine", *Feminims.* 358-60.

Mohanty, Talpade, Chandra. "Under Western Eyes: Feminist Scholarship and Colonial Discourses", *Postcolonial Theory—A Reader*, Ed. Padmini Mongia. London: Arnold, 1996. 172-97.

Rao, Ramachandra K. "Tagore's Chitra—An Appreciation", *Triveni*, Jan-March 1980. www.yabaluri.org/TRIVENI/CDWEB/tagoreschitra anappreciationjan80.htm. Accessed Dec. 2011.

Shukla, Reshu. "Tagore's Chitra: An Epitome of Love, Truth and Beauty", *Perspectives and Challenges in Indian English Drama.* Ed. Neeru Tandon. New Delhi: Atlantic, 2006. 149-56. www.dailypioneer.com – 4 Dec. 2011. Accessed Dec. 2011.

3 A Web of Socio-Psycho and Cultural Aspects in the Plays of Girish Karnad

G.A. Ghanshyam

A group of people, a race or a community forms a society, which has its own social and moral codes, tradition and culture. The individuals comprising the society follow its codes and culture ingrained in their life and psyche. In fact, society and culture are the key factors giving shape to the psychology of its people. The same also stands for society and culture, for it is its members who influence and create them.

Every society has its codes and principles, its own tradition and culture. The culture specifications of every society bind its people together in unity. They decide the psychology of the people, their character, attitude, beliefs, superstitions and way of life. Inherent in the myths, legends, folklore and theatre; society and culture finds an apt representation in religion, arts and literature.

Indian society is a tradition bound society with a rich cultural repertoire. Unique in its diversity, Indian society is unified in a single thread of tradition running through its culture and society. Spiritual, patriarchal, ritualistic, idealistic; Indian society is hierarchal in structure and conventional in culture. Here it wouldn't be a cliché to say that since literature mirrors society so Indian literature also abounds in glimpses of its society and culture, in representation of its psychology.

If society is a creative agent, then culture is its handmaid. Complementary in nature they both influence and create character. It is said Indian drama apart from being a form of entertainment and source of pleasure, also, "comprehend whole arc of life, ranging from the material to the spiritual, the phenomenal to the transcendent, and provide at once relaxation and entertainment, instruction and illumination" (Iyengar, 1).

Indian English drama is replete with instances of life in its truest essence laying bare all its innate and implicit social and cultural characteristics, psychology and nature. The extensive use of tradition, myths, legends and folklore by contemporary dramatists like Girish Karnad indicates to the very important triangular points of intersection that is social, cultural and psychological factors distinguishing the society and its people.

Girish Karnad, a major dramatist has significantly gone back to the roots and re-created for us the rich and vibrant picture of Indian society, culture and its people. In all his plays he genuinely portrays the Indian way of life with all its positive and negative aspects, its tradition and their relative contemporary importance and relation.

Culture defines society. The cultural ethos of every society is unique in its form and essence representing the character of its people, their experiences and beliefs. Myths, legends and folklore are in fact the embodiments of these cultural ethos that represent the underlying values and principles of life, the shared experience of the race, the rules and the codes of society. Girish Karnad has time and again returned to eternal roots of his cultural tradition, taking inspiration from mythology and folklore.

Myths, Folklore and Legends

Myths are an integral part of the culture and are in fact the projection of individual and social dynamics. For the playwright, myth has a, "palpable presence" and he "experiments with it within his genre by relating, interpreting, revisioning and re-fashioning it within the structural framework of his art" (Chakravartee, 182). Karnad also takes his inspiration from the rich tradition of India's past and weaves it through the web of his imagination into tales of his own. Karnad's first play *Yayati* is a story taken from the *Mahabharata*. The mythical story is a tale of responsibilities, sacrifice and self-realization. The play *The Fire and the Rain* is also taken from the forest canto of *Mahabharata*. It is based on the myth of Yavakiri and also includes the myth of the conflict between Indra, Vishwarupa and Vritra in the Epilogue. Karnad's plays, *Bali—The Sacrifice* and *Flowers: A Dramatic Monologue* are mythical tales taken from a Kannada and a Sanskrit epic respectively.

Folk imagination is at once mythopoeic and magical. In the folk mind, one subsumes the other. Folk belief, besides being naïve, has a touch of poetry about it which works towards a psychic adjustment. All folklore is religious, often based on animism because the primitive imagination extends its vision from the natural, in which it is steeped and with which it is saturated, to the supernatural, which to the folk mind is only an extension of the former (Rangan, 199).

Folklore is in other words the cultural and social construct that provides a definite shape and image to the moral and ethical codes engendered by society and followed by the individual. *Hayavadana* and *Naga-Mandala* source their origin from the folklore tradition of India. *Hayavadana* is based on Thomas Mann's translation of the Sanskrit 'Vetal Panchavimashati', which forms part of Kshemendra's *Brihat Katha Manjari* and Somadeva's *Kathasaritsagara*. Karnad's *Naga-Mandala* is inspired by the snake myths prevalent in South India. It is a dramatization of two folk tales of Karnataka. In fact Naga Cult is a kind of worship practiced in Kerela.

Girish Karnad has written plays that owe their source to Indian history. Weaving his tales around legendary figures drawn from varying periods of Indian national history Karnad has given a contemporary interpretation. According to Nietzsche, "History is necessary to the living man in three different ways: in relation to his action and struggle, his conservatism and reverence, his suffering and his desire for deliverance" (Nietzsche, n.p). In other words the past help us to comprehend the present. Karnad's *Tughlaq* was inspired by the historical character of Muhammad-bin-Tughlaq, the fourteenth century sultan of Delhi.

In *Tale-Danda*, Karnad takes his inspiration from a historical movement that took place in Kalyan in 1168 A.D., Karnataka. Basavananna, the great Sharana poet saint and his movement to eradicate caste differences forms the main theme of the play.

Religion, Ritual and Superstition

India is a nation richly imbued with religious sentiment and belief. According to M. Rajeshwar, "Most Indians are at least in theory religious in outlook" (Rajeshwar, 24). In Indian society one's faith is often more than just a personal inclination for it defines an individual's identity. Every aspect of life in India is associated with religion intertwined with which are numerous rituals and superstitions. Forming a part of the cultural identity of India it shapes and constructs the distinct identity of the individual.

In *Hayavadana* the presence of goddess Kali reveals the religious sentiment prevalent in Indian society, culture and psychology. Devadutta prays to the goddess to win the hand of Padmini in marriage. Later he beheads himself as an offering to the goddess. Divine intervention unfolds the central theme of the play, 'incompleteness' and quest for completion. The theme also reveals the Upanishadic principle that visualizes the human body as a symbol of the organic relationship of the parts to the whole.

Religion and ritual not only form a part of the narrative of Karnad's plays but are also integral to the dramatic representation of the plays, a take off of the folk theatrical tradition of the country. *Hayavadana* begins with an invocation of Lord Ganesha, the first to be worshipped among the gods and the remover of all obstacles.

If *Tughlaq* shows the hypocrisy and misuse of religion, then evolution and transformation of religion forms a part of the play *Tale-Danda*. Superstition an innate characteristic of traditional and orthodox religion finds a reflection in *Naga-Mandala* wherein Kurudava gives the aphoridiasic root to Rani giving a new twist to the tale. The reference to a Yaksha woman enticing Kappanna, the son of Kurudava also reveals predominance of superstitious belief and belief in the supernatural elements.

Sacrifices also form a part of such religious practice as seen in the obliteration of the self physically in *Hayavadana*, the snake ordeal that Rani undergoes in *Naga-Mandala*, the seven years Fire Yagna in *The Fire and the Rain*, and the daily ritual of sanctification, adornment and worship of Lord Shiva in *Flowers: A Dramatic Monologue*.

Spiritual thought and wisdom inherent in religion are also incorporated into the theme of the plays. The emphasis given to intellect or the mind over matter is inherent in Indian socio-psycho and cultural context is evident when in *Hayavadana* Devdutta says, "According to Shastras, the head is the sign of a man..." (Karnad, *Hayavadana* I, 146). The theory of Karma, Ahimsa, Balidan, Varna, etc. also echoes through the various narratives of Karnad's other plays. The Hindu spiritual belief in yoga, self restraint, selflessness and sacrifice of self is re-iterated in the plays. The unrestrained, selfish enjoyment of sensual pleasures of Yayati is disapproved of and so is the egoistical attainment of knowledge for power as in the characters of Raibhya, Yavakiri and Paravasu; while the selflessness, compassion and love of Puru, Nittilai and Arvasu are commended in life. Attainment of true knowledge does require sacrifice but here it means a surrender of self: the sacrifice of false ego, sensuous pleasures, ambition and pride. "True sacrifice is that of love especially that which is for the benefit of humanity" (Nair, 248).

Socio-cultural practices like Sati, Varna and the Partriarchial moral codes are portrayed with remarkable clarity and preciseness by the playwright in plays *Yayati*, *Naga-Mandala*, *Tale-Danda*, *The Fire and the Rain*, etc. The Bhagavata thus says in *Hayavadana*, "...Padmini became a sati. India is Known for its pativratas, wives who dedicated their whole existence to the service of their husbands;" (Karnad, *Hayavadana* II, 177). In context of the patriarchal social order that subjugates and alienates a woman, Karnad comments on the role of Appanna and Naga in the play *Naga-Mandala* that they represent the twin roles of the husband, "as a stranger during the day and as lover at night" (Karnad Author's Introduction, 19).

Idealism

Idealism forms the core of Indian culture and psyche. Karnad portrays this important aspect of Indian society in *Tughlaq* where it is misguided, in *Tale-Danda* where it is shattered and destroyed by violence and blood shed by the traditionalists, in *Bali—The Sacrifice* where it reveals the stark realities of human instincts contrasted with bare ideology which finds an echo in *Flowers—A Dramatic Monologue* wherein idealisms of faith come in conflict with basic human desires of the senses.

Ideals form the basis of the various principles and codes conceptualized and formulated by Indian society and practiced through culture that creates and shapes the typical Indian psyche. Yet idealism is often manipulated for selfish ends as in the case of the Yayati who takes advantage of Puru's devotion and reverence for him as a son to transfer his curse onto him; or the two friends Devdutta and Kapila who sacrifice their lives in front of goddess Kali but hide their real motives, "The rascals! They were lying to their last breaths" (*Hayavadana* I, 142). Tughlaq, who uses prayer to fulfill his own vested interest to gain sovereignty, etc.

As per the traditional scales of social roles and culture, the individual holds a subordinate position to society, community or family. In *Naga-Mandala* Rani and Appanna conform to their social roles and obligation as husband and wife even though both are aware of the truth of their relation.

Indian society is traditional and an individual is still governed by societal roles and norms that ensure a continuity and survival of its cultural mores. Eric Fromm assigns a creative role to society and culture which moulds and holds a tremendous influence on an individual's psyche. 'We are what we believe in and where we live in.' So, society and culture makes a person and are generic in quality holding true for all persons belonging to that community or society.

Girish Karnad has minutely and with expert precision depicted the social, cultural and psychological aspects of Indian society and character in his various plays. Taking his source from the soil of India he has not only revived tradition and culture through his plays but has also provided us with a glimpse of the past relevance in contemporary times and the essential process of evolution of life, society and culture, and thereby psyches of the people.

WORKS CITED

Chakravartee, Moutushi. "Myth and Reality in Hayavadana and Nagamandala". *Girish Karnad's Plays: Performance and Critical Perspectives*. Ed. Tutun Mukherjee. Delhi: Pencraft International, 2006.

Iyengar, K.R. Srinivas. *Drama in Modern India*. Bombay: The P.E.N. All India Centre, 1961.

Karnad, Girish. "*Hayavadana*" *Collected Plays*, Vol. I. New Delhi: OUP, 2006.

——. Author's Introduction. *Three Plays*. Delhi: OUP, 1993.

Nair, Rama. "Ritual as Self-Discovery in The Fire and the Rain". *Girish Karnad's Plays: Performance and Critical Perspectives*. Ed. Tutun Mukherjee. Delhi: Pencraft International, 2006.

Nietzsche, Fredrich. *The Use and Abuse of History*. Indianapolis: Bobbs-Merrill Educational Publishing, 1957.

Rajeshwar, M. "Psychoanalysis and Indian Writing in English: Promises and Possibilities". *Indian Writing Today*. Ed. C.R. Visweswara Rao. New Delhi: IAES, 1996.

Rangan, V. "Myth and Romance in Nagamandala or their Subversion". *Girish Karnad's Plays: Performance and Critical Perspectives*. Ed. Tutun Mukherjee.

4

New-Morality in Girish Karnad's *Tughlaq*

Shivaji Shankar Kamble

Bhalchandra Nemade, a serious critic, advanced the term New Morality as a modern literary value to set a very high premium on the morality of the writer. Nemade dichotomizes morality into two divisions, viz., old morality and new morality which is more akin to Mahatma Phule's true morality and false morality, expressed in his book entitled *Sarvajanik Satya Dharm* (The Universal Religion of Truth). According to Phule, Morality, as expressed in *Ramayana* and *Bhagavata* is unreal, untrue and unbelievable; however, what annoys Phule here is false and unreal morality of spurious, wicked and bogus scriptures. For example, in an imaginative (romantic) *Ramayana*, Ravana had ten noses, twenty eyes, twenty ears and twenty hands but only one anus and two legs. It seems unnatural and magical. Phule objects to *Seeta Swayamwara* (system of choosing bridegroom); Rama's being monogamous, on the ground of false morality and prefers true morality in Aesop's stories.

The writer has to employ his own scale of values, which are based on the original social values. Since literature is an art form the writer must imply a plane, a condition which goes beyond social values. This is what Nemade means by the morality of a writer.

It is impossible to grasp what Nemade really had in mind, when he spoke about New Morality, without considering Gandhi's view of morality and the imperative need for moral commitment to self-chosen values. True morality, for Gandhi-New Morality, for Nemade—consists not in following the beaten track, but in finding out the true path for ourselves and fearlessly following it. Gandhi's moral concern, like Jotirao

Phule, tended to simultaneously subvert Brahminic and Kshatriya orthodoxy following the basic construction: centrality of the periphery of Indian culture New Morality proved to be *avant-garde* nature of *Satyashodhak* movement and Gandhian way of life.

Indeed morality is an adherence to personal value judgement. Values are general principles, guidelines and standards to regulate our day-to-day behaviour. As a moral idea and general conception, values include interests, needs, preferences, attitudes, sentiments and dispositions. It means that values are means to achieve desires, dreams, hopes and ideals of life which expresses moral imperatives. Independence, fraternity, justice, equality, friendliness, desires, objectives, interests, needs, ideals, wealth and general tendencies are some mentionable values (Rawat, 93).

Jnanpith Awardee Girish Karnad is the most outstanding dramatic genius of the post-Independent Indian literature. His historical play *Tughlaq* is a great classic in Indian dramatic literature. It deals with the life, visions, ideals and dreams of Muhammad-bin-Tughlaq, an extraordinary intellectual, dreamy-eyed idealist and *avant-garde* medieval Muslim monarch, who dissuades his mind from the rosy, revelry and pleasure-loving life and roseate to bring about social change, Hindu-Muslim unity, peace, prosperity, progress, equality, freedom and to transform his state into 'Utopia' like a regardful regal ruler. Unfortunately, he is misunderstood by his people. Therefore, Karnad desires to remove all the untruths and misunderstanding about him and suggests rethinking and reconstructing the history in general and Tughlaq in particular, who is verily, an apostle of modernity and new morality.

The royal declaration in the opening scene tells that the Hindus are exempted from the Jizia-tax, which was imposed on the infidels for the permission to live by the previous Muslim rulers. But Tughlaq has strong individual values and his vision is enlarged by Greek literature, Al Mutazi's philosophy, Sadi's poems, Aflatoon's (Plato) poetry, Sukrat's (Socrates) wisdom and Zarathustra or Buddha's vision. Therefore, he wants to treat all his subjects equally and stunningly states that 'Hindus are also human beings' (Karnad, 2). But the retrograde people think that the act of abolition of Jizia-tax is against the tenets of Koran. As a true votary of new-morality, modernity and the vulgar herd, Tughlaq does not want to follow the age old customs like Jizia-tax. On the whole, to destroy Jizia-tax and to treat all the subjects equally on humanitarian ground is Tughlaq's supreme personal and collective value of judgement.

'Freedom of Expression' is another shining personal value of judgement of Tughlaq. Under this concept, he gives a right to his subjects to criticize the Sultąn and give voice to their grievance openly. Certainly such a democratic rarity in medieval age is like a dream world. Aziz, a Muslim washerman, takes unfair advantage at a snail's pace by disguising himself as a Brahmin named Vishnu Prasad of Shiknar, files a case against the government with back dated false documents. The Kazi-i-Mumbalik studies the case carefully and orders adequate compensation to Vishnu Prasad for illegal misappropriation of his land by the government officials. Tughlaq admits his mistake and obeys the impartial decision of Kazi-i-Mumbalik willingly. In this regard, he says, "May this moment burn bright and light up our path towards greater justice, equality, progress and peace—not just peace but a more purposeful life" (Karnad, 3). Thus he follows justice without any consideration of might, weakness, influence, religion and creed which is unique and unwanted in the annals of history. Thus, he unveils the unvarnished truth that example is better than percept. Indeed this is his personal value of judgement which is more akin to Mahatma Phule and Mahatma Gandhi in the true spirit.

Aziz and Azam, the two cheaters, follow the path of violence for power and success. Both have their own wicked philosophy and morality about world of success and politics in which virtuous have no place. They believe that one can get greatness by stealing, robbing, killing and misusing power. In this regard, Aziz says, "a man must commit a crime at least once in his life-time. Only then will his virtue be recognized!.... Now all you have to do to become a saint is rape.... What's the point in raping for sheer lust? That's a mug's game. First one must have power—the authority to rape! Then everything takes on meaning" (Karnad, 57). This is a dishonest man's destructive philosophy of life, which directly affects the ideal edifice of Tughlaq. Therefore, Aparna Dhawadkar points out, "power for Aziz is also a kind of licensed evil that need not be naturalized through discourse. To rape a woman only out of lust is a pointless game" (52). Indeed Aziz and Azam are the representatives of false morality, and both upset the applecarts of Tughlaq.

Shifting capital of India from Delhi to Daulatabad is a prudent political decision of Tughlaq. Besides the security of nation, he desires communal harmony, peace, prosperity, progress, equality and unity in the company of Daulatabad based Hindus. His decision displays that he wants to create an 'utopia' in his kingdom. Verily he wants to get closer to hearts of Hindus in Daulatabad. This is his ideal passion which represents an excellent example of his new morality. It is true that people suffered unspeakable miseries due to his dangerous decision, albeit, he had made a lot of arrangements like food, clothing, medicine, etc. on the route to Daulatabad for his subjects. As an ideal king, he does everything lovingly, sympathetically and sociably for his people, nonetheless, he is considered manic maelstrom. But one cannot deny his honest purpose behind it except his Machiavellian maneuvers.

Because of the zeal of giving and teaching new things to people, Tughlaq introduces several novel schemes. Introduction of copper currency is one of them. It is one of the most daring monetary experiments through which he wants to build a passionate relationship of love, trust, faith and mutual understanding between the ruler and ruled for 'a new future for India' (4). Another important thing is that he makes *Namaz* (prayer) compulsory. He allows people to pray five times a day, even to read Koran in the streets also. But his enemies use prayer as an instrument in order to eliminate their political and religious enemies. Misuse of prayer or religion for one's personal end is a false morality.

Tughlaq spends 'Sleepless nights' because his mind is preoccupied with the thought of regeneration of his country and countrymen. He does not want to waste his time in sleep, marriage and breeding. Infact, he believed that he has only one life to live and so much to do in it. Therefore, he prays to Almighty to save him from the sleep so that he may think about his people all twenty-four hours of the day (Sequeira, 59). To get more time for the welfare of his subjects, he discards all mundane pleasures and pompous life. To be honest, 'the idealist in him is restless and cannot sleep' (Rajgopalachari and Krina, 27). It means that Tughlaq is ready to immolate not only his sleep but life also for the betterment of his subjects. This is his commitment towards his subjects and a fine piece of new morality.

There are two types of enemies of Tughlaq, viz., political and religious. Ain-ul-Mulk is his political enemy, who wants to capture the throne of Delhi, whereas Sheikh-Imam-ud-din is Tughlaq's religious enemy, who defames Tughlaq by accusing him publically, regarding his many misdeeds. Tughlaq desires to overcome these two enemies. So he sends Sheikh-Imam-ud-din as his emissary of peace against the approaching army of Ain-ul-Mulk. But he is murdered treacherously on the battle-fied. Then Ain-ul-Mulk is defeated but Tughlaq pardons him. To pardon is an excellent way to conquer an enemy. However, Tughlaq sacrifices Sheikh, the saintly man, in order to save his State from the false religion. In fact he thinks that peace, humanity, generosity and forgiveness is more important than religion. These qualities of Tughlaq elevate the golden lace on his personal value judgement.

While communicating with the young guard on Daulatabad fort, Tughlaq advices that young generation should not be regardless to reality and objects of life. Everyone should try to clasp the whole world in one's palm like a rare diamond and live for achieving ideals rather than being brainless cattle. Impossible quest for novelty should go on. Such a new morality is presented in form of advice by Tughlaq.

'Impartial justice' is another crowning element of new morality of Tughlaq. After the murder of Najib, Tughlaq loses his faith and decides to work with sword instead of words. He finds that people can understand whip and his enemies can understand only the language of sword. Such a destructive kind of morality emerges in his mind. However, when Tughlaq finds his stepmother guilty in Najib's murder, without any hesitation, he punishes her severely. This incident shows his impartial justice, honesty and deep love for ideals. Indeed these values are versions of new morality.

In sum, Girish Karnad believes that the existence of dramatist implies community and his group consciousness. So he employs his own scale of values, based on the original social values. While presenting socio-political reality, he compels society to fight against moral insensitivity, inhuman customs and cultural lethargy of the times. However, he gives thoughtful analysis of the subject, taken from history, particularly for understanding the present and preparation for the future. This is his ethical commitment to his medium. As far as the protagonist Tughlaq is concerned, he loses all the religious, ethical and community values and support which is similar to the Indian experience of the sixties. Thus, Karnad uses his creative energy for instilling a sense of social consciousness about social reformation and regeneration among the masses of the contemporary world. This is his personal value judgement, reflected in *Tughlaq*.

WORKS CITED

Dharwadkar, Aparna. *Historical Fictions and Post-Colonial Representation: Reading Girish Karnad's Tughlaq,* in PMLA, Vol. 110, No. 1, Jan. 1995.

Karnad, Girish. *Tughlaq*, 24th Impression 2001. New Delhi: Oxford University Press, 1975.

Nemade, Bhalchandra. *New Morality in Contemporary Marathi Fiction*, in Vagartha, No. 18 and Indian Literature, Sept-Oct. 1978.

Rajgopalachari, M. and Krina, N.A. *Karnad's Tughlaq: A Critical Note*, in Indian Scholar, Vol. 11, No. 1, Jan. 1989.

Rawat, H.K. *Sociology: Basic Concepts*, Jaipur: Rawat Publications, 2007.

Sequeira, Isaac. *Review of Tughlaq* in Gray Book, Vol. 2, No. 1, Spr-Sum. 1973.

5 Indian Regional Drama—The Trilogy of Satish Vyas's Two Act Plays

Indira Nityanandam

Gujarati Theatre has had a vibrant past and continues to do so even today. From the traditional five-act full-length play to the popular twentieth century, one-act play, from closet drama to that written to be staged, from the literary to the slap-stick variety, Gujarati literature has plenty of all of them.

Satish Vyas is an acclaimed figure in Gujarati Literature. As a teacher of repute, he brings to his plays a rare combination of two worlds—that of academics and of art and makes his plays present a just and lively image of the predicament of modern man. The one-act play today occupies a legitimate place in literature. It is no more used as a curtain-raiser. Satish Vyas attempts a variation of this when he writes two-act plays. As A.K. Singh says, in his introduction to the trilogy, "The dramatist understands, perhaps, the inability of busy modern men who increasingly display lack of sustained savouring of a work of art. He packages his thought in dramatic garb for his audience who have just about one hour and a half for a performance."

The history of the one-act play as a genre in Gujarati is a very short one. Like many other literary forms, this too has been imported from the West. However, the form in Western literature too is only about a hundred years old. Attempts have been made to trace the origins of the one-act play to the Mystery and Morality plays of pre-Elizabethan England. Here the stage was broken into a series of platforms set about a town square or else the actors toured the streets from point to point on elaborately decorated carts or 'pageants'. A drama played in this way had to be episodic; it may even seem to us now to be a large number of short one-act plays strung together by the Bible theme. However, we can certainly see that both in theme and structure as well as in language and technique they are far apart. Later, we had the Drolls and the Burlesques and even later the Curtain Raisers. Though there may be some similarities between these forms, the one-act play of today has come a long way from these so-called precursors. It is said that when W. Jacob's *Monkey's Paw* was first staged (on 6th October, 1903), the audience was so impressed by it that they left the theatre without waiting for the actual three-act play. The curtain raiser had become the main play. Since then, many dramatic associations of Great Britain like the Little Theatre and Art Theatre and later British Drama League and Community Drama Association instituted annual prizes for the best one-act play of the year. It is generally believed that they contributed in no small measure to the development of this genre. In Indian Literature, Bharata in his *Natyasastra* listed four kinds of one-act plays—*Vyayog, Utsrishtikand, Bhana and Vithi.* However, most critics firmly believe that none of the shorter plays of even the great playwright Bhasa can be considered one-act plays in the contemporary sense of the term. Whatever may be the source, the modern one-act play occupies an important place in twentieth century literature in many parts of the world. The reasons for this wide-spread popularity may not be hard to find. The popularity of the radio as a means of entertainment also contributed to this trend. Moreover the impatience of twentieth century audiences, who were not willing to spend three hours watching a full-length play, also contributed to making them highly receptive to and appreciative of this new genre.

The one-act play is not just a shorter version of the full-length play. It is as distinct from the full-length play as the short story is from the novel. A true one-act play cannot be enlarged, lengthened or padded up to make it a full length play. Bhanuprasad Choksi in his attempts to define the characteristics of this genre in *Maro Priya.* Ekanki (*My Favourite One-Act Plays*) says that it should have a single dramatic situation, a single incident, a single point of view, etc. Dr. Mafatlal Bhavsar believes that the duration of the play can be from five minutes to one hour. Unity, singleness and economy provide the backbone to this form. It is an undeniable fact that this form is written to be staged and hence some contemporary Gujarati playwrights believe that no attempt should be made to restrict this form to strict literary rules. When one considers the difference between reading a play and watching it on stage, one can recall the words of Granville-Barker who envisages the task before the reader:

> He must, so to speak, perform the whole play in his imagination; as he reads, each effect must come home to him; the succession and contrast of scenes, the harmony and clash of the music of the dialogue, the action implied, the mere physical opposition of characters, or the silent figure standing aloof—for that also can be eloquent. (84)

In the one-act play, it can be reiterated that staging of the play seems to be more the rule than the exception, specially in Gujarati. Jaswant Rekhdiwala believes that the Gujarati playwrights continue to imitate the Western dramatists in almost all aspects of this form, both thematically and stylistically. The eight characteristic features that are associated with the full-length play are equally important for this form. They are: plot, character, dialogue, milieu, language and style, aim, stage directions and *rasa*. Reiterating the importance of the stage as an intrinsic part of any play, J.L. Styan writes:

> In the true magic of the theatre...the good dramatist perfectly crystallizes his thoughts and feelings, and at the same time grants his audience some common material of human life for recognition and understanding, for that unique quality of sharing the experience of others.... It may or may not be easy to read, but it will certainly be alive in the theatre.... Its quality is to be measured by the only test—performance in the theatre, and when we read a play critically, we are first and foremost making this test of stageworthiness in our imagination. (14)

Satish Vyas, the well-known dramatist and critic, in his path-breaking collection of contemporary one-act plays *Aadhunik Ekanki*, describes the major differences between drama and the other forms of literature. He believes that drama reaches the audience 'double filtered' because the actor contributes in no small measure to the effectiveness of a play. In ancient Indian drama criticism, visualization was considered of paramount importance and hence 'aangikam' is a major challenge to the actors. To Vyas, there is no category that can be called literary or closet drama. Any play that is not stageable is not a play at all. When asked, in an interview, why he chose to write two-act plays he replied, "Where do spectators have time to sit for a three hour performance? One-act plays are many a times limiting in scope. It is more convenient to express oneself in say an hour and a half or two hours. That is how I have ended up writing only two-act plays without a single three-act play to my credit" (160-61).

The three plays under consideration here are *Jal ne Parde* (translated as *Mist of Tears*), *Angulimal* and *Kamroo*—both having the same titles in English. The plays were published in 2005 and 2006 in Gujarati and translated into English in 2008. One realizes the limitations of reading a text in translation, but a good translation can contribute in tremendous measure to an aesthetic appreciation of a text and this translation does succeed in doing that to a great extent. In order to appreciate these plays, a certain knowledge of Gujarati literature is essential. This is particularly relevant if one wishes to understand the milieu, the culture in which the play is set. *Jal ne Parde* deals with the loneliness of the Gujarati poet, prose writer and dramatist Kant, whose religious conversion continues to haunt his readers and admirers even after almost a century. Like Eliot's conversion twice, Kant too embraced Hinduism again. Born in 1867, as Manishankar Ratnaji Bhatt, Kant is accepted as one of the greatest poets in Gujarati. The early deaths of people close to him—his father, his two wives, his son Pranlal, the poet Kalapi—left a vacuum in him which even time could not fill. In fact, the friendship and mutual artistic contribution make the two poets an inseparable pair. Satish Vyas says that his play is an attempt to understand that vacuum. There have been earlier plays based on writers like Kabir, Narmad, Jaishankar Sundari, etc. In Europe, there have been plays like Brecht's *The*

Life of Galileo, Eugene O'Neill's *Long Day's Journey into Night*. This play too is probably in the same tradition. Vyas is able to portray the inner turmoil that Kant faces when he decides to convert to Christianity. The poet conveys his views from his first publication to his visit to Kashmir at a much later date. The narrator who represents the inner being of the poet Kant and the poet himself are the only two characters. Interestingly, all the other characters are evoked through the poet's solo performance on the stage. The playwright is able to re-create each relationship aesthetically: the soft, mellow love for his first wife, "Fresh jui flowers everyday.... Flowers everyday, you must be wondering why? Oh! Na'di, every night is our honeymoon night" (9), the agony of watching his mother after his father's death, "Stop hurting my mother. Stop smashing her hands on the floor.... Why do you have to rub it (chandla) off?..." (8), his sorrow at the death of his first wife, "Na'di, why did you suddenly go away like this?" (20) and again, "The world is forlorn without my beloved. All happiness is lost but my life continues to roll" (21) and at the death of his son, "Pranu, why did you have to depart like this?... My care, my sitar have gone waste... The music of my life has died down..." (24). It is during these moments of sorrow and pain that he reads the Bible and gets some solace from it. Gradually, he is drawn more and more towards Christianity: "...it is true that the religion of one's birth is supreme but for me Christianity is auspicious. It is now my religion" (25), and later "Our religion has changed from today. Actually more than changed, we have understood the true meaning of religion" (32). Vyas is able to present the turmoil that Kant undergoes when he finds himself ostracized by friends and relatives, even by his own wife who refuses to share his room or even cook for him. Though the conversion is not and should not be of consequence to anyone else, Kant finds himself having to bear the brunt of reactions of all around him. The play captures this angst. As Avadesh Kumar Singh says in his Introduction to the English translation of the trilogy,

> *Mist of Tears* exists at multiple levels, as a play, as a biography and a piece of criticism. Despite being the biography, the play does not meddle with facts. It is this

> fidelity to facts and their interpretation that make this play a creative critical milestone of Gujarati literature. By eschewing the temptation of writing a critical treatise on Kant, the playwright has served as a model for all those with their books without any perspicuity and interpretation keep adding to already multiplying burden on the world of criticism. (XIII)

On reading *Angulimal*, the first question that rises is whether a writer can create in literature a character who already exists in the collective consciousness of the race and yet claim that he (this character in literature) has nothing to do with the original character. Or is the readers' appreciation or perception of the play guided and clouded by all that he already knows. The answers to these questions may be the guiding force for our appreciation of this play which retains the original title in the translation too. Angiram, the protagonist, firmly believes that work is not essential for a human being:

> There are so many who don't work. To begin with, the king doesn't do any work. The head-priest simply lolls in the temple and eats. Nor do birds and animals work. Why, then, do you insist that I work? (55)

Angulimal is a commentary on present-day politics of democracy which is based purely on the number game. Angiram justifies his 'no-work' policy and goes to the extent of chopping off the fingers of the panchayat members when they point fingers at him. Angiram becomes Angulimal and the Anguli Purana becomes the epical saga which celebrates valuelessness as it is concerned only with the end and not the means. The play seems to move from a feudal pre-democracy society to a contemporary democratic set-up. With Gaya being the locale "the dramatist has suggested the state whose malaise plagues all states of the country and even beyond...", says Singh (VIII). Moral anarchy is prevalent and very soon Angiram becomes a psychic case. The political game continues as the trade-off—the buying of fingers goes on. Divide and rule seems to help in this political game. As fingers are chopped off, the chorus sings,

> Little finger or middle finger,/ straight finger or crooked finger, Short finger or long finger,/ Half finger or full finger,/ fat finger or thin finger,/ male finger or female finger,/ healthy finger or ailing finger,/ true finger or false finger,/ ...they want fingers,/ they like fingers,/ .... Fingers are his life./ Fingers are his God./ Say Jai Angulimal/. (80)

The chanting of Buddhist chants in the background draws attention to the tragedy of this modern Angulimal who does not have a Buddha to redeem him. The play ends with the stage crowded with fingers pointing at one another and the chorus chanting:

> It's a Hindu's, a Muslim's/ a high caste's, a low caste's/ ... Aimed at one another,/ cursing one another,/ dispersing, extending,/ such hollow fingers,/ such useless fingers!/ Not men but fingers.... (102)

The third play in this trilogy is Kamroo which is a "disguised critique of feminism in its extremist form" (Singh, IX). As women blame men for their suppression and exploitation, they conceive of a world without males. In fact, this world admits no male gender, not even male trees and birds. The play begins with a song describing the natural beauty of the land called Kamroo and a group of dancers each with a lamp, performing a slow dance. The world of Kamroo, ironically, comes from *Kama* or the desire for natural physical gratification. The suppression of natural instincts is clearly unnatural and so lesbianism is seen as the alternative. Enacting a play is important to every playwright and so we have Bhamini saying, "A play is effectively taught through performance. Then it becomes easy to understand the play" (136)—almost voicing Vyas's own point of view that

> It is deeply satisfying to see many of my plays being performed repeatedly. It is all the more heartwarming when the performance matches your expectations or sometimes even surpasses it. I attribute the popularity of my plays to the convenience they offer for performance, the emotions that they convey, experimentation of themes and their quick pace. (Interview to the translators, 159)

Vyas is also happy that this play was staged in the Gujarat Samachar and INT competitions where it won prizes. As Shakespeare would say, 'The play's the thing'. Gradually realization dawns that motherhood is a natural instinct and that state is not possible without the presence of a man. The word man ceases to be taboo as stories of the Nath community are narrated, and gradually the presence of a man in their midst is discovered, the pregnancy and birth of a male child being the culmination. Kamini declares, "I declare each one of you free. You may go where you like" (157). In attempting to translate words which have gender in Gujarati was certainly a daunting task for the translators, but which they seem to have done with aplomb.

The importance of dialogue in a play is beautifully summed up by Prof. Eric Bentley when he writes of Ibsen:

> An Ibsenite sentence often performs four or five functions at once. It sheds light on the character speaking, on the character spoken to, on the character spoken about; it furthers the plot; it functions ironically in conveying to the audience a meaning different from that conveyed to the characters. (82)

Good dialogue should be able to throw out a sub-textual stream of images. Satish Vyas is able to do this excellently and the English translation is able to capture most of it.

The study of drama has to include a study of the theatre of that period and Gujarati theatre today is prepared and well-equipped for such plays. Vyas has also placed his plays in the contemporary context—social, political, moral, religious, etc.

WORKS CITED

Bentley, E.R. *The Modern Theatre*. Cambridge: Cambridge University Press, 1948.

Boulton, Marjorie. *The Anatomy of Drama*. London: Routledge and Kegan, 1960.

Granville-Barker, H. "Shakespeare's Dramatic Art", *A Companion to Shakespeare Studies*. Ed. Granville-Barker and G.B. Harrison, 1934.

Vyas, Satish. *Aadhunik Ekanki*. Ahmedabad: Gujarat Sahitya Parishad, 1984.

——. *A Trilogy of Two Act Plays*. Translated by Rupalee Burke and Darshana Trivedi. Ahmedabad: Divine Publications, 2008. (These plays were published individually in Gujarati)

Styan, J.L. *The Dramatic Experience: A Guide to the Reading of Plays*. London: Cambridge University Press, 1965.

6 Subaltern Historiography: Girish Karnad's *The Dreams of Tipu Sultan*

Abha Shukla Kaushik

The term Postcolonial does not lend itself to any fixed definition. Postcolonial discourse, sharing the mood of post-modernism and questioning the continuation of hierarchies, does not merely suggest a reversal of the many binaries that exist in the contemporary world. Postcolonialism is basically a shift in perspective. It is difficult to isolate postcolonial literary theories as something that is purely literary in nature. The interdisciplinary nature of the theory forbids their purely literary use. The fact that the term lends itself to more than one interpretation allows its use in different contexts. It is an interdisciplinary field that sometimes encroaches upon what can be identified as cultural studies, feminist studies, dalit movement, etc. Postcolonial investigation actually connects the literary with the sociological, the historical, the cultural, the political and the economic.

One of the early attempts to theorise postcoloniality is made by Bill Ashcroft, Gareth Griffith and Helen Tiffin in their book *The Empire Writes Back: Theory and Practices in Postcolonial Literatures*. Later Edward Said, Homi Bhabha and Gayatri Chakravorty Spivak emerged as the main voices.

The word postcolonial can be understood by drawing on both—the Commonwealth including the erstwhile colonies, and the more complex use of the word post as something which involves the past as well as the present. In the context of postmodernism and poststructuralism it is difficult to accept any post something as that which comes after something. Beginning of the post-independence phase in a country need not mean the beginning of postcolonial period. The many discussions regarding the term postcolonial make it clear to us that in the field of literary theories, this term is very rarely being used to denote something that comes after colonialism. With the dropping of the hyphen, the term postcolonialism is effectively being used as an always present tendency in any literature of subjugation marked by a systematic process of cultural domination through the imposition of power. The unhyphenated postcolonialism goes beyond the point of independence in the colonies which makes it possible to recognise differences. Two important trends that can be discerned are that it defies the linearity of history and accepts the notion of opposition as well as complicity among the colonised.

Postcolonial discourse offers certain theoretical models which can be used in the discussion of literary texts which come either from the colonial period written by the colonised or the coloniser or from the postcolonial contemporary world. Different texts therefore, can be read differently by using the perspectives of writers from the former colonies. Postcolonial literary criticism has primarily suggested a way of reading differently the colonial texts by reading differently and hence challenging any accepted mode of reading is an important feature of postcolonial criticism. Postcolonial critics challenge the identities imposed by the Western discourse on the third world. Gayatri Spivak writes about the continued subalternisation of the so-called third world literatures. Third world literature deals with the nation, with colonialism; with the trauma the colonial era has created in order to receive recognition in the international scene. In these literatures the desire to show one's own culture as a very distinctive culture overshadows the concern for raising questions regarding the impact of colonialism on these cultures. Discussion of literatures from India especially of creative writing in English in India therefore feels obliged to make a reference to the Indianness of experience that is presented through such literary works so that most of the novels written in the first half of twentieth century cannot but mention the freedom struggle as it was the social reality of the time. Later the focus shifted to discussing what was lost or gained by the colonial experience.

There is a very strong tendency among the postcolonial writers to rework the texts belonging to the colonial period. A re-reading of the different texts from the colonial era not only explores the various modes of representations of the colonised subjects but it also challenges the tendency to project coloniser as a unified subject superior to everyone else.

What needs to be stressed in any work dealing with colonisation and decolonisation is that the play of power in the colonised societies was very complex. The relationship between the coloniser and the colonised was never completely on the basis of oppressor—victim opposition but required at times the involvement of colonised at different levels. Actually there is a continued presence of power structures in what is common-sensically held as colonial and the subordinated. These power structures have a strange way of repeating themselves in different contexts with different coordinates and this is an important issue which cannot be overlooked. Different situations of structural domination do exist. There is always a possibility of the victim of one kind of exploitation acting as the agent of oppression in another system of discrimination. These power structures are so linked with one another that mentioning the subaltern history of the margins of modernity without bearing in mind the complex structures of the post-colonised societies in the contemporary world will not be very helpful.

Although most of the works on post colonialism have been produced in English, post colonialism as a theme is not anymore an area associated only with the British Empire or relevant only to English language. Economic exigencies and globalisation have resulted in a blurring of distinction between what was formerly identified as a colonial country and what is now seen as a powerful partner.

Locating the text in the social, historical, cultural, temporal context therefore becomes important. Edward Said gives greater responsibility to a literary critic by asking him to read a text contrapuntally. Deriving basically from the principles of comparative literary criticism, contrapuntal reading involves reading simultaneously from a different area or from a different period to throw more light on the interconnectedness of literature and history, of the centre and the margin. Subaltern historiography becomes a power tool in the hands of writers to do this. The historian in the subaltern historiography creates a place for the subaltern in history there by going against the norm of traditional history writing. The concept can be understood clearly if we look at one of the contemporary plays *The Dreams of Tipu Sultan* written by Girish Karnad, a well-known name in Indian theatre.

The Dreams of Tipu Sultan can be described as the long-awaited history play in which, after dealing with pre-colonial Indian history in two earlier works, i.e. *Tughlaq* and *Tale-Danda*. Karnad confronts British colonialism in its crucial early stages of military expansion. Karnad strongly felt that Tipu needed to be given his due as a major figure in Karnataka history, as a visionary, and a patriot and this play was written basically to revise his image. The 'dreams' of the play's title refer to a secret record of Tipu's dreams maintained by him, found after his death. These 'dreams' have been used like a metaphor by Karnad to show the 'real' man behind the image of the warrior, by looking into the inner aspirations of Tipu.

In many important respects Tipu Sultan follows the model of the history play established in *Tughlaq* and *Tale-Danda*. It draws upon a range of historical sources to present convincing portraits of the principal characters, but creates an imaginative plot and resonant dialogue to contain their experience. It deals with a controversial protagonist who can be characterized in radically opposite ways, depending on the observer's viewpoint —as a heroic figure of anti-colonial resistance comparable to the Rani of Jhansi in one perspective, and a treacherous but fallible and even foolish adversary in another.

Hussain Ali Kirmani, a person from the margin, employed by the British to write history, among the play's characters enables Karnad to reflect on the process of history-writing and the many conduits of history—oral and written, unofficial and official, objective and subjective, dominant and subaltern. The play also juxtaposes larger-than-life figures such as Tipu, Haider Ali, Nana Phadnavis, Lord Cornwallis, and Arthur and Richard Wellesley against a large cast of less prominent historical individuals like Kirmani, Tipu's principal queen and sons, numerous courtiers, and military officials, as well as ordinary citizens and soldiers. The result is a historical reconstruction that succeeds as a dramatic fiction through its multiple of voices. Kirmani in the play is reluctant to write the history of Tipu Sultan because he understands that the British have already presented Tipu as they want him to be seen. When Mackenzie asks him to write a history of Tipu Sultan he says "Yes. For you, he's made up of bits of evidence, bits of argument that prove your side was right. And that's what I don't understand. You have your version of history, all worked out. Why do you want my side? Why do you care?" (8).

Tipu Sultan stands apart in Karnad's works because as a play about colonialism it has to grapple with the inescapable psychodrama of East vs. West, Europe vs. the non European other, white vs. non-white, and colonizer vs. colonized. Avoiding any partisan parade of heroes and villains, Karnad creates ambitious and determined players in both camps who are sucked into the vortex of a major transitional moment in Indian history, politics, and culture. There are several important strategies at play in portrayal of Tipu Sultan that unfold simultaneously.

Karnad interlineates 'textualized' history with legend, lore, and memory because all these modes of transmission are germane to story of Tipu. The ruler's fabled persona as the Tiger of Mysore thus figures prominently in the action, both as oral legend and as military reality that the English must contend with. Karnad also casts his protagonist in multiple and contradictory roles—as a beloved ruler, legendary warrior, loving father, and visionary dreamer, but also as the Machiavellian schemer who plots with the French against English, the defeated soldier who enters into humiliating treaties with the enemy, and the gullible commander who is eventually betrayed by his own side. He has to agree to the humiliating terms of the British because he knows that "...several of my officers had already started secret negotiations with him. I knew who they were. My trusted officers. Yet I couldn't expose them without bringing the whole edifice down" (52). The perceptions of Tipu that have the greatest energy, however, are those with Brechtian-materialist overtones: they underscore Tipu's excitement over the 'new ideas' of Europe, his understanding of political economy, his interest in the link between commerce and empire, and his desire for an up-to-date army in his analysis. He tells his children "I've had two teachers in my life. My father, who taught me war, and the English who taught me trade. They taught me that era of camel is over, that it is now the age of sailing ship" (35). The tragedy of Tipu's fall is not only that it made way for a full-scale colonial takeover, but that it destroyed a visionary who shared the modernizing impulse of the European Enlightenment, and could meet the English on their own terms much to their chagrin.

Karnad's portrayal of English characters, is more in line with the conventional view of colonial conquest and the attendant cultural relations. Ethically, the main English characters in the play are rational, calculating, pragmatic, and ruthless, although their resentment of Tipu's apparent invincibility is also an aspect of what Homi Bhabha terms 'colonial ambivalence', while their racist contempt for all natives anticipates the unqualified colonialist denigration that Edward Said calls orientalism. Mornington sneers at Tipu's rising power and influence, "we have driven the French and Dutch out of India, contained the Portuguese. Is there any reason why we should tolerate an upstart native" (56). Karnad's principal thematic argument is a familiar one; the English succeeded in India not only because of their superior weapons and warfare, but because of their ability to play off members of the native ruling elite against each other. Tipu tells as much to the Maratha leader Haripant,

> What you've got is only a restitution of your earlier possessions. And in return you have given the English new territories: Salem, Dindigul, the Malabar coast with its coconuts and pepper and its magnificent ports. You are back where you were while English now have entire

> coastline of India. And remember, they are sea-faring power. Mine is landlocked kingdom, so I thirst for the sea, for today the sea is the power, to prosperity, you have the whole of the western coast. And instead of keeping the English out, you've permitted the shark into your waters and are trying to swim along with it. (54)

This accounts for the crucial quadrangulation between the Wellesleys, Tipu Sultan, the Nizam of Hyderabad, and Nana Phadnavis, and the dynamics made interesting from the perspective of the postcolonial present because it depicts the decentered nature of power relations in the absence of 'national' idea. Karnad's Tipu is a proto-nationalist who resists as long as he can the Englishman's schemes to rob his land, even as he understands that English 'believe in the destiny of their race' (51) and are willing to die in faraway places for their dream of England. At home, however, his appeals to a common faith fail to rally the Muslim Nizam to his side, and the instinctive hostility between Hindu and Muslim princes alienates him from the Marathas, although he issues a prophetic and purely political warning about England's territorial ambitions. The pained scenes of Tipu's peace treaties with the English emphasize that a complex, civilized, and prosperous culture was betrayed into subjection because of the pursuit of petty self-interest by key functionaries. He not only has to concede half of his territories, and most of his wealth to the British who are supported by the Nizam and the Marathas but also has to send two of his young sons aged seven and eight years as 'hostages'. He has to face a personal tragedy too at the time as his wife the queen dies. He is traumatised and ashamed of what he has to do. He says "Oh God! God! Why didn't I die before I heard these words? Ruqayya Banu, why didn't you take me with you? How did I come to this?" (48). In hindsight, the 'traitorous' collaborations between English and native armies across racial and cultural lines becomes the perfect prelude and antithesis to the invention of India-as-nation by nineteenth—and twentieth-century nationalists.

The play has scenes from the present which show Hussian Ali Kirmani's attempts to write an 'objective' account of the dead Tipu for the English, and then there are also intermittent scenes from the past which portray the sultan. He is the first nationalist who dared to look the British in their face, who does not want to

> ...spend the rest of my life looking with anxiety at the English for smiles of approval or frowns of displeasure? Today I am the only one in India who won't bow and scrape before them. So they want to humiliate me. I'm told England is buzzing with stories of what a monster I am and how I need to be subdued. (60)

This gives the play a powerfully elegiac quality. Kirmani as a participant-observer in Tipu's tragedy, shows that the matter of history consists not of facts (which concern the English) but also with the memories of fabled ruler that are fading all too quickly. The play begins and ends with memory: Kirmani and Colin Mackenzie serve as the chorus for a highly selective and reflexive history that unfolds cyclically, beginning with the day of Tipu's last battle and returning to it via crucial stages in his slide towards defeat and death. He lost not because he was weak but because he was betrayed by his own men. According to Kirmani,

> Mir Sadiq's conduct of the war was so openly treacherous that his own troops lynched him. Nadeem Khan, the Qilledar, has ordered a pay parade for his troops at very moment of British assault, thus taking them away from the battlefront. Poornaiya slipped with alacrity into the post of Prime Minister under the new regime. Qamaruddin was by his side. The battle of Seringapatam was lost before it had begun. (64)

This proves the point that colonialism thrives on the tenet that the centre at times invites selected members from the margin to be its inhabitant so that the rest of the margin could be marginalized. Besides, elite natives found the structure of the colonial institutions useful to strengthen their own positions.

In subtle moves, Karnad also reveals that the interests of the appointed historian are at variance in some respects with 'actual' history. Kirmani disclaims that Tipu ever sent an emissaries to Malarctic, the French governor-general of Mauritius, whereas the very first scene with Tipu shows him talking about Malarctic's role in arranging a royal delegation from Mysore to France. Tipu's dreams-partly narrated and partly enacted are political allegories of his reign; some contain imaginary characters while others conjure up key historical figures like Lord Cornwallis and Haider Ali. The last dream is the most poignant because it is a fantasy of victory in the midst of defeat and death. The insertion of this dream text into history introduces a level of experience even more evanescent than memory, and makes *The Dreams of Tipu Sultan* almost a poetic play. Karnad has raised many questions through the play regarding the British Colonial policy of divide and rule; the short sightedness of Marathas, Tipu's lack of killer instinct, etc. but he leaves many loose ends never imposing his own conclusions so that the reader or viewer can draw his/her own.

WORK CITED

Karnad, Girish. *The Dreams of Tipu Sultan* and *Bali: The Sacrifice*. New Delhi: Oxford University Press, Fifth Impression, 2009. All quotations are from this edition.

7 Habib Tanvir's *The Living Tale of Hirma*: Interrogation of the Popular Discourse of Democracy

R.T. Bedre and *K.U. Gangarde*

Habib Ahmed Khan (1923-2009), who later took the pen name as Tanvir, is ranked with Sisir Bhaduri, Utpal Dutt and Prithviraj Kapoor as the pioneering actor-managers in Indian theater (Wikipedia, 1-6). He could be called as the inaugurator of the theater of roots movement which is said to have begun in 1970s. Associated with the Progressive Writers' Association and Indian People's theater Association (IPTA) in India and Royal Academy of Dramatic Arts (RADA, England) for acting and Bristol Old Vic theatre School for direction, Late Habib Tanvir had been more popular for his path-breaking experiments with the non-professional Chhattisgarhi actors than for his playwriting, direction, poetry, acting and journalism. As an actor, Tanvir was also part of Richard Attenborough's masterpiece *Gandhi*. Like Girish Karnad, Tanvir too realized that the Western models cannot suit the Indian sensibility; he turned to the indigenous arts.

Like his Bengali counterpart, Badal Sircar, Tanvir had been in discussion more for his experiments in the performance of plays than his plays. His first play *Agra Bazaar* (1954) was performed with the local residents and folk artists from Okhla village in Delhi and students of Jamia Milia Islamia, his plays *Gaon ka Namm Sasural, Mor Naam Daamad* (1972) and *Charandas Chor* (1975) brought into limelight the native chorus technique like Nach. In early seventies he switched to Chhattisgarhi, a local language from Hindi and then to Pandavani, a folk singing style from the region and temple ritual. Spontaneously pro-improvisational, utter simplicity in style, presentation and technique, and yet powerfully experimental are the hallmark of Tanvir's productions. His notable performances are *Mitti ki Gaadi* based on Shudraka's Sanskrit play *Mrichakatika*, *Ponga Pandit*, *Jisne Lahor Nahi Dekha* (a rendition of Asghar Wajahat's work), *Kamdeo ka Apna Basant Ritu ka Sapna*, an adaptation of Shakespeare's *A Midsummer Night's Dream*, and *Zahareeli Hawa*, the Hindi translation of the Canadian Indian playwright Rahul Verma's *Bhopal* based on the Bhopal Gas Tragedy.

During his lifetime, Tanvir won several national and international awards for his contributions to the performing arts. Tanvir was recipient of awards like Sangeet Natak Akademy Award (1969), Sangeet Natak Akademy Fellowship (1996), Padma Shree Award (1983), Padma Bhushan Award (2002), and Kalidas Samaan (1990). He also enjoyed the honor of being nominated as member of Rajya Sabha from 1972-78.

However, it doesn't underestimate the rich content of his plays. Tanvir's dramatic corpus is not prolific as he authored very few plays, though he adapted and produced many plays. The most discussed among his plays are *Agra Bazaar, Charandas Chor*, and *Hirma Ki Amar Kahani*. He also wrote his only English play, *The Broken Bridge* in 1995. The first of these, *Agra Bazaar* is based on the works and times of the plebian 18th century Urdu poet, Nazir Akbarabadi. Tanvir's second play, *Charandas Chor* appeard in 1975 is an idealized presentation of a thrifty thief who tries to be honest and dooms himself. Like *Ponga Pandit*, Tanvir's *Charandas Chor* had invited wrath of certain religious groups. The last of these, *Hirma ki Amar Kahani*, has been translated into English as *The Living Tale of Hirma* by Anjum Katyal and Pratibha Katyal in 2005. An attempt is made herein to focus on Tanvir's ambivalent treatment in this play which offers a critical insight in the issue of the Accession.

As the play is set in the Accession times, it describes the conflict between the reluctant princely states and the Government of India on the issue of Accession. The semi-historical setting of the play, like those of Girish Karnad's plays, facilitates the readers/viewers to look at the process of Accession from an objective viewpoint, to use Brecht's term 'complex seeing'. Such semi-historical setting distances the contemporary viewers from the times and assesses the issues of the time. This ambiguity in the treatment and the approach is well reflected in a choral song in the play:

> ...There was dark and there was light
> And the light was dark as night
> Tell me how would you describe it?
> Know your goal, oh my heart, know your goal [...].
> (Tanvir, *The Living Tale of Hirma*, 10)

Hirma Dev Singh Gangavanshi, the ruler of the state of Titur Basna is the protagonist in the play. The Government of India forcibly and tactically and gradually makes him merge his state into the Union of India. The play enacts and dramatizes the attempts from both sides to achieve their respective goals. Both parties hide their overt intentions in the name of interest of the tribal subjects. On the one hand, Hirma (referred in the play) tries to cash his command and popularity over his people to retain his state, on the other hand, the government uses its power, the bureaucracy and some dissident elements of the Titur Basna. Hirma wants to retain his state and property, while the government wants to replace his rule with democracy. Kalhan, who is an old friend of Hirma, is the representative of the government. He is the collector of the district and later deputy commissioner, and is the counterfoil to the character of Hirma. Kalhan rightly reveals the government's designs:

> [...] the biggest issue facing me was how to replace the system of feudalism with democracy. This question faces me even today. The entire population of the state of Titur Basna is adivasi. This is a fact. Its whole life is according to the adivasi system, and one cannot label adivasi system a feudal system. But we saw feudalism in the adivasi rule of Titur Basna, and we began to work hard to introduce democratic values into this rule [...]. (9-10)

Like most rulers of the time, Hirma too strives to be independent and challenges the government plan to abolish his state. Hirma, like representative of all the princely states argues with Kalhan:

> Why are you people playing games with me? You speak of democracy, and in the name of democracy, you destroy a princely state. You depose a rightful king whose right to rule goes back for generations, and replace him with a man who cannot take my place as long as I'm alive. And today you come and tell me that I should get out of jail and exile myself? And this while the entire populace is clamouring for me? They consider me their Maharaj, Mahaprabhu, Mahapurohit and Bhagwan! You tell me if Bhagwan leaves their midst, who will the people call on, who will they turn to? (33)

In order to save his estate, Hirma, when put in exile, begins his hunger strike and demands that he should be allowed to lead the traditional Dussehara procession, and when allowed to do so, he reveals that he will take the idol of Danteshwari Devi with him on which all adivasis declare to follow him where he goes. This move of Hirma brings Kalhan on back foot. To escapes this crisis, Kalhan suggests Hirma to contest elections to plead his demand, Hirma tries that too, when failed, he joins the opposition party, and makes his personal issue as a people's movement. Kalhan narrates:

> Hirma and his supporters joined the opposition party. There were new demands raised by their party. The issue of Hirma's estate was turned into a people's movement which spread throughout Titur Basna. Baigin Bai meanwhile organized a separate women's political wing. She dressed them all in red saris and soon the streets of Rainapur were filled with thousands of red sari clad women agitators. The New Year brought fresh problems. (43-44)

When Hirma's political efforts do not bear fruits, he converts his attempts into people's Movement. At his orders, his adivasis subjects begin movement of non-cooperation and disobedience. They prevent the government trucks carrying paddy. The women organization led by Hirma's half wed wife Baigin Bai begins to oppose government policies. Patwari and government servants are asked to leave villages, people are told not to pay taxes, and the clerks are prevented from preparing the list of the farmers who have to pay the taxes. At first the demand was for ancestral property, then the throne and now for the self-government. He categorically tells Kalhan:

> The world that existed before you people came. If you leave us alone, even today it is possible to achieve. I didn't ask them to stop the levy, merely to reduce it. I didn't ask them to stop the requisition of paddy, merely to reduce it. I'm only interested in the throne to the extent that I can restore to the adivasis their land, their self rule, and their rights. Had you done that, I would have had no complaints against your government. You accuse me of hampering your work. I say that you are the one who has been continuously hampering me and will continue to hamper me in the future. (56)

On the other hand, Kalhan, the collector of Rainapur, plays his power game systematically. First, he captures the property of Hirma in the court of words and he was not allowed to do anything without the advice-cum-permission of the court. Hirma is replaced by his good-for-nothing brother Bira. When Hirma's attempts were nonviolent, he and his adivasi followers are made targets of the shooting by the government officials.

In fact, Tanvir turns the present play into a theatre of debate where the characters debate the merits and the demerits of the tribal system and proposed democratic setup. In the play, the playwright, through the character of Hirma, offers a criticism of the democratic rule where selfishness, corruption, and delay in execution prevail. Thereby one sees the other evil side of democracy, which promised a lot to the innocent masses but fulfilled little. A scene in the State Assembly exposes the defects of democratic system. The supporting members of the assembly describe the functioning of the democratic setup. The first member states it and demands reversal of government. He also points out the corruption:

> Honourable speaker, sir. Many promises were made to us before the elections. Ten months have passed since this government has formed. Not one promise has been kept to date. Instead, the people are being subjected to all kinds of torture and oppression. Even the one or two incidents I am aware of are enough to make the blood run cold. For hundreds of years, the adivasis have considered the land on which they live their own, and they thought of the jungles as theirs by right. For ages, they have been settling their own domestic, property and land disputes through their panchayat. But now their lands have been snatched from them, and their right to the jungle and its produce has been taken away. It has been said that they have cut down the jungle. We demand our jungle back! (38-39)

The Assembly member highlights the features of the adivasi life and also describes how the new government system has changed it. He also points out how the public property is looted in the name of the welfare schemes. He narrates:

> Traditionally, the adivasis held full rights to all the riches of the forest: Lac, *harra*, honey, gum, mango, berries, *tendu*. They subsisted on the sale of this produce, a little cultivation and some hunting. Now all this is forbidden to them. Yet a few middle men and contractors are legally permitted to profit from the forest. Illicitly, hundreds of contractors and complicit of government employees and forest officials are hacking down trees on a large scale. They are embezzling lakhs from the government funds. Doesn't this harm the forest? But let a single adivasi attempt to cut down a few trees and cultivate land according to his traditional way of life, and he is punished. It is said that he is destroying the forest. As a result he is being forced to turn from agricultural to manual labour. And all the while, his own jungle, his own wealth, is being swallowed by rich *seths*. And the *Sarkar* is totally indifferent.
>
> Earlier, the villages used to resound with the music of *mandar* and *manjira*. Now they are as silent as graveyards.

> For ages, the songs and dances of the people have been flourishing in the districts of Titur Basna. Instead of giving them the chance to develop further their art and culture, which is inseparable from their way of life, their farming and hunting and daily routine, is being destroyed. Instead of creating a healthy environment for these arts, which are linked to their daily life, they are being reduced to mere exhibitions in big cities once or twice a year. Adivasi cultural wealth is wiped out, in return for a smattering of awards to a few individuals. (39-40)

The same member also voices the complaints of many like Hirma Dev Singh whose estates have been snatched away by the government. He advocates for such states:

> ...It is a matter of great shame that a decent, upstanding, sensible gentleman should be declared insane, and his personal wealth, his by right of inheritance, should be forcibly taken away from him. And what is more, that this should be propounded by taking advantages of this for the elections. He is promised that if he should help the government in the election, his property will be restored to him. And after all this, Sarkar Bahadur blatantly refuses to relinquish his estate. (41)

The government representative, the minister tries to answer these questions. His reply reveals government's indifference towards the problem of the people. Justice in the every matter is denied in the name of procedure, to be exact, delaying the matter is the style of the government functioning. The first member who is also representative of the adivasis rightly points out: "Your committees and your deliberations are nothing but a screen from behind which you hunt your prey. You can no longer hide behind them" (43).

While protesting Hirma Dev Singh's men forming the opposition, the Minister exposes Hirma's designs quite openly. He terms it as a feudal conspiracy. He does not mince words while exposing the designs of Hirma's to the house:

> ...This entire drama that has been enacted before us is nothing but a feudal conspiracy. The erstwhile maharaja

> of Titur Basna, my good friend Shri Hirma Dev Gangavanshi, is clearly behind this. He is fighting for his ancestral property. He wants to re-establish feudal rule in the state. And yet he claims that he's doing it for the people. If this had not been so, these worthy gentlemen would have worked side by side with us, given us suggestions and advices, guided us. But these gentlemen are not interested in this. This is why they played their trump card and taken us by surprise. (42)

While criticizing the government process of accession, Hirma Dev Singh exposes the corruption in the bureaucratic schemes. He puts the failure of government policies in fulfilling the promises of development of adivasis Hirma makes the collector certain:

> ...I only know that all your schemes were failed, and your politics has been a failure. If even a small fraction of a huge budget of two crores which has been allocated for the development of Titur Basna had been used, we could have built a road of pure silver from Rainapur to Rainapur! (36-37)

The most important aspect of the play of all is that it offers an opportunity to look at the accession issue from both points of view objectively. The play debates the popular idea of public interest. So far the historical records and the popular literatures have portrayed the rulers of the erstwhile states as villain of their subjects. The picture is also painted that the cruel rulers opposed the public will of their majority subjects to join the Indian union like the rulers of Junagarh State and Hyderabad State. So far no one listened to the pangs/agonies of those rulers who lost their ancestral estates and prerogatives.

The central idea of the play is contrast. The play enacts this contrast of the parties—the Government of India, through in bureaucratic setup and the rulers of the states. This central argument of the play is well stated in a choral song in the play:

> Two kinds of people in this world
> Listen and hear us out
> Two kinds of people in this world

Those with money and those without
Heaven for one is hell for another
A feast for one means famine for another [....] (43)

The final truth of the play is stated by Kalhan who later becomes the deputy commissioner. "Every man is bound to do his duty. Trouble starts when the duty of man clashes with that of another" (54). To conclude, the play challenges the popular belief and discourse of democracy and offers an audience to the erstwhile rulers of the Indian princely states.

WORK CITED

Habib, Tanvir. *The Living Tale of Hirma.* (Trans.) Anjum Katyal and Prabha Katyal. Calcutta: Seagull Books, 2005.

http://en.wikipedia.org/wiki/Habib_Tanvir. Accessed on 06/06/2011.

8 The Tragic Dilemma of Larins Sahib

Basavaraj Naikar

Whereas the Indian English drama is very poor in comparison with the Indian English fiction and poetry, historical-political drama is the poorest. None can fail to notice the paucity of historical and political drama in Indian English literature. The reason for the conspicuous paucity are obvious enough. First of all, writing plays happens to be generally more difficult than writing fiction. Then writing plays in English is more difficult than writing plays in regional languages. Even if the plays are written in English, the chances of performance of such plays are very rare in the Indian context. Even if the performances of such plays are arranged, the response of the audience is restricted to the intellectual class. Secondly, writing a historical play requires a deep knowledge of history, historical imagination and a definite historiography—qualities conspicuously missing in the modern Indian English writers. Viewed against this background, Gurucharan Das's *Larins Sahib* happens to be a very significant historical play in Indian English which successfully captures the mood of the pre-Mutiny colonial encounter between Indians and the British and the dilemma faced by Henry Lawrence in the peculiar colonial situation. Henry Lawrence has been a very popular figure in the British India and a subject of literary depiction by many writers like Tom Gibson and Parrington.

Although the colonial encounter between the Indians and the East India Company provides the general background of the play, the main action focuses on the dilemma of the eponymous hero Larins Sahib who is torn between his professional loyalty to the East India Company and his sympathy for the Sikh King Dalip Singh. The play captures the ambivalent relationship between the colonizer and the colonized, which is marked by political contempt and hatred on the one hand and by emotional sympathy and understanding on the other. The dramatist has brought out the ambivalence of colonial relationship very clearly and convincingly.

The play dramatises the conflict between two forces, i.e. the British Imperialism represented by the East India Company with all its authorities like Hardinge, Currie and Elliot, and the Indian King Dalip Singh, son of the late Maharaja Ranjit Singh. Henry Lawrence who is known for his administrative efficiency and dutifulness is promoted as the Regent of the Sikh Kingdom and directed to be the caretaker of Dalip Singh, the minor son of the late Maharaja Ranjit Singh. The dramatist depicts the character of Henry Lawrence with remarkable clarity of motivation. Right from the beginning of the play we learn that he is known for his sympathy for and understanding of the native problems of India. It is precisely for this non-imperialistic habit that he has become a butt of ridicule among the East India Company officials. When Lord Hardinge, Governor-General camps at the bank of the Sutlej, half way between Lahore and Delhi on 20th March of 1846, he is eager to meet Henry Lawrence and discuss the details of administration of the Sikh Kingdom with him. Everybody has heard about his reputation and admires him for his efficiency. As Elliot describes to Lord Hardinge, Henry Lawrence "has built up a phenomenal reputation. Just two years on the border as a minor clerk with the Revenue Survey, and he's become a legend. I believe he's on the first-name terms with most of the nobility of the Punjab. They swear by him and the peasantry of the Ferozepur district thinks he's some kind of saviour" (3). Hardinge seems to be silently impressed by Elliot's description of Henry Lawrence's legendary reputation. But he exhibits a colonizer's contempt for the colonized country right from the beginning of the play: "Damn these bloody tribes! Damn this bloody country. Damn the whole world" (2). He continues to curse India because "Everything in India is second-rate. Even Travellers' best becomes second-rate in India" (2). Such a man with such contempt for and prejudice against India cannot like the look of Henry

Lawrence on his first meeting with him. He chides Henry Lawrence, "Why, this is disgraceful. You look like a bloody native. Your hair needs cutting. Your boots need shining, your shirt needs buttons.—(Softly) I hope your breeches stay up" (4). Henry Lawrence, though a servant of the East India Company is known for his sympathy for Indians and for his adoption of Indian dress which make him unpopular with his own British officials and colleagues. Currie comments upon him to Lord Hardinge, "Your Excellency, we should be thankful Mr. Lawrence is at least wearing his regimental colours. Normally, I am told, he finds native dress more comfortable" (4). In recognition of Henry Lawrence's remarkable ability, he is appointed by Lord Hardinge as the regent of the North-West territories of India: "In consideration of your generous services in the Punjab, in view of your knowledge of the North-West territories, I, Henry Hardinge, the Right Honourable Governor–General of India and Her Majesty's Most Honourable Privy Council hereby appoint you Agent of the Honourable East India Company to the Government of His Highness Dalip Singh, the son of Maharaja Ranjit Singh.... Come on, show some sign of life. You're promoted to the Residentship...the destiny of the entire North-West is now in your hands" (9). Henry Lawrence has to accept the responsibility of residentship, although he does not fully subscribe to the official view of the East India Company. The victory of the East India Company over the Punjab Kingdom is a matter of pride for Lord Hardinge who attributes the success to the military record of the East India Company. But Henry Lawrence does not feel proud of the achievement of his government, as he knows that "There's a difference however, between greatness and military records.... When their army is betrayed by their own leaders, it is hardly a feather in our cap" (7). He believes that there is no cause for joy "for a fairly fought battle would have resulted differently" (7). His conscientiousness has made him know the harsh truth that Maharaja Ranjit Singh's kingdom lost the battle on account of internal betrayal rather than on account of the so-called military prowess of the East India Company. But the defeat of the Punjab Kingdom is attributed by the British officers to the colonizer's racial superiority and civilizing mission. As Currie explains it, "It is clearly a matter of racial superiority. Every pagan power, no matter how formidable in appearance, must succumb to the civilizing mission of the white races" (7). But Henry Lawrence looks at Indians and their life from a sympathetic and humanistic point of view. He shows the remarkable perceptiveness of an inside-outsider in his grasp of the political events of the Punjab, "Ranjit Singh died seven years ago. Since his death there's been chaos everywhere and a fierce struggle for succession. The Sardars have been quarelling like dogs. And understandably, Sir. For he not only created the Punjab from a mass of petty states but in fact his personality united the kingdom. He established no institution, which could live apart from him. When he died, the Punjab died" (8). But his sympathetic interpretation of the Punjab situation is not viewed sympathetically by the East India Company. Currie accuses him that he "seems to have become a true oriental: he argues through the method of contradiction" (8). Whereas Henry Lawrence finds dignity in the life of Indians, Currie states that "I find no dignity among people who eat with their hands" (8). He further considers Henry Lawrence a clown and an orientalist thereby giving vent to his imperialistic contempt. He half-heartedly sanctions a native officer Sardar Sher Singh as assistant to Henry Lawrence. He feels the white man's burden of administrating India efficiently but at the same time fears the possibility of contamination with the inferior native culture. His warning to Henry Lawrence testifies to the fear, "A word of advice, Mr. Lawrence. I hope you will restrain your orientalism and keep the natives at a distance. Keep them in their place if you have to rule them" (11). Henry Lawrence being appointed as the Resident of Lahore goes there along with his native officer Sardar Sher Singh. He knows the enormity of his responsibility and decides to do his best to continue the work of the one-Eyed Lion of Punjab.

After assuming charge of the Punjab as Resident, Henry Lawrence has to face a number of challenges in his administration. The conflict between Christian culture and Sikh culture and that between British law and Sikh law create a variety of problems for him. For example, when a small detachment of English soldiers was crossing the Shah' alami Gate, the road was blocked by a couple of cows. The officer in command ignorant of the Hindu reverence for cows cleared the street the quickest possible way by shooting the cows. The Hindu religious sentiments being deeply hurt, the natives create a grand hullaballoo over the vulnerable issue. The resultant chaos and confusion generate a lot of tension to Henry Lawrence whose prime duty as a Resident is to maintain perfect peace and harmony in the kingdom. He, therefore, rushes to Rani Jindan Kaur to explain the unhappy event and wants to apologise publicly the next morning. Obviously, the Rani and her Wazir Lal Singh feel angry and hurt by the unhappy slaughter of cows. Thus in addition to cultural conflict, there is also a legal conflict. Lal Singh insists that the young officer who killed the cow should be tried according to Sikh law. But Henry Lawrence clarifies the point that it is not possible. "I'm afraid that may not be possible. He can only be tried according to the rules of the Honourable Company. However, I intend to deal with him as severely as I can. Please rest assured that this will not happen again" (23). Thus two law systems operating simultaneously in the kingdom of Punjab pave the way for a great deal of confusion. In spite of Henry Lawrence's willingness to apologise publicly, the Sikh authorities are not pacified easily. They want to avenge it in their own way. Lal Singh bursts out furiously, "The son of a pig; I'm going to burn the Residency tonight" (23). Not only that, but he wants to conspire with Tej Singh against the British. Henry Lawrence who understands the sensitivity of the cow-issue takes the young officer Lumsden to task. He slaps him and even threatens to suspend him from duty if he repeats the mistake. But the other officers of the East India Company are not very sympathetic towards the Indians. Abbot, for example, wonders, "...why in heaven's name are the niggers so touchy about the cows?" (26). He exhibits his religious superiority when he says, "The natives aren't Christians, sir. Their odious religion has thousands of ugly Gods and rituals. We aren't expected to know them all, are we?" (26). But Henry Lawrence can understand the positive side of the Indian behaviour and contrasts it with that of other people in the world. Referring to Lumsden's folly, he clarifies certain aspects of Indian behaviour, "Mr. Edwardes, I am less concerned with the integrity of Mr. Lumsden than with the fact that there are at least a thousand persons outside who would be glad to have his head. Fortunately Indians are civilized people, and don't resort to violence easily. In other land, by now we would have been burnt alive" (28). He further advises his colleagues to serve India whole-heartedly or return to their own country.

Rani Jindan is impressed by Henry Lawrence's sympathetic understanding of the natives of Punjab. She is, therefore, eager to befriend him. Assuming the disguised identity of a singer called Zubheda Begaum, she meets him privately at night and gifts a diamond to him as a mark of her friendship with him. She tells him how the diamond belonged to her late husband and how she values it greatly. She further requests him not to wear it publicly but to keep it as a memento of their friendship Henry Lawrence seems to be deeply impressed and touched by the Rani's gesture. His sympathy for India enables him to talk philosophically about the Punjab. He thinks that emperors like Alexander, Kanishka, Harsha, Timur and Babur may come and go, but the peasant of Punjab will remain permanently. "Yes, the Punjab peasant will always be there. Isn't it reasonable then, that we win him to our side? To win him, we must work for him, for his sake. The memory of the British should rest in the peasant's heart, in his timelessness" (38). But such a sympathetic point of view of a servant of the company is not accepted as a sincere one by Sher Singh who sees an element of hypocrisy in it and who thinks that "even the wisest men forget where good ends and power begins" (39). The diamond which is secretly given to Henry Lawrence by Rani Jindan with a warning not to wear it publicly symbolises the bond of friendship between the two. But Henry Lawrence who is flattered by the precious gift forgets her warning and wears it publicly, thereby attracting the attention of the courtiers of the Kingdom.

Within the Kingdom, there are antagonistic forces working against each other. Whereas Sher Singh is a confidant of Henry Lawrence, Tej Singh and Lal Singh identify themselves with the natives now although they have betrayed the Kingdom to the enemy in the past. It is this internal division in the Kingdom that complicates matters for Henry Lawrence and aggravates the misunderstanding between the colonizers and the colonized. When Henry Lawrence sincerely tries to apologise to the public of Lahore about the inadvertent killing of a couple of cows by one of his officers and promises not to allow any repetition of such mistakes in future and even permits concession on land revenue for one year, the people are happy and cheer him heartily. But Tej Singh and Lal Singh take advantage of the generosity of the British officers and create confusion in the mob by shooting at Henry Lawrence and other British officers. Fortunately Henry is not hurt, but they are puzzled by the confusion created by the conspirators. Lal Singh and Tej Singh accuse Sher Singh as a 'spoon' of the British. Sher Singh, in turn, accuses Lal Singh as a traitor turned Wazir. Lal Singh and Tej Singh are not really sympathetic to the Rani although they pretend to be her well-wishers. They ask Sher Singh to tell Henry Lawrence to return the Kohinoor diamond to them so that they can blackmail the Rani. Thus both Lal Singh and Tej Singh behave like perfect opportunists.

Meanwhile Lawrence tries to win the hearts of the native population by wearing the typically Indian garments including the *chogah*. But the Rani dissuades him from doing that on account of the possibility of the Sardars' resentment to it. But Henry Lawrence dreams of building bridges, roads and canals in the Punjab and make it sing with joy. He wants to continue the welfare activities of the Lion of Punjab. The Rani, of course, lends her moral support to his plans. Henry Lawrence seems to have fallen in love with Rani Jindan without his knowing it.

Lumsden, a hater of natives, has again acted high-handedly by killing twenty-four people to curb the violence at Shah Alami Gate. When Lawrence remonstrates him for behaving so irrationally, he answers, "Yes. The filthy native needed to be taught a lesson" (49). His answer obviously indicates the callousness of a colonizer towards the colonized and provides a sharp contrast to Henry Lawrence's sympathetic approach to life. Henry Lawrence is so angry with him that he instantly terminates his services at Lahore and sends him to Calcutta.

Henry Lawrence's long experience in India has enabled him to understand the contrast between British administration and Indian administration. He knows that the cultural difference between the two peoples comes in the way of natural understanding and rapproachment. He, therefore, tries to conduct the Durbar in a typically Indian fashion by having the divan and cushions covered with colourful velvet with gold initials H.L. Embroidered on them so that he can rule the natives better. "That is the way to rule India...with dignity. I must also get the Residency exterior lifted a bit. Yes, Indians like colour, pageant, style. They respect it. That's authority for them. This place looks like a barracks—no wonder they think us odd. They like to be ruled through the heart; we rule through the head. They like to be dealt with at the personal level; our basis of administration is impersonal law. They respect tact; our laws and settlements are crudely blunt" (52). A strict administrator, Henry Lawrence has had Wazir Lal Singh arrested for the conspiracy of firing at the Shah' alami Gate. But Sher Singh warns him to be cautious about Lal Singh and get him released lest he (Lawrence) should get into trouble. He explains how Wazir Lal Singh is a very influential and dangerous traitor and how he can harass Lawrence in a variety of ways. But Lawrence turns a deaf ear to Sher Singh's warning.

Henry Lawrence conducts the Durbar in an Indian fashion and hears the cases. He exhibits his humanitarian attitude when a poor woman comes to the Durbar and complains about the sickness of her child. In spite of the absurdity of her request, he sends her away with a purse of money and with an advice to seek a doctor's services. But he behaves like a strict administrator when he hears the case of a young Hindu widow who refused to commit *sati* when her husband died. Henry Lawrence asks for her opinion. But unfortunately she refuses to talk with anybody. When he seeks the opinion of two brahmins there, they opine that she should be burnt alive as it happens to be the Hindu custom. He further opines that a wife is a personal property of a husband who can even throw her into a well.

Henry Lawrence is so angry with these brahmins that he threatens to throw them into a well. He tells them that according to the British law the punishment for a man who burns his wife is death by hanging. He wants to put an end to the irrational and inhuman practice of *sati* and declares, "Sher Singh, we are issuing a proclamation: *sati* is with immediate effect abolished in all provinces and districts of the Punjab. And the Hindu Reform Bill is with immediate effect extended to all parts of the Punjab" (56). His decision to abolish *sati* is not only bold but very admirable. Similarly he emerges as a strict administrator when he orders Lal Singh and Tej Singh to be brought up before the Durbar. In spite of Sher Singh's warning against disgracing them, Henry Lawrence makes three charges against them: one, of an attempt to abduct His Highness Maharaja Dalip Singh and subvert his Raj; two, of conspiracy of firing at the English officers; and three, of exploiting the war against the English to subvert the Raj. But Lal Singh and Tej Singh do not answer him. On the contrary they spit at him contemptuously. Henry Lawrence, therefore, orders them to be put into lock-up. Thus, he enjoys the dispensation of justice as well as being addressed as the 'Angrez Badshah'.

But Henry Lawrence's sympathy for the natives and his strict administrative actions are not approved by the authorities of the East India Company. He is, therefore, called by the Governor-General Hardinge at Calcutta to answer the charges levelled against him. He goes there wearing a *chogah* on his head and is, therefore, not easily recognised by Hardinge. When he is properly recognised by the authorities after a little while, Hardinge asks him sarcastically, "Good God man, what are you up to? Where did you get these silly robes? This isn't a fancy-dress party. Still haven't learnt to be a soldier, have you?" (60). Lord Hardinge is excited about the annexation of Sind to the Company and has been dreaming of conquering the beautiful Kashmir, by managing some sort of arrangement with Gulab Singh. His imperialistic pride, tact and aggressiveness are evident in his words, "I know it is a delicate matter. India's a delicate matter. Don't forget gentlemen, we're the greatest power on this earth today. Everything we do is a delicate matter" (61).

Hardinge is not bothered about justice, mercy or fairness. A representative of the East India Company, he has a predatory approach to India and gets angry with Henry Lawrence who believes in justice, fairness, sympathy and love in spite of being an agent of the company. Henry Lawrence is charged with six mistakes: one, the unauthorised and unnecessary arrest of their most faithful allies in the Punjab Kingdom, Wazir Lal Singh and Army Commander Tej Singh; two, the unsanctioned release of one month's revenue of Lahore district; three, unbecoming behaviour in the 'cow-row'; four, pre-emptory dismissal of Lumsden, one of the their best officers of the company; five, employing and favouring Sher Singh, a native officer and six, accepting valuable gifts without informing the Headquarters. But Henry Lawrence refuses to accept them as charges but considers them only as questions. He answers the questions one by one. He defends his arrest of Lal Singh and Tej Singh on the grounds of treachery and attempt to subvert the Raj of His Highness Dali He says he has waived the revenue of the Punjab until a just settlement of the problem. He wants to honour the promises and treaties with the leaders of the Punjab. He is against separating the young Maharaja Dalip from the mother and Regent Queen Jindal on legal grounds. Henry Lawrence refuses to give the diamond (Kohinoor) to Hardinge on the ground that it is a symbol of the bond of friendship between the Rani and himself. He explains, "That won't be possible, sir. The Jewel isn't mine. It belongs to the Rani and the Maharaja's family. It was only loaned to me as a symbol of her faith in us" (67). Thus, Henry Lawrence maintains his sterling integrity on account of which he has become a very popular officer in the Punjab. Lord Hardinge cannot but admire him. As Elliott confesses, "...I feel we owe Mr. Lawrence our congratulations. In no part of India is there so much popular sentiment in our favour. It's all due to him. He's a hero there, sir" (67-68). Lord Hardinge invites him to dinner in a mood of appreciation.

Henry Lawrence's desire to win the hearts of the natives of Punjab through fair dealing, his extraordinary respect for the late One-Eyed Lion of Punjab make him almost crazy and inebriated with power. His vanity is bloated beyond proportion. That is the reason why he wants to be addressed as 'Angrez Badshah' and be dressed in the garments and ornaments of the late Maharaja of Punjab. Sher Singh feels shocked by Henry's craziness. But Henry is not in a position to listen to him or anyone. He appears to be intoxicated with power and hence grows megalomaniac: "Angrez Badshah; Angrez Badshah; (Puts his hand with the diamond condescedingly before him.) Bow down to the Angrez Badshah; Bow down, you Lal Singh and Tej Singh. You can kiss the jewel. The Punjab is mine, as surely as the Kohinoor is mine. Where is my Rani? Oh, she's in the harem, is she? So much the better. Where is my son? Aslee Let him slee He needs his slee The tribes are restless? We shall teach the tribes. They are dealing with a great Badshah of a great land. Let's go on to battle. The new Lion has come. (And he yells) Arhh!" (70). Obviously Henry tries to overreach himself by identifying himself with the late Maharaja of Punjab and dreaming of becoming a new Lion. The power has gone to his head.

But he is totally independent in his actions. His megalomania is going to be curbed by the East India Company. Although he wants to do a lot of good to the Punjab and win the hearts of the native population, he is a puppet in the hands of the East India Company, which has its own imperialistic policy. Henry has to act according to the instructions of the Governor-General Lord Hardinge. Although Wazir Lal Singh and the Commander-in-Chief Tej Singh are traitors according to Henry Lawrence and Maharaja Dalip Singh, they are said to be close allies of the Company Government and useful to it in many ways. Henry Lawrence becomes helpless in this context and has been forced to cancel the arrest of these traitors and to apologise to them publicly. Not only that, he has to honour them with titles along with other thirteen nobles. He has placed the name of Tej Singh at the top of the list of nobles to be honoured. He, therefore, calls a special Durbar meeting chaired by His Highness Dalip Singh and attended by the Regent Rani. After explaining the purpose of the meeting, he announces the award of the title to Tej Singh, "The first and foremost Sardar of our court, the brave and noble Sardar Tej Singh, the Commander-in-Chief of the Khalsa, is to receive the first honour; from today he will be addressed as Raja Tej Singh" (72). Henry Lawrence has to ensure the loyalty of the nobles of Punjab by honouring them with titles and for making use of them for the imperialistic cause. In spite of his love for the Punjab, he cannot be a native, but has to be an agent of the Company, and execute the directions given by the Governor-General. But the dramatic change of his attitude towards the traitors like Lal Singh and Tej Singh is not liked by the Regent Rani and His Highness Dalip Singh, as they attribute it to his loyalty to the Company. That is the reason why His Highness Dalip Singh embarrasses Henry Lawrence by insulting Tej Singh deeply. When Lawrence personally takes the golden plate containing the saffron to Dalip, the latter, instead of applying it on Tej Singh's forehead snatches the plate from Lawrence and turns it upside down over the head of Tej Singh. Then, he kicks Sardar Tej Singh with his left foot. Tej Singh loses his balance and falls down. There is great laughter in the Darbar. Obviously, Lawrence is as much embarrassed as Tej Singh is humiliated by this unexpected act of the young Maharaja. Lawrence, therefore, dismisses the Durbar.

Lawrence knows that Dalip is too young to know why he humiliated Tej Singh by kicking him publicly. He guesses that Dalip must have been schooled by the Rani. When he meets the Rani, she confesses that she did the schooling and that there was a reason for that. Referring to Tej Singh, she says, "That son of a pig deserved it. You want to know if I put Dalip up to it. Yes. I did. And I'm not at all sorry or ashamed for what my son did" (75). She accuses Lawrence, "You Angrez have been helping that traitor from the very beginning. Now you've made him a Raja. It's disgusting! Half the Punjab knows he's a scoundrel and just because he does your dirty work.... And apologizing to Lal Singh like that. I've never been so humiliated" (75). But Lawrence accuses her that she has insulted the Company Government. He further orders her to go far away from her son, i.e. to Sheikhupura, because she is a naughty woman and a troublemaker. The Rani tells him not to separate her from her son. But Lawrence's loyalty to the Company Government has hardened him against the Rani. The transformation of his attitude to the Rani is very unexpected and dramatic. He is silent with embarrassment. But the Rani loves him as an individual though not as an agent of the Company. She wishes to use the personal intimacy to her political advantage. She says, "I want to love you. Why are you sending me away? Don't you love me any more?" (78). She is angered by his silence. But suddenly she become aware of her political identity and threatens him, "You can't do this to me! Angrez or the Angrez's father can't touch me. Does the Angrez realize who I am? (Slowly, deliberately imperiously). I am the Mother of the Punjab. I am the wife of the one-Eyed Lion. You won't dare! I am the Mother of the Khalsa. Touch me and you'll have mutiny on your hands. Once I leave, a curse falls on the Angrez. And the first one to go will be you, Larins" (78). But Lawrence remains helplessly silent. When she realises his deep-seated loyalty to the British Government. She understands the futility of having friendship with him. She, therefore, asks him to give back her diamond to her. But he refuses to give it to her. "I can't. The Governor-General has promised it to Queen Victoria" (79). The Rani curses him for his betrayal of faith and mannerlessness. She analyses his behaviour properly, "You are intoxicated Larins! Something demonic is urging you on to your destruction. Believe me. (Pause) God, now I understand your robes, your Durbars and your 'Angrez Badshahs'. It all fits. And your obsession with my late husband. You're drunk, my friend. Power's gone to your head. And you've forgotten your manners" (79). She is so angry with him that she calls him 'dirty and cruel'. Her young son Maharaja Dalip also hates Lawrence for his high-handed behaviour and pro-British attitude. Lawrence insists that the Rani should leave Lahore on the same day. As the last attempt, she declares her love for him once again and asks him to take her to England or Nepal, "Larins, I've an idea. Why don't you take us to England? Let's leave this dirty place to the Angrez, come. (Lawrence shakes his head.) Why, what's the mater? All right, then we can go to Nepal" (81). But Lawrence flatly refuses to oblige her, because his professional loyalty to the British Government triumphs over his private passion for the Rani. The Rani, therefore, helplessly bids goodbye to him and goes away from there. Henry Lawrence is torn between two loyalties, i.e. private attraction for the Rani and the professional duty to the Company. He has to sacrifice the private loyalty to the professional one.

Lawrence's behaviour with the Rani appears rather callous and mannerless even to Sher Singh who has so far been a loyal assistant of Lawrence. He is deeply hurt by the imperialistic attitude of Lawrence paving the way for annexation of the Punjab Kingdom to the East India Company. He bursts out helplessly and angrily, "Ranjit Singh is dead today!... The Punjab is dead today!... You've banished the Mother of the Punjab. Time is up. His Highness is too young to know what he wants. The Punjab is now another pawn in the Angrez's game" (81). He further accuses Lawrence of callousness in separating the mother from the son and of lack of capacity for friendship. The height of his anger could be seen in his frontal attack on Lawrence; "You hypocrite! You never loved anyone. You don't deserve anyone's friendship. You are incapable of giving. You turned a hypocrite when you saw how powerful you'd become. You imagined you had become Ranjit Singh" (82). Sher Singh wants to sever his friendship with Lawrence because the latter is evil and ambitious. He analyses Lawrence's behaviour almost brutally, "It's a matter of choice. You've chosen. You could have chosen the way of the heart. Because she was your friend—you won't deny that? Or you could have chosen to obey your country's order. Your duty to her or your duty to *your* queen. You've chosen. In my terms, Larins Sahib, it's a choice between the Punjab and England. Your Queen and my Queen. That's where we part. I won't have anything to do with the Company Raj. Farewell!" (83-84). Just as Lawrence has made his choice, Sher Singh also makes his choice and declares his intention of fighting for the Rani and against the British Raj, "We are enemies. Farewell, Larins Sahib. Before I leave, let me tell you: I shall return. When I do, I shall be on the other side. I shall come to revenge my queen. So be prepared. I shall be armed and the whole Punjab army will be behind me.

The Angrez will be thrown out of the Punjab or I shall die. Larins Sahib, you've made a man of me and I thank you. It was another Sher Singh who wanted to be an English gentleman. He's as dead as the One-eyed Lion. You taught me the magic of the Lion's name, Larins Sahib. Now you know what I shall do: I shall shout (and he shouts.) 'Come on men. Take your swords. Remember the Lion, and save your land.' I shall rally every son and father. We shall kick out the Angrez. And we shall save our land. Farewell, Larins Sahib, we shall meet on the battlefield again" (85).

Henry Lawrence has lost his very confidential friend Sher Singh because of his deep seated imperialistic attitude. Although Lawrence tried to understand the native problems of Punjab, he did not choose the way of the heart, but instead chose the way of the head. He has grown conceited without knowing it. Intoxicated with power, he dreams of being a second Lion of the Punjab. The power seems to have gone to his head. That is the reason why he has lost the sympathy of both the Punjabis and the Company Raj alternately. He is nearing his *hubris.* Although dejected by Sher Singh's final departure from him, he soon recovers his composure. A glow returns to his face. He goes to the mirror again and adjusts his *chogah.* Then he swaggers about displaying his jewel triumphantly. He boasts of himself," But I still have the Punjab. Let them go away. I don't need them. I don't need the Rani; nor Sher Singh. I have the Punjab, Angrez Badshah! The New Lion is here. I am the Punjab!" (86). It is precisely at this moment of enactment of power-drunkenness, the balloon of his vanity is punctured. He receives a special mail from the Governor-General at Calcutta through a special messenger. Although Edwardes hesitates to read the letter as it is marked as 'personal and confidential', Lawrence orders him to open it and read out the contents. Accordingly Edwardes reads the letter loudly, "My dear Lawrence, I regret to inform you that the Court of Directors of the Company are persuaded that the Government of India no longer require your services in the Punjab. Mr. Currie will temporarily assume charge at Lahore until a suitable successor is appointed. He will prepare grounds for the formal annexation of the Punjab. You are requested to proceed to Calcutta at the earliest" (86). Now Lawrence's humiliation is complete. His intoxication with power is totally washed out. He orders Edwardes, "You'd better go now, Edwardes. I'll take off the Lion's *chogah*. It's grown too hot for me" (86). His removal of the Lion's *chogah* is symbolic of his loss of power and reputation. The termination of his services in the Punjab by the Directors of the Company appears to be the right kind of punishment for his hauteur. In this sense, Henry Lawrence becomes a tragic figure. Like most of the tragic heroes, Lawrence is forced to sacrifice his power for the temporary pleasure of megalomania. The play *Larins Sahib* thus shows the operation of the law of life punishing the man when he loses the right perspective and behaves irrationally.

WORK CITED

Das, Gurucharan. *Larins Sahib*, London: Oxford University Press, 1970. All quotations are from this edition.

9 The Generic Constructs of the Ideas of 'Patriarchs' and 'Deviants' Re-orienting Dattani's *Where There is a Will* and *Dance Like a Man*

Saptarshi Mallick and *Dibyabibha Roy*

Mahesh Dattani's dramatic canvas is coloured with real life conditions and the livid experiences related with urban cosmopolitan and middle class Indians. The issues dealt by Dattani in his plays, are radical, unconventional, contemporary and free from taboos. Homosexuality, lesbianism, child sexual abuse, communalism and gender discrimination are some of the areas that get addressed in his plays preparing the stage for a specific realism on the lines of Ibsen and Shaw. For him human beings are an integral part of the society and consciously or unconsciously the creeping influences of societal set up, determine the fabric of relationship around him. Dattani explores the dichotomy between male and female roles within the archetype of family managed by male members in the context of the Indian society.

The society at large has never been able to re-define the externally constructed notions of masculinity and femininity. Men had been viewed as the source of support and had been seen as a guardian of the female race. He had been the chief bread-earner of the family and therefore, the unrecognized familial law had put the encumbrance of being the head of the family on the males. This is specifically true of the Indian society which has always been embedded into stereotypes. We have always found men to be at the zenith of power and supremacy. The women had always remained at the background, either as a moral support to their men or as an innocent confidante, of course with certain exceptions. Indian society had always been therefore a phallocentric one where any deviations on the part of gender or sexuality had been a source of ridicule or scorn.

John Beynon in "Understanding Masculinities" observes:

> The [still] widely accepted view among the general public is that men and women fundamentally differ and that a distinct set of fixed traits characterize archetypal masculinity and femininity. This is reflected in popular sayings such as 'Just like a man!' or 'Just like a woman!' and in the kinds of features found in popular magazines along the lines of 'How manly is your man?', with a list of attributes to be rated or boxes to be ticked. Masculinity and femininity are often treated in the media as polar opposites, with men typically assumed to be rational, practical and naturally aggressive and women, in contrast, are held to be expressive, nurturing and emotional. (56)

In Indian English literature it is difficult to find writings where the notions of deviations and the deviants are revered. Sometimes in the garb of humour and sometimes with 'philosophical twists' (Raina, 449), there has been very little focus on the idea of subverting the patriarchal stereotypes. Asha Kuthari Chaudhari regarding the choice of setting and the themes of Dattani's plays observes,

> ...Dattani unambiguously chooses his location within the dynamics of a pre-existing structure of the contemporary urban Indian family which then turns into the site of the ensuing conflict, within his narrative. With newer realities piling on the older, 'acceptable' realities, his plots and subplots often work to destroy the very edifice in which they situate themselves, blasting the given stereotypes that shape the structures. (25)

Dattani treats men as gulls of their own fates, shows them as formidable authoritative figures of the family and at the same time, he creates other male characters that question the normative roles of the men or become social deviants who raise the questions on the hegemonic social structure and in a way subvert the socially constructed stereotypes.

In an article "Men will be men...stuck in patriarchal role", Nandita Dasgupta writes, "She may have got rid of her meow, but he's stuck with his alpha roar. For men there seems to be no other way to be. Sure he may wax his chest and do the washing up today, but he's still trapped by patriarchal stereotypes and continues to play protector, procreator and provider" (Dasgupta). Dattani's male characters are as much interesting as his female characters are. In *Dance Like a Man*, *Where There is a Will*, *Do the Needful*, *On A Muggy Night in Mumbai*, *Bravely Fought the Queen* or *Tara*, the men in his plays are presented in a different charisma. The men are stuck in their roles of power and authority that do not fall in the line and choose to be fallouts or deviants from their stigmas of normative heterosexual roles. Dasgupta in her article quotes Roop Sen, who conducts workshops on gender imaging and roles, "We question the stereotype. Because if you're not in the mould, every part of you is questioned. If you're anything else, you're demasculinised" (Sen). Therefore when we find the reflections of the aggressive, heteronormative portrayals of men like Amritlal Parekh and Hasmukh Mehta, we also find the 'demasculinised' Jairaj and Ajit, or a Nitin and Alpesh in his plays. It is actually the subversion of the masculinity that the heterosexual men exemplify and irrevocably we realize how futile their 'alpha roars' are.

In *Where There is a Will*, Dattani's dramaturgy weaves a tapestry of philosophical insight and social consciousness which is a rare one. The play focuses on the assertive figure of a staunch patriarch, Hasmukh Mehta, who is seen working within the traditional roles of a patriarchal society in the first act. Sita Raina in her "A Note on the Play" in *Collected Plays* says,

> *Where There is a Will* has several interesting aspects. Mahesh described it as the exorcism of the patriarchal code. Women—be it daughter-in-law, wife or mistress—are dependent on men and this play shows what happens when they are pushed to the edge. What interested me particularly was its philosophical twist. To be the watcher of one's self is to make intelligent changes in this life.... Consequently, when he became the watcher of his actions,

> he perceives that his desire for control has led him to be victim of his own machinations unlike Kiran who uses power play to essentially improve her relationships. (449)

The play, set in a lavish house of Hasmukh Mehta, portrays an elite society of a Gujrathi family, where the father is seen to be the dictator. Each of the four characters in the play, Hasmukh, his wife Sonal, his son Ajit and his daughter-in-law Preeti, 'provides an appropriate foil to his/her counterpart'. (Agarwal). From the beginning of the play, we find Hasmukh Mehta exercising his hegemonic control over the family and its members to establish his own conception of 'self' which he has drawn from his father. He thinks that it is he who had made a living for his family. He scorns his son Ajit and he continuously curbs his right at home; does not allow him to speak to his friends on business matters nor does he allow him to talk to government officials. He claims that he is "trying to fill up empty spaces" (458) in Ajit's mind but actually he allows no independence. He proclaims: "I, Hasmukh Mehta, have every right. It's my phone you are using in my house, and it's my business secrets you are leaking to government officers, and my typists your friend is flirting with" (458), but being unaware he himself jeopardizes his own life on having an affair with Kiran Jhaveri who, as Ajit says after the death of his father, is "...not a who-is-he, she's a who-is-she...Yes. Yes. She's a marketing executive turned company director—and my late father's mistress" (485). Hasmukh Mehta is in control of the two distinct spaces in his life; his public and private domains. The former being his successful business career and the latter his family and his relationship with his wife and son which is apparently complete and perfect. However he has his own grievances:

> Why does a man marry? So that he can have a woman all to himself? No. There's more to it than that. What? Maybe he needs a faithful companion? No. If that was it, all men would keep dogs. No. No, I think the important reason anyone should marry at all is to get a son. Why is it so important to get a son? Because the son will carry on the family name? (*Pause*) Why did I marry?

> Yes, to get a son. So that when I grow old, I can live again through my son. Why did my father marry? To get me. Why did I marry? To get Ajit... (*An expression of distaste appears briefly on his face, then he coughs.*) Then I should be a happy man. I've got a loving wife who has been faithful to me like any dog would be. (475)

To him, his wife is nothing more than a faithful dog although it is Sonal who keeps a track of everything in his life, his blood pressure, his tablets and his heart attacks. But Mehta is perhaps no exception. Beena Agarwal therefore rightly comments, "Hasmukh's statement (regarding his wife as quoted above) strikes a tone of sarcasm and sexual colonialism" (109). In *Tara* too we come across Patel who too nurtures similar thoughts regarding his wife:

> Patel: Bharati, put down that phone!
>
> Bharati: How dare you run my life!
>
> Patel: Oh, for God's sake! You're getting out of hand! (343)

The wives, in Indian society can perhaps only be busy with the household chores and continue to be a 'faithful' follower of her husband. It takes only a few characters like Jaya (in Shashi Deshpande's *That Long Silence*) to realize that "Man and woman...I realized the deep chasm between the two. They are separated for ever" (Halder, 102). Mehta is no different from the likes of Amritlal Parekh, Jiten and Sridhar. A man becomes a 'man' as a result of the sociological processes as soon as he starts growing. They imbibe their masculinities as soon as they enter the social life. Beynon says, "Men are not born with masculinity as a part of their genetic make-up; rather it is something into which they are acculturated and which is composed of social codes of behaviour which they learn to reproduce in culturally appropriate ways" (What is Masculinity? 2). Mehta a victim of the ideology, an order of the society that he has perhaps been subjected to. He accuses his wife of her incapabilities: "When we were newly married, I used to joke with her and say she was as good as gold. But that was when we were newly married. I soon found out what a good-for-nothing she was. As good as mud. Ditto our sex life. Mud. Twenty-five years of marriage and I don't think she has ever enjoyed sex. Twenty-five years of marriage and I haven't enjoyed sex with her" (473). He has his wrath against his son too whom he considers nothing: "If you are you, you are nowhere. You are nothing just a big zero. No matter what you do, you'll remain a zero. Over the years you'll just keep adding zeroes to your zero. Zero, zero, zero" (461), but that is not all for him. The mercenary Mehta means nothing more than money, "On their own, the zeroes don't mean a thing. But if there's a number one standing before all those zeroes, then they really add up to a lot (461), and we realize how "Money has made him stubborn" (472), and he rests his power play on his money and on his being a man just as Amritlal Parekh in *Dance Like a Man*, who resists his son from taking up dance as his career because for him, "It doesn't give you (his son, Jairaj) any income" (415). In a recent Hindi film *3 Idiots*, we find how a father almost forces his son to take up engineering as his career whereas he wants to pursue Literature. In the long run, he succumbs to his own patriarchal image when his son commits suicide for not being able to cope with the pressure that his father has been exercising over him. To most fathers, as to Mehta, sons are sources of investments and they want their returns of their own investments: "Who is Ajit? Isn't he my son? No. He's just a boy who spends my money and lives in my house. He doesn't behave like my son. A son should make me happy. Like I made my father...happy. That is what I wanted my son to make me. (*Gets a little worked up*.) But he failed! Miserably! He has not a single quality I look for in a son! He has made my entire life worthless! He is going to destroy me!" (475). But these father figures do not realize that their sons are different. The collapse of the traditional world as it comes in conflict with the modern sensibilities is also Dattani's perception of subversion, which has time and again cropped up in his *Dance Like a Man*. Referring to John MacInnes's work, *The End of Masculinity* (1998), Beynon argues that "Young men are no longer happy to be defined solely by their occupations, as were their fathers, certainly their grandfathers before them. They are instead (or so the rhetoric would have us understand), happy to swap domestic and other roles with their partners, while both heterosexual and homosexual men can now adopt an extended range of lifestyles (if, of course, they have the resources.)" (*What is Masculinity*? 5). Therefore, when Hasmukh Mehta dies in the play, Ajit nearly breathes a sigh of relief, because at the core of his heart he knows that he has no father who would now try to mould him according to his whims and fancies and there would be no one on whom his life can be modelled any more. In *Dance Like a Man*, too the situation, is no more different. Amritlal has always detested his son's decision to take up dancing and that too under the guidance of an effeminate *guruji* or teacher. According to him, dancing is an arena devoted entirely to women and he relegates it to a "craft of the prostitutes". Amritlal, like all fathers in the society had expected his son to be a 'man'.

> Amritlal: I thought it was just a fancy of yours. I would have made a cricket pitch for you on our lawn if you were interested in cricket. Well, most boys are interested in cricket, my son is interested in dance, I thought. I didn't realize this interest of yours would turn into an...obsession.
>
> Jairaj: Didn't you have your obsessions?
>
> Amritlal: If you mean my involvement in fighting for your freedom, yes, it was an obsession.
>
> Jairaj: You had yours. Now allow me to have mine. (414-15)

Playing games within the heterosexual matrix is supposed to construct a man as he leaves his boyhood and enter the stage of adulthood. When Chandan (in *Tara*) helps his mother in knitting, Patel vehemently opposes his act: "But you (Bharati) can think of turning him into a sissy—teaching him to knit!" (351), and when Chandan says that's 'unfair', he is ordered to go to his room. Any representative from the patriarchal sphere is strongly opposed when there is any sort of role reversal. The fathers fail to understand that post independence with the breakdown of the agrarian setup, there has been an exodus from villages to towns which indicate that with the growth and development of education and the employment opportunities, the young men today have become individuals and can make their destinies without their support. In a recent Hindi film *Paankh* (2010), the protagonist, Charlie, a boy, is made to act in films as a child artist as a girl. In the film, his mother, who is actor, past her prime, makes him do this. As a result, he never indulges in sports and becomes a victim of ridicule. As he grows up, he is stuck in a limbo, he cannot understand in which domain does he fit best: is he a boy or a girl? His father vehemently opposes his wife, but in vain. No one ever asks him, what he wants to be and he too is left with no freedom to have his obsession fulfilled. However, Chris Haywood and Máirtín Mac Ghaill observe:

> In western schools, boys' identities may be worked out in age-specific ways that may not correspond to society's manly ideals. For instance, in research with younger children in a primary school, we found that many of the young boys were not interested in (hetero) sexual relationships (72). It was intriguing that not only did many of these boys find sexual relationships with girls boring but expressing an interest in girls was itself a sign of femininity. Instead 'boyness' was often demonstrated through 'playing', in the classroom, playground or at home. Fascination with cartoons, computer games and board games that contained a high content of violence, aggression and toughness were juxtaposed but carried with it a 'benign boyness' that was inclusive of girls and other boys.... Therefore 'boyness' may not be necessarily captured by the adult-defined and applied category of 'masculinity'. (72)

While Connell in *Masculinities* talks about the importance of sports which enhances the masculinity:

> The construction of masculinity in sports also illustrates the importance of the institutional setting. Messner emphasizes that when boys start playing competitive sport they are not just learning a game, they are entering an

> organized institution. Only a tiny minority reaches the top as professional athletes; yet the production of masculinity throughout the sports world is marked by hierarchical, competitive structure of the institution. (35)

The son in the family is supposed to be the harbinger of peace and prosperity which is in tune with his traditional roles of a protector and provider. Even today, the society, represented by these patriarchs, denies accepting any deviations on the part of a son. To Amritlal, his son's decision to grow long hair 'to enhance his *abhinaya*' (416) is 'abnormal'. In an encounter between the two,

Amritlal:	I have never seen a man with long hair.
Jairaj:	All sadhus have long hair.
Amritlal:	I don't mean them. I meant normal men.
Jairaj:	What are you trying to say?
Amritlal:	All I'm saying is that normal men don't keep their hair so long.
Jairaj:	Are you saying that he is not...(Realizes the implication.) Are you saying...?
Amritlal:	I've also noticed the way he walks.
Jairaj (*angrily*):	This is disgusting! You are insane! (417)

Amritlal's concern has always been to make his son a 'man'. He questions Ratna (Jairaj's wife), 'Do you know where a man's happiness lies?' and he immediately answers 'In being a man'. But Dattani creates a parody of the fact of being man. Later, in the second act of the play, Jairaj converses with his daughter Lata regarding an 'erotic numbers', we see that Jairaj has hardly accepted his father's proposals.

Lata:	Daddy, you make it sound so crude. 'Erotic numbers'?
Jairaj:	There's nothing crude about it. I danced the same item. For the army. A friend of ours arranged a programme and the money was good. Your mother was too scared and they only wanted a woman. So I wore your mother's costume, a wig and... whatever else was necessary to make me look like

> a woman, and danced. They loved it. They loved it even more when they found out that I was a man. (435)

The male playing the role of a woman is found in the *puranas* too. Ruth Vanita observes that the medieval Hindu scriptures bear testimony to the fact how God Ayyappa was born out of the intercourse between Lord Shiva and Lord Vishnu when the latter took the form of a woman. She states,

> The story of Shiva's attraction to Vishnu's Mohini form is related in at least three *puranas* which date approximately fro 850 to 950 AD. ...The traditional interpretation of the story is that Vishnu's leela (play) is to make Shiva forget that Mohini is Vishnu and thus become attracted to Vishnu's Mohini form, it is noteworthy that in this version as well as in Telegu versions, it is Shiva who asks Vishnu to assume his Mohini form, because Shiva missed seeing it earlier and heard about its beauty. So Shiva is aware of the ambiguous nature of this male-female form. In the context of religious drama where men and boys traditionally played, and still often play, female roles, audience awareness of and response to the man disguised as a woman would be comparable to Shiva's.... The stories suggest the fluidity of gender in sexual interaction. (Vanita, 80)

It is noteworthy here that Mahesh Dattani himself played the role of Dolly in North London rehearsal room in 1996. Michael Walling, the director, writes:

> Because this was a male body, the element of performance was even more pronounced. And clear than it was with a female actor. Moreover, the fact that a male actor was able to portray the female character was deeply subversive of the gender norms which the play dissects and questions. ...the characters are men and women because they are playing *roles*. (69)

But the irony remains in Jairaj's leaving his paternal house to carve a niche for his own but unfortunately he and his wife come back 'defeated'. Amritlal accepts them but his acceptance is tinted. "I have been wise enough to invest my money in the right places. But don't think you have a right to all my wealth. I have far better things to do with it than hand it over to you" (425). The authority of a patriarch is always in terms of his wealth. And transaction he makes, he always equates it with monetary aspects. This is true for Hasmukh Mehta as well. However, if Amritlal's happiness was to make his son a 'man' snatching him away from the clutches of dancing, Hasmukh's happiness lies in perverse domination. He says to his son: "Just polish my shoes every morning and I'll be happy" (458). In asserting his power and wealth, Hasmukh Mehta never leaves a stone unturned to criticize his wife and son. For an apparently well-established business man, his private life seems to echo sense of waste for him. In his solitude he recalls his bygone days:

> We made money! I remember we used to spend half the night going through our accounts and counting our profits. The other half of the night we would dream of being millionaires! (*Puffs on the cigarette again.*) Then when I was twenty-one, the greatest tragedy of my life took place. I got married to my wife, Sonal...the following year Ajit was born. Tragedy after tragedy.... Forty-five years old and I'm a success in capital letters. Twenty-three years old and he's on the road to failure, in bold capital letters! At his age, I was a mature responsible man, not eating my father's head and nibbling at papads! (464)

Hasmukh Mehta's soliloquy echoes the basis of patriarchy as does Devraj Gowda's (*Do the Needful*) when he readily accepts his wife's inability to have been a perfect housewife. When Prema Gowda says that "I should have been a proper housewife" her husband replies, "Good. I am glad you realize your mistakes" (121). If we consider Hartmann's definition of patriarchy as "a set of social relations between men, which have a material base, and which, though hierarchical, establish or create interdependence or solidarity among men that enable them to dominate women." Again, if we consider that "Control is maintained by denying women access to necessary economically productive resources and by restricting women's sexuality" (German), we find that Sonal and Preeti are rendered almost unproductive, if not otherwise productive in their domestic 'labour'. The likes of Sonal and Preeti (*Where There is a Will*), Kusumben Patel and Prema Gowda (*Do the Needful*) or Dolly and Alka (*Bravely Fought the Queen*) represent the silent victims of patriarchy. A similar set-up is also noted in *Tara*. As German observes, "The greatest disadvantage that the housewives suffer is not that they are exploited by men, but that they are atomised and cut off from participation in the collective action that can give confidence to fight back against the system" (German). Thus, it is the complete assertion of patriarchy and their masochistic claims on their women and their sons that these characters seem to implement their rights and powers as patriarchy in the Indian society still refers to the "father (the 'patriarch') ruled not only the women in the family but also the younger men.... The patriarch's power derived from his possession of wealth produced..." (German). In the play *Do the Needful*, although we do not come across a staunch patriarch as Amritlal or Hasmukh, yet the fathers in the play, Chandrakant Patel and Devraj Gowda, are always exhibiting their respective catalogue of personal property to get their daughter and son married, not knowing their wishes and not considering whether or not they want to participate in their dealings. It is later that we come to know how, Dattani makes Lata and Alpesh, not just victims of the institution of marriage but how they remain in the wedlock only to make a mockery of it.

John McRae in his essay "We Live in the Flicker: Reflections in Time on the Plays of Mahesh Dattani" observes that the playwright has the ability to laugh at himself and therefore his plays have no pretences. He writes,

> He knows where he stands and has no need to pretend that he is any other than who he claims to be—no pretence: he sees himself as he sees the society he lives in, from within, and for all its good, bad and indifferent qualities and flaws. Who else would dare to put the two different taboos of our times, money and death, together

> in what purports to be a romantic comedy? He did it effectively in *Where There is a Will....* (62)

Dattani himself in an interview with Abhijit Sen said that he was not placing himself on any particular side of the characters that he creates. He said, "I place myself on the side of truth" (Interview with Sen). Therefore he proclaims to write about the truth that he perceives. And the truth that comes out of his portrayals of the patriarchs is that although they assert their rights on the family, they hardly realize how hollow their rights are. Dattani succeeds in depicting not only the claims of the males over others but he subverts them either comically or in the garb of a philosophy, for the readers to unearth or the audience to note.

Dattani's dramatic strategy comes to a crescendo in the second half of *Where There is a Will*. The first act has seen Hasmukh Mehta in his self-proclaiming role revolving his wand of control. It is in the second half that Dattani utilizes his creative potential to the fullest. The man who was so dominating in the first act is reduced to the figure of a ghost in the second after his death. In his invisible self he becomes an observer of his actions and in a way this illumines his realization of the self deeply. Hasmukh is a diabetic and has a high blood pressure, he suddenly dies and the scenario at home changes overnight. He realizes that the 'garb of authority maintained...was a method to save his own inner self from the clashes of the outside world" (Agarwal, 110). It is only after the death that his nature comes to light and the comments present a mockery and subversion of his parental authority. Sonal, the naïve wife of Hasmukh, hardly realizes that her husband is dead and is instead anxious for his tablets. The second part of the first act begins with the ghost of Hasmukh Mehta. He says, "It feels good to be dead" (479) and the audience/readers are expected to see through the death as the decline of the patriarchy in the household. A dead man, Hasmukh still refuses to admit the natural behaviour of his bereaved wife: "She cried at all the appropriate moments. I even got a mention in the newspapers. (*Picks up a paper cutting.*) 'Garmrnt Tycoon Dead'. That felt good" (479). Even after being dead he exercises his rights to judge his wife's emotions and the news of his death in the papers makes him satisfied. But he hardly realizes what he has done to the family. It is his 'will' that runs havoc. He asserts, "What about all my money? ... I don't think they deserve all that money. None of them have worked it, especially not my son. Neither he nor my daughter-in-law will get what they were after —my wife is also in for a great shock. You see, I have made a special will! (*Laughs*). They are going to hate me for doing this to them!" (479). The 'special will' leaves no room for his family members to enjoy his wealth. The otherwise naïve Sonal too has to cry out, "He has ruined us!" (480). The new order in the play is introduced with the entry of Kiran Jhaveri, who has been appointed as the trustee of the will. Kiran is like Lalitha in *Bravely Fought the Queen*, whose microcosmic intrusion depletes the macrocosmic family of Hasmukh Mehta. Mehta realizes how his authoritative control has been reduced to nothing. He comes to understand that his measures to control the economy of his family with his invisible presence only break the wall of his illusions in the responses of Sonal, Ajit and Preeti. Sonal becomes conscious of her own freedom; Preeti's concern has only been money. Mehta's place in the family is taken up by Kiran, almost as the matriarch who is in control of the Mehta family.

> Kiran: My main duty is to run the Mehta group of industries on behalf of Ajit Mehta. I have the authority to make all the major decisions in the interest of the companies. My duty also extends to training Ajit Mehta and eventually delegating most of my responsibilities to him in places. (492)

But Kiran, who had earlier won the heart accolades of Mehta comes up with the shocking revelation to Sonal: "Mrs. Mehta, no woman has an affair with an older man, especially a married man, for a little bit of respect and trust. It was mainly for money" (506). Preeti, the otherwise naïve and calm daughter-in-law of Mehta is thwarted by the mistakes that her husband has committed which has left them paupers especially when she is conceiving: "[And] I hate you for that! Oh! I curse you! Look what you've done to your wife and child! Made them paupers! All because you answered back your father! Doesn't that hurt you?" (502), but we realize later that Ajit's resistance has been his blessing as Kiran observes, "He may not be the greatest rebel on earth, but at least he is free of his father's beliefs. He resists. In a small way, but at least it's a start. That is enough to prove that Ajit has won and Hasmukh has lost" (510) echoing Foucault's observation that "Where there is power, there is resistance, and yet, or rather consequently, this resistance is never in a position of exteriority in relation to power" (95). Thus, the collapse of patriarchy becomes visible with Kiran's declaration. Women have always remained in the periphery as far as the patriarchal society is concerned and "Neither education nor economic independence would help them in gaining their dues unless male ego undergoes complete change and transformation" (Vishnu, 150). Samita Sen observes, "The independent Indian state considered the granting of equal political and civil rights to women adequate. But without questioning the family's authority, women cannot assert and realize their rights" (224). Thus, when Kiran shares her past with Sonal and tells her that she is lucky as she is 'educated', we learn the agony of a woman caught in the web of a man's world:

> Kiran: ... I learnt my lessons from being so close to life. I learnt my lessons from watching my mother tolerating my father when he came home every day with bottles of rum wrapped up in the newspapers. As I watched him beating her up and calling her names! I learnt what life was when my mother pretended she was happy in front of me and my brothers, so that we wouldn't hate my father.... Yes, Mrs. Mehta. My father, your husband—they are weak men with false strength. (508)

The 'will' in the play therefore is both the legal document and Hasmukh Mehta's wish to control the lives of his family members even after his death. But his authority is toppled and "amidst the complicated confabulations that are necessary for the comic design of the play, (as) the protagonists begin to search for the self" (Chaudhari, 82-83), Hasmukh Mehta too realizes the futility of his efforts. Asha Kuthari Chaudhari observes, "The will, here, becomes the iconic instrument to power (through wealth), and shapes and reshapes the destiny of the family/familial relationships after his death. But the irony is that Hasmukh, to give the devil his due, transfers this controlling power to a woman and changes the entire fabric of the monolith that he is trying to preserve; immediately opening up the spaces for the individual identity he has all sought to deny" (83). Sonal and Kiran come together and their "collective force born out of long annals of exploitation and suffering, is an effort to abolish sexual colonialism. Their collective voice is a declaration of woman emancipation against the 'will'of Hasmukh" (Agarwal, 114) and in the liberation of all these characters, Subir Dhar finds, is also the defeat of Mehta. He adds,

> This domineering husband, heavy father and tyrannical boss is gradually dwarfed and diminished to the point of insignificance. Of course he never quite loses our sympathy for he is given an engaging comic vitality and verve (both in the flesh as well as a spectre), but we cannot help being unused when we hear that his erstwhile family has made plans to cut down the tamarind tree in the garden—his last terrestrial haunt. The truth underlying the comedy is serious enough: the man who could rule over his family even after his death is exposed at the end to be what he really was—a comitragic weakling who had constantly quested for a father-substitute, a man who was rude to everyone because he was insecure himself, an unfaithful husband who didn't really want a mistress "... [but] a woman who would father him." (80-81)

The reversal of patriarchal order marks *Bravely Fought the Queen* too. Baa takes over the reigns of the family after the death of her husband and becomes the patriarch in the guise of a woman. Nagpal observes, "She (Baa) has become a repository of all the male values in the family. This is why she urges Jiten to beat up Dolly even though she is pregnant" (89). Dattani is a 'craftsman' and not merely a writer (as he himself said in an interview with Anita Nair) (5) and therefore what emerges out in his plays is not a one-dimensional aspect of patriarchy but patriarchy in its 'varied manifestations' (Nagpal, 89). Baa has internalized the male violence that she had been a victim of and so is Bharati in *Tara* who could say nothing to her father who being an influential person had ruined the life of little Tara. Chandan and Tara had three legs when they were born and the blood supply to the third leg was from Tara. But Bharati's father and Bharati herself instructed Dr. Thakkar to "risk giving both legs to the boy" (378) and to this the doctor readily complied for his own mercenary interests. The wish for a grandson and an heir makes Tara a victim of gender discrimination and here it is not only the men involved but Tara's own mother who too agrees to the unethical decision to see her son survive. Dattani thus brings out the role played by women in inflicting pains on the women too through his various dramatic strategies and it is here that his subversions are revealed. Santwana Halder quotes a famous anthropologist: "The supposition that a society's rules of conduct are exclusively or predominantly male-made is preposterous. The fact that the codification of the rules and the supervision of their observances very often are male prerogative should not lead us to make the mistake of the cock parched on the hedge crowing because the hen laid an egg" (107).

What therefore starts as a portrayal of staunch patriarchy in most of the plays, opens up new domains of study. In this chapter, I have tried to highlight the face of patriarchy as stereotypically presented and then tried to show how Dattani subverts the norms to present the alternative views. Thus, what emerges out is a new definition of masculinity not merely as an antonym of femininity but paves a way for men to break their 'alpha roars' and do what they would perhaps like to do. And as for the females, they can opt for a path of their own too, breaking their silence and the performative roles that they have always played, knowingly or unknowingly; willingly or unwillingly.

Observing on his play *Tara*, Dattani argues,

> The play is misread and people tend to focus on the medical details but that is not really what the play is

> about. It is a metaphor either for being born equal as male and female and sharing so much more and with the surgical separation comes a cultural distinction and prejudices as well, but on another level, it could also deal with the individual having the male and the female self is, whether your gender is male or female, is definitely given the lower priority. (Qtd. By Halder, 110)

Dattani also argued that the biological polarities between males and females are necessary for the union of one another but the cultural differences that society creates are artificial and these demarcations actually "hinder the natural unions of male and female whether it's body-to-body or within oneself" (Halder, 110). Dattani criticizes the 'forced harmony' between the two sexes and his plays are an expose on the doctrine of *Ardhanarishwar*, which finds place in Brihadaranya Upanishad too:

> He (self, *Viraj*) was not at all happy. Therefore a person (even today) is not happy when alone. He desired a mate. He became the size of a man and wife in cold embrace. He divided this body into two. From that (division) arose husband (pati) and wife (patni). Therefore as Yajnavalkya said, the body (before one accepts a wife) is one half of oneself, like the half of a split pea. Therefore this place is indeed filled by a wife. He was united with her. From that (union) human beings were born. (190)

Thus, it is the societal pressures and prejudices that create the division between the sexes and in complying with the norms, men and women suppress their innermost desires which get silenced in the long run of performance of their gendered scripts and as a result when one gets prioritized, the other voice becomes inaudible. Dattani portrays the dilemma of the 'men' caught in the web of the self-created images of patriarchal roars.

WORKS CITED

Agarwal, Beena, "*Where There is a Will*—A Comic Caricature of Patriarchal Authority", *Mahesh Dattani's Plays: A New Horizon in Indian Theatre*. Jaipur: Book Enclave, 2008.

Beynon, John, "Understanding Masculinities", *Masculinities and Culture*. Buckingham: Open University Press, 2002.

——. "What is Masculinity?", *Masculinities and Culture*.

Brihadaryanaka Upanishad. (I, iv, 30) *The Upanishads*, Swami Nikhilananda. Kolkata: Advaita Ashrama, 2008.

Brown, John Russel. *The Oxford Illustrated History of Indian Drama*. USA: OUP, 1995.

Chaudhari, Asha Kuthari, "The Setting: The Constructed/Deconstructed Family", *Mahesh Dattani: An Introduction*. Delhi: Foundation Books, 2005.

Conell, R.K., "Social Construction and Gender Dynamics", *Masculinities*. UK: Polity Press, 2nd ed. 2005.

Dasgupta, Nandita, "Men will be men...stuck in patriarchal role", TNN, March 8, 2010. 22nd May, 2010. <http:// timesofindia.indiatimes.com/ India/men-will-be-mem-stuck-in-patriarchal-role/articleshow/ 5656040.cms>.

Dattani, Mahesh, *Collected Plays*. Vol. I. New Delhi: Penguin, 2000. The further citations from the same book have been put in parenthesis.

Dattani, interview with Abhijit Sen at Ramkrishna Mission at Narendrapur, Kolkata on 29th of April, 2010.

Dhar, Subir, "*Where There is a Will* and *Bravely Fought the Queen*: The Plays of Mahesh Dattani". *The Plays of Mahesh Dattani: A Critical Response*, R.K. Dhawan and Tanu Pant, eds. New Delhi: Prestige, 2005.

Dhawan, R.K. and Tanu Pant (ed.), *The Plays of Mahesh Dattani: A Critical Response*. New Delhi: Prestige Books, 2005.

Foucault, Michel, "The Deployment of Sexuality: Method". *The History of Sexuality*. Vol. I. *An Introduction*, trans. Robert Hurley. New York: Vintage Books, 1990.

Haywood, Chris and Máirtín Mac an Ghaill, "Troubling School Boys: Making Young Masculinities". *Men and Masculities*.

Halder, Santwana, "Gender Discrimination in Mahesh Dattani's Tara: A Study of Prejudice in Patriarchal Society", *The Dramatic World of Mahesh Dattani: A Critical Exploration*, Amar Nath Prasad, ed. New Delhi: Sarup Publishers, 2009.

McRae, John, "We Live in the Flicker: Reflections in Time on the Plays of Mahesh Dattani", *Mahesh Dattani's Plays: Critical Perspectives*. Angelie Multani, ed. New Delhi: Pencraft International, 2007.

Multani, Angelie, ed. *Mahesh Dattani's Plays: Critical Perspectives*. New Delhi: Pencraft International, 2007.

Nagpal, Payal, "Consuming and Selling Women: An Analysis of Gender Play and the Politics of Capitalism in Mahesh Dattani's Bravely Fought the Queen", *Mahesh Dattani's Plays: Critical Perspectives*, Angelie Multani, ed. New Delhi: Pencraft International, 2007.

Raina, Sita, "A Note on the Play", *Collected Plays*. New Delhi: Penguin, 2000.

Reddy, Venkata and R.K. Dhawan, eds. *Flowering of Indian Drama: Growth and Development*. New Delhi: Prestige, 2004.

Sen, Roop, is a counselor in Kolkata and the quote is from his byte in Dasgupta's article "Men will be men...stuck in patriarchal role", TNN, March 8, 2010. Accessed on 22.05.2010. http://timesofindia.indiatimes.com/India/men-will-be-mem-stuck-in-patriarchal-role/articleshow/5656040.cms.

Sen, Samita, "A Father's Duty: State, Patriarchy and Women's Education". *Education and the Dispriviledged: Nineteenth and Twentieth Century India*, Sabyasachi Bhattacharya, ed. New Delhi: Orient Longman, 2002.

Vanita, Ruth, "Bhagavata Purana: The Embrace of Shiva and Vishnu (Sanskrit)". *Same-Sex Love in India: A Literary History*, Ruth Vanita and Saleem Kidwai, eds. New Delhi: Penguin, 2008.

Vishnu, Ashwini Kumar, "The Man, The Mistress, The Will: The Motifs in Mahesh Dattani's *Where There is a Will*". *The Dramatic World of Mahesh Dattani: A Critical Exploration*, Amar Nath Prasad, ed. New Delhi: Sarup Publishing House, 2009.

Walling, Michael, "Everyone will be in Costumes! And will have Masks on!: Gender and Performance in Bravely Fought the Queen." *Mahesh Dattani's Plays: Critical Perspectives*. Angelie Multani, ed. New Delhi: Pencraft International, 2007.

10

A Drama of Disabilities: Mahesh Dattani's *Tara*

Vivekanand Jha

When Indian English Drama was struggling for survival and identity Mahesh Dattani made an incarnating presence in the arena of plays. His movement has further bolstered with the achieving of Sahitya Akademi Award, first time in the history of Indian English Drama. Before eminence of Dattani on the spectrum of the stage, Indian English Drama was merely confined to diverse phases of imitations and translations. The credit goes to him for bringing the profile of Indian English Drama at par with Western or European practice and tradition. He made an exploration, experimentation and innovation with the existing touchstone of the plays and consequently his plays turned diverse in art, craft, themes, techniques and styles. Indian English Drama once on the verge of extinct has wholesomely groomed under the umbrella of Dattani and the seeds of stagecraft sown by Dattani turned from sprout into the tree of mushrooming leaves and fruits.

No trace of superfluity and overabundance is found in his plays and his dialogues are to the point, clear and crisp. The dialogues of his plays are directed towards suiting the needs of every character and they bear the stamp of suitability, appropriateness and pertinence. They carry the sense and sensibility of homogeneity emanating from heterogeneous emotions and feelings. Every words of his verbal communication are colloquial, appealing and most of the sentences used by him are aphoristic, full of adages and axiomatic. M.K. Naik presents short survey of the dialogues and language used by Dattani in his plays in the following words:

> Dattani's dialogue is crisp and entirely functional, making for quick exchanges between characters, though long monologues are also employed wherever necessary. The style is an interesting mixture of modern English colloquialisms ("shit", "what the fuck"), Indianisms ("eat my head", "we are honoured with your presence"), and words and expressions from Indian languages. Actually three Indian languages are drawn upon: Hindi, Gujarati and Kannada. (Naik, 209)

Successes became darlings for Mahesh Dattani after he turned the first playwright writing in English to receive the central Sahitya Akademi Award for his collection *Final Solutions and Other Plays* in 1998. This highest award for a literary work in the country opened a new door for debate, analysis and critical appraisal of dramas in the spectrum of Indian English Literature. Mahesh Dattani speaks in a conversation in the wake of receiving Sahitya Akademi Award:

> Well, I think this has been really the kind of endorsement that Indian English Theatre in the country has been looking for because up till now it seems as if it belonged to a fringe section of society and that it was seen as not quite theatre, not quite art, that it was more of a kind of theatre club kind of thing. And perhaps justifiably so. I am not saying that its not entirely unwarranted that feeling and opinion. But I think since so much has actually happened and there has been a serious attempt to, you know, have a kind of movement in this direction. Because there are enough English speaking people and there are enough people who want to do theatre, and right in the language, so this has been a kind of endorsement of that effort. (Angelie, 130)

Dattani was avid viewer of the dramas right from his childhood. Even if he was in Bangalore he used to watch frequently staging of the dramas by the theatre-companies of Ahmadabad and Mumbai. His attachment to theatrical background ultimately made him versatile and multifaceted personality. One of the key of Dattani successes as a dramatist has been his launching of own theatre company, Playpen. He is not writing to be read rather than to be performed but he writes because he is a dramatist and he has a theatrical background. Beena Agarwal gives appraisal of Dattani's dramatic art and craft:

> Dattani's dramatic art is inspired by the mission to communicate profound meaning through his plays and, therefore, he exhibits keen awareness for the direction and stage performance of his own plays. His sensitive dramatic self is a fine synthesis of a dancer, director, actor, playwright, audience and commentator moving collectively towards a single direction. (Agarwal, 24)

In a benevolent and professional measure Dattani launched his own theatre studio, Playpen in 1984. It has opened new opportunity not only for Dattani but also for other amateur and professional artists. Dattani has spiritual, physical and mental affinity and attachment with this theatre group as it has given him new-fangled deference, direction and dimension in the dome of English Drama. Every play composed by Dattani has been performed and it has remained haunting spots for the overseas playwrights and artists. The number of courses concerning with drama's study and workshops have been organized in this mansion of dramas. Dattani never wrote for targeted readers, audiences and spectators and themes of his dramas signify and appeal to worldwide community. This is the reason he has picked English language as means of communication to convey the voices of his passions, emotions and feelings. He kept himself adhered to the great degree of professionalism in performing the play and he admits himself totally soaked into theatrical world:

> My milieu is theatre, you can't operate in isolation. I do want a theatre movement to happen. The major block for that is lack of sound training and professionalism. We have the talent, but theater is more than that, it's a craft of communicating through the language of action. (Dasgupta)

Dattani is the dramatist of contemporary realities and most of his plays are based upon the burning issues of the society.

He advocates for the well being and fundamental rights of the common people, aggrieved and diseased. He is exclusively and explicitly known for incorporating debatable, controversial and radical themes into his plays. The corpus of themes that represent his plays are complexities of human relationship, mess of the modernism, communal tension, issue of similar sex and homosexuality, sexual abuse of child, gender hierarchy and identity, power play within the family, morality of middle class people, unprivileged section of society, conflict between tradition and modernity, patriarchy, eunuchs, woes of women, issue of child-labour, interpersonal relationship, identity crisis, pressures of the past, compulsions of the HIV positive sufferers. The themes Dattani plays emanate from the social issues that disturb his mental, physical and spiritual equilibrium. He confesses his thematic preoccupations in a revealing interview:

> They invariably do. Social issues move me and I like to examine an idea from different angles. The plays where the content came first are On a Muggy Night and Final Solutions. As for the latter, I was asked to write a play about communal tension, and I said 'what can one write about that other than platitudes? But out of that churning emerged' 'Final Solutions' Sometimes the characters spoke to me first, as in Tara and On a Muggy Night. In Dance Like a Man, the plot emerged out of a flashback structure where the same actors play different generations. Sometimes images make the first impact; then, the set. (Dattani-in Hindu Online Ed.)

Though the plays of Dattani hardly exhibit any sense and sensibility of rural India but a closer look at his plays divulge that most of his plays are rooted in urban setting of India rather than inferring themes from Western civilization. He has hardly spent life in countryside and he passed most of his life drifting from one city to another and his personal experience and encounter with those cities come into display into his plays. In an enlightening interview he justifies the facts that compel him to compose the plays based on the life of urbanity:

> I think the old cliche...about writing what you know best holds good for any work or for any art (drama or

> literature). I think one has to be true to one's own environment. Even if I attempted writing a play about the angst of rural Indian society, it wouldn't ring true, it would be an outsider's view—I could only hope to evoke sympathy, but never to really be a part of that unless I spend a lot of time there. I think there are enough issues and challenges in urban Indian society (the milieu I am a part of) and these automatically from the content of my work. (Dattni—Interview by Erin B. Mee)

The performance in the play is all important for Dattani and is prerequisite condition and benchmark for its success. He wants himself to be both beginning and denouement of his play. His play is consummate combination of writing and directing and he seeks more enjoyment in directing the play rather than writing it. This is one of the reason his play has scaled the height of national and international popularity. Dattani admits in an interview:

> When I'm directing a play, I feel like I'm a complete human being. That makes me happy. And also when I meet people with a passion. It reaffirms all that I do. I'm enjoying what I'm doing and don't want to do anything else. (Dattani-Profile by Anita Nair)

He considers himself as a dramatist more than a writer. There were very few writer who opted to write plays in English in India and this is one of the reasons he preferred to become a pioneer playwrights rather than a writer of other English genre. The first collection of plays published By Dattani is *Final Solutions and Other Plays* in 1998 which he managed to get published when he was approached by Mr. Padmanabhan of East West Press in Chennai. Because it was this publication that bagged him the Sahitya Akademi Award. On winning of this award only, Penguin approached him for a collected works edition.

> Well, I had no choice because my interest lies primarily in drama. So I didn't have a choice, that oh, I will write for drama, I will write a novel or I will write poetry. It has always been drama from the beginning because that's

> where my focus is and I began writing for the stage quite later, later in my career so to say in theatre. I began as an actor, then I moved on to direction and then finally because there is a dearth of scripts written originally in the English language, Indian scripts. That's why I decided to try my hand at it. (Angelie, 130)

Besides prolific and prominent Indian playwrights writing in English, Mahesh Dattani is also well-known as a stage director and actor, screen writer and film maker with numerous scripts and productions to his credit. His plays have been anthologized in single volume called *Collected Plays* by Penguin. Most of his plays have been translated and performed in other regional languages of India and have been incorporated in the curriculum of numerous Indian and foreign universities and schools. He made his presence felt in the filmdom with the film *Mango Souffle* and it was displayed in numerous international film-festivals and pronounced best motion picture at the Barcelona Film Festival 2003. His film *Morning Raga* remained cynosure of the Cairo Film Festival in December 2004 and it registered the award for best artistic contribution. More importantly its script has been archived by The Academy of Motion Pictures, USA and it was accepted by Oscar Academy for nomination of the award. He has worked in partnership with various international theatre companies and his recent achievements are stage adaptation of Paolo Coelho's bestseller classic, *The Alchemist* and composing of the script of Brief Candle, directed by Lillete Dubey. He has explored and experimented with writing, directing, acting, performing, teaching and running workshops with consummate perfection, beauty and truth. Dattani enjoys every moment and facet of creativity and reveals his passion in an interview:

> I guess it's all momentary. A bit like when you are eating *bhel puri*, you enjoy it more if you are not thinking of chocolate mousse! So I am passionate about it all, but seriously, all my interests seem to feed my primary interest of seeing my works on stage. As one philosopher put it—all forms of entertainment are like playing with the shadows of life. All things beautiful in this world are

> transitory by nature. And there is nothing so immediate and ephemeral as theatre. To me it is a search for beauty as much as it is a search for truth. We can only experience them in the shadows that our art generates. (Dattani-conversation with Lakshmi Chandra)

The themes of his plays bear the testimonial of varying tone, temperament and treatment. Dattani expanded his range and canvass of creativity from stage Plays to radio and screen Plays. He has an ability to amalgamate the traditional beliefs with ultramodern disposition and conviction. His plays are heavily charged with socio-political, emotional, physiological and psychological issues. The theme of family covers the large chunk of plays wherein characters are found struggling and wrestling with one another. The best example of such play is *Tara* which circles around the grave and traditional issues of gender biasing. The son and daughter delivered from same womb are preferentially treated by no less than parents themselves in the intoxication of superstition and ancestral beliefs and the daughter is sacrificed for the short-term benefit of the son. The play is contextual and relevant in the light of the burgeoning incidents of foeticide and widening gap in the sex ratio of male and female child. On the question of what gave him the idea for the play, *Tara*, Mahesh Dattani:

> Well, basically, it began with, you know, reading an article in a medical journal about Siamese Twins being separated, and, of course, they were invariably of the same sex and there was this thing about a fused leg and which had the qualities of both left and right so there had to be some careful consideration as to which twin was supplying the blood to the leg and the journal went into the detail because obviously it was a very unique operation and separation. Although that was the inspiration but I think by then having written *Dance Like a Man*, I was prepared to take on the gender issue head on, and I think that was a powerful metaphor. Again, you know, the play is misread and, you know, people tend to focus on the medical details but that's really not what the play is about. It's a metaphor either for being

> born equal as male and female and sharing so much more and with the surgical separation comes a cultural distinction and prejudices as well, but on another level, it could also deal with the individual having the male and female self and half the female self is, whether your gender is male or female, is definitely given the lower priority. (Angelie, 130)

The play, overall, deals with pain, predicaments and disabilities and their adverse repercussion on the well-being of characters. The play reveals how the impact of children's disability plays havoc with every member of the family. The strain on the parents and its effect on their marriage life are prettily conspicuous in the play. The conjugal crack is created between the couple who were once tied in a knot though being from two distant states, cultures and tradition. The high degree of desperation and frustration is noticed in every member of Patel's family and they seem to be reeling under perpetuating stress.

Time, techniques, music, costume and lighting play pivotal role in the play in ascertaining stage directions, the language, characters, motivations and actions. The lighting is aptly used for switching from one action to another. The music in the play determines the mood and temperament of certain characters. The playing of music in the drama reveals taste and psyche of both Chandan and Tara. Dattani has pertinently applied the references of Western classical music in the play. The music composers that Dattani talks about in the play are Beethoven and Brahms. Both were German and the music of Brahms was influence by Beethoven. Tara has special affinity with Beethoven as he composed his magnum opus only after he turned deaf at the age of twenty and Tara identifies her own disability and seeks solace with that of Beethoven who achieved his greatness when he was not able to hear his own creation. Whenever Tara finds herself in the situation and position of deep distress, dejection and despondency she prefers to give her ears to Beethoven music. Once Tara is found hating the music of Brahms but after being convinced by Chandan that even music of Brahms appeals to high tragedy and romance she acceded to listen him too.

> The concept of time and place is greatly challenged by various dramatists, with openness for experimentation like Mahesh Dattani's multi-sets and layered scenes. Experimenting with multi-level staging, moving back and forth in time to create a kaleidoscopic montage effect in drama all work exceedingly well for Dattani. He also shows a great liking for dance and music, whether in the background or directly linked to the setting. With the multi-level staging, often with each stage depicting a different time and place-playing with the concepts of past, present, and future, one finds conversations overlapping and flowing into each other, with underlying metaphorical implications. (Sitanshi, 162)

To look son and daughter with biased and discriminating eyes has been traditional and age old custom in India and it has been tagged with rites and rituals of life. Parents think their daughter of alien home as one day she would be married and go to her husband. They have superstitious and mythical belief of being ultimately emancipated at the hands of their son. This fact pertaining to illusion of life is optimally exploited by Dattani in this play. The whole drama is circling round one dark secret and its revelation. The twin: Tara and Chandan were successfully operated and separated by Dr. Thakkar. The twins had three legs between them and the third leg was supplied by Tara's blood system. The probability of the leg's survival was greater with Tara. But Bharati and her influential father were hand in glove to undertake the risk of supplying the third leg to Chandan. In the pursuit of procuring this malicious design the doctor was bribed with a plot of land in Bangalore by Bharati's powerful and politician father. Patel couldn't object muscularly enough and he also ultimately became accomplice of this nasty conspiracy. The leg that had survived only for two days with Chandan could have accompanied Tara's forever. Tara is devastated by this revelation. Further elucidating the context of gender discrimination in the drama Dattani speaks in an interview:

> Well, I think it is the revelation in the end about, you know, Tara's love for her mother which uptil then was unquestionable. She suspected her father for having done something, you know, was in someway, but she had no idea what it was, but her love, her mother's love was unquestioned and she did not question that, so when she comes to know of the truth of what we, I mean, we only have the father's version. We don't know whether that is the real truth or no. again, but it does sort of break her away like a shooting star from the mother, and I think with that she—that's tragedy, she dies. We don't know how she dies, but we know that's the end of Tara, and I think that's somehow all the attitudes towards Tara and the relationship between her mother, her father and her brother, which we see through the play. In hindsight you could see where it was coloured or where it was blinkered or where it was being compensated for. (Angelie, 130)

Bharati has to pay disproportionately for committing one mistake or sin of denying one leg to her daughter, Tara. Because of the physical disability the Patel's family is pitted into a vicious circle and irresolvable imbroglio. The conjugal and married life of both Bharati and Patel is jeopardized and they are found on bitter terms and quarreling with each other. Thus as result of physical disabilities of Chandan and Tara, the married life of Bharati and Patel suffers a spiritual disability. Bharati exhibits pretentious, crafty and compensatory love for Tara so much so that although donor for kidney transplantation of Tara has been found yet Bharati is adamant to donate her own kidney to Tara. Bharati tells to Tara she is donating her kidney to her to compensate for the injustices that have been done by Patel with Tara. The donation of kidney to Tara by Bharati witnesses another case of disability in the drama and Bharati suffers nervous breakdown. Thus, it can safely be suggested that Mahesh Dattani's *Tara* is knitted into the web of disabilities and diseases.

WORKS CITED

Agarwal, Beena. "Dattani's Theatrical Art and the Tradition of Indian Theatre", appeared in *The Dramatic World of Mahesh Dattani: A Critical Exploration,* Amarnath Prasad (Ed.), New Delhi: Sarup Book Publishers Pvt. Ltd., 2009.

Dasgupta, Uma Mahadevan. "The Minute I Write a Play, I Want to Direct It." 2001.

Dattani, Mahesh. "Invisible Issues: An Interview with Mahesh Dattani by Erin B. Mee", appeared in *Mahesh Dattani's Plays Critical Perspectives*, edited by Angelie Multani, New Delhi: Pencraft International, 2007.

——. "The Invisible Observer"—a profile by Anita Nair, http://www.anitanair.net/profiles/profile-mahesh-dattani.htm.

——. In conversation with Lakshmi Chandra. http://www.scribd.com/doc/54543266/Dattani-Interview-Muse-India.

——. 'I do not write merely to be read', A Conversation with Tutun Mukherjee, *The Hindu, Online Edition of India's National Newspaper,* Monday, 26 July 2004, http://www.hinduonnet.com/thehindu/mp/2004/07/26/stories/2004072601790100.htm.

Multani, Angelie—A Conversation with Mahesh Dattani, the Journal of the School of Language, Literature & Culture Studies (JSL), IV.

Nai, Naik and Narayan, Shyamala A., *Indian English Literature 1980-2000*; New Delhi: Pencraft International, 2007.

Sitanshi, Talati-Parikh, "Modern Indian Drama". King, Kimball (ed.): Western Drama through the Ages: Four great eras of western drama.

11 Expanding the Space of Patriarchy: A Study of Select Plays of Mahesh Dattani

Raichel M. Sylus

Dramatists like Mahesh Dattani, Manjula Padmanabhan and others have kept Indian drama in English alive by offering their mite to keep its tale trailing through. One among the promising dramatists of modern India, Mahesh Dattani, has ventured deep into the recesses of the present Indian social set up. Dattani, who has sown the seed for the Modern Indian Theatre, has also been acclaimed as the master creator of the contemporary form of theatre. One of India's best and the most serious of contemporary playwrights, founder of the playgroup "Playpen" and the first playwright to be the winner of the most coveted Sahitya Academy Award, is still active in the field of film making and play writing.

The contribution of Dattani to Indian drama has been manifold with conventional themes like family relationship, morality and identity, blending of the old with the new ones and concentrating exclusively on the upper middle class society. His themes are akin to many other dramatists writing in English. Yet, Dattani differs in one aspect—his honest portrayal of the everyday issues in an Indian family set up and in the Indian society. There are no solutions from Dattani but there are issues, which erupt from all aspects that point out to the inconsistencies prevalent in the contemporary Indian subcontinent.

Dealing with the most compelling issues rooted in the present social milieu, Dattani portrays a rainbow of characters who are striving to expand their 'space'. His characters bring honour to his plays and his works are read across the globe for the same. He remarks: "I talk about the areas where the individual feels exhausted. My plays are about such people who are striving to expand 'this' space. They live on the fringes of the society and are not looking for acceptance, but are struggling to grab as much fringe-space for themselves as they can." It is Dattani's desire that if drama has to exist as an art form, then it has to take up social issues to captivate the mind of the audience towards the play. His selection of the urban social set up in the current scenario and establishment of an identity for himself, and for the characters who long for a space are matters of concern in his works. Herein lies the fame of Dattani.

Sheila Ruth, in her essay on "The Dynamics of Patriarchy", gives the traits of an ideal patriarchal male. According to her he "...must be not only brave, but never-timid; not only independent, but never-needful; not only strong, but never-weak. Committed to victory in battle, which is his first priority, he is a man of constraint and restraint, for violent emotions of any kind might deter him from his rationally designed course or strategy" (48). While these are supposed to be ideal traits that profess his individual excellence as a male in the community, these traits themselves prioritize his role in the family and the community.

The characters in his plays make the reading an enjoyable one and the characters take all the sympathies. His deft construction of characters especially the women folk helps the readers to analyse women through the prism of modern cultured, activated Indian society. By unraveling the skeleton in the cupboard, an open secret of the middle class society, all the well-known and the unknown shams are now on the streets. Dattani says that he is "fascinated by women who make their choices given their limited resources and circumstances but my choice of women as central characters is purely an artistic choice and in no way am I trying to take on a cause. I am free to show men and women with failings and strengths without being overwhelmed by political implications". He thus explores a gamut of human relationships touching upon vital and sensitive themes like religious tension, gender issues, marginalization and morality.

The middle class milieu, which Dattani has acclaimed as his own, has been subjected to him in all his plays. The experiences of living in the borderline have been portrayed in his plays—by exploring stage spaces and by his use of legitimized Indian English. Being a versatile personality, he adorns various mantles whenever necessary to empathize with the characters and not sympathize for them. The never-ending struggle of the contemporary Indian families trying to create their own space is the subject matter of all his plays.

Dattani's *Where There is a Will* elaborates the colourless relationships between the couples that comprise the family and hints at the pathos—the kind of bonding between Kiran and Sonal. Sonal here is a traditional woman portrayed with contempt. Dattani makes use of the space as much as possible to reveal the characters and their ideas. He creates an apparent picture of gender and gender roles in the play—what happens when the man is the head and the reversal, when the woman takes over his charge. It is a representative picture of a domineering husband. The dynamics of power and the domination within the family is the gist of the play. The story is a humorous one where the rich business man in the play tries to have control of the family even after his death through a will. May be he wanted to extend his space even after his life on earth by being a ghost and dominating the family.

The story of *Where There is a Will*, his first play is deeply rooted in the Gujarati family setup and it is about the maneuverings of a dysfunctional Indian family. The trouble that is to follow in the play has been introduced ominously in the first part of the play, as if setting the tone to the play. The over smart and astute Kiran Jhaveri is an epitome of Dattani's women characters in the way that she longs for an identity. In the process of exploring the dichotomy between the male and the female roles in a family solely dominated by male members, Dattani portrays Ajit, who in this play stands as a testimony to the patriarchal dominance of his autocratic father. On the other hand, Hasmukh Mehta is a representative of the patriarchal society who opines that a father chooses the best for his son. His confidence is so strong that he feels Ajit will not be able to make spaces for himself in the future without the presence of his father. He quips: "If you are then, then you are nowhere. You are nothing just a big zero" (461). Having stood as a subaltern who cannot speak boldly to his father, Ajit talks back to his father. Hasmukh still tries to gain control of his son.

"We are all living out a dead man's dream" is a lucid statement of Ajit's comment on his dead father's will. The will is so written that even after Hasmukh's death, the members of the family are bound by the will. The play is an apt portrayal of how an individual is suppressed by the patriarchal foibles in the family. There is a dire need for the individuals to come out of the spaces of their dining room, bedroom and the decorated room. The literal expansion of space at home will not yield results. What is necessary is the space to live life freely and help others live happily.

Dance Like a Man is a play on the conflict between tradition and modernity. Home, the sweet home that all Indians aspire to be in, is crucial to the existence of three generations of its occupants. Dattani opines, if it is the pigeonholing of masculinity within a Hindu undivided family. The characters battle against the society that prevents them from reaching out to the roots. Jairaj the protagonist fights against the society to win respect for himself. This is a different play in this sense. Dattani opines in one of his interviews that *Dance Like a Man* is "a battle against society". It is an outcome of his learning Bharatanatyam in his early twenties. The play also focuses on the space made available to women in the patriarchal society. It is based on a traditional South Indian backdrop with the power struggle rooted in Indian ambience.

Amritlal Parekh, in the play, has the sole authority of a father. Jairaj, the protagonist, who goes against the cultural dynamics of the society has strict rules to be followed. For Parekh, Bharatanatyam should be taken up as a hobby. Amritlal is of the opinion that Jairaj has to stop the dance once he is grown up. He says:

> Jairaj: You promised you would allow me to continue with my hobbies.
>
> Amritlal: That was when you were a boy and dance was just a hobby. Grow up Jairaj. (422)

The reason that Asha Kuthari Chaudhuri gives for Amritlal's behaviour is that "The underlying fear is obviously that dance would make him 'womanly'—an effeminate man—the suggestion of homosexuality hovers near, although never explicitly mentioned" (68). His son's monetary dependence on him has also been exploited. This conflict aggravates the son who remarks: "Reform! Don't talk about reform. If you really wanted any kind of reform in our society, you would let them practice their own art" (416). The patriarchal code is steeped in tradition and authority in the Indian society.

There is a need for a change to a person like Jairaj to expand the space in the family and come out to enjoy individuality. In this manner, Dattani has higlighted a son's plight in the family, and how Jairaj's attempt to escape from the shackles of the father turns out to be in vain. It is also to be noted that Jairaj has lost his ability and identity as a dancer because of his father's capability in ruling over the family.

Tara, a play about a typical contemporary urban Indian trying to create a new identity is a play with a woman as protagonist. The first scene is set in London with Chandan. He recalls his childhood with his sister Tara Patel, a Siamese twin and dramatizes all, through a series of flashbacks. The injustice is by none but their own mother. It exposes the existing patriarchal stereotype of the typical Indian mind, which always vies for a boy child than a girl. The play looks at an Indian family trying to cope with the trauma of freak children and their struggle for survival. While Dr. Thakkar, the doctor who operated the twins receives winning accolades, the twins are in the boiling cauldron of gender prejudice.

Dattani gives a very enclosed space to this play. Tara is entangled within the enclosures of the Patel household. Roopa is the only person through whom she has contact with the outside world. Tara is not welcomed outside, in the streets and as usual, she has to face the ridicule. It is a revelation to many that the life of girl children is affected due to gender bias even among urban educated families. Agarwal quotes Gayatri Spivak's view on patriarchy. She quotes that "all subjugated classes of society are not permitted to speak of their rights and duties.

They are left to survive in the confined spaces of domesticity, kept in dark to bear the burden of patriarchy in silence and sobbing" (69).

While *Tara* is a play based on gender bias, Bharati in the play suffers under the hands of patriarchy even after her marriage. Mr. Patel takes sole authority in making decisions in the family. While Bharati is ready to donate her kidney inorder to save the life of Tara, her fear of expressing her desire to her husband suppresses her and she maintains absolute silence. This is another way of patriarchal injustice meted out by the husband to the wife. This gives rise to the reason for such a behaviour of a husband in an Indian household—that a woman is preferred based on the child she has begotten. Most of the Indian families prefer a son to a daughter.

In *Final Solutions*, Dattani talks about the subordination of women. Though the play is couched in the present, it also goes back to the past events. Hardika is a living embodiment of the past adorned with her past guilt. The fact that the action takes place in the house of the Gandhis is itself a mocking statement contrary to what is happening outside. It is Javed and Bobby who come to dispel the space inside by entering in from the outside space. It is an example of the communal clashes prevalent in the outside world. The cloistered space at home has become a place to seek for a space. Now it has become a cluttered space of oppression. Smita once comments saying that she should runaway from home as Javed did—not literally running away but to go out for five minutes and come back after getting fresh air. It is an indication for her desire to have more space for her which she does not have. While the older generation in the play tries to make up by adjusting to the family situation, the younger or the contemporary generation tries to create a room of its own.

All the plays of Dattani are hence a voice of the voiceless and unvoiced. The marginalized are always marginalized. Looking at the point of view of the readers themselves, it is no wonder that they are helpless on the issues raised by him. Raising up issues in works like these kindle fuel to the fire already burning around and it is in the hands of the readers to help these most vulnerable victims. For plays to be meaningful, they should be not mere descriptive representations but ensure justice and equity that eludes most people today.

Unseen readers are sure to shower praises on Dattani when they read his plays—not for any reason but for his true and honest portrayal of the society. His characters stand apart in the fact that they have an urge to survive and succeed. They present themselves isolated in time and space.

Women want to build a world where exploitation, oppression and intolerance do not exist. They want a world where integrity, diversity and the rights and freedom of all are respected. He speaks to a wider audience and his issues are those that are very much in existence in the common society. It may seem as a theme that hardly inspires a writer. Patriarchy has lent itself a good deal in examining the predominant role of men in the Indian set up. Hence the need of the hour is not to appreciate patriarchy, but to elaborate and create a space for women to hold a good position in spite of the patriarchal set up. Patriarchy should not be subjection or oppression for women, it should elevate the status of women and create a special and desirable way towards their upliftment.

Having given a new dimension to Indian theater, the readers hope that many more Dattani's will rise to the occasion to fill in the expanded space created by Dattani. As remarked by Anita Nair, Dattani does not try to reform the society or to purge it but hopes to give the audience a tint of what exactly they are. As all of Dattani's plays end with a question, it is a question to be posed to ourselves "How far is the creation or the expansion of the space by Dattani in his plays helped in the upliftment of his characters?"

WORKS CITED

Agrawal, Beena. *Mahesh Dattani's Plays: A New Horizon in Indian Theater*. Jaipur: Book Enclave, 2008.

Chaudhuri, Asha Kuthari. *Mahesh Dattani: An Introduction*. New Delhi: Foundation Books, 2005.

Dattani, Mahesh. *Collected Plays*. New Delhi: Penguin, 2000.

Kumar, Gajendra and Uday Shankar Ojha ed. *Indian English Literature—A Post Colonial Response*. New Delhi: Sarup and Sons, 2005.

Ruth, Sheila. *Issues in Feminism. An Introduction to Women's Studies*. California: Mayfield, 1990.

Talwar, Urmil and Bandana Chakrabarty. *Contemporary Indian Drama Astride Two Traditions*. New Delhi: Rawat Publications, 2005.

12

Magnum Opus of Man-Woman Relationships in the Background of Indian Sensibility in Girish Karnad's—*Hayavadana*, *Naga-Mandala*, *Tughlaq*, *Yayati*, *The Fire and the Rain* and *Tale-Danda*

Saurabh Mishra

Drama in India stands as the tallest and richest tradition. In fact the very spirit of the Indianness coins by the virtue of traditions, beliefs and values which the drama propagates. Tracing its roots in the revered Vedic era, drama has been celebrated throughout the ages. *Ramayana*, *Mahabharata* and the holy *Bhagavad-Gita* have been the epitomes of various dramatic plots. These have for long been used for promoting sensibility of issues prevailing in the society. The great sage, Bharat Muni, in his great treatise *Natyashashtra* dictates: "Theatre is life. There is no art, no life, no craft, no learning, and no action which cannot be seen in it." Ideally qualifying drama as the most genuine and reverberating aspect of the earliest form of literature in India.

The origin of drama in the world is mostly rooted in the religious instincts of people. In England the development of drama had larger contribution from the 'Church'. The 'Miracle' and 'Morality' plays drew heavily from the religious elements; written mostly by the clergy men. Likewise in other countries like Egypt and China drama grew on the similar lines. In India drama originated and came to be enacted in temples. Bharat

Muni in 7th century A.D. propounded his theory of drama in *Natyashastra*. According to his philosophy-Lord Brahma poured the nectar of all the four Vedas (Sama, Yajur, Rig and Atharva) to form the new Veda—the fifth one: Natya.

Indian 'English Drama' was structured on the various European Models and plots of Sanskrit plays. The peregrination of Indian English Drama has been the canvas portrayal of diffidence until the literary wizards like—Rabindranath Tagore, Sri Aurobindo and Harindranath Chatopadhyay occupied the stage in the pre-independence era. Largely the plays were inspired in soul from the deep rooted beliefs and values of the Indian soil. In the post-independence era the trend of translation of plays from various original vernacular forms of language to English was in vogue. The prime flag bearers of the genre were some great playwrights like—Girish Karnad, Mohan Rakesh, Badal Sircar, Mahesh Dattani, Uma Parmeswaran and Vijay Tendulkar.

Girish Karnad has been the playwright who impacted the Indian English Drama in a big positive way. Through his first play—*Yayati* in the year 1961, Karnad embarked on what was going to be a splendid set of contribution to the Indian English Drama. He has to his credit eight plays, out of these five were translated into English—*Tughlaq, Hayavadana*, *Naga-Mandala*, *Tale-Danda* and *The Fire and the Rain*. Karnad's plays carried a deep sense of Indian orientation and served as an appropriate instrument to quench the literary thirst with a new vision, perfectly incarnated in myths and legends of India.

Being a convincing voice of the era Girish Karnad has through his plays been able to convey beautifully the various shades of 'man-woman relationships'. It would be apt to term that he had the connoisseur's eye in visualizing the under lying currents in the relationships of the characters of his play. The fabulous blend of myth and folklore made his creations churn out the crux of man-woman relationships. These would though appear complex in display, but are simple to comprehend and correlate. The power of communication that his characters imbibed from his outstanding yet simple style of creation had a phenomenal effect on the audience.

I

The 'Man-Woman Relationships' in his plays have received a meticulous treatment. *Yayati* displays the complex structure of relationship between the trio of Devayani, Sharmishtha and king Yayati on one hand and Puru and Chitralekha on the other. In *Naga-Mandala*, relationship of Appanna, his wife Rani and the Nag is portrayed. *The Fire and the Rain* is indeed a bouquet of relationships which rotate around-Paravasu, Vishakha, Raibhya, Yavakri, Nittilai and Arvasu. *Hayavadana* focuses on Padmini a newly wedded wife, Devadatta—the husband and Kapila the friend of Devadatta. In *Tughlaq*, we find the relationship between the stepmother and Muhammad the son being exhibited. In *Tale-Danda*, King Bijjala and Rambhavati the queen are shown in various shades of matrimonial bond. Also Sovideva's relationship with his mother Rambhavati is explored. Latiamba's and Madhuvarsha's fiasco is also seen in the shade of Kalavati and Sheelavanta, along with Sovideva's neglect of his wife.

The relationship universe which surrounds Karnad's characters is the main thread which builds around their appeal and charisma. His characters being reared from the mythological bank of Indian sensibility are upfront in construct and dialogues. The man-woman relationship canvas which these characters contribute to is varied and multifaceted. Ranging from the husband-wife relationship to stepmother-son saga, Karnad has also been able to project general perceptions of people in their times about the man-woman relations. Although women are the underdog in most of the relationship portrayals he has also touched the sensibility of man in contrasting shades. Karnad has also depicted the levels in relationship response of his characters which are segregated—age, caste and social acceptability wise.

The character of king Yayati is beautifully laid out amidst the longing for the lost youth and the encounter with three women—Devayani, Sharmishtha and Chitralekha. The cord of love, extra marital relationship and incest is featured through the three female characters respectively. Devayani's relationship with Yayati is based on theme of love. Her devotion and affection towards young Yayati, her savior, is marred by the presence of Sharmishtha. Yayati and Sharmishtha are shown to be in an extra marital relationship, which Devayani couldn't bear and hence—Shukracharya out of his extreme love for his daughter Devayani curses Yayati to become old.

The triangle of love thus formed between them is ousted by Shukracharya's curse of old age on Yayati. The loss of youth acts heavily upon the psyche of Yayati and he loses trace of his affections. Devayani who was taken over by the youth of Yayati and fell in love with him; she is now seen horrified by the curse of old age being enacted upon him and runs away. The matrimonial relationship between the two is seen to be shattered because of Yayati's extramarital affair and Devayani's impulsive behaviour. Yayati failed to realize the sacrosanct nature of matrimonial bond (forming relationship with Sharmishtha); he was taken over by the love for carnal pleasures. Devayani too failed to realize the importance of marriage, her love to Yayati proved to be an outwardly attraction only. She could not bear the old and worn out face of Yayati. The relationship status is flawed from both the ends and denies the tenets of Indian sensibility; hence it reached a sudden inappropriate end.

Shukracharya and Devayani exhibit the father-daughter relationship. The decision of Shukracharya to allow Devayani to marry Yayati, shows the extreme love and faith of father in his daughter's decision. This shows the maturity of relationship, in the context of patriarchal Indian sensibility. The daughter is shown have found respect for her decision by her father; even though it was against the prevalent caste system of times. Where one could marry in one's caste only. Shukracharya's maturity and patience to handle situation at hand is appreciable. Contrary to this mature decision stands his pronouncing of curse of old age upon his son-in-law Yayati. The curse proves to be decisive in a negative sense for Devayani; bringing even more sorrow and despair to her. Here it is also important to discuss that Shukracharya's wrath was subjected to Yayati only. Sharmishtha is not taken under the ambit.

Sharmishtha and Yayati are shown in out of social bounds relationship. This brings curse upon Yayati, making him old.

Being an adulterous bond in nature and appearance—Yayati and Sharmishtha relationship yet survives through the rough times of Yayati's old age curse. Sharmishtha stands tall against the odd encountered by Yayati and agrees to follow Yayati to hermitage to wash off their sins. The contrasting effect so built is realization of the fact that true love survives in wake of any storm. Although immoral, the relationship between the two is shown to be more than carnal pleasure and bodily charm. The love of Sharmishtha and Devayani to Yayati gives two shades of matrimonial aspect of man-woman relationship.

Puru and Chitralekha are seen in another deeper and darker shade of relationship. Their matrimonial bond is shown to be devastated by Puru's exchange of his youth with his father's old age. Chitralekha a newly married young lady finds it hard to bear with the sudden loss of youth in Puru; after her initial acceptance. The situation of exchange comes all of a sudden to her and she accepts it initially. The gravity strikes the cord of her heart and mind when she encounters Puru's old face—"Don't come near me...go away from here...Don't touch me!" (75). Her disbelief and horror gives way to the Indian sensibility of an ideal wife; she asks Puru to not come near her and leave. This sudden shock leaves her longing for reversal of the act. In her devastated relationship she finds no console. Her agony ends in self infliction-committing suicide.

Puru though sacrifices his youth for the happiness of his father, fails to care about the needs and sentiments of his young bride—Chitralekha. Chitralekha's repeated requests to Puru, not to lose his youth, are turned down by him. Desparation makes her decide to leave the kingdom which she is not allowed to do. Her appealing falling on deaf ears makes her choose the only possible option of liberation from this now turned worthless life—committing suicide. Even her death made no effect on old Puru, who could only shed a tear on her death and realize what catastrophe has befallen only after the return of his youth by Yayati.

This matrimonial bond features neglect by Puru of Chitralekha, in wake of his duties towards his father. Indian sensibility has played a large role in deciding actions of Puru.

His exchange of youth with his father reflects the Indian sensibility of a true son, sacrificing the entirety for the welfare and need of his father. But on the other hand he defies the Indian sensibility of an ideal husband; his failure to be an ideal husband—the protector, the lover, the comforter, towards Chitralekha.

Yayati and Chitralekha, reflect upon the father and daughter-in-law relationship. Yayati's blind self-interest ruins the life of Chitralekha. Yayati is seen to be completely disjointed from the Indian sensibility of a father-in-law. He fails to ensure and protect the interests of his son's bride. In fact he is real root cause of Chitralekha's misfortune. Complete lack of sympathy towards her and the ardent attitude preaching to live up to the name of the Bharatha family makes him even worse. Chitralekha's unstable and shocked state of mind can be seen by her act to offer herself to Yayati. Neither will you return Puru's youth nor will you accept me!... Of what use am I to your garland of victories? All of you have achieved your objectives. Who needs me now? You have your youth; Pururaj has his self-sacrifice, but what am I to do? (87). Realising which she later commits suicide. Even the shocking display of Chitralekha's mental state couldn't move Yayati. Remorse dawns on him only after the death of poor Chitralekha. The character of Yayati is shown as a complete dominating patriarch.

Karnad in *Yayati* has coined each character with diverse engagements and leaves his audience pondering over the complex situations in the man-woman relationship. All through the scope of this drama Karnad beautifully contrasts the situation of each character with either—passion, neglect, devotion and remorse under the umbrella of patriarchal set up of Indian sensibility. The adultery of Yayati, haste of Devayani, Sharmishtha's craving for Yayati, Puru's neglect of Chitralekha, Chitralekha's suicide and Yayati's remorse leaves a deep impact.

II

Hayavadana bears the plot which hatches the relationship saga of: Devadatta, Padmini and Kapila—the friend of Devadatta. Padmini is the limelight of the relationship.

Devadatta has already fallen in love fifteen times before he nurtures affections towards Padmini. Devadatta's love and affections are impulsive and resultant of fascination for beauty rather than love for Padmini. His erratic nature is evident from his vows of sacrifice to goddess Kali and lord Rudra; if he gets Padmini as his wife. The relationship quotient in terms of his contribution is invisible. His raw and rustic responses right from the initiation of relationship till the end are non-contributive in handling of odds which erupt.

The relationship between Padmini and Devadatta is shown in the state of misery and dilemma. Padmini is shown to be in an existing fondness for Devadatta, due to his intellectual capabilities, but she is also seen wanting for the perfect body of Kapila. This dilemmatic longing for the best of the two men creates the drift in the relation of husband-wife. The Indian sensibility of dharma strictly prohibits the idea of being in love out of the institution of marriage. Although since this play raises this question; sensibility of Draupadi's relation with Pandava's couldn't be passed on here. As even there Pandava's and Draupadi's relation was not the one which could pass the test of Indian sensibility. Polyandry is strictly prohibited in the Indian institution of marriage. Hence, suffering with 'confusion of affections' in relationship Padmini loses the faith of Devadatta, who in fit of jitters sacrifices his head to goddess 'Kali'.

Padmini is seen diseased with the desire for brain and brawn. She is unable to contain her insatiable self. The episode at the Kali temple brings forth the desired equation in the heart and mind of Padmini. Her subconscious act of putting the wrong heads on the wrong body signifies her internal desire to achieve perfection in her matrimonial relation. Padmini brings out the thought of search for completeness in relationship; searching for a soul mate—one who satiates the parched soul. Indian sensibility promotes no one is complete, except the almighty. Hence to search for perfect being is nothing but a wish for a mirage. Termination to such a desire evokes cataclysm. She ends up in a devastated state—sans Devadatta, sans Kapila, sans everything she desired and had; indeed a broken self.

Kapila's love for Padmini is—fascination for her beauty; same is reciprocated by Padmini for him—love for his muscular body. Having had the most of intellectual Devadatta Padmini craves for the other man in her life (Kapila). The episode of Fortunate Lady's flower marks the creation of lecherousness in her heart and soul for Kapila. Her lustful eyes fall upon the fit muscular body of Kapila and she craves for his physical perfection. Lust is differentiated from love here in both the relationships that Padmini aspires for. Karnad has made the point when even disguisedly blessed with the desired combination; Padmini lurks in dilemma.

Too much of free and willful interaction sprouts affections; as has been the case with Kapila and Padmini. Kapila and Padmini's relationship is expressed as cognizance of all those diversions and lures which encompass a common man's matrimonial world. These are hazy and taboos, but charming and tempting enough to catch upon people. Such relationships result in a nullified meaning, both socially and mentally. The common man's world is aptly suited in the choice of the names of the characters by Girish Karnad. Karnad in an interview said —"In Sanskrit, any person whose name you do not know is addressed as 'Devadatta'. Kapila means dark and therefore earthy and Padmini is the name of one class of women in Vatsayana's Kamasutra" (Bernett New Quest).

Thus in *Hayavadana* we find the epitome of Padmini's greed for perfection and the ensuing pitfall in her relationship with Devadatta. The situational creation is of prime importance in bringing out the desires, along with a note of sensibility which always acts upon the characters in the drama. The construct is meticulous and provides an opportunity to evaluate the acts of the characters and the Indian sensibility in instant comparison of the man-woman relationship in the drama.

III

A unique display of son and stepmother relationship forms the cue in the man-woman relationship in one of the most celebrated work of Girish Karnad—*Tughlaq*. The stepmother here is seen to have a concern for Tughlaq's life. She is seen to be bothered about his orientation towards life. The character of Tughlaq though is unresponsive and suspicious towards her, which culminates in the decree of her publicly humiliating and cruel death. The story builds environ of suspicion, gruesome deaths, treachery and tyranny at large; in the guise of general public welfare.

Relationship of mother and son detailed in the drama is no exception to it. In scene two, Tughlaq treats her without any seriousness. Her advices and concern for well-being of her son is taken in mockery as false hoods by Tughlaq. He does not confide in her concerns. Strikingly, both these attitudes are unwarranted according to the Indian sensibility of stepmother-son relationships. The concern of Tughlaq's mother fails the sensibility of jealousness, competition and animosity generally associated with the Indian culture. Relationship of lord Rama and Kaikai (third wife of king Dashratha) and Dhruva and Suniti (second wife of king Uttanipada) are conspicuous examples of hatred and disgust of a stepmother towards son and reciprocation of likeability from son towards the stepmothers.

Tughlaq poses a cold response to the opposition of his stepmother towards his uncanny ways of rule. In her statement—"It's only seven years ago that you came to the throne. How glorious you were then, how idealistic, how full of hopes. Look at your kingdom now. It's become the kitchen of death" (*Tughlaq*, 65). She praises his ideals with which he ascended the throne of Delhi; his deeds did not match those ideals now. The gruesome and Machiavellian actions that had become the part and parcel of his daily conduct of affairs of the state are in lot of contestation from public at large; therefore mother desist him from such acts.

Voice of mother fails to make any impact on Tughlaq; as he is surrounded and advised by people who had started to believe in his theories and designs making them even more vicious. The influence of Najib for instance proves to be stronger on the mind of Tughlaq rather than the pleadings and advice of his stepmother. Even the advice of intellectual like Barni fails to persuade Tughlaq. In such desperation and left with no other option the stepmother gets Najib (one of the confidants of Tughlaq) assassinated. In her bid to save her son from the clutches of such people as Najib, the mother takes the extreme step, showing her intensity of concern. Tughlaq on the other hand guided by his instincts of mistrust towards stepmother sees—animosity and treachery in the killing of Najib. On coming to know that his stepmother had made it happen, Tughlaq decrees her to be stoned to death in public. The concern for well-being of her son is rewarded by claims of her being adulteress and finally decree of her humiliating death. Thus in *Tughlaq*, Girish Karnad has built an opposite case to the Indian sensibility of relationship of stepmother-son.

IV

In *Naga-Mandala*—Rani, Appanna and the Nag occupy the centre stage of man-woman relationship. The relation of Rani, the central character in the drama, with Appanna is plagued with disharmony and neglect. Appanna is a mature man as compared to Rani, a newly wedded ignorant girl. Rani a new entrant to the matrimonial world is inflicted by an extreme neglect and mental exploitation at the hands of Appanna—her husband. Appanna's neglect of Rani is caused by his involvement in an out of bond relation with another woman. The adulterous ways of Appanna create a lull in his relations with Rani. The core factors of—love, concern, protection and togetherness are absent in their mutual relation. Onus of this unnatural relation structure belongs to Appanna. He being a matured youth well versed with the ways of the world should have made relation turn the right way. Rani's immature nature is hardly to blame for any relationship discord.

The plot of the drama focuses upon the state of young married girls who are subjected to sheer neglect. The expectation built on the part of Rani is of concern and company; the bare minimum for such a relation to flourish. The imprisonment of Rani by Appanna, while he is away, is inhuman and unwarranted. This reflects the caging of the aspirations of Rani. Appanna and Rani share a constrained relation of a cruel master

(Appanna) and a humble and obedient servant (Rani). While Appanna is seen busy in his relations with concubine, Rani's plight is heart moving and presents the picture of women in such relations. She has no one to share her fears and loneliness with. The status of wife conferred on her by virtue of the social bond is reduced to—a prisoner, a maid and a human without feelings and demands or expectations. Being ill treated and tortured by her husband, her conjugal rights remain unconfirmed. She bears the brunt of the situational and cultural factors in the male dominated patriarchal Indian society.

The Naga comes as the harbinger of change in her life. The Naga is developed as a conscious character that finishes the trouble of Rani's life. The old woman who gives the potion to Rani—is symbolic of care and guidance which one woman offers to the other, seeing her plight. The Naga is the symbol of freedom and respite for Rani. He fulfills her barren life with seeds of love, care and affection. It is made possible through the character of Naga that Rani achieves completion in her womanhood. She now is no more a solitary prisoner; but a loving wife and a to be mother, too. Dollors Collellmir says—"Thus, from the philosophical and mythological point of view, there is reason to say that the Cobra causes Rani's intergration at different levels, the physical, the emotional, the spiritual and the intellectual, and that he has given her the chance to choose and achieve liberation" (7).

The symbolism of Naga is chosen very deftly by Karnad; it appeals to the connotation of Indian sensibility of snakes to be able to transit in human shape and back to the original form—the 'Ichadharai' ones. Naga acquires the shape of Appanna, while he is with Rani, since Rani would disown any unknown man. This scripture is not new to the Indian mythology; there have been many such cases of alien acquiring the shape of husband of a devoted wife. Lord Vishnu posed as Jalandhar the husband of pious Vrinda, thereby tricking her of her virtue which was source of Jalandhar's strength. Connecting the Naga and Rani's plot with the Indian mythology, we find that the women are taken to be the source of providing strength to the husbands. Husbands on the contrary may be following evil ways of life. The unparallel structure of man-woman relationship is the cause of distance in the relations expressed in the drama.

Naga is sacrificial figure which aims to comfort Rani. Important to note here is that the compassion developed in Naga is not automated, but by virtue of the magical herbs given accidently by Rani. This shows that the male figures are insensitive towards the sufferings of their counterparts; it's only some magic which could create the empathy in them for their women. Rani is a very powerful description of Indian female. She depicts—softness, sensitivity and longing for affections on one hand and depicts the incarnation of goddess on the other. Either she is too weak or too strong. In any of the case she is not taken up by other normal male counterpart in the society. She is out reach of normal ways of life.

To summarize the effect of man-woman issues in the drama *Naga-Mandala* it would be correct to term the situation of Rani as a 'Solitary prisoner' dominated and crushed by Appanna transforms to a new level of avatar of 'Goddess' who is served and obeyed by Appanna. Girish Karnad in this drama has maneuvered the man-woman relationship such that the plight of the downtrodden female changes to a visibly powerful figure. Karnad himself commented on the role and significance of the tale saying—"They also express a distinctly woman's understanding of the reality around her, a live counterpart to the patriarchal structures of the classical texts and institutions. The position of Rani in the story of *Naga-Mandala*, for instance, can be seen as a metaphor for the situation of a young girl in the bosom of a joint family where she sees her husband only in two unconnected roles—as a stranger during the day and as a lover at night. Inevitably, the pattern of relationships she is forced to weave from these disjointed encounters must be something of a fiction. The empty house Rani is locked in could be the family she is married into" (Karnad "Author's Introduction"). He has thus made the character of Rani develop from the nothingness—scratch in the relationship cordon to the only meaningful entity.

V

In *Tale-Danda* we find the relationships being discussed in the background of casteism. It is a wonderful treatise to see the sound application of casteism as a factor in the development of the plot by Karnad. The relationship of King Bijala and Rambhavati the queen takes up the disparity of man-woman relations as has been observed in the previously discussed plays. The King doesn't treat the queen as an equal. It is by the virtue of king's wishes that the queen performs her acts. The relationship between Bijala and Rambhavati is not painted evenly in the same colour it has its good patches too. Rambhavati recalls in Act-I—"Suddenly, you were as you used to be in those days—our early years together, when you'd talk and talk and insist on my listening" (15). To this Bijala responds in a different tune rebuking the entire womenfolk—"Is that all you have to say? Doesn't anything interest you women except marriage and husbands and children?" (15). Rambhavati also angrily responds—"Have you left us anything else?" (15). Her extreme displeasure is mark of change from tolerance to intolerance of the male hegemony. Still her neglect and unparallel status by the king, is responded by the inevitable compliance of king by her. Her compliance is not the resultant of her willfulness but of the fear and unsaid mandatory devotion. In one such conversation with her son Sovideva the queen expresses her displeasure about the treatment by the king—she says, "What am I to do? Do you think your father ever listens to me?" Thus leading to the contemplation that the underlying sensibility of the society rules the chord of relationship between a man-woman, this irrespective of the status of the couple involved.

Sovideva the son of King Bijala, is seen to be closer to his mother than his father. Rightly, so under the Freudian 'Oedipus Complex', this describes a son's affections towards his mother and anger and hate towards father. Sovideva confides his anguish and plans to his mother—the queen. The queen ideally supports the son but subject to the liking of his father—the king. She says "Do as you wish. Just don't upset your father, that's all. He turns his bad temper on me and I can't take it any longer"

Sovideva's relationship with his wife is also of the same order and kind as that between the king and the queen. Sovideva too is seen to offer neglect and lower status to his wife, he is also seen to rebuke and scold her. Sovideva exiles his wife to her father's house without bothering to call her back. Again we see the other factor—Indrani, the prostitute being responsible for the differences in the relationship. Substitution of Indrani in the life of Sovideva in place of his wife shows the primary value of the relationship is not due to love care and affections but instead carnal pleasure. Sovideva admits the same when he says to Manchanna—"Yes. And see our Queen again! She is our Queen after all, frigid bitch though she is". This testifies the denouement of the disparity of status in man-woman relationships in India and women being treated as unequal in the patriarchal society.

The next episode involves portrayal of man-woman relationship amidst the casteism factor. Madhuvarsha and Lalitamba fiasco is coupled with the Kalavati and Sheelavanta marriage. Karnad has given a new shade to the relationship scenario in this plot of the drama. Here 'Hypergamous' marriage is set up between Kalavati and Sheelavanta. The whole plot depicts the Indian sensibility of cateism in the man-woman relations in the Indian society. The marriage between a Brahmin's daughter and a Cobbler's son is Hypergamous.

Madhuvarsha and Lalitamba are Brahmins by caste and are the parents of Kalavati. The episode of the clash between the two parents on the issue of their daughter's marriage is an important one. It reflects the concern in mother's heart for the patriarchal decision of the father. Lalitamba, the mother is gravely concerned of the outcome of the marriage. She fears that her daughter who is so tender would not be able to cope up with the tough and debased lifestyle of a Cobbler's family. In Act-II, scene V, she exhibits her fear that the girl—"can't stand the smell of the leather" (40). But the father Madhuvarsha is concerned about the social prestige in the 'Sharana' fraternity. He stresses that because of such a marriage—"the orthodox will see this mingling of castes as a blow at the very roots of Varnasharama dharma" (38). Haralayya—the father of

Sheelavanta, who is also a Sharana, voices his concern on the marriage saying that—"Rivers of blood will flow if the marriage takes place" (41). Madhuvarsha overrules the twin concern of Lalitamba and Haralayya; deciding to conduct the marriage. The male dominance of Madhuvarsha works and hence the female concern is put aside rudely—"Woman, I said hold your tongue" (41). The ownership and concern of children in the man-woman relationship is also subject to the social constraint of male dominance in the relationship.

Thus, in *Tale-Danda* we are introduced to an altogether different shade of man-woman relationship which has casteism and parental concern at its back. Karnad has been once again successful in bringing out the Indian classification of patriarchal dominance in the man-woman relations. Bijala and Rambhavati's relation is also a reflection of same male hegemony. Sovideva too, exercises his machismo towards his wife and the poor being suffers at his hand. Madhuvarsha proves to be an irresponsible husband and father. He is atrocious in his behaviour towards his wife and dominant in imposing his decision of marriage. Lalitamba is a dedicated woman, who is bullied by her husband, and in the process unable to exercise her right to protect the welfare of her daughter. Her right is usurped by the dominance of Madhuvarsha.

VI

The Fire and the Rain introduces a complex plot filled with relationships which are based largely on the components of hatred, jealousy, revenge and lecherousness. The relationship web is woven such that it represents consistent cycle of hate and jealousy. Paravasu and Vishakha are shown to share the matrimonial bond. The relationship between the two is shown to be in a different pattern as compared to the earlier discussed ones. Paravasu who has attained the chief-priesthood is away from his hermitage. In his absence, his wife Vishakha is shown to have been lured and courted by her past lover Yavakri. Her disrepute reaches Paravasu who then plans to visit his wife denying all the constraints of the Vedic ritual. Getting to know about the circumstances under which she was attracted towards

Yavakri; Paravasu believes her. This is totally against the Indian sensibility of unequal status adorned on women by men. Paravasu behaves contrary to the normal code. Vishakha in Act-II says to Paravasu—"Something died in your father the day the King invited you to be the Chief Priest. He's been drying up like a dead tree since then. No sap runs in him (pause). On the one hand, there's his sense of being humiliated by you. On the other, there's lust. It consumes him. An old man's curdled lust. And there's no one else here to take his rage out on but me (32). Paravasu believes her word to word and as a result of which he is convinced of the evil in the mind of his father Raibhya. The connect in the relationship of Paravasu and Vishakha shown here by Karnad is out of tune with the notion of general Indian sensibility as shown in the case of Puru, the compassion—towards his father rather than his wife Chitralekha in Yayati. Vishakha on the other hand is shown to be a woman dedicated to the husband. She gets lured by the pleadings and advances of her past lover Yavakri. Her initial withdrawal from the trap shows that her sensibility protected her initially from being in an immoral relationship, but in the end the lure proved to be stronger and won.

Yavakri the past lover of Vishakha is disturbed and parched for vengeance against her husband and father-in-law. The chance meeting with Vishakha, is taken by him as an opportunity to guide his vengeance against the wrong doers. Yavakri, feels doubly offended when he learns that his love Vishakha has been married to his foe's son-Paravasu. Yavakri projects his love to Vishakha and makes her the suitable vehicle for the accomplishment of his revenge on Raibhya.

Thus the bond that Yavakri tries to revive is no more due to the past affection, but just as a step towards his revenge. He uses Vishakha as an instrument in his fight against Raibhya and Paravasu. He is unconcerned about the effect of such an immoral relation on Vishakha's life. Instead he focuses on gratifying his hunger for her flesh and thereby debasing her and avenging his father's insult. Yavakri turns out to be an irresponsible man who didn't care about the woman who willingly sacrificed her piousness to fulfill his love. Vishakha is shown to be lured into the trap of Yavakri, but prior to it she refuses Yavakri any favours and dismisses his moves. The initial refusal and the later self initiation show the dilemma in Vishakha's mind. She is bounded by the general schema of a married woman and hence she refuses to accept Yavakri advances but her environ, wherein Paravasu has left her alone for seven years and Raibhya is casting an evil eye upon her, makes her shed her schematic boundaries and decide against the very notion of piousness of a married woman. Vishakha's wish to take revenge against her polluted environ makes her go out of the sacrosanct relation of marriage.

Raibhya's relationship status with Vishakha is also the depiction of the pathetic state of affairs for women in the male dominated Indian society. Being in the status of father-in-law to Vishakha, Raibhya is expected to offer care and protection as the father does to his daughter. Instead he subjects her to physical torture and also casts his evil eye on Vishakha. This is reflection of the treatment of women as instruments of pleasure and subjects of exploitation. The complexity of the situation expresses the feeling of hatred and being offended in father (Raibhya) by the son (Paravasu) and since both have no direct opportunity to conflict; poor Vishakha becomes the subject of learned Raibhya's hatred and lust. Hence, is created the wish to avenge in Vishakha. She not only creates relations with Yavakri which hurts the male ego of both the characters, but also tells Paravasu of the lust of his father. The resultant patricide by Paravasu shows what women can achieve anything if they are subjected to such a great emotional and physical exploitation. The chaos created in relations by women reflects upon the whole clan and which echoes the Indian sensibility of the Sanskrit phrase—"yatra naryastu pujyante ramante tatra devta"! (It is where women are respected and worshipped, that the gods reside).

Another totally different relationship aspect devoid of revenge, the central theme of the play, is that of Aravasu and Nittilai. The relationship is based on love and sacrifices totally opposite to the ones depicted earlier in the same play. Nittilai is a sharp contrast to the character of Vishakha. She is shown to be the ideal Indian woman. Her calm and composite nature speaks volumes about the dignity and responsibility she shoulders for everyone else's sake. She is dedicated towards the benefit of all those who are related to her and the society as a whole. Nittilai's dedication and love towards Aravasu is undeniable, still she refuses his advances before marriage. After her marriage to an elder person whom she doesn't love, Nittilai, rushes the help of Aravasu but when he tries to be intimate with her she refuses and says in a serious voice "Aravasu, when I say we should go together—I don't mean we have to live together—like lovers or husband and wife. I have been vicious enough to my husband. I don't want to disgrace him further. Let's be together—like brother and sister. You marry any girl you like" (42). She is very clear about her role and duties. Aravasu understands and respects her stand, but she lacks the same understanding by her brother and her husband. The brother and husband of Nittilai make her the object of their false vengeance—"[...] the brother knocks Aravasu down and pins him to the ground. The husband pulls out a knife, grabs Nittilai by her hair and slashes her throat in one swift motion. He then let's her drop" (58). Aravasu could not marry Nittilai as he was busy cremating the body of Yavakri and as a result couldn't reach on time where the elders of Nittilai were waiting. The importance of things other than Nittilai in Aravasu's life depicts the lack in relationship. Whereas Nittilai's selfless reaction to help Aravasu when she heard he was in dire need, confirms her commitment level. The unequal empathy in the relationship speaks of disparity in man-woman relationships.

In a nutshell Girish Karnad has shown the man-woman relations in different frames of vengeance and mistrust. All the characters and the relationships shared between them, in the play, are pre-occupied with hatred and will to take revenge, except the one between Aravasu and Nittilai. But, even these characters could not be spared of the evil effect of their environment and are seen to be helplessly crushed by the bulldozing of negativism all around them.

VII

At large the analysis of 'Man-Woman Relationship' in the works of Karnad results in reflection of deprived and pathetic situation of the women in the Indian society. Same is felt by C.N. Ramachandran for the female characters in Karnad's dramas—"the worst sufferers are women...who are caught up in a whirlpool of Hindu patriarchy, and are sucked down helplessly" (28). The psychological context of that may be traced to the development of the 'Schemas'. The promotion of any relationship in any society is largely dependent on creation of these schemas. Karnad has empathetically disposed the contemporary dilemmas in context with the fables and myths of Indian society. Karnad values past in his scripts. He himself has attached significance of correlation between the past and the present—"The past is never totally lost; it coexists with the present as a flow. A rich variety of theatre form still exists, with a continuous history stretching over centuries" (Introduction, 11).

His depiction of various issues has been able to touch the chord at the heart of audiences. Relevance of issues such as—adultery, misconceptions, frigidness, revenge, domination and exploitation in contemporary scenario is root of his exemplary success on the platform of Indian English Drama.

The irresponsible and insensitive men characters loom large in his scripts. The likes of—Appanna, Bijjala, Puru, Madhuvarsha, Paravasu, Raibhya, Tughlaq, Yavakri, Devadatta, Yayati, Kapila, Aravasu and Sovideva prove to be brusque, vehement and totally aloof from any concern towards the womenfolk. Their treatment of the women in relationship is no more than the master-slave bond irrespective of the level or junction of engagement. It appears to be a waste of the very spirit of relationships. In this context it is appropriate to refer to what Simone de Beauvoir says about woman's role as the husband conceives it in the marital relationship. She views:

> A husband regards none of his wife's good qualities as particularly meritorious; they are implied by the institution of marriage itself...he is still more profoundly ignorant of her dreams, her fancies, her nostalgic yearnings, of the emotional climate in which she spends her days. (492)

Female characters are mostly suppressed, dominated and eclipsed by the male hegemony. They appear to be generally feeble to launch themselves and their causes. Chitralekha, Nittilai, Padmini, Rambhavati and Latiamba and the likes are soft in—attitude and in their actions too. They feel the pain of oppression by the male counterparts, but could do little to defend against them. Although, Rani and Vishakha show some challenge and are successful in either effecting a change in the attitude or destroying the entire clan.

Their treatment in drama has caused the desired catharsis of realization. These works are indeed master piece creations, which express plight of women and promote awakening in the society. Man-Woman issues addressed by Karnad are very objective in nature. A comprehensive evaluation of all these characters points out the significance of contribution and abilities of women in general and hence appeals towards achieving respectfulness and parity in relations.

WORKS CITED

Abrams, M.H., *A Glossary of Literary Terms*. 6th ed. Bangalore: Prism Books, 1993.

Babu, M. Sarat. *Indian Drama Today: A Study in the Theme of Cultural Deformity*. New Delhi: Prestige Books, 1997.

Bhatta, S. Krishna, *Indian English Drama: A Critical Study*. New Delhi: Sage Publishers, 1987.

Bhatia, Nandi, Ed. *Modern Indian Theatre: A Reader*. New Delhi: Oxford University Press, 2009.

Bocock, Robert. *Sigmund Freud*. New York: Routledge, 2002.

Chari, A. Jaganamohana. "*Hayavadana* and *Naga-Mandala*: A Study in Postcolonial Dialectics". *The Plays of Girish Karnad: Critical Perspectives*. Ed. Jaydipsinh Dodiya. New Delhi: Prestige Books, 1999.

Dass, Veena Noble. "A Re-Reading of Girish Karnad's Plays with Reference to Myth and Folktale". *Flowering of Indian Drama: Growth and Development*. Ed. K. Venkata Reddy and R.K. Dhawan. New Delhi: Prestige Books, 2004.

Dhanavel, P. *Indian Imagination of Girish Karnad: Essays on Hayavadana*. New Delhi: Prestige Books, 2000.

Dhawan, R.K., 50 Years of Indian Writing, *IAES*, New Delhi, 1999.

Dollors, Collellmir. *Mythical Structure in Girish Karnad's Naga-Mandala.* de la Universitat de Barcelona, 7.

Freud, Sigmund. *Civilization and its Discontents.* New York: W.W. Norton and Company, 1961.

Ghosh, Manomohan, (edited and translated) *Natyashashtra Ascribe To Bharat-Muni* (A Treatise on Ancient Indian Dramaturgy and Histrionics), Volume I & II, Varanasi: Chowkhambha Sanskrit Series Office Reprint, 2007.

Iyengar, K.R.S., *Indian Writing in English*, New Delhi: Sterling, 1985.

Jain, Jasbir. "The Curious Journey of the Indian Drama in English". *Contemporary Indian Drama: Astride Two Traditions.* Ed. Urmil Talwar and Bandana Chakrabarty. Jaipur: Rawat Publications, 2005.

James, R. Bernett. "An interview with Girish Karnad", *New Quest.* No. 36, Nov.-Dec. 1982.

Karnad, Girish. *Collected Plays.* Vol. 1 & 2. New Delhi: Oxford University Press, 2005.

——. *Yayati.* Delhi: OUP, 2007.

——. *Tale-Danda.* Delhi : Ravi Dayal, 1993.

——. *The Fire and The Rain.* New Delhi: Oxford University Press, 1998.

——. *Three Plays: Naga-Mandala, Hayavadana, Tughlaq.* Delhi: Oxford University Press, 1995.

——. *Tughlaq.* Madras: OUP, 1972.

——. "Author's Introduction" *Three Plays: Naga-Mandala, Hayavadana, Tughlaq.* (Eighth impression) New Delhi: Oxford University Press, 2002.

——. "Introduction", *Three Plays.* New Delhi: Oxford University Press, 1994.

Naik, M.K. *A History of Indian English Literature*, New Delhi: Sahitya Akademi, 1995.

Ramachandran, C.N. "Girish Karnad: The Playwright in Search of Metaphors," *The Journal of Indian Writing in English.* 22. 2: 1999.

Simone de Bauvoir, *The Second Sex*, Trans. & Ed. H.N. Parshley, Harmondsworth: Penguin Books India Ltd., 1974.

13 Feminist Articulations and Transgendered as Victims in Mahesh Dattani's *Tara* and *Seven Steps Around the Fire*

T. Sasikanth Reddy

Mahesh Dattani is one of the promising Indian English playwrights voicing for the marginalized victims through the experimental fragmentary settings in his theatres. Most of his plays are a true reflection of his time, place and socioeconomic background. When he won the Sahitya Akademi award for his *Final Solutions* and Other Plays, the Akademi commended that his plays "probe tangled attitude in contemporary India towards communal differences, consumerism and gender...a brilliant contribution to Indian Drama in English" (Mangayarkarasi, 222).

Dattani's plays are the postmodern attempts that try to map the cultural shifts occurring in the urban India. Sudha Rani in her critique on Mahesh Dattani, considered him: "a society and...chooses expressionism to illustrate the continuous struggle of urban Indian in familial, social and cultural modernist artist who in such a critical cultural situation selects different forms other than realism to depict the spheres to treat his individual identity" (Rani). Dattani, the voice of India, is a contemporary social reformer. He has dealt with diversity of themes. He is an authority as a dancer, director, playwright, audience and commentator. He is innovative in the use of dramatic techniques. He has set the direction of new drama which attempts to eliminate the difference between page and stage. The dominant thing in Dattani's plays is the struggle between individual and the society. He is of the view that there should be coordination between social conventions and consciousness of human dignity. According to him social myths need to be reinvestigated to save humanity. His characters are mouth-piece to represent the voice of common man crushed under the wheels of exploitation of elitists.

Dattani's plays can be analyzed through the poststructuralist perspectives like gender theories. Hence, the gender schema approach born out of sex role theories of mid 80's has been chosen to study the major characters in Mahesh Dattani's *Tara*, reflecting the gender issues as social trauma. As *Tara* is the stage play of multi-level sets the gender issue discussed as content is also multi-layered. Sandra Lipsitz Bern one of the cognitive psychologists of Cornell University popularizing the gender schema theory views as, "the process by which a society transmutes male and female into masculine and feminine is known as the process of sex typing" (Bern, 354). From this point of view the author tries to discuss the characters of Tara and Chandan born as conjoined twins representing both female self and male self and explaining how male has more privileges over female self in all cultures and this sex typing is deeply rooted in man-woman psyche of Indian cultures. Tara the play's title character is to be studied as the victim of this collective consciousness of the social system.

Dattani has presented the bizarre reality of the woman playing second fiddle to man. The play *Tara* opens with Chandan changed into Dan in order to absolve himself from the guilt of his sister. He has to bear the brunt of his grandfather's cruelty. He considers himself responsible for his sister's death. In this play Dattani plays with the idea of female infanticide that is prevalent among the Gujratis and also suggests Patel's hegemonic patriarchy when he insists that proper division in the gender be made. *Tara* gives us a glimpse into the modern society which claims to be liberal and advanced in its thought and action. In a society which claims that its mothers are educated today have "Devis" like Durga, Kali, Saraswati, Lakshmi, etc. whom not only women but men also pay obeisance, differentiate between a male child and a female child. All the propagandas of equality be male and female, equal opportunities to women in all the fields are belied. Dattani's deep preoccupation with gender issues leads to the emergence of the idea of the twin side to one's self-quite literally embodied in one body and the separation that follows. Dattani mentioned in one of his interviews with Lakshmi Subramanyam: "I see Tara as a play about the male self and female self. The male self is being preferred in all cultures. The play is about the separation of self and the resultant angst" (Subramanyam, 134). Erin Mee writes in the note of the play: "*Tara* centres on the emotional separation that grows between two conjoined twins following the discovery that their physical separation was manipulated by their mother and grandfather to favour the boy [Chandan] over the girl [Tara]. Tara, a feisty girl who isn't given the opportunities given to her brother [although she may be smarter] eventually wastes away and dies. Chandan escapes to London, changes his name to Dan, and attempts to repress the guilt he feels over his sister's death by living without a personal history, woven into the play are issues of class and community, and the clash between traditional and modern lifestyles and values" (Mee, 320).

Tara is the play about a female self viewed through a male self and the irony is both selves are born as conjoined twins, medically called 'Siamese twins' but they were miraculously separated to survive. The physical separation was made through the surgery. As Dan recollects: "like we've always been Inseparable. The way we started in life. Two lives and one body in one comfortable womb. Till we were forced out—and separated" (Dattani, 325).

The story line clearly indicates that when Chandan and Tara turn fifteen they start realizing the adulthood as man and woman constructed on them by their parents, Patel and Bharati who are educated but the social thrust of sex typing phenomena drives them to be discriminating between their children favouring the male child. Bharati's father is also an influencing factor in this misdeed. The twins were conjoined from the chest down though they did not share any vital organs. The conjoined twins were about to be separated but there was a complication as there were three legs. Bharati and her father influenced the doctor by bribing him with three acres of prime land in the heart of the city, Bangalore, so that Chandan might have two legs, the weaker third leg would survive on the girl. Yet, Chandan's body rejected the second leg that was later amputated. Dattani has well pointed out that the biologically conjoined twins never experience natural or sex favouritism but socially nurtured gender favouritism. The mother, her father and the surgeon collaborated to afford the male with better chances. They reflect the social milieu that is always male specific.

Bern's gender schema theory discloses the intricacies of patriarchal society under which both sexes are cognitively schematic to influence any individual to favour the particular gender, male. There is a paradigm in the collaboration of mother, father, grandfather and the male Doctor, Thakkar in favouring the boy, Chandan against the girl, Tara. The system still prevails to treat Tara as subaltern. Bern states: "A schema is a cognitive structure, a network of associations that organizes and guides an individual perception.... Schematic processing is thus highly selective and enables the individual to impose structure and meaning onto the vast array of incoming stimuli" (Bern, 355). She further views it as a "constructive process where in what is perceived is a product of the interaction between the incoming information and the perceivers preexisting schema" (Bern, 228). This perception would help one know the subtleties of gender construct occurred among the characters of Patel's family and so is the society at large.

Bharati tries to shed her burden of guilt by showing maternal love and concern for her daughter and to assert her moral superiority over her husband. She also tries to expatiate by the act of donating kidney to her daughter which was ultimately futile. Dattani establishes that mother and daughter relationship is ultimately subordinated to the directives of patriarchy. All cultures and all countries by establishing values, roles, gender perception, prescribe unequal means. Dr. Thakkar occupies the one on the highest level throughout the play. Tara and Chandan are conjoined, Siamese twins who must be separated to survive. The dichotomy between the twin 'gendered' selves is recognized, and a physical separation is made through surgery "Like we've always been inseparable. The way we started in life. Two lives and one body in one comfortable womb. Till we were forced out—And separated" (Dattani, 325).

Mr. Patel, an emblem of male chauvinism, maintains his absolute authority in the decision-making about the family. Bharati is a pathetic victim of patriarchy. She was exceptionally conscious for safety of Tara, not for the sake of Tara but for her own sake. It was irony of fate that Chandan and Tara were entwined in such a way that their separation was impossible. Chandan enjoyed greater preference and Tara was left to enjoy the position of a subaltern. The effort to separate them through surgery left Tara cripple for life. The suffering of Tara and Chandan is a symbolic justification of the perception that the grace of the relationship exists not in their separateness but in their moving in a coordination or interdependence. The famous theatre director Erin Mee writes: "Dattani sees Tara as a play about the gendered self, about coming to terms with the feminine side of oneself in a world that always favours what is 'male', but many people in India see it as a play about the girl child" (Mee, 320).

Tara was more enthusiastic and full of jest and spark of life. She had high aspirations which she could not accomplish because of her handicapped state while the boy was comfortably ensconced and had come to terms with his handicapped life. Why was then Tara denied the privilege of the good leg. Why? Is it because she was a girl? Is being a girl in the society a curse. Why so much partiality and differentiation done to women in the country which has rich heritage and where women are otherwise placed on the pedestal. Dr. Thakkar belied his godly profession and led himself to be bribed by Bharati's father into becoming an accomplice in the bizarre act of severing the leg. He should have upheld his profession by denouncing the decision at his inception whereas he in a way took Tara's life by severing the leg. His wise decision could have given Tara a safe, secured and complete life. Patel meanwhile seems much beleaguered: "Yes, call me a liar, a wife beater, a child abuser. It's what you want me to be! And you. You want them to believe you love them very much" (Dattani, 354). Again he tells

Tara: "Tara, please believe me when I say that I love you very much and I have never in all my life loved you less or more than I have loved your brother. But your mother..." (Dattani, 354).

This is why the play generates a death like response from Tara when she learns the truth, she was discriminated against, because of her gender, but not by her father—it was Bharati's decision that deprived her of what she wanted more than anything else in the world—a second leg. Bharati's father further strengthened his indulgence for male grand child by leaving his property after his demise to Chandan and not a single penny to Tara. Patel's attitude has also been negative. He blames his wife and father-in-law for the damage done cannot be denied. The fact that male is always given the greater chance is obvious from Patel's planning for Chandan's education and future career. No consideration whatsoever for her feelings! Tara is the victim of this collective social system. Her father, Mr. Patel, is not much different from his wife, though Bharati is guilty of a more serious crime against Tara. He continuously and doggedly favours Chandan when it comes to giving him higher education abroad, and a career.

Patel: You are turning them against the whole world.

Bharati: I am doing that.

Patel: Yes! Look at the way you treat Tara. As if she is made of glass. You coddle her, you pet her, you spoil her, she's grown up feeling she doesn't need any one but you! (Dattani, 352)

But Tara could have made her defiance, her strength and fight the society to etch a place of her own. Tara is discouraged openly, not withstanding her feelings in the matter, even though she is more intelligent, sharp and witty and would perform well if given opportunities in life. Economic and cultural factors have been responsible for the antipathy against and inferiorization of the girl child. All these factors combine to create the social system in which the girl child has to live and die. Tara is killed by social system, which controls the minds and actions of the people. The trauma of coming to know the role her mother had played in her life, and the discrimination become too much for her. And why is she killed? Tara is not wanted. Girls are not wanted.

> Tara: Oh! What a waste! A waste of money. Why they spend all the money to keep me alive? It cannot matter whether I live or die. There are thousands of poor sick people on the roads who could be given care and attention, and I think I know what I will make of myself. I will be a carer for those people. I...I will spend the rest of my life feeding and clothing those...starving naked millions everywhere is talking about. (Dattani, 370)

The above statement shows that Tara is not deterred by the injustice done to her by her parents but she presents herself as an empowered lady to face all the hurdles. She also shows sympathy towards the downtrodden. She was bubbly and energetic girl who had all the qualities of a normal girl. If she had been given moral support by her parents, she might have shone like a star as her name signifies. Her life was a burden on this earth. This made her lose interest in life altogether. Further she refuses to go to physiotherapy or fill forms for college.

> Tara: How do you expect me to feel anything for anyone if they don't give me any feeling to begin with? Why is it wrong for me to be without feeling? Why are you asking me to do something that nobody has done for me? (Dattani, 380)

Tara was a bright and shining star which was a source of cheerfulness and happiness of the family. A complete life could have done wonders and she would have scored the limits which her brother Chandan couldn't have. Tara is potentiality sacrificed on the altar of gender. Identity crisis becomes a chain with which a female is fettered when the question of choice between male and female arises.

The central idea of the play *Tara* is that the society can accept and tolerate male though he is physically challenged and when Tara turns fifteen she becomes the victim of gender biased system promoted by male dominant generations. The tragedy is that she could not survive. The play ends with the note of failure on the part of Dan, saying: "I move. I move, without meaning. I forget Tara. I forget that I had a sister—with whom I had shared a body, In one comfortable womb, till we were forced out—and separated" (Dattani, 381). But Dattani says that he didn't contend with such a note that male self is very much privileged over female self and hence, he just idealistically intends to anticipate the better understanding among the gendered sexes on the basis of humanist perception, as Dorothy Parker has written, "my idea is that all of us men as well as women, should be regarded as human beings" (Beauvoir, 280-85). At last the play extends a little to show, "Tara walks into the spot without limping. Dan also appears without limp" (Dattani, 354) and Dan speaks to Tara, "Forgive me for making it my tragedy. Tara embraces Dan...they hug each other tightly" (Dattani, 380). This fantasy scene implies that Dattani's creative consciousness longs for the reunion of all the sexes at a single point of humanism. It would be fruitful if gender study thus expands beyond feminist consciousness to assert the socialist need of humanism. For, this gender study must transcend all sexual and cultural politics to promote the humanist concern among the people of different sexes.

Dattani's polemical work *Seven Steps Around the Fire* throws light on cruel upper class mentality and mystery created in the life of marginalized for the sake of their social prestige. Elitist can do anything to get power. After getting power they become devilish to sustain the same. As a result of this, they create complexities in the life of marginalized and they even don't bother about it. They treat marginalized category as puppets. Mystery is omnipresent in the play. From the beginning to the end there are mysteries about the murderer of Kamala, a eunuch, relationship of eunuch among themselves and the disturbed relationship of elite class people. The play talks about uninterpreted social myths which result in the mysterious existence of marginals. Dattani in *Seven Steps Around the Fire* takes up a issue that is beyond the zones of social behaviour.

Dattani has tried to explore the community of eunuch and their existence in mysterious social milieu in India.

The play *Seven Steps Around the Fire* revolves around the third gender which is the community of eunuchs and their existence on the fringes of Indian milieu. This play carries more messages than the central issue of the murder of a transgendered. The play presents the transgendered as the victims of the society which has its own fixed notions about his/her social status. It is a paradoxical situation where the singing and the dancing of the transgendered at a marriage for blessing a newly married couple is believed to assure parenthood to the couple. So it is not a complete banishment of them from society's circle. Their visibility does not cause any embarrassment or mishap. Yet they are restricted in social function. In this way they are objects of mistrust, ridicule and contempt. They are social victims and exist only on the margins. Asked whether he considered himself a lone speaker of gender issues in the current Indian dramatic scene, he replies: "I wish more people would explore aspects of sexuality rather than just sex, to that extent, I'm alone" (Phatarphekar, 25).

Uma, a Ph.D. scholar in Sociology, the wife of the Superindent of police Suresh Rao, and daughter of a vice-chancellor, is researching the community of eunuchs and is following up the murder of a beautiful eunuch Kamala. Constable Munswamy assists her, set to the task by his boss in order that he may keep her out of trouble in her sleuthing. The eunuch community that inhabits tiny pockets of Indian cities treads areas that are generally brushed aside to the fringes, the margins of the society, as it were. This is literally a no man/s land in many senses of the term, and no woman/s either. The correlative of these grey zones is, of course, another of Dattani's pet concerns.

Uma [voice-over]. Case 7. A brief note on the popular myths on the origin of the hijras will be in order, before looking at the class gender-based power implications. The term hijra, of course, is of Urdu origin, a combination of Hindi, Persian and Arabic, literally meaning neither male nor female. Another legend has it that god Rama was going to cross the river and to exile in the forest. All the people of the city wanted to follow him. He said "Men and women, turn back." Some of his male followers did not know what to do. They could not disobey him. So they sacrificed their masculinity, to become neither men nor women, and followed him to the forest. Rama was pleased with their devotion and blessed them. There are transsexuals all over the world, and India is no exception. The purpose of this case study is to show their position in the society. Perceived as the lowest of the low, they yearn for family and love. The two events in mainstream Hindu culture where their presence is acceptable—marriage and birth ironically are the very same privileges denied to them by man and nature. The play opens with the chanting of Sanskrit marriage mantras that fade out to the sound of the rustle and hiss of a fire. After a significant pause, the action begins. Uma is in the police station, to visit the cell of Anarkali, a hizra—an accused who she is to interview. Munswamy is highly amused at Uma/s reference to Anarkali as she himself preferring the neuter it. Dattani has immediately entered into questions of gender assignations from the second line of the play. Munswamy piously declares that a lady with antecedents like Uma should perhaps look at more acceptable cases.

Madam, if you don't mind me saying, why is a lady from a respectable family like yourself...? There are so many cases. All murder cases. Man killing wife, wife killing man's lover, brother killing brother. And that shelf is full of dowry cases. Shall I ask the peon to dust all these files? (Dattani, *SSAF*, 7).

Marginalized even in crime, the community Uma focuses upon and tries to investigate has grown around itself thick and impenetrable walls of incomprehensible myths and superstition so that it may survive in isolation. Munswamy points out; it would be simpler and more honourable for Uma to study mainstream crime. Even Munswamy hates calling himself as brother by Anarkali.

Anarkali: We make our relations with our eyes. With our love. I look at him, he look at me, and he is my brother. I look at you, you look at me, and we are mother and daughter. Oh, brother, give me cigarette, na.

Munswamy: Shut up. And don't call me brother. (Dattani, *SSAF*, 11)

Anarkali's yearning for various relationships like brother, sister, mother and father suggest that they have equal desire for the protection of personal relationships. When Uma offers Anarkali that she would like to be her sister, she [Anarkali] is overwhelmed but fears of consequences of it "Oh! You are only being kind—Don't hurt my heart" (Dattani, *SSAF*, 13). She is torn between the fear of social code and legal provisions but finds consolation in the love and sympathy of Uma "But I will tell you because you are my sister" (Dattani, *SSAF*, 13). Anarkali's reaction whose own neutral ground has taught her to be wary of these very components. She is immediately on her guard and inaccessible—spitting venom and abuse, and in the process laying bare a number of unpalatable truths.

Then Anarkali changes tactics and decides to use the operating power situation to her own benefit by manipulating Uma to obtain her freedom, money and even cigarettes. The conversations that Uma has with Anarkali reveal many of the veiled truths that lie shrouded within the multiple layers of myths and cultural beliefs and at the same time problematising relationships within accepted norms. Jeremy Mortimer observes in the note about the play:

> Mahesh's plays often feature characters who are questioning their identity, and who feel isolated in her marriage, and in this sense of isolation makes her empathise with Anarkali, the hijra she befriends. (Mortimer, 4)

The play moves in the form of investigation of the case. Uma decides to visit Shivaji Nagar to see Anarkali's friend Champa. Uma offers the bail amount to Champa for the release of Anarkali. Uma first suspects that the rivalry between Kamala and Anarkali was responsible for the murder.

Champa: Oh, may you have a hundred children! I knew that you are a social worker.

Uma: You will bail her out?

Champa: What a question to ask!

Uma: She-she didn't really kill Kamala, did she?

Champa: What difference does it make whether she did or no?

Uma: I certainly don't want to help anyone who is a murderer!

Champa: Yes, yes. That won't suit you. No. She did not kill Kamla. They were sisters.

Uma: If I give you the money, will you go to the court and get her release orders?

Champa: Did I come begging you—please give me money to save my daughter? Huh? (Dattani, *SSAF*, 24-25)

The intervention of Salim in search of one particular photograph brings complication in the play. Uma in her quest to unveil the mystery of Kamala's murder, sustains the grace of an essentially good human being.

Anarkali: Would you have believed me? Anyway, what is the use of all that? What does it matter who killed Kamla? She is dead—So many times I warned her. First I thought Salim was taking her for his own pleasure. When she told me about Subbu, madam, I tried to stop her. I fought with her. I scratched her face, hoping she will become ugly and Subbu will forget her. He wanted to marry her.... I was there at their wedding...she gave me picture to show to Champa. I saw the men coming for her. I told her to run...[cries for a while]. Here, madam, take this. (Dattani, *SSAF*, 41)

Uma enquires at Mr. Sharma's place about the identity of Salim and the secret of his relationship with Kamala. The appearance of Subbu the son of the minister who for the first time appears almost at the end of the play, adds a complication in the play. In the meantime Anarkali was bailed out. She was ordered to wear special ghagra on the occasion of the marriage of chief Minister's son Subbu. Mr. Sharma is all the time apprehensive about the revelation of the truth. So Mr. Sharma does not want the entry of the hijras.

> Uma: Mr. Sharma, what have you got to lose? The marriage ceremonies are done. You should be happy. Just let them dance a little. Is that asking for too much?...
>
> Mr. Sharma: Er...maybe I overeacted. After all, their presence is expected. I will give them some money....
>
> Champa: Thank you, sir, but we must sing and dance to bless this house and the handsome couple.
>
> Mr. Sharma: Well, all right. Just one number and you will get your baksheesh.
>
> Anarkali: Where are the newly married? They must be here.
>
> Mr. Sharma: Oh! (Dattani, *SSAF*, 39)

Subbu comes forward looking at them. With the dancing Anarkali, the vision of dead Kamala start haunting his mind. The play ends in Subbu's suicide using, strategically, Suresh's gun and the final revelation by the hijras.

> Uma: Of course Mr. Sharma couldn't have it—totally unacceptable. So he arranged to have Kamla burned to death. But Salim had to tell him about the picture. Mr. Sharma simply had to have that picture. He sent Salim to threaten Anarkali and Champa—He did get the picture eventually—after losing his son. What a price to pray! And now he will be arrested and tried for murder. (Dattani, *SSAF*, 41)

In the end one can say that there is also the special connotation to what it means to be a eunuch in the Indian context, and the strong identifying marks revealed in how they speak, walk, clap or sing. These are unmistakable marks that the eunuch assume to formulate a distinctive identity that sets them apart as a community in India and are easily recognized by the Indians. Dattani's emphasis on the unseen, invisible and even unspoken nature of such identities, on the issues that are swept under the rug and presumed non-existent by the majority begins to work in the conjuction with phenomenological absence as his female protagonist Uma Rao begins her investigation on the community.

WORKS CITED

Beauvoir, Simone de, "Woman and Other", (ed) Dennis Walder, *Literature in the Modern World: Critical Essays and Documents,* New York: Oxford University Press, 2004.

Bern, Sandra Lipsitz, "Gender Schema Theory: A Cognitive Account of Sex Typing", *Psychological Review*, 1981, Vol. 88. No. 4.

Dattani, Mahesh, *Collected Plays*, New Delhi: Penguin, 2000.

——, *Seven Steps Around the Fire, Collected Plays,* New Delhi: Penguin India, 2000.

Mangayarkarasi, T., "Tensions and Conflicts: A Critical Responses to Mahesh Dattani's Final Solutions" Published in the Proceedings of National Seminar on *Indian English Literature: Theme and Techniques*, St. Xavier's College, Palayamkottai.

Mee, Erin, "A Note in the Play", *Collected Plays, Mahesh Dattani,* New Delhi: Penguin.

Mortimer, Jeremy, *A Note on the Play in Mahesh Dattani, Seven Steps Around the Fire, Collected Plays,* New Delhi: Penguin India, 2000.

Phatarphekar, N. Pramila, "Mahesh Dattani; 10 Questions" *Outlook*, 26th July 2004.

Rani, Sudha, "Expressionism on Contemporary Indian English Stage". <http://www.museindia.com/showfeature3.asp?id=669>

Subramanyam, Lakshmi, ed., *Muffled Voices: Women in Modern Indian Theatre*, New Delhi: Shakti, 2002.

14

Genesis of Titles and Evolution of Themes in the Plays of Girish Karnad

Krishna Singh

Girish Karnad, a versatile genius acclaimed as a noted actor, producer, director, TV artist and cultural administrator occupies a prominent place in Indian English Drama. His plays are the medium through which he discusses socio-political and cultural problems of India conforming to the tradition of Henrik Ibsen, John Galsworty and G.B. Shaw. Karand is appreciated as a playwright of myths and legends, history, subalternity, castesim, rituals, feminism, cultural issues and humanism. Despite these cultural roles Karnad definitely brought revolution in Indian English Drama—discarding Eurocentric models and techniques altogether; boldly advocated and used Indian myths, legends, folk tales, history, socio-political and contemporary issues with Indianized English and folk theatre conventions with the motive to de-colonize Indian English Drama, he gave it a new shape—Postcolonial Indian English Drama in the real sense. All his plays from *Yayati* to *Wedding Album* illustrate this hypothesis. His views expressed in prefaces, introduction to his plays and interviews also endorse the argument. Hence Karnad's role as a de-colonizer of Indian English Drama is to be explored in the present chapter. Even the titles of Karnad's plays are pregnant with the body of thought which can be expanded into several volumes. The titles are apt and very suggestive; they epitomize the Indian subjects and sensibility and rooted in the cultural past of the country go beyond the limits of time and space. They connect one world, i.e. of myth, legend, history or folk-lore to another world, i.e. modern with its own characteristics and problems. They are well-chosen to co-relate past with the present continuous. Titles are named after a mythical-legendry-historical or folklore character or a socio-political issue of the contemporary India. They instantly connote the proposition of the play, though the treatment often reverses the traditional message, yet elaboration, exemplification and conclusion (without offering any clear cut solution) make his plays more suggestive and thought provoking which leads to public discourse regarding problems raised through his plays. His plays are real problem plays in which contemporary socio-cultural and political problems are dealt with dramatic action and final solution is left to the audience.

Yayati (1961) the first play of Karnad ges its title from the myth of Yayati which figures in Adiparva of *Mahabharata*. Karnad has reinterpreted the myth of Yayati to give it modern meaning and significance. It is self-consciously existentialist drama on the theme of responsibility and human relationship. Yayati—the unheroic hero stands for modern man inhabited by worldly desires, sensual pleasures, and irresponsible exercise of power and utter forgetfulness of the imperishable values of life. The play also deals with question of woman's struggle for emancipation and identity in orthodox Indian society. Karnad himself has commented on the genesis of the plot of *Yayati*:

> The story of King Yayati that I used occurs in Mahabharata. The King, for a moral transgression he has committed, is cursed to old age in the prime of life. Distraught at losing his youth, he approaches his son, pleading with him to lend him his youth in exchange for old age. The son accepts the exchange and the curse, and thus becomes old, older than his father. But the old age brings no knowledge, no self-realization, only the senselessness of a punishment meted out for an act in which he had not even participated. The father is left to face the consequences of shirking responsibility for his own actions. ("Afterword" to *Yayati*, 73)

The play reflects the stressful situation while he was writing the play. The play enabled him to develop a set of values rationally. Karnad was not satisfied with the traditional glorification of son's obedience, contrary to it he connects the story with real life situation. He deviates from the original story—in *Mahabharata* King Yayati has five sons; after the older four refuse their father, the youngest Pooru yields to his entreaties. Karnad has restructured the story as an ironic drama of discontent, futility and death. Yayati is self-centred epicurean who invites the curse because he fails to overcome his lust for Sharmishtha (the Asura Princess who is rival and slave of his wife, sage Shukracharya's daughter Devayani) although Devayani has warned him about the dire consequences of his transgression. Pooru is a philosopher who feels unsettled by the questionable legitimacy of his birth, and oppressed by the weight of dynastic tradition. Pooru accepts the curse of his father and ends the play on a note of stark bewilderment, unable to peruse the point of what he has endured. Karnad's version of the myth makes itself an original due to his rejection of traditional glorification of son's 'self-sacrifice' and, against the backdrop of lust, jealously, and racial tensions, the tragic choices with which the young Prince and his bride Chitralekha are closely confronted. Devayani, the Brahmin Queen, Sharmishtha, the slave Princess, Chitralekha, Pooru's new bride succeed in subverting the male world through an assertion of their rights and privileges. Chitralekha emerges as a New Woman who defies all sorts of traditional taboos and subjugation and overtly fights against them to secure "room" for her. She condemns Pooru's decision and Yayati's false rhetoric for the sake of dynastic glory. She is a woman who lives in the real world and confronted with practical problems after Pooru's decision. But she never yields before them and rather prefers to die. In the Prologue to *Yayati* Karnad has explained the choice of an ancient myth: "We turn to ancient lore not because it offers any blinding revelation or hope of consolation, but because it provides fleeting glimpses of the fears and desires sleepless within us. It is a good way to get introduced to ourselves" (6).

Tughlaq (1972) deals with the life and turbulent reign of Mohammad-bin-Tughlaq and title of the play is named after him which is apt and epitomizes the life and history of Tughlaq and suggests multiple connotations. *Tughlaq* is a historical play which confines, for the sake of dramatic precision, to five years reign of Tughlaq from 1327-32. The action begins in Delhi in

1327, then on the road from Delhi to Daultabad and finally in and around the fort of Daultabad. *Caligula* legend supplied the substance for the play and Camu and Sartre accounted for the existentialist character of Karnad's plays. History plays were also written before Karnad but there was no serious attempt to relate history to modern problems and sensibility. Karnad himself has commented on the genesis of the play and its multifold meanings:

> What struck me absolutely about Tughlaq's history was that it was contemporary. The fact that here was the most idealistic, the most intelligent king ever to come on the throne of Delhi...and one of the greatest failures also. And within a span of twenty years this tremendously capable man had gone to pieces. This seemed to be both due to his idealism as well as the shortcomings within him, such as his impatience, his cruelty, his feeling that he had the only correct answer. And I felt in the early sixties India had also come very far in the same direction—the twenty year period seemed to me very much a striking parallel. (Qtd. in Murthy, Viii)

> And when I came to Tughlaq I said Oh! Marvelous! That is what I wanted. In those days existentialism was very much in the air. To be considered mad was very much fashionable. Everything about Tughlaq seemed to fit into what I had read was the correct thing to do, which was to be mad and do impossible things and so on. So I started reading about Tughlaq. But as I started reading about Tughlaq, I suddenly realized what a fantastic character I had hit upon, I started with Ishwari Prasad and then went on to all the contemporary material and suddenly felt possessed. I felt this character was growing in front of me. (Qtd. in Tilak, 25)

The play has an interesting story, complex plot and scope for spectacle and several dramatic conventions. Further the play is of the sixties, and it reflects, observes U.R. Anantha Murthy: "the political mood of disillusionment which followed the Nehru era of idealism in the country" (viii). Though Karnad denies having contemporaneity of the play in mind, it attracted the attention of the audience. As regards Tughlaq's idealism, scholarship, visionary temperament, zeal for innovation, religious tolerance and generosity, Karnad closely follows historical sources. A rationalist in politics and religion, Tughlaq was a victim of the wrath of orthodox Muslims like Barani thought him a non-believer in Islam. Karnad depends on ancient historical sources in delineating Tughlaq's character and ignores modern researches which help in presenting Tughlaq's character in an unbiased manner. According to both history and Karnad, Tughlaq is guilty of patricide and fratricide, a ruthless monarch who murders on suspicion and inflicts untold sufferings on his subjects by change of capital and introduction of token currency. His reign was full of rebellions. In history as well as in Karnad, Tughlaq has been presented as a bundle of contradictions and paradoxes which are put to great artistic and dramatic use. For dramatic purposes, Karnad deviates from the history. The episodes of Aziz and Aazam too have been included with a view to creating humour, irony, paradoxes, parallels to highlight Karnad's account of Tughlaq's administration. But the play is, comments U.R. Anantha Murthy: "more than political allegory. It has an irreducible, puzzling quality which comes from the ambiguities of Tughlaq's character, the dominating character of the play" (viii). All the characters are dramatized aspects of his complex personality; they also exist in their own right. The character of Tughlaq has been projected in great psychological depth signifying philosophical questions on the nature of man and the destiny of a whole kingdom which a dreamer like him controls. The external action throughout enacts the inner drama of Tughlaq. Both Tughlaq and his rivals appear to be idealists; yet, in the pursuit of ideal, they perpetrate its opposite. The whole play is structured on these opposites: the ideal and real; the divine aspiration and the deft intrigue.

Hayavadana (1975) gets its title from the Sanskrit words, i.e. *Haya* (horse) and *Vadana* (head)—the story of horse-headed man which constitutes the sub-plot of the play. The plot of *Hayavadana* is based on Thomas Mann's *The Transposed Heads*, adapted on a tale from Somdeva's *Brihadkatha Saritsagar*, an ancient collection of stories in Sanskrit. The Sanskrit tale, narrated by a ghost to an adventurous king, gains a further mock-heroic dimension in Mann's rendering. The original poses a moral problem whereas Mann uses it to ridicule the mechanical conception of life which distinguishes between body and soul. Mann laughs at the philosophy which holds the head superior to the body. Mann further maintains that the human body is fit instrument for the fulfillment of human destiny. Even the transposition of heads will not liberate the protagonists from the psychological limits imposed by nature. The central episode in the play—the story of Devadatta and Kapil is based on a tale from *Vetala Panchavimshika*, but Karnad has borrowed it from Thomas Mann's mock-heroic transcription of the original Sanskrit tales—*The Transposed Heads* whereas the sub-plot—the horseman's search for completeness is Karnad's original invention. *Hayavadana* is essentially a play on the search of identity in a world of tangled relationships. Devadatta, the intellectual, and Kapil, the man of body, are very intimate friends. Devadatta marries Padmini. Kapil and Padmini fall in love with each other. The two friends kill themselves. In a highly comic scene which is of great significance Padmini transposes their heads, giving Devadatta Kapil's body and Kapil Devadatta's. It results in a confusion of identities, which reveals the ambiguous nature of human personality. The situation gets complicated. They fight a duel and kill themselves again. Padmini performs *sati*. Karnad delves deep into the traditional myths to spell out modern man's anguish and dilemmas that are created in his mind. In *Hayavadana* he is seized with the theme of incompleteness, "mad dance of incompleteness" (57) and depicts Devadatta, Kapil and Hayavadana (horse-man) yearning for completeness. Karnad's play in a characteristic way begins where the 'Vetal' story ends. "How would the woman take it if it really happened and would it ultimately solve the problem for her," are the fascinating questions the artist in him faces. Shubhangi S. Raykar analyses thus: "In all his plays Karnad takes this kind of leap from the original story and develops it further...this further development is the play of the artist's imagination and it challenges the glib solutions offered in the original stories" (*SRS*, 48). Kirtinath Kurtkoti rightly commented that the play is a, "world of incomplete individuals, indifferent gods, dolls that speak and children who cannot, a world indifferent to the desires and frustrations, joys and sorrows of human beings" (*KK*, vii). The use of folk-theatre conventions, i.e. use of masks, curtains, dolls, the story-within-a-story transport the audience into a bizarre world. The theme of extra-marital relationship is also treated which develops complication and entanglement in human relationship.

Naga-Mandala (1990) is a richly textured dramatic transmutation of two folk tales of Karnataka. The title is apt and well-chosen to deal with the story of Naga with its symbolic connotations. It deals with gender-bias and the subjection of woman in patriarchal Indian Orthodox society. The female protagonist—Rani and Kurudavva, other female character, are generic creations who stand for Indian woman. Though the play is a richly textured dramatic transmutation of two folk tales of Karnataka, Karnad delves deep to explore contemporary socio-cultural and philosophical concerns giving them modern validity. Rani is placed in a world where orthodox social conventions, cultural taboos and coercive forces work; patriarchy is established which proves greatest blow to the existence of Rani. Apart from overt patriarchy, she is socialized to internalize the male superiority—an invisible conspiracy to derogate and marginalize her position in the society. She adopts new ways to transcend age-old subjection of woman. Rani is surrounded by evil social forces where she finds herself helpless; tortured by alienation and despair but she never surrenders and continues her struggle for identity—as a woman, as a wife and as a mother. Karnad's solution appears, at the first observation odd, unconvincing and unconventional violating traditional mode of treatment. Message is clear: despite alienation, despair and antithetical conditions a woman must continue her struggle for her existence and transcend "nothingness" in life and manipulate co-existence as a means for self-existence. Patriarchy, socio-cultural practices, parents of Rani, Appanna, Village Elders, Naga, Dog, and Mongoose, etc. are the tools to perpetuate exploitation of Rani. Like Kate Millet's *Sexual Politics* (1969), Karnad's *Naga-Mandala* exposes the mechanisms that express and enforce the relations of power in society and further analyse the social arrangements and institutions as covert ways of manipulating power so as to establish and perpetuate the dominance of man and the subordination of woman.

Prologue introduces Four Flames, which are animated, symbolic representations employed to report the sufferings of women. Man and Story are identical to Greek Chorus, throughout the play they go on commenting and supplying important information and remain on the stage. Act I unfolds Rani, well-known for her tresses; married to a man who was "rich and his parents were both dead" (27); Rani's parents are least concerned about the character and wrong doings of Appanna, they are equally responsible for her atrocities, after marriage they never visit Rani. Neither welcome ceremony, nor bridal song is there. Rani is nonplussed to hear: "Well, then, I will be back tomorrow at noon. Keep my lunch ready. I shall eat and go" (27). He pays no attention to her, goes out, shuts the door, and locks it from outside and goes away. She runs to the door, finds it locked. She doesn't know what is happening and stands perplexed. She can't even weep. She goes and sits in a corner of her room, talks to herself indistinctly; tired and exhausted goes into sleep; sees nightmares, cries for parents. Next morning when Appanna comes, Rani tries to explain the pains of loneliness, and tries to win the sympathy of Appanna, he very coldly rebukes. He finishes his meal and goes out, locks her. Thus the days rolled by. Rani, mechanically, goes into the kitchen, starts cooking and talks to herself. She becomes a caged bird whereas Appanna is a philanderer; regularly visits his concubine. Kurudavva emerges as the rescuer and friend to Rani; sensing Rani and her husband have no physical relation, she decides to help Rani. Rani is treated in a slavish manner, imprisoned like a caged bird, neither is she allowed talking to outsiders nor is any outsider allowed to do the same. Despite her chastity and fidelity, she is forced to face the Naga Ordeal. In course of time, Rani becomes pregnant. It is news of joy for her as a fulfillment of a woman's dream. But her search for identity as a mother is not fulfilled; on the contrary, Appanna reacts violently on knowing her pregnancy as he had never made love with her. He is out of himself, calls her a strumpet, a whore, drags her out of the house, and threatens to give her extreme punishment for cuckolding him. Appanna publicly questions Rani's chastity and registers a case in the village court where Village Elders sit to judge. Rani is forced to face an Ordeal to prove her chastity. Rani finally accepts Cobra who gave her love and motherhood: "You don't know how heavy you are. Let me get used to you.... This hair is the symbol of my wedded bliss. Live in there happily, for ever" (64). Rani's acceptance of Naga as her own is a curt reply to the question of extra-marital relation in which only males are allowed to go freely, even after getting married, to concubine (as Appanna does) whereas the yardstick of morality is imposed upon women. J.D. Soni judiciously comments that Karnad in the play tries to "fuse artistically dialectical relationship between tradition and modernity" (76). A. Jagmohanchari has studied *Hayavadana* and *Naga-Mandala* as post colonial dialectics. The post colonial matrix "embedded in the play *Naga-Mandala* opens up yet another space for the working out of the theme of patriarchal oppression.... This (Appanna's) vulgar display of power instead of love and treating woman as a disposable object accrues to him owing to the post colonialist ethos and the mystique of tradition" (182). Krishnamayi attempted to redefine the insurgent female psyche in an androgenic milieu and concluded: "Gender equality still remains a myth...the discussion of the relationship between man and woman have been prescribed by man not by woman. Her limits have been imposed on her by man who is ruled by the mastery-motive. She accepts it because of biosocial reasons" (64-65). Karnad himself commented: "They (tales) also express distinctly a woman's understanding of the reality around her, a lived counterpart to the patriarchal structures of classical texts and institutions" ("Introduction", *Three Plays*, 17). Prem Sagar observes, "*Naga-Mandala* presents a tale of male chauvinism to give the message that it debilitates and degrades both sexes" (Preface).

Tale-Danda literally means death by beheading. Offering one's head, either on completion of a vow or in penitence, was a common practice in medieval Karnataka. Basavanna often uses the word to express his outrage at a particularly unpleasant situation or accusation, to mean something like 'May my head roll' or 'I offer my head'. The play draws its title and story from the life of Kannada saint Basavanna who resisted ideologically against the prevailing evils of caste hierarchy. Explosive situations after the official endorsement of Mandal Commission Report and Mandir issue in 1989 motivated Karnad to concentrate on subaltern issue. And the historical context, deeply implanted in his mind, which proved catalyst to the plays of Karnad was predominated with, Karnad himself explains: "...tensions between the cultural past of the country and its colonial past, between the attractions of Western modes of thought and our own traditions, and finally between the various visions of the future that opened up once the common cause of the political freedom was achieved" ("Introduction", *Three Plays*, 1). Drawing our attention to the genesis of the present, the play illuminates the endemic affliction of the caste and class politics infecting our body politic in the medieval period of history. It was the strong sense of history, which has nurtured in Karnad a dominant will for social justice, a sincere compassion for the socially oppressed and subaltern. Karnad doesn't offer any solution to the problem; but raised the subaltern issue for discussion and common consensus. Under Basavanna, a social reformer of the 12th century assembled a congregation of poets, mystics and social revolutionaries and philosophers who formed the *Lingayat* faith, giving impetus to courageous questioning and social commitment. The abolition of caste, equality of sexes, rejection of idol worship, repudiation of Brahminism, and of Sanskrit in favour of the mother tongues, i.e. Kannad; were the main tenets of subaltern revolution. The resentment reaches its climax when Madhuvarsa, a Brahmin gives his daughter Kalavati in marriage to an untouchable—Sheelvanta. This last act opposing caste hierarchy, not just in theory but in practice also, brought down upon the wrath of orthodox; the movement ended in terror and bloodshed. The playwright wants to suggest that whenever such important issues are not considered seriously and solutions offered by these thinkers go unheeded, disastrous results would follow again.

The play reveals, in the name of Varnashrama Dharma, lower caste people are socialized to internalize the reigning superiority of upper caste. Mallibomma though adopts *Lingayat* faith, but can't even think of entering Jagdeva, a Brahmin's house. King Bijjala tried to ascend to higher Varna from barber to Kshatriya but failed:

> For ten generations my forefathers ravaged the land as robber barrons. For another five they ruled as the trusted feudatories of the Emperor himself. They married into every royal family in sight. Bribed generations of Brahmins with millions of cows. All this so they could have the caste of Kshastriya branded on their foreheads. And yet you ask the most innocent child...what is Bijjala?...instant reply will be barber. One's caste is like the skin on one's body. You can peel it off top to toe, but when the new skin forms, there you are again; a barber—a shepherd. (14-15)

Among subalterns tribals, shepherds, cowherds and low caste untouchables figure. Resistance has two forms: ideological and physical. It was *Lingayat* faith (Shaivistic) in sharp opposition to Brahminical faith; (better known as Sanatan Dharma) founded on humanitarian grounds, open to all groups, austerity in living, trying to crumble the wall of untouchability, exposing rigidity and discrimination in traditional faith. They rejected anything "static in favour of the principle of movement and progress in human enterprise" ("Preface" *Tale-Danda*). They tried to come out of caste venom and religious fanaticism. The devotee of the faith was called *Sharana*. Antagonistic forces are *vis-à-vis* to gain power—hence hegemonic war begins. Physical resistance of *Sharanas* comes to dismal end. It was a conflict between deep-rooted orthodoxy and new and innovative ideas. The movement was not matured enough. Even Basavanna doubts the success of the marriage—i.e. hypergamous (*Pratilom*); it (movement) went into young hands of Jagadeva—a violent revolutionary who kills King Bijjala and finally commits suicide. *Sharanas* lost their drive, mutual differences and infights, prompt reaction from orthodox against *Sharanas* led by young Sovideva;

Basavanna's resignation from the movement and power politics bring failure to the subalterns' resistance.

The violent reaction of Brahmins suggests even now subalterns are no match to defy the exploitation and discriminating behaviour of the orthodox Hindu society. Basavanna observes: "we have a long way to go" (39) "we are not ready for the kind of revolution this wedding is. We haven't worked long enough or hard enough" (44). Damodara Bahatta, Queen's priest and Manchanna Karmita, a Brahmin adviser to the King represent Hindu fanaticism and strongly plead for conformity with Vedic tradition—a measure to suppress subaltern revolution. Sovideva, the Prince wins the game of power politics exploiting the Hindu Brahminical sentiments; subtly used to perpetuate Vedic traditions. With the coronation of Sovideva the triumph of the oppressor rings loud. Sanskrit chanting from ancient scriptures denotes the re-establishment of caste order at least for the time being till another revolution. Pranav Joshipura has criticized the play: "...instead of deliberating on how to abolish the Varna system, Karnad presents it in a startling manner without any solution...to treat an age-old problem without suggesting any solution raises serious doubts about the capacity of a writer" (69). Karnad who extends the tradition of Henrik Ibsen and G.B. Shaw obviously leaves it to the audience to decide; yet he gives remedial suggestions through Basavanna's speeches. Basavanna's doubts, concerns and embarrassment regarding subaltern revolution clearly reflect platwright's concerns. Vanashree Tripathi judiciously comments: "*Tale-Danda* highlights the neglected portion of history that has immense bearing on the history and politics of contemporary times. Focusing on the class, caste, and gender configurations in A.D. 1166, the play proves the subalterranean and insidious motivations driving the diverse caste groups in complex power equation" (28). Rupalee Burke finds Karnad a playwright with a difference whose motive behind playwriting is to catch the:

> Pulse of the socio-cultural-historical-political facets of India and Indian life...his plays have always aimed at providing message in the contemporary context.... In

> *Tughlaq* and *Tale-Danda* Karnad employs history to comment on the pathetic and corroded state of Indian modern day politics, and through which he engages in an intellectual debate of our time. (105-07)

Basvanna's vision of egalitarian society and spiritualized politics was the vision of Karnad himself, expressed by Bijjala: "Basavanna wants to eradicate the caste structure. Annihilate the Varna system. What a vision! And what prodigious courage! And he has the ability.... All hard-working people from the common stock. They sit together, indifferent to caste, birth of station (15). *Tale-Danda*, Karnad acknowledged in an interview, "is not necessarily an attack on caste. It is a question of 'Why', why is it that some of our problems seem perennial" (Reddy and Dhawan, 138). He raises many questions and few oblique suggestions are provided but more are left to the audience to think and get them resolved.

The Fire and the Rain (1998) is a very apt and thought-provoking title which has deep, symbolic and allegorical meanings. The 'fire' in the title of the play is the fire of lust, anger, vengeance, envy, treachery, violence and death. The 'rain' symbolizes self-sacrifice, compassion, Divine Grace, forgiveness, revival and life. *The Fire and the Rain* is a far more successful play; Karnad draws upon a story from Chapters 135-38 of the Vana Parva (Forest Canto) of the *Mahabharata*. It is narrated by the ascetic Lomasha to the Pandavas during their exile. But in the best traditions of modernism, Karnad gives a contemporary meaning to an old legend, which stresses the dangers of knowledge without wisdom and power without integrity. The myth cautions about the misapplication of power that human beings receive from the gods after great penance. Yavakri, the son of sage Bhardwaj, acquires knowledge of the Vedas directly from Indra after ten years of rigorous penance. Though his father warns him regarding acquisition of divine power, Yavakri uses it to molest the daughter-in-law of sage Raibhya, whom he resents. Raibhya in retaliation creates a demon (*Brahma Rakshasa*) and a spirit in the form of his daughter-in-law, Vishakha, both of whom pursue Yavakri and kill him. Bhardwaj curses Raibhya—that he will die at the hands of his own son—and then kills himself in remorse. Sometime later Paravasu indeed mistakes the deerskin his father Raibhya is wearing for a wild animal, and accidentally kills him. Involved with his younger brother Aravasu in a fire sacrifice, Paravasu initiates another cycle of evil when he falsely accuses the latter of patricide (hence of brahiminicide). Aravasu then begins his own penance to the Sun God, and when granted a boon, asks for Yavakri, Bhardwaj, and Raibhya to be restored to life. Lives that were destroyed due to human lapses are restored through divine intervention. Karnad has forged closer connections between the principal characters and created them into rounded personalities. Yavakri and Vishakha are not strangers but lovers whose relationship both precedes and follows. Vishakha's marriage to Paravasu, making her more than merely a passive object of Yavakri's lust. Her marriage itself appears to be an arid contract: after a frenzy of sensual gratification Paravasu has left Vishakha to Raibhya's care, and the relationships between the three are startling in their lovelessness and malevolence. Similarly, Paravasu kills his father out of hatred rather than ignorance. Karnad has also invented a love episode between Aravasu and a tribal girl Nittilai, and develops a contrast between the life of discipline and sacrifice with the life of instinct and emotion—opposition between Brahmin and Sudra, with Aravasu working as a connective link between the two appositive worlds. Karnad's note on "Drama and *Purushartha*" in *The Fire and the Rain* endorses his unequivocal interest in the doctrines of *Purushartha* towards which a work of art should draw mankind.

The Dreams of Tipu Sultan (1997) draws its title and story from the history of Tipu Sultan. It follows the model of the history play established in *Tughlaq* and *Tale-Danda*. It was first written as a radio play for BBC to celebrate the fiftieth anniversary of independence in 1996. Later it was entirely re-written for the stage. The plot obviously deals with some aspects of Indo-British relation. It primarily explores the secret inner world of a man whose public life was a continual war against British colonialism. Tipu Sultan is viewed as one of the most brave warriors, political visionary and dreamer; one of the most politically perceptive and tragic figures in modern Indian history.

Bali: The Sacrifice has drawn upon the thirteenth century Kannad epic *Yashodhara Charite* by Janna, which in turn refers back through an eleventh century Sanskrit epic by Vadiraja to the ninth-century Sanskrit epic *Yashastilaka*, by Somdeva Suri. The play is a tribute to astuteness and sensitivity of Mahatama Gandhi that he saw so clearly the insistence of non-violence to the "cultural and political survival of India" (Karnad, *Two Plays*, 69). It explores the existential dilemma of passion and violence posed by an ancient Jain myth. The myth is less concerned with actual violence than with the morality of substitution, which permits violence, a wider and subtler play by masking its true nature. Violence has been the one of the crucial subjects of debate in the history of Indian civilization. Vedic sacrifices, conducted by Brahmin priests, involved the slaughter of animals as offerings to the gods, which the Jains found repugnant. To the Jain, indulging in any kind of violence, however minor or accidental, meant forfeiting one's moral status as a human being. Later Buddhists too advocated non-violence. The issue found some resolution when the Brahmins renounced blood sacrifice. Miniature figurines, made of dough, were substituted for live animals, a practice that continues to this day. Despite this change, Jains objected to this process of substitution that carries the original violent impulse within them which was no less dehumanizing. Karnad came across the myth of the Cock of Dough when he was in his teens and the myth littered with discarded drafts of dramatized versions of it. The myth revealed unexpected meanings with long ponderings over it and *Bali: The Sacrifice* is the result of over two decades evolution. Karnad transforms the story of the dough figurine that comes alive at the moment of sacrifice into a mature philosophical exploration of love, jealously, desire, betrayal, and violence between men and women who are bound by the ties of blood and marriage, or encounter each other in the perfect freedom of anonymity. Novelty of the play lies in the unconventionality of its major characters, and the seriousness with which it yokes intimate personal acts to structures of religious belief and practice.

The two short monologues in English—*Broken Images* (2004) and *Flowers* (2004) form a radical addendum to Karnad's forty-years career as a playwright because they initiate new subjects and forms. The title of *Broken Images* is derived from Karnad's study of spilt personality—disintegrated due to complex mind sets and takes up a debate that has grown edgier since independence—the politics of language in Indian literary culture. Manjula Nayak, the play's only character, is a successful author of short and long fiction in Kannada and teacher of English in a Banglore college, succumbs to the temptation of larger audience and money making; involves in plagiarism and exposed later. It deals with problems of authenticity and bad faith created by globalization, through a confrontation between a writer and her electronic image. When Karnad takes on literary politics in the play he immediately relates language to genre. The central issue in the play doesn't involve drama at all but the radically unequal status of fiction written in two contemporary languages, Kannad and English. *Flowers* (2004) in contrast, returns to the world of folktale, and is the first work in this genre to focus on male rather than female desire, thus registering a small but important shift in Karnad's dramaturgy. The tiltle is very apt and symbolic; it is offered for devotional purposes as well as for sensual desires. The legend of Veeranna on which the play is based belongs to the Chitradurg region, and became widely known when a Kannad writer T.R. Subbanna included it in his novel *Hamsageete* (1952). The married priest has been passionately in love with a mistress to whom he takes the offerings from the temple after the every prayer. One day the *palegar* (chieftain) discovers a hair in the *prasada* and demands an explanation from Veeranna, who claims that the hair belongs to God. Challenged by the chieftain to prove the truth of his claim the priest in turn challenges God to display hair or accept his head in punishment, and enters a meditative trance to the accompaniment of Venkatashubhayya's song. When the chieftain arrives the next day to expose Veeranna's lie, the *shivalinga* has indeed sprouted long silken hair, and when (urged by the singer) he pulls out a tuft to test its authenticity, blood begins to ooze from the crown of the *lingam*. Over-whelmed by a sense of sin at having injured his deity, Veeranna beheads himself in the sanctum. The conflict between religious devotion and erotic love—mingling of spiritual and carnal is central. The miracle of the *shivalinga* confirms the power of the priest's worship and marks him as one of the chosen, but it also ends his life.

Wedding Album (2008) is the latest play of Karnad. It's a delightfully poignant tale of love and longing in a shining India. It explores the traditional Indian wedding in a globalized, technologically advanced India. The *Wedding Album* which is structured into nine scenes deals primarily with women and their two different worlds, i.e. traditional and modern cyber world. But both of them merge into each other. Even the traditional elder women are fused with energy, hope and modern sensibility. Younger sorts enjoy liberty in education, love, courtship via 'distance' technology; and marriage. The play marks the highest evolution of feminine psyche. The backdrop of the play is unlike of *Yayati, Hayavadana, Naga-Mandala,* and *The Fire and the Rain* which also treat feminine issue. It deals with middle class Saraswat Brahmin family—an epitome of multiculturalism and cosmopolitan ideology. The play also examines the fundamentalism of the Hindu middle class family weakening. The family comprises Father Nadkarni, a doctor, Mother, an intelligent housewife, progressive in her ideas who sacrificed her talent for the sake of the family, conscious of children's career. Hema, the eldest daughter married and lives in Australia; Vidula, younger daughter has done BA in Geography, Rohit, son who writes stories and script for teleplays, is seeking better future prospects and Radhabai, a cook in Nadkarni's family is antitype of rest of the women. Vidula Nadkarni is exposed to modern education, social culture and science and technology. She is twenty-two and half; has done BA in Geography and presently doing nothing. She is the product of modern cyber world. She regularly visits to Internet Café to find her life partner. To the surprise of Pratibha Khan she, "agrees to consider marrying a man whom she has never met...in this day and age?" (8). Like Westernized Indian youths, she is facilitated by video tapes, SMSs, phone calls and webcam to decide her husband. Aswin

Panje, a Sarswat Brahmin is her choice, finally their marriage is materialized. Unlike Vidula, Pratibha Khan is a modern self-made Oriya woman of forty who develops her own business in Bangalore and takes tough decision to marry a Khan. And for being successful producer of television serials, she understands the psychology and emotional appetite of the audience and rejects out rightly the story of Vidula as a possible theme for future episode: "Pratibha: Rohit, we have an audience which is predominantly young. College going. Or young professionals. Westernized. At least potentially" (8). She has a practical approach to life. She wonders over Vidula's decision to marry a man without meeting him. Pratibha is an important figure in modern corporate world symbolizing modern Indian woman's emerging role and image. Hema, though born in modern age, educated and married and lives in Australia, is rooted in conservative practices and customs of Sarswat Brahmin family. She disapproves Rohit's advances to Isabel, a Christian girl. She is satisfied as a housewife. As a fair sex, she has bitter experience of how, first, her father-in-law observes her body; secondly, Vivan, a young boy, younger to her son feels crazy for her: "Vivan: The moment I saw you the other day, I fell desperately in love. I want to die kissing you. I want to die with my hand inside your blouse..." (45). She feels humiliated and slaps on his cheek. These two instances prove a woman is always a prey to male sexual desire irrespective of age or relation. Mother is a fusion of tradition and modernity. She maintains age-old social conventions prevalent in Saraswat Brahmins. The most remarkable feature of her character is that she understands the need of the time and proper human resource development. Despite limitations of middle class family, she has "skill at management" (91). She is talented who sacrificed it for the sake of the family. She has learnt a lot from life. Consequently, she insists on, especially to Vidula, to make sound career and become self-reliant: "Mother: ...so many opportunities in today's world. We couldn't even dream of such world...there are lots of openings in America.... Don't throw away your talents in just bearing children" (90). Mother has developed a cosmopolitan vision which refutes any caste or religious distinction: "I don't see any difference between Christian girls and Hindu girls these days" (43). Radhabai, Mira and Vatsala have been characterized to depict first set of woman in Indian society. Mira and Vatsala regiser their presence in Scene Three. They are generic and typed characters. Radhabai, a widow, is a cook in Nadkarni's family who takes personal care of the family and serves delicious dishes to children and is reminded of her own daughter Yamuna she has shamelessly left, naked and abused on the road. At the end of the Scene Nine she finds her daughter in the street below in a very pitiable condition: "Radhabai: ...There she was—this mad woman—stark raving mad. Shouting foul abuses at the kids who were throwing stones at her.... Yamuna! She was shouting and screaming: Where is Amma? Where is Amma's house" (92-93). Radhabai is paralyzed to see her and avoids meeting her eyes apprehending the loss of job; and engages in kitchen menials. The gloomy image of the widow and her mad daughter figure in the last page of the wedding album leaves us to think over their lot seriously.

Karnad is widely known as a playwright, but he is also a highly talented film-maker, a versatile actor, an able cultural administrator, a noted communicator and a person of wide accomplishments and interests. Based on his serious explorations of folklore, mythology and history, the subjects of his plays reflect the problems and challenges of the contemporary life, and endeavour to forge a link between the past and the present. The creative intellectual that Karnad is, he obviously, "views the subjects of his plays from his own perspective, develops them in the crucible of his own imagination and personal experiences, and employs them as a medium to communicate his own-independent and original feelings, thoughts and interpretations" (Girish Karnad).

WORKS CITED

Burke, Rupalee. "India Then and Now: The Contemporary Relevance of Girish Karnad's *Tale-Danda*", *Studies in Indian Drama in English*. Eds. Prasad, Amar Nath and Saryug Yadav. Bareilly: Prakash Book Depot, 2003.

Dharwadker, Aparna Bhargava. Ed. With an Introduction *Collected Plays.* Vol. One: *Tughlaq, Hayavadana, Bali: The Sacrifice, Naga-Mandala.* New Delhi: O.U.P., Fourth Impression, 2008.

——. Ed. With an Introduction Collected Plays. Vol. Two: *Tale-Danda, The Fire and The Rain, The Dreams of Tipu Sultan, Two Monologues, Flowers, Broken Images.* New Delhi: O.U.P., 2005.

"Girish Karnad" <karnatakavision.com/girish-karnad.php> 20 Oct. 2010.

Jagamonarchari, A. "Karnad's *Hayavadana* and *Naga-Mandala*: A Study in Post Colonial Dialectics" *New Directions in Indian Drama.* (Eds.) Pandey, Sudhaker & Barua, Freya. New Delhi: Prestige, 1994.

Joshipura, Pranav. "*Tale-Danda:* A Problem Play", *Indian English Drama: Critical Perspectives.* (Eds.) Dondiya & Sunderan. New Delhi: Sarup & Sons, 2000.

Karnad, Girish. *Yayati.* New Delhi: Oxford University Press, 2008.

——. *Tughlaq.* Chennai: Oxford University Press, 1998.

——. *Hayavadana.* Chennai: Oxford University Press (Fourteenth Impression), 1998.

——. "Introduction" to *Three Plays: Naga-Mandala, Hayavadana, Tughlaq.* New Delhi: O.U.P., 2002.

——. Two Plays: *Dream of Tipu Sultan, Bali: The Sacrifice.* New Delhi: O.U.P., Fourth Impression, 2005.

——. *Tale-Danda.* Delhi: Ravi Dayal, 1993.

——. *Two Monologues: Flowers, Broken Images.* Collected Plays. Vol. Two: *Tale-Danda, The Fire and the Rain, The Dreams of Tipu Sultan, Two Monologues, Flowers, Broken Images.* (Ed.) With an Introduction by Dharwadker, Aparna Bharagava. New Delhi: O.U.P., 2005.

——. *Wedding Album.* New Delhi: Oxford University Press, 2009.

Krishanamayi. "Redefing the Insurgent Female Psyche in an Androcentric Milieu" *The Indian Journal of English Studies.* Vol. XLI, 2003-04.

Kurtkoti, Kirtinath. "Introduction" to *Hayavadana.* Chennai: Oxford University Press (Fourteenth Impression), 1998.

Murthy, U.R. Anantha. "Introduction" *Tughlaq.* Chennai: Oxford University Press, 1998.

Raykar, Shubhangi S. "The Development of Girish Karnad as a Dramatist: *Hayavadana*" *Contemporary Indian Drama.* (Eds.) Pandey, Sudhaker & Taraporewala, Freya. New Delhi: Prestige, 1990.

Reddy, K. Venkata and Dhawan, R.K. (Eds.) *Flowering of Indian English Drama: Growth and Development.* New Delhi: Prestige, 2004.

Sagar, Prem. (Ed.) *Naga-Mandala* (Narain's Series). Agra: Lakshmi Narain Agarwal, n.d.

Soni, J.D. "Girish Karnad's *Naga-Mandala*: An Experiment in Technique", *Indian Writing in the New Millenium*. Ed. Dhawan, R.K., New Delhi: Indian Association for English Studies, 2000.

Tilak, Raghukul. *Tughlaq: A Critical Study*. New Delhi: Rama Brothers, 1998.

Tripathi, Vanashree. *Three Plays of Girish Karnad: A Study in Poetics and Culture: Hayavadana, Tale-Danda, The Fire and the Rain*. New Delhi: Prestige Books, 2004.

15 Beyond Broken Columns: Mahesh Dattani's *Final Solutions* and the Quest for 'Horizontal Comradeship'

Abin Chakraborty

> The eyes are not here
> There are no eyes here
> In this valley of dying stars
> In this hollow valley
> This broken jaw of our lost kingdoms.
>
> T.S. Eliot (Eliot, 84)

These lines may well be uttered by the agonised family members of Ishrat Jahan and three other Muslims who were killed on 15th June 2004, in a fake encounter conducted by the currently jailed IPS officer D.G. Vanzara who had staged this murderous drama, according to Magistrate S.P. Tamang, to get promotions and win the favour of his superiors (*Times News Network*). Just as Eliot's hollow men lament the collapse of an earlier existence marked by the illuminating presence of faith, we along with members of Ishrat Jahan's family, may also mourn the collapse of the secular fabric of India which has been repeatedly ravaged by the spectre of communalism, aided by governmental institutions and members of administration such as D.G. Vanzara. It is these examples of administrative collusion which exacerbate those forces of marginalisation which push certain sections of the society to the peripheries by subjecting them to various kinds of deprivation and injustice. And these processes thus lead to what Pramod Nayar calls 'postcolonial subalternization' (Nayar, 69) which inevitably fosters a sense of unbelongingness in the minds of these subalternized sections that ruptures the 'imagined community' of the nation. These incidents are actually indicative of the conflict between the constitutionally determined secular national structure of India and the discourse of communalism, which obviously threatens to destroy that secular fabric altogether. It is this conflict, along with its terrible consequences, which are insightfully explored in Dattani's *Final Solutions* (*FS*, 2000), which brings into focus the entire discourse which makes possible either the destruction of Babri Masjid or the carnage in Gujrat and also seeks to imagine ways in which a new future beyond fissures may be created.

Such an attempt, however, must always take into account the entrenched discourse of Hindu nationalism which has been cumulatively created by nationalist historiography on the one hand and the rise of Hindu nationalism on the other. As Partha Chatterjee illustrates with numerous examples, a number of major Bengali thinkers and authors began by imagining the nation as a primarily Hindu entity, within which however, even originally anti-Hindu and anti-Brahmin religions like Buddhism, Jainism or Sikhism could be subsumed, and placed both Islam and Christianity as alien forces which could not be included within the imagined community of India. While a Bholanath Chakravarti could claim during a meeting of the Adi Brahmo Samaj, in 1876 that: "The cruelty of Yavana [Muslim] rule turned the land to waste" and that "The resumption of good fortune was initiated the day the British flag was first planted on the land" (Chatterjee, 93-94). Tarinicharan Chattopadhyay, in 1878, in the eighteenth edition of the *History of India*, would claim, while castigating the Mahmud of Ghazni, "Of all Muslims it was his aggressions which first brought devastation and disarray to India, and from that time, the freedom of Hindus has diminished and faded like the phases of the moon" (Chatterjee, 103-04). Furthermore as Partha Chatterjee has shown, such remarks were preceded and followed by the construction of Muslims as "fanatical, warlike, bigoted, dissolute and cruel" (Chatterjee, 102), who were, time and again, opposed by Hindu kings who would be celebrated as pious, determined, dauntless and yet unfortunate individuals, embodying that heroism which would be required for national liberation. Interestingly, such classifications directly stemmed from contemporary colonial historiography of India which was itself motivated by a vilification of Islam and especially Mohammad, determined by a Orientalist discourse that went as far back as Dante and Spenser. And it was their division of India into a classical Hindu ancient past, a dark Muslim Medieval age and a British induced Renaissance, which was accepted and applied by Indian historians who did not bother to interrogate the categorisations and their bases. Partha Chatterjee therefore notes:

> For Indian nationalists in the late nineteenth century, the pattern of classical glory, medieval decline, and modern Renaissance appeared as one that was not only proclaimed by modern historiography for Europe but also approved for India by at least some sections of European scholarship. What was needed was to claim the agency for completing the project of modernity. To make that claim, ancient India had to become the classical source of Indian modernity, while "the Muslim period" would become the night of medieval darkness. (Chatterjee, 102)

So pervasive was the effect of this paradigm of nationalism that, at least in Bengal, this narrative, as appropriated by schools and colleges and literary creations "went virtually unchallenged until the first half of the twentieth century" (Chatterjee, 110). This is quite blatantly manifested by the later writings of Bankimchandra, especially such novels as *Rajsingha, Anandamath*, etc. As Tanika Sarkar has shown, these texts present the Muslims as the Hindus' hated historical adversary who must be confronted to ensure the Hindus' own survival. Throughout Anandamath, therefore we keep hearing the refrain, "Kill the low Muslims", which is even elaborated into virulent rhetorical questions such as these:

> How does the Muslims ruler protect us? We have lost our religion, our caste, our honour, and family name, and now we are about to lose our very lives...how can Hinduism survive unless we drive out these dissolute swine? (Sarkar, 180)

Such strategies and statements continued to be adopted in contemporary Bengali theatre as well and all such exclusionary and divisive representations created, from the very inception of Indian nationalism, a certain void that not only widened later but also ensured the eruptions of communal conflagrations which keep harking back to the notion of historical origin as a marker of modern identity. As Partha Chatterjee explains:

> Buddhism or Jainism are Hindu because they originate in India, out of debates and critiques that are internal to Hinduism. Islam and Christianity came from outside and are therefore foreign. And 'India' here, is the generic entity, with fixed territorial definitions, that acts as the permanent arena for the history of the jati. (Chatterjee, 110)

Unfortunately, such a conception of national community remarkably tallies with Savarkar's concept of Hindu and Hindutva which are the basis of the attempt to make India a Hindurashtra, almost in the manner of the German Aryan state under Hitler and his Nazi party. Savarkar stated:

> A Hindu means a person who regards this land of Bharat Varsha, from the Indus to the Seas, as his Fatherland, that is the cradle of his religion. (Veer, 1)

Savarkar's definition of Hindutva, through the notions of 'Karmabhumi' and 'Punyabhumi', as Peter Van Der Veer observes, "equates religious and national identity: an Indian is a Hindu—an equation that puts important Indian religious communities, such as Christians and Muslims, outside the nation" (Veer, 1). This stance becomes all the more evident when Savarkar, further elaborates his position and states:

> A Hindu therefore, to sum up, the conclusions arrived at, is he who looks upon the land that extends from Sindhu to Sindhu—from the Indus to the seas—as the land of his forefathers—his Fatherland (Pitribhu); who inherits the blood of that race whose first discernible source could be traced to the Vedic Saptasindhus and which on its onward march, assimilating much that was incorporated and ennobling much that was assimilated,

> has come to be known as the Hindu people, who has inherited and claims as his own the culture of that race as expressed chiefly in their common classical language Sanskrit and represented by a common literature, art and architecture, law and jurisprudence, rites and rituals, ceremonies and sacraments, fairs and festivals; and who above all addresses this land, this Sindhusthan as his Holyland (Punyabhu), as the land of his prophets and seers, of his godmen and gurus, the land of piety and pilgrimage.... All these essentials could be summed up by stating in brief, that he is a Hindu to whom Sindhusthan is not only a Pitribhu but also a Punyabhu. (Savarkar, 115-16)

Since, Muslims and Christians, even if they are born in India, have Mecca or Jerusalem as their Holyland, they are thus identified as non-Hindus and by definitions, non Indians, according to Savarkar's logic. He makes this all the more clear as he states:

> That is why in the case of some of our Mohameddan or Christian countrymen who had originally been forcibly converted to a non-Hindu religion, and who consequently have inherited, along with Hindus, a common fatherland and a greater part of the wealth of the common culture—language, law, customs, folklore and history—are not and cannot be recognised as Hindus. For though Hindusthan to them is Fatherland, as to any other Hindu, yet it is not to them a Holyland too. (Savarkar, 113)

It is on the basis of this logic that M.S. Golwalkar would go on to assert:

> All those not belonging to the national, i.e. Hindu race, Religion, Culture and Language, naturally fall out of the pale of real 'National' life.
>
> We repeat: in Hindusthan, the land of the Hindus, lives and should live the Hindu Nation—satisfying all the five essential requirements of the scientific nation concept of the modern world. Consequently only those movements are truly 'National' which aim at re-building, revitalizing,

> and emancipating from its present stupor the Hindu Nation. Those only are nationalist patriots who, with the aspiration to glorify the Hindu race and Nation next to their heart, are prompted into activity and strive to achieve that goal. All others are either traitors or enemies to the national cause, to take a charitable view, idiots. (Noorani, 20)

Such a vision of Hindu nationalism, as evident from the remarks, refuses to acknowledge non-Hindus as Indians and according to Golwalkar, if these communities indeed must stay, they should exist as completely subservient, subjugated peoples, almost as the Jews were in Hitler's Germany:

> The foreign races in Hindusthan must either adopt the Hindu culture and language, must learn to respect and hold in reverence Hindu religion, must entertain no idea but those of the glorification of the Hindu race and culture, i.e. the Hindu Nation and must loose their separate existence to merge in the Hindu race, or may stay in the country wholly subordinated to the Hindu nation, claiming nothing, deserving no privileges, far less any preferential treatment—not even citizen's rights. (Noorani, 20)

These statements obviously emphasise the fascist nature of such enterprises which becomes further evident from Golwalker's other statements:

> To keep up the purity of the Race, and its culture, Germany shocked the world by her [sic] purging the country of the Semitic Races—the Jews. Race pride at its highest has been manifested here...a good lesson for us in Hindusthan to learn and profit by. (Noorani, 20)

Such statements form the discursive framework for the rise of Hindu fundamentalism in India which has produced a retrograde, revivalist, fascist nationalism which has grown in strength across India and has produced in the minds of religious minorities a haunting sense of insecurity which has only been intensified by such occurrences as the demolition of the Babri Masjid or the burning of missionary Graham Staines. These discursive frameworks and the kind of actions they instigate are integral to the processes of postcolonial subalternization as a result of which the new subaltern begins to feel a sense of unbelongingness owing to the multiple deprivations and injustices that he is subjected to and they may well generate a sense of hostility towards the nation-state in question. This is precisely the context that Dattani seeks to explore in the play where two Muslim boys, chased by a fanatic mob that keeps baying for their blood, seek shelter in the house of Ramnik Gandhi. Considering the fact that Gandhi is called the 'father of the nation', the domestic space of the Gandhi household becomes symbolic of the nation-space of India itself and the issue of the Muslim boys seeking shelter in the house becomes tied up with the broader framework of creating an inclusive secular nation which can accommodate Muslims and other religious minorities as equal citizens. Such an ideal, however, is rudely shattered at the very beginning as the symbolic representation of the nation-space is fearfully disrupted by divisive religious forces. It is these forces which vehemently assert themselves through the chorus as they collectively assault Javed and Bobby simply for being Muslims after spewing hatred through their frenzied responses and questions:

> Chorus 1, 2, 3: This is our land! How dare they?
>
> Chorus 1: It is in their blood!
>
> Chorus 2, 3: It is in their blood to destroy!...
>
> Chorus 1: (pounding with his stick) Send... them...back. *Pause.*
>
> Chorus 4: (questioning) Send them back?
>
> Chorus 2: (pounding with his stick) Drive...them...out. *Pause.*
>
> Chorus 5: (questioning) Drive them out?
>
> Chorus 3: Kill the sons of swine! (*FS*, 168-69)

Through these comments Dattani foregrounds that communal discourse which identifies Muslims as an inimical, hostile group of people who should have all gone to Pakistan after Partition. M.S. Golwalkar had identified the whole Muslim population of Post-Partition India as "internal threats" who had all voted for Pakistan and wrote:

> Has their old hostility and murderous mood, which resulted in widespread riots, looting, arson, raping and all sorts of orgies on an unprecedented scale in 1946-47, come to a halt at least now? It would be suicidal to delude ourselves into believing that they have turned patriots overnight after the creation of Pakistan. On the contrary, the Muslim menace has increased a hundredfold by the creation of Pakistan which has become a springboard for all their future aggressive designs on our country. (Golwalkar, 119)

These dialogues inevitably register the sense of fear and awe generated by the hateful, vindictive voices of people like Golwalkar who want to ruin India's secular fabric by making it a 'Hindurashtra', following perhaps the same pattern that Hitler's NAZI party used to create a supposedly pure and powerful Germany by annihilating the supposedly corrupting presence of the Jews. The communal ideology that has been developed through the texts of Golwalkar and others bears uncanny resemblance to the NAZI project and it is as a result of such ideological mobilization that Javed and Bobby's identity as Muslims endangers their lives in the same way that Ishrat Jahan's was by her identity as a Muslim. And it is in this context that the oft-repeated concept of one's 'own people' becomes significant. Instead of operating as an inclusive signifier of all Indians the term becomes fractured into communally polarised opposites of 'us' and 'them'—an opposition that ruptures the nationalist dream of 'unity in diversity'—and places the minority communities in that unnarratable space of incomprehensibility where they are identified, in the words of Gyanendra Pandey, as "'populations' within nation states" whom the state wishes to "destroy...because they are collectivities with 'different' (not to say, abnormal) values, customs and practices" (Pandey, 274).

One of the strategies through which is this is done is the repeated reference to the trauma of partition which becomes one of the many available tools of communal polarisation. As Vasanthi Raman notes:

> A macabre way, in which partition has resurfaced in the lives of Indian Muslims, particularly since the 1990s, is in the metaphor of a mini-Pakistan. Partition is almost reenacted every time there is a riot and Muslim areas have been affected.... The language and the slogans of the Hindu right wing during the series of riots since 1992, when the Babri Masjid was vandalized, unabashedly recall partition. (Raman, 276)

The same process is also highlighted in the play through Hardika, who had herself been victimized by the communal frenzy during Partition and her diary becomes a window through which those troubled times are poured on to the stage:

> He said he was happy that we were rid of the Britishers. He also said something which I did not understand then. He said that before leaving they had let loose the dogs. I hated to think that he was talking about my friends' fathers...but that night in Husainabad in our ancestral house—when I heard them outside—I knew that they were thinking the same of us. And I knew I was thinking the same, like my father. (*FS*, 167)

Her fears are concretized by the destruction of the Krishna idol which not only represents the antagonism between warring religious communities but also symbolizes the absence of love which is reinforced by the rupturing of the records of love songs.

> Lying about like pieces of glass, Shamsad Begum, Noor Jehan, Suraiya. The songs of love that I had learnt to sing with. Those beautiful voices. Cracked.... (*FS*, 167)

Hardika not only adored these Muslim singers but even aspired to be like them in the future. This substantiates that sense of a syncretic culture where so many diverse strands could merge together on the basis of that shared universal human emotion of love which was also the subject of their songs. However, as the records are cracked by the thrown stones we also witness that rupture of our syncretic culture which is also responsible for the ongoing politics of estrangement, hatred and conflict that feeds itself through the resurrection of traumatic memories of the past to harden communal hatred within individuals. Hardika herself has become so prejudiced by these traumatic events that she not only despises the two young boys but even asks Ramnik to shut the door against them so that they may be slaughtered: "How could he let those people into my house? They killed his grandfather" (*FS*, 179).

Her unfeeling, seemingly inhuman prejudice is born out of that binary of 'us' and 'them', generated by divisive, fundamentalist discourses and the opposition to the entry of those two boys in the house, also represents symbolically those aforementioned exclusionary narratives that identify the Indian Muslims as aliens who belong outside the realm of the "real National life", specifically Pakistan. As Hardika says "I cannot forget, I just cannot forget" (*FS*, 223), we are confronted with a vision of entrenched ruptures and we realize why Renan said that "Forgetting…is a crucial factor in the creation of a nation" (Renan, 11). In fact, as Hardika demonstrates, lack of forgetting transforms the nation into, what Bhabha calls, "a liminal signifying space that is internally *marked* by the discourse of minorities, the heterogeneous histories of contending people, antagonistic authorities and tense locations of cultural difference" (Bhabha, 148).

This is definitely true for India and they are most visibly and terribly foregrounded during the riots, which are often found to be instances of organised violence, instigated chiefly, by various militant Hindu fundamentalist organisations in the past three decades. In fact, ever since independence India witnessed a steady rise of the discourse of majoritarian communalism which inevitably developed a sense of fear, humiliation and consequent resentment in the Muslim communities that became all the more acute in the wake of the violent communal politics that gripped India since the 1980s, culminating in such barbaric deeds as the demolition of the Babri Masjid and the consequent riots as well as the genocide of 2002. It is this mentality which is voiced by the Muslim Chorus:

Chorus 1, 2:
They hunt us down!
They're afraid of us!
They beat us up!
We are few!
But we are strong!
They beat us up!
They're afraid of us!
They hunt us down!
They want to throw us out! (*FS*, 179)

Wrongs without redress breed revenge. Suppression of religious identities because of fundamentalist activities breeds an opposed fundamentalism that can only drag us into an endless cycle of vitiating violence. This is precisely what happens in case of Javed who becomes part of a riot-rousing group with its own fundamentalist agenda as a result of that ambience of unbelongingness which a Muslim often has to face and which is exemplified in the text through the episode involving the delivery of a letter. As Javed opens the gate to deliver the letter, a man comes out and orders him to go back after leaving the letter on the wall. And he only picks up the letter after cleaning and wiping both the letter and the place on the wall where it was kept. Such an incident offers just one glimpse of the kind of prejudice an Indian Muslim has to confront at times which is re-emphasised by Aruna's own reluctance to offer them water or milk and the way in which she delicately separates the glasses touched by the Muslim youths as she considers their touches to be as contaminating as the touch of a lizard. Such alienation becomes all the more acute for the Muslim underclass, to which Javed obviously belongs, because not only are they cut off from the mainstream of Indian society but their mere survival is under threat on account of the growing saffronisation of even those sources of daily labour through which they could hope to eke out an existence. As Anand Chakravarti reports, following the Gujrat genocide,

> The poor Muslims here are not only economically marginalised but, as Muslims, they are also subject to

> virulent social ostracism and hate by Hindus, including many among dalits and those adivasis who claim to be Hindus. The irony is that, generally speaking, these dalits and adivasis share the same life chances as those of poor Muslims. The latter are, therefore, alienated not only from the fruits of their labour but also from even those who share the same material circumstances. They are despised, hated, and humiliated in village communities and urban neighbourhoods in which they have lived for decades or even generations along with their Hindu neighbours. (Chakravarti, 4246)

He goes on to report how at the insistence of the Vishwa Hindu Parishad, a key component of the Sangh Parivar, several local establishments, run by the Gujrat Industrial Development Corporation, sacked their Muslim labourers, immediately after the riots. It is these actions and gestures that doubly alienate members of minority communities who find respite through the seductive rhetoric of an opposed fundamentalism which virtually drugs them into an amoral trance that renders possible the committing of immoral acts, including those terrorist strikes which continue to lacerate our times:

> I was swayed by what now appears to me as cheap sentiment. They always talked about motherland and fighting to save our faith and how we should get four of theirs for every one of ours.... 'The time has come', somebody would say. 'This is jehad—the holy war! It is written!' 'Yes', I would say. 'I am ready, I am prepared!' (*FS*, 205)

However, as the tense of Javed's statement itself indicates, he 'is' not any more what he once 'was'. As one who has peered into the abyss and come back, Javed indeed emerges as a heroic character whose very rejection of the fundamentalist indoctrination opens the space for that world beyond communal polarisation which is sheltered alike from the ingrained prejudices that govern Aruna as well as those wounds of past which continue to traumatise the likes of Hardika. It is through the friendship and bonding of Javed, Smita and Bobby that this hope is realised on stage which also indicates Dattani's hope that it is perhaps through the youth that India can dream of a future of tolerance and forgiveness, unfettered by the shadow lines that keep us apart. This is emphatically articulated by Bobby who deliberately places the idol of Krishna on his palm, disregarding Aruna's prejudices, and states:

> He doesn't cringe from my touch. He welcomes the warmth of my hand. He feels me. And he welcomes it!... You can bathe Him day and night, you can splash holy water on Him but you cannot remove my touch from His form. You cannot remove my smell with sandal paste and attars and fragrant flowers because it belongs to a human being who believes, and tolerates and respects what other human beings believe. That is the strongest fragrance in the world! (*FS*, 224-25)

It is this humanistic faith which unites Bobby, Javed and Smita. Together they represent that sense of 'horizontal comradeship' (Anderson, 8) which is supposed to be the foundation of any nation and which can counter those processes of postcolonial subalternization, generated by vertical hierarchies of power, which give rise to various divisive forces. Through them we are taken to those 'in-between spaces' which, according to Homi Bhabha "provide the terrain of elaborating strategies of selfhood—singular or communal—that initiate new signs of identity" (Bhabha, 1), away from the binaries of communal conflict. Through his young characters Dattani perhaps seeks to foreground the possibility of a new India, not directly scarred by the trauma of Partition and its aftermaths, which is willing to move beyond engraved barriers in search of better times. And the location of the young characters, as the harbingers of such change also perhaps indicates the responsibility that the youth must shoulder to move beyond the morass of communal hatred. However, as Derrida has shown, all textual strategies of thematic cohesiveness are disrupted by gaps, silences or spectral figures, banished to the peripheries, which haunt our apparently unified structures (Derrida, 46). The figure of the dead pujari exercises a similarly 'hauntological' (Derrida, 63) presence in this particular play and produces that unbalancing moment which 'exposes the grammatological structure of the text' (Spivak, 1).

Where does his corpse lie in this ethic of tolerance and forgiveness? How will his family members respond to either Javed or that acquaintance of his who committed the murder? Will they be able to forgive or remain entrapped in that same cycle of sterile hate? This particular textual ghost thus lays bare a series of unquiet debates about public posture and private response, between forgetfulness and forgiveness, between love and justice. Dattani, as ever, does not provide us with final solutions and faithfully holds a mirror up to the complexities that confront us.

It is as an illustration of these complexities that in the final scene Hardika, after she learns from her son how her family members had burned Zarine's father's shop, is able to ask her son:

> Hardika: Do you think...do you think those boys will ever come back?
>
> Ramnik: If you call them, they will come. But then again—if it's too late—they may not. (*FS*, 226)

Ramnik's reply is characterized by a cautious balance that enunciates at once both the possibility of an inclusive future based on forgiveness, tolerance and compassion as well as the difficulties that lie in the way; difficulties that have been further intensified owing to the unprecedented, televised, state-sponsored carnage in Gujrat, the rise of international Islamic terrorism as well as the emergence of Hindu terrorist groups in India. Ashis Nandy, in a seminar after the Gujrat carnage worryingly observed:

> The forces the Gujarat violence might have released are a different kettle of fish. They seem to have done what the Partition riots did. Also, given that they have been arguably the first video riots in India—riots taking place in front of TV cameras—their impact will be pan-Indian and international. The minorities all over the country have seen the experiments in ethnic cleansing and the attempts to break the economic backbone of the Muslim community. The sense of desperation brewing among the Gujarati Muslims is likely to be contagious.

> I wonder what we should do with 120 million bitter Muslims, a sizeable section of them close to desperation. Will it be another case of Palestine now onwards, at least in Gujarat? Prima facie, Modi has done his job. The Sangh Parivar's two-nation theory is genuine stuff and has already initiated the process of a second partition of India, this time of the mind. We, our children and grandchildren—above all, the Gujaratis—will have to learn to live with a state of civil war. (Nandy, para 25-26)

However, following the example of Barack Obama we should also recall for our reading the words of Martin Luther King Jr.: "I refuse to accept despair as the final response to the ambiguities of history. I refuse to accept the idea that the 'isness' of man's present nature makes him morally incapable of reaching up for the eternal 'oughtness' that forever confronts him" (Obama, para 13). Despite the ambiguities raised by the figure of the dead pujari or ceaseless spiral of violence that entangles us, we can still hold on to the image of Bobby, Javed and Smita playing and splashing water among each other as the symbol of that 'oughtness', away from the frictions of our current 'isness'. It can operate as that icon of what Paul Ricoeur calls 'appeased memory' (Ricoeur, 11) born out of the recognition of mutual loss and the willingness to move beyond recrimination and prejudice which enables the logic of forgiveness to penetrate the logic of justice on the level of "matters that can only be symbolical" (Ricoeur, 9). Just as in the face of widespread despair, following the horrors of World War I, Tagore had uttered the hope of sprinkling the sacred water of worship "to sweeten the history of man into purity and...make the trampled dust of the centuries blessed with fruitfulness" (Tagore, 51), we too may hold on to Dattani's image of youthful conviviality and harmony as the symbolic precursor of a time when, after traveling the wasteland of communal conflicts, we too will find our path to that rose-garden, to learn 'to care and not to care' (Eliot, 98) and say with him: "Shantih, Shantih, Shantih" (Eliot, 75).

WORKS CITED

Anderson, Benedict. *Imagined Communities: Reflections on the Origin and Spread of Nationalism*. London: Verso, 1983.

Bhabha, Homi. *The Location of Culture*. New York: Routledge, 1994.

Chakravarti, Anand. "Doubly Alienated Muslims: Some Implications of the Gujarat Carnage". *Economic and Political Weekly*, Vol. 37, No. 41 (Oct. 12-18, 2002), 4246-4248. Accessed from <http://www.jstor.org/stable/4412723>. Accessed on May 24, 2010.

Chatterjee, Partha. "The Nation and its Fragments", *The Partha Chatterjee Omnibus*. New Delhi: Oxford University Press, 1999. 1-282.

Derrida, Jacques. *Specters of Marx*. London: Routledge, 1994.

Ghosh, Ajit Kumar. *Bangala Nataker Itihash*. Kolkata: Bengal Publishers, 1946.

Dattani, Mahesh. "Final Solutions", *Collected Plays*, Vol. 1. New Delhi: Penguin, 2000, 159-226.

Eliot, T.S. *T.S. Eliot: The Complete Poems and Plays*. London: Faber and Faber, 2004.

Golwalkar, M.S. "Extract from *Bunch of Thoughts*", *Hindu Nationalism: A Reader*. Ed. Christopher Jaffrelot. New Delhi: Permanent Black, 2007. 117-38.

Nandy, Ashis. "Obituary of a Culture". 10 Dec. 2009. <http://www.india-seminar.com/2002/513/513%20ashis%20nandy.htm>.

Nayyar, Pramod. *Postcolonial Literature: An Introduction*. New Delhi: Pearson Education, 2008.

Noorani, A.G. *The RSS and the BJP: A Division of Labour*. New Delhi: Leftword, 2000.

Obama, Barack. Nobel Peace Prize Acceptance Speech. Oslo, Norway. 10 Dec. 2009. <http://www.brahmmajanen.blogspot.com/>, 10 Dec. 2009.

Pandey, Gyanendra. "Afterword: Communalism after Communalism", *The Gyanendra Pandey Omnibus*. New Delhi: Oxford University Press, 2008. 262-82.

Raman, Vasanthi. "The Surang (Tunnel) of Madanpura: Partition Motif in Banaras". *The Partition Motif in Contemporary Conflicts*. Ed. J.S. Tiwari and Ben_Ari Eyal New Delhi: Sage Publications, 2007. 260-282.

Ricoeur, Paul. Interview with Sorin Antohi, *Memory, History, Forgiveness: A Dialogue between Paul Ricoeur and Sorin Antohi*. Budapest, 10 Mar. 2003. <www.janushead.org/8-1/Ricoeur.pdf>. 8-25.

Sarkar, Tanika. "Imagining Hindurashtra: The Hindu and the Muslim in Bankim Chandra's Writings", *Making India Hindu*. Ed. David Ludden. New Delhi: Oxford University Press, 1996. 162-84.

Savarkar, V.D. *Hindutva—Who is a Hindu*. Bombay: Veer Savarkar Prakashan, 1969.

Spivak, Gayatri Chakrabarty. Translator's Preface to Jacques Derrida's *Of Grammatology*. Baltimore: John Hopkins University Press, 1997. x-lxxxvii.

Tagore, Rabindranath. *Nationalism*. New Delhi: Macmillan, 2001.

Times News Network. "Ishrat shootout was staged, says Gujrat court". *The Times of India*, Kolkata, September 8, 2009.

Van Der Veer, Peter. *Religious Nationalism: Hindus and Muslims in India*. New Delhi: Oxford University Press, 1996.

16 *Silence! The Court is in Session*: The Muted Spaces of Violence Camouflaged in Camaraderie

T.R. Muralikrishnan

Vijay Tendulkar's play *Silence! The Court is in Session* projects the dual perspectives in dealing with the social issues particularly the women in general. The psyche of the society to hush up things remains a dominant idea through out the play and the double standards while dealing with woman issues offering a clichéd naïve assurance that it is after all a play, a 'game' largely calls for an analysis of the disturbing subtext. The attempt made here is to look into those spaces in the play which generally goes unnoticed for want of merit from the thematic perspective. The dramatist has carefully loaded the play within the play not in the conventional sense but to explore the male psyche which denies freedom of choice for women in matters of sex, motherhood, profession and creativity. The silent spaces are those that remain part of the enactment of the play, indirectly contributing to the overall progress of the play, at the same time, for a critical viewer they assume prime importance.

Leela Benare's physical proximity with the on stage characters such as Samant and Rokde are vital. Men, in this play, find it difficult to share intimate spaces with women in public but they desire close relation in private as it is the case with Prof Damle. The moment Benare touches her own stomach there is a meaningful nervousness. She knew there was some thing to hide. The room of the mock trial has a faulty bolt since it slips itself and it traps the inmates. Benare tries many times to walk out but all ended up unsuccessfully. The 'caged' bird did sing at the end;

The parrot to the sparrow said,
'Why, oh why, are your eyes so red?
'Oh, my dear friend, what shall I say?
'Some one has stolen my nest away'....

The mundane middle class conversations centre on, '*pan*', 'garlands for hair', 'puja', 'tea with sugar or *gur*', 'snacks', 'puffing pipe', 'ear pick', and 'game of cards'. The characters find it best to spend time to talk about all that. The quality of topics remains superfluous though they pretend to be sensitive to bigger issues of life. The public exhibition of love and care between Mrs. and Mr. Kashikar invite attention to the projection of family affection among popular culture. They want others to acknowledge it but deep inside the truth is something else. The subtle winking of Karnik and Ponkshe carry significance since the plan to trap and expose Benare is part of the inner play project. The gavel used by the 'judge' Kashikar is only to silence the women in the group. The *Geeta* is replaced by the Oxford English Dictionary at the time of taking vow. That means only the size matters and not what it contains. The small bottle of TIK 20 inside the purse of Benare later turned out to be effective evidence against her.

As Anita Singh (2009) states, "Feminist theatre argues that for over two millennia, since even before Aristotle wrote out his *Poetics* or after Bharata's *Natyashastra* and the dramatists that followed; dramatic text and performances were dominated by male ideologies. In response, feminist theatre evolved not only to share the tragically under represented experiences of women living in a patriarchal society, but also to create a theatricality that would subvert traditional theatre's most sacred traditions". The play reveals that at the operational level the liberal outlook spread by the brave new generation does not hold any significance. Each artist represents an unfulfilled dream. A sense of ennui pervades their lives. Sukhatme has proved quite inefficient as a lawyer. The Kashikars are childless. Ponkshe is a failed scientist and Karnik is a failed actor. Rokde does not have an identity of his own. Amongst themselves even, they do not have anything but hatred for each other. The adoption of Rodke by the Kashikars is only to make a slave out of him. In act two Samant gives an account of a poor woman, a widow, who is charged with infanticide. The tolerance of Kashikar reaches the limit when he admonishes his wife to keep quiet. He observes that she can neither keep quiet at home nor there at the court. She in turn complains that Kashikar is scolding her at every step and she does not know how to swallow all these insults.

> Kashikar: It'll add that bit of variety, I would say.
> Mrs. Kashikar: Exactly.
> Kashikar: What do you mean, exactly? Hold your tongue. Can't say a word!...
> [Mrs. Kashikar is silenced.] (21)

Similarly, later Mrs. Kashikar offers to do something on her own but her husband says no and she is silenced. Further, in a later sequence Kashikar observes, "Silence must be observed while the court is in session. Can't shut up at home, can't shut here. ... Mrs. Kashikar: So what? Scolding me at every step!" (28). However Kashikar does not wait for anyone to express his opinions: "An opinion is an opinion. I don't wait for any one's permission to give it" (68). Similarly, when tirades of insulting remarks are directed at Benare by Samant, Benare gets furious. But Kashikar warns her to be quiet. Interestingly Mrs. Kashikar too joins the male group to taunt Benare. She asks why Benare should get angry if her conscience is clear. When Sukhatme calls Benare 'a girl', Mrs. Kashikar objects to it and expresses that she must be called a 'young lady'. But Sukhatme wants to know why she is not married. Mrs. Kashikar says it is simple thing that anybody who really wants to marry can do so in a flash. "It is the sly new fashion of women going for job and earning makes everything go wrong. That is how promiscuity has spread throughout our society" (54). Earlier her husband had voiced a similar opinion on women: "...our society should revive the old custom of child marriage. Marry off the girls before puberty. All this promiscuity will come to a full stop" (52). The verbal violence against Benare reflects the male centered perspective of the society in dealing with woman, especially while taking up discussion on man-woman relationship. To top it all, the words of Manu are partly quoted,

"*Na stri Swatantryamarhati*", 'woman is not fit for independence'.

The entire dramatic sequence centers on the play within the play. At the beginning the original understanding is to do a rehearsal of the play they are going to present later in the evening. The announcement says that 'The Sonar Moti Tenement (Bombay) Progressive Association' will stage a 'Mock Law court' that night at eight o'clock. Benare tells Samant that the objective of the programme is to spread enlightenment. The trial is against President Lyndon Johnson of the US for producing atomic weapons. The actors are to great extent amateur and they are only good at expressing bits of wisdom on dramatic art. Rodke's remark on Karnik is significant. Karnik says that when he sees public formalities between husband and wife (Kashikars), he suspects something quite different in their private life. Rodke takes exception here and says, "That's the effect of modern theatre!" (12). Later, Karnik asks Mr. Kashikar to look at things from the audience's point of view. Karnik's words are significant, "Will someone please tell me what this Modern Theatre is supposed to be? People just play with words without knowing what they mean. I do what seems right with me" (15).

Sukhatme jeers at Karnik for being a man of the modern theatre but looking at things from the audience's perspective. Karnik retorts at Sukhatme saying that people just play with words without knowing what they mean. When Samant was given the role, Karnik asks him if he has ever seen a play. Sukhatme teases Karnik by observing that it is a good thing that Samant has not seen a courtroom in a play. This will help him in keeping away from all wrong notions about it. Karnik is the one who is excited about doing a rehearsal by bringing an imaginary case against somebody. He says that in drama theory this is called visual enactment. The intolerable cruelty towards Benare continues with the explanation that it is after all a game. However, the rules of the game favour only the dominant group and not the 'accused'. The institutionalization of woman as thing to be harassed continues unabated when Benare is reprimanded more than once and the privileged positioning of the court of law is invoked to settle scores against Benare. In the third act, Benare tries to express herself to the audience her true feelings and concerns. This speech is more of an inner drama than the externalized version of it. All the other people sit motionless. This phase helps the audience to listen to the woes of a silenced woman. For the real audience the play comes to an end here though a man comes in to enquire whether 'The Living Courtroom' has begun. Thus, Tendulkar has created a masterly stroke at the end to culminate the play. Anita Singh (2009) opines "'Herstories' or women centered drama is hinged on revelation and recognition of the assumed perceptions on the differences between men and women. These devices along with a preference for non-linear plots and open ended conclusions as opposed to climaxes are just some of the elements that comprise feminist theatre."

Benare is an educated woman about thirty-four years old. Her life was not entirely smooth as she wanted it to be. She was exploited by her maternal uncle and the entire family took opposition to her proposal of marrying him. Despite this she pursued her studies and became a schoolteacher. Her liking of Prof. Damle ended up in rocks as he exploited her sexually but when she got pregnant he shied away from the alliance. As she puts it at the end, "I offered my body on the altar of my worship. And my intellectual god took the offering—and went his way" (75). She got associated with an amateur dramatic alliance, whose prime purpose was to educate the public with social and current issues. Benare was originally reluctant to perform the role of an accused but this reluctance was ignored. The playwright endeavours to create a game—like atmosphere. But soon the imaginary charges lead to personal dilemmas. The play is long drawn exposition of Benare's true understanding of the society. Her words at the beginning about herself are significant, "My life is my own-I haven't sold it to anyone for a job! My will is my own. My wishes are my own. No one can kill those-no one! I'll do what I like with myself and my life!" (5). Benare is seen in a mood of gaiety, but she gets treated badly by her co-artists. They venomously attack her under the guise of a 'trial play'. The play thus moves from the talkative and mirthful soul to a gloomy, shocked and shattered entity. She is pregnant, she looses her job, and her character is exposed.

There are innumerable instances where the characters come with superfluous philosophical treatises for supporting the cause of woman oppression which Benare scoffs at as "straight out of a school composition book". "Sukhatme: Motherhood is pure. Moreover, there is great-er-a great nobility in our concept of motherhood. We have acknowledged woman as the mother of mankind. Our culture enjoins us to perpetual worship of her" (30). Sukhatme's speech as the counsel for the prosecution is another example: "Sukhatme:... If it is encouraged, there will be no such thing as the institution of marriage left. Immorality will flourish. Before our eyes, our beautiful dream of society governed by tradition will crumble into dust. The accused has plotted to dynamite the very roots of our tradition, our pride in ourselves, our culture and our religion.... Woman bears the grave responsibility of building up the high values of society..." (71).

The speech made by Benare to signify the suppressed conscience of women remains one of the charming utterances in the play: "Life is a poisonous snake that bites itself. Life is a betrayal. Life is a fraud. Life is a drug. Life is drudgery.... Life is a very dreadful thing..." (73). She wanted to die, but she could not. The judgment seems absurd. Mr. Kashikar says: "The crimes you have committed are most terrible. There is no forgiveness for them.... No memento of your sin should remain for future generations. Therefore this court hereby sentences that you shall live. But the child in your womb shall be destroyed..." (76). Her idea of rosy life was the one she wrote in the school book: "The grass is green/The rose is red/The book is mine/Till I am dead" (9).

But every single book got torn one by one and she did not know where. But she is still there. She is not dead. She has been betrayed by her co-artists and all of them a failure in the field of art and science and more importantly in life. Her defeat in the battle is already destined. As Shubha Tiwari (2007) states, "The problem with Leela Benare is that she is too much of a woman. She is sexually alive. She needs to fulfil her desires. And above everything else, she is not ashamed of her instincts. She is not submissive". Such frankness and openness will not be tolerated in a male dominated society. The value systems dominate the woman both at the psychic level and at the social level. Benare is juxtaposed with Mrs. Kashikar so as to make the divide clear. Benare has violated the social taboo. Mrs. Kashikar is middle aged, married, a house wife but childless. Mrs. Kashikar has damaging view against Benare. She does not hesitate to say that these young unmarried girls get everything without marrying. She shows her doubt, how can Benare remain unmarried till the age of thirty-four? "The two female characters, Benare and Mrs. Kashikar, are poles apart from each other in respect of their personality and view of life. Whereas Benare posses an assertive personality, Mrs. Kashikar lacks that assertiveness. The authoritative nature Mrs. Kashikar tries to flaunt is not an integral part of her character, rather a sham. Her very venture to establish herself as a strong personality is blotted out by characters like Benare and Mr. Kashikar" (Guha, 2011). The last speech of Ms. Benare was skillfully constructed by Tendulkar. It echoes the irony, sorrow lampoon present in Indian society. Benare says, "But I was ignorant instead; I threw myself off a parapet of our house—to embrace death. But I didn't die. My body didn't die I felt as if its feelings were dead—out they had not died either then..." (74). As Megha Trivedi (2009) observes, "Benare is a prey of male chauvinism; she is used simply to gratify the quench for bodily thirst and deserted at the end to her own destiny. Man has all the rights to be sinful in the society. He can be harsh, notorious and innocent too. All the rights are reserved specially for him. On the other hand, a woman must be deserted, abandoned, ignored, thrown away and should be tainted for her sins. There is no escape for her in our society. She must be brutally destroyed for her actions both physically and mentally."

Rajni Singh Solanki (2009) cites the 'Introduction' by Arundhati Banerjee who maintains that "the accusation brought against Benare at the beginning of the trial turns into the verdict in last because contemporary Indian Society, with its roots grounded firmly in reactionary ideas, cannot allow the birth of a child out of wedlock. This very, reversal in the attitude of the authorities expresses the basic hypocrisy and double standards on which our society is founded. In the course of court proceedings, Benare's private life is exposed and publicly dissected revealing that she is a woman of loose character, Tendulkar displays, the psychological violence that makes a female individual as helpless as Lachrymose. The play points out the intricate levels of insensitivity looming large in the society for the cause of woman. The writer has successfully overcome the conventional temptation to make it a propaganda play. The theme is fit for sermonizing on the travails of a free thinking woman. But Tendulkar gives it a new dimension by exploring the silent spaces in the making of the play. He merges the dominant theme with the innovative stagecraft. The mock court is only a device to demarcate the narrow line between illusion and reality. Tendulkar has exposed the bitter middle-class morality that suffocates the desires of Benare to mother a child in the play. Tendulkar does not suggest any solution to the problem. Mr. Kashikar, the judge, who silences his conscience himself, is a representative of the middle class, who remain silent despite all challenges. Quite ironically the troupe is titled 'progressive' though the acts are astonishingly regressive.

WORKS CITED

Dass, Veena Noble. "Women Characters in the Plays of Tendulkar," *New Directions in Indian Drama*, ed. Sudhakar Pandey & Freya Barya. New Delhi: Prestige Books, 1994.

Guha, Tandrima. "Vijay Tendulkar's Silence! The Court Is In Session: A Socio-Linguistic Study" MS Academic Vol. 1, No. 4, July 2011. <http://www.msacademic.net> 2 Aug. 2011.

Singh, Anita. "Aesthetics of Indian Feminist Theatre", *Rupkatha Journal on Interdisciplinary Studies in Humanities*, Volume I, Number 2, Autumn 2009. <http://www.rupkatha.com/journal> 18 Jan. 2011.

Solanki, Rajni Singh. "Exploitation of women in three plays of Vijay Tendulkar the playwright" Shodh, Samiksha aur Mulyankan (International Research Journal Vol. II, Issue 6 (Feb., 09-April, 09). <http://www.ssmrae.com> 18 Jan. 2011.

Tendulkar, Vijay. *Silence! The Court is in Session*, trans. Priya Adakar Calcutta: Oxford University Press, 1978.

Tiwade, Kavita. "Subjugation of woman in Silence! The court is in the session" Indian Streams Research Journal Volume I, Issue-VII August 2011 <http://www.isrj.net> Accessed on 13 Nov. 2011.

Tiwari, Shubha. "Silence! The Court is in Session: A Strong Social Commentary", *Contemporary Indian Dramatists*, New Delhi: Atlantic Publishers, 2007.

Trivedi, Megha. "Silence! The Court is in Session: The Quintessence of Gender Discrimination", *The Indian Review of World Literature in English*, Vol. 5 No. II – July, 2009, http://www.worldlitonline.com. 18 Jan. 2011.

17

Rhetoric of Desire and Despair: Badal Sircar's *That Other History* in Existential Vision

Nirban Manna

In the novel *Death in the Afternoon,* for Ernest Hemingway, the elegant spectacle of the valiant bullfighter flirting with death is a metaphor for a true artist and an 'authentic' individual as well. This compulsive confrontation of life and death ennobles the art, artist and the world. In the formative years (1957-70) Sircar was desperately seeking this courageous and elegant bullfighter in himself and in his art. Through the Writer in *Evam Indrajit*, Badal Sircar shows off his own desire, "The audacious assertion of life claims immortality in its brief spark. These are sparks. I have to write my play on the story of the claims of immortality of these brief sparks..." (*Evam*, 43). In *Evam Indrajit* (1965), *Shesh Nei* (There's No End, 1970), *Pagla Ghora* (The Mad Horse, 1967) *Tringsha Shatabdi* (The Thirtieth Century, 1966) he recurrently returned to the theme of existential question, nihilism and guilt-ridden impotent middle class individual. His heroes struggle towards a new understanding of "being for self" (Sartre's term for 'consciousness') in terms of the 'Other'. *Baki Itihas* or *That Other History* (1967) is no exception. Here Sharad (Though in Bengali version, it was Sharadindu and V.L. Doshi in his translation curtails the name) witnesses the vicious presence of evil in the pathway of human existence. In *Evam Indrajit*, Indrajit during his conversation with the writer directly raised the problem of evil in this godless universe but in *That Other History* Sircar demands the individual responsibility towards the evil.

Indrajit: I read a long time ego that all those atomic weapons are controlled by buttons. And there are interlocking systems so nobody can spark off an atomic warfare by pushing the wrong button. Just imagine, a minor oversight could destroy the whole world!

Writer: So?

Indrajit: Nothing. This priceless, invaluable life—about which we think so much, measured and count... (*Evam*, 40).

Indrajit questions the validity of living under the shadows of death. And nobody can forget how Camus begins his *The Myth of Sisyphus*. He too asks the same fatal question—to live or to die.

In the existential philosophy, this dilemma is the final stage of the 'definite awakening'. Camus elucidates the destiny of the war between man and the universe in the following ways,

> Weariness comes at the end of the act of a mechanical life, but at the same time it inaugurates the impulse of consciousness. It awakens consciousness and provokes what follows. What follows is the gradual return to the chain or it's a definitive awakening. At the end of the awakening comes, in time the consequence: suicide or recovery. (*Myth*, 19)

In *Caligula*, Cherea, assessing Caligula's dilemma says, "To lose one's life is no great matter.... But what's intolerable is to see one's life being drained of meaning, to be told there's no reason for existing. A man can't live without some reason for living" (Act II, 21). Here lies the question of voluntary death and living in an absurd life. By suicide an individual confesses that life is intolerable to him. And instinctively he counters it, ridicules it by suicide as Kirilov in Dostoyevsky's *The Possessed* did. And thereby he freed himself from the clutches of absurdity; it is one kind of revolt against absurdity of world. But the absolute rebellion and sarcasm to absurdity lies not in this blunt escape but living and loving the world. The defence against nihilism and self-destruction is the test of intellectualism of an absurd hero. For Heidegger, Camus and Sartre, death is the ultimate victor and the incarnation of the ultimate evil which terminates all of possible meaning, our struggle and our freedom. Thus Sartre says, "Thus the very existence of death alienates us wholly in our own life to the advantages of the Others. To be dead is to be a prey for the living" (B&N, 695). The only essence of humankind lies in the constant struggle against death. Badal Sircar in his *That Other History* elaborates the two kinds of gestures towards life and death. One is represented by Seetanath who ridicules the absurdity and cruelty by voluntary death. And on the other hand, Sharad represents the absolute revolt and freedom.

In Enugu, some months before Sircar had written *That Other History*, he scribbled an important section of Charlie Chaplin's *The Autobiography* in his diary. "Over the years I have discovered that ideas come through an intense desire for them; continually desiring, the mind becomes a watchtower on the look for incidents that may excite the imagination—music, a sunset, may give image to an idea" (*Hijibiji*, 266). Sircar's deep mediation on the nature of death was excited by news of a man's suicide read in France. In his diary written on 23rd January 1964, he scrawled his ideas in random ways, "A picture comes. A story of man's suicide read in a newspaper. An imagination—first scene, the wife's opinion. Second imagination—second scene. And the last scene—the version of the ghost of the dead" (*Hijibiji*, 230). Sircar in *That Other History* directly spelled out the story as it is experienced by him during a creative process. The news of suicide comes to a couple, Vasanti and Sharad, and the wife is asked by her husband to weave a story from her own point of view. Act I consists of the enactment of Vasanti's opinion about Seetanath's suicide. She holds the domestic unhappiness as the cause of the suicide. Then the husband weaves a story. Sharad blames the "Lolita Fixation" as the cause of the man's suicide and in Act III, the dead man appears before Sharad and justifies his voluntary death as a revolt against the evil that gnaws human existence from the dawn of the civilization. Here Seetanath and Sharad engage in a dual. While Seetanath insists that living in this cruel world is utter absurdity, Sharad asserts that redemption lies not in death but in the constant struggle with death. In the course of the debate Sharad for the first time encounters that he has been caged in his egotistic world and dragging drab meaningless world. He realized that man is born by chance, lives by encounter and dies by accident. Persuaded by Seetanath's discursive logic, Sharad confronts the dreadful presence of evil and decided to rebel against the hackneyed living by committing suicide like Seetanath. But it's the chance appearance of his friend Vasudev that saved him. It is not avoiding death by chance; but the main emphasis is on the fatal knowledge that Sharad comes to know. Now on, he has to carry the absurd world with the realization of its 'no-thing-ness' (Sartre's term).

The whole matrix of *That Other History* structurally follows Camusian thought of suicide. In *The Myth of Sisyphus*, Camus says,

> There are many causes for suicide and generally the most obvious one were not the most powerful. Rarely is suicide committed...through hypothesis. What sets off the crisis is almost unverifiable. Newspaper often speaks of 'personal sorrow' or of 'incurable illnesses'. These explanations are plausible. But one would have to know whether a friend of the desperate man had not that very day addressed him indifferently. He is the guilty one. For that is enough to precipitate all the rancours and all the boredom still in suspension. (13)

Here Vasanti's version confirms Seetanath's 'personal sorrow' and Sharad's 'incurable illness'. But the ghost's version nullifies all the hypothetical discourses and narrates an existential version of the event. Sircar in an interview with Biplab Chakraborty acknowledges the similarity of *That Other History* and *Evam Indrajit* with *The Myth of Sisyphus* (Pessimism, 169). The whole story is an enactment of a creative process happening within the mind of Sircar. In this way Sircar himself becomes the character in this play. Sharad and Vasanti are none but Sircar himself. The play is about the process of creating an art from a stimulus. In the process of a Sircar's creative adventure to write a story from a stimulus, he ultimately discovers a philosophy of life at the end. The story begins with the stimulus of an image of man committing suicide, and then the writer himself makes 'a feminine domestic story' to be told through Vasanti, then proceeds to a 'mature psychological realism' of Sharad, and ultimately sneaks into an existential supra-realism narrating the archetypal conflict of life and death. Thus in the process of storytelling Sircar arrives at the fatal question of validity of living an absurd life in the face of gnawing evil.

The play opens with a setting similar to Coward's 'drawing-room comedies' where a middle class couple, Sharad and Vasanti start their usual Sunday business. Their conversation ranges from the payment of the electric bill to the wedding invitation. Initially they have planned to take a short holiday trip to Botanical Garden and Diamond Harbour, but ultimately decide to stay in the home. Then Vasudev, the colleague from Sharad's college, came to their house for morning tea. In a jocund holiday mood they have started their usual Sunday. We come to know that Vasanti is a creative writer and her recent story in a magazine is quite a successful attempt. Vasudev insists her to write a similar smash hit. But Vasanti says that she is out of any theme.

When Vasudev has retired, Sharad gives Vasanti a clue from the newspaper for her next story. The short news covers the suicide of their distant acquaintance Seetanath. Vasanti starts weaving a story. Her narration is supported by visual representation. Her version determines domestic unhappiness as the cause of Seetanath's suicide. With the lights slowly fading, the setting shifts to the house of Seetanath and his wife, Kanak (in original Bengali version her name was Kana). Here Seetanath and Kanak are seen struggling with their poverty. They have been scrimping and saving all the year to build a house of their own. Kanak is more obsessed with the economic security than Seetanath. She carefully cherishes the dream of having a home of her own on a newly bought land. Like Mrs. Thurlow in H.E. Bates' short story *The Ox,* Kanak is obsessed with a secure future. Kanak is a woman with an unthinking singleness of purpose to save enough money to build a home. She has been denying herself from minimum lavishness for that. She reacts hysterically when anything is said against her dream. And she knows her obsession and holds her deprived childhood responsible for that.

Seetanath: OK. But tell me, why is having a house of your own so important to you, Kanak?

....

Kanak: You could have understood it, if you had grown up in the kind of condition in which I did...Never had anything which I could tell mine—my very own. Let alone a room, but not even a simple sari or a blouse. Nothing! Not even a dirty little piece of string belonged to me. (Act II, 6)

We come to know that due to sheer poverty, Kanak's sister had disgraced herself by becoming mistress of an evil man. But to Kanak her sister had done nothing wrong. She did all to survive and for a good life. Thus to Kanak, the desired home is the realization of her possessed dream. And to Seetanath, his wife is his only love. But suddenly this love story takes a twist when the bailiff appears on the gate. The bailiff brings the court-summon for an unpaid mortgage repayment. Seetanath tries his best to hide the truth, but Kanak ultimately comes to know that her dream is on mortgage, she also discovers that Seetanath has been lying about saving money and now, she is left with nothing. In a hysteric fit she locked herself behind the doors. Then an old man appears on the gate to unfold Seetanath's lie. He is the father of Kanak. He has been constantly blackmailing Seetanath for money for long. Seetanath has been so far giving the money to cover the truth about her father's character. Seetanath has thought that the gambler father had caused enough shame to Kanak, so he lied to Kanak that her father had died in an accident. The sole purpose of Seetanath was to see Kanak happy, but in the course he has drained the money saved for the home and mortgaged the house. When the old man goes out, Kanak comes out of the room with a suitcase in her hand; she is about leave Seetanath to go to Seetanath's rich friend, Nikhil to seek her desired security. She has decided to take the profession that her sister had shown her. In sheer shock Seetanath committed suicide by stabbing with a kitchen knife. In Vasanti's opinion Seetanath was pushed to the edge of perpetual stillness when Kanak had deserted him. Here a happy conjugal life is destroyed by a crude revelation. But the version is weak, melodramatic and unconvincing story justifying a suicide for the cause of personal sorrow. The best criticism of Vasanti's story could be found in Sharad's comment in the beginning of Act II.

While in Vasanti's version it is the outer world which is vulnerable, in Sharad's version, it is the 'inner storm' that creates the deadly vortex in Seetanath's life. In response to Vasanti's melodramatic story, Sharad says; "Well, I feel that when a person commits suicide, he is usually victim of some severe mental disorder. Deep inside him this thing is eating him. His nerves get highly strung and snap at the slightest jolt. In short he is very sick mentally" (Act II, 10). Sharad's version uses the setting of Vasanti's story and here Kanak is seen discussing about Seetanath's bizarre behaviour in last few days with Vijay, Seetanath's colleague from the school. Here we see that Seetanath has decided to expel a student, Ashok because Ashok is caught reading Nabokov's *Lolita* in the class. While everybody including Vijay and the school secretary, Vidhi*babu* regards Seetanath's decision as heavy punishment for venial offence, Seetanath is seen adamant to punish him. Actually Lolita is a stimulus for Seetanath's long standing hidden guilt consciousness which was initiated ten years ago in the jungle of Chambalgad. Kanak narrated that ten years ago, Kanak and Seetanath went to Chambalgad to spend their summer vacation, and they befriended the forest officer Banwarilal and his little daughter Parvati. In the dark forest, in a hysteric fit, Seetanath raped Parvati. There in the heart of darkness, Seetanath realized his darkest evil in his heart. From then on he has been haunted down by the guilty feeling. He ripped all the relationship and memories related to Chambalgad and he shunned all the physical intimacy with his wife. Through perseverance he tried to control his sexual perversion. But Seetanath couldn't come out of the incident and the guilt feeling. Vijay Knows that Seetanath preoccupied with some thought often scribbled the name Parvati and Chambalgad in the paper. Neither Vijay nor Kanak know what exactly happens in Chambalgad. But in the end he confesses, "Day and night that ugly poisonous virus grew in my body—like some horrendous germs it spread though my system—multiplying in thousands, millions each moment" (Act II, 16). Thus Seetanath is well aware of the Humbert within himself. By punishing Ashok, he wants to punish none but himself. His hatred for *Lolita* is his personalized guilt ridden psyche. He says in a fit of rage, "This is very mild punishment what he did. Actually, he should be tied to a post in the street and horsewhipped" (Act II, 11). But he realizes his mistakes at the end—one was punishing Ashok wrongly for his own guilt, and the other was to run way from the guilt. After a fiery debate over this issue of crime and punishment, Seetanath goes out to calm his mind. But he returns with a greater realization that Parvati was not an isolated event, but it is an expression of the poison ivy rooted deep in his psyche. He realized that he is suffering from dreadful pedophile disorder called Lolita fixation. He confesses before Vijay the sin he had committed in Chambalgad and says that Parvati is still living within him. He admits that when he has gone to the school secretary, Vidhi*babu*'s house, he saw Vidhi*babu*'s young granddaughter, Gouri. He says, "Yes, Vijay! Gouri!! Parvati may have dissolved into past but Gouri is in the present—today—now! Parvati was the victim of some dacoit. But who can tell what is in store for Gouri—what will be her fate" (Act II, 17). Vijay tries to encourage Seetanath to overcome his guilt consciousness, but Seetanath has already decided to kill the devil on which he has no control, he wants to end all his torment and to save the little girl, Gouri from his perverted scheme.

Like Nabokov's Humbert, Seetanath too is under the strong obsession of the pedophiliac fixation. Both know their guilt and call their obsession as 'devil'. Seetanath's guilt gnaws him when he associates himself with Hurbert's crime. There are several similarities between Seetanath and Humbert. They are as follows—

1. Both are suffering from sexual perversion of pedophilia.
2. Humbert for the first time discovered the 'devil' in him in his relation with Annabel and here Seetanath in his relationship with Parvati.
3. After 24 years Humbert came under the same obsession when he saw Lolita, here after 10 years, Seetanath was tormented when he had seen Gouri.
4. Both saw in their second victim, the reflection of the first; Humbert saw Annabelle in Lolita, and Seetanath saw Parvati in Gouri.
5. Both practiced temperance to curb their fixation.
6. While Humbert is convicted in court, Seetanath punishes himself by committing suicide.
7. Both are married persons and their wives don't know about the disease.

As in Akira Kurosawa's *Rashomon* (1950), the devil's gate is the gateway of each narrative and the storytelling returns to the gate after each of the three versions, so also in *That Other History* the couple's apartment is the gateway of narratives. Sircar after the each narrative returns to the couple to narrate the last few lines of their versions. Sircar uses this technique deliberately to impute the sense of continuation and make the impression that the audience is viewing nothing but a version or opinions of truth. This technique is also used to comment on the version. Whether it is Sharad's criticism of Vasanti's story in the beginning of Act II or Vasanti's reaction to Sharad's version in Act III, it is nothing but audience reaction to both versions. Vasanti's doubt over the possibility of Sharad's justification is nothing but to build the dramatic tension and to let the story roll further. As Sharad became angry when he had been criticized so also did Vasanti when she was criticized for being 'melodramatic' and 'unrealistic'. Actually both imply a subjective impression of the objective event. In Vasanti's version, we find a feminine domestic story emphasizing on the economic security, the misunderstanding between husband and wife. Here the female character Kanak covers the central stage, while the male protagonist Seetanath is sidelined. On the other hand in Sharad's version Seetanath, who is like Sharad a teacher and has the habit of collecting newspaper-cutting, takes the central stage. While to a female it is the outer world which is vulnerable, to a male it is the inner world. Each protagonist of the respective versions is the subjective projection of the narrator himself or herself. In his production in 1967, Sombhu Mitra experimented with this idea. He employed one actor to play the role of Sharad and Seetanath and one actress to play Vasanti and Kanak. Each narration is the ejaculation of the subjective self of the narrator. And both are caged in their arrogant egotistic perspectives of respective gender, family and world. But in Act III, with the encounter of Sharad and the ghost of Seetanath, Sircar stretched the narration beyond ego and superego to the realm of an objective knowledge of human existence. Here Like the woodcutter's version of *Rashomon,* Seetanath's version is the binding force that resolves the conflict of all the versions of a truth. As in *Rashomon* with the woodcutter's version in the end, we realized the presence of evil in every human being, so also after the ghost's version in this play, we realize the audacious spark of human resistance to the evil in the universe.

Act III opens with the concluding narration and the critical remark of Vasanti's on Sharad's version. Sharad realizes that slowly he is becoming obsessed with Seetanath and his idea of suicide. He confesses that he is too obsessed to sleep in the night (18). His obsession with the idea of suicide causes Seetanath's ghost to appear before him. G.J.V. Prasad in his article "The Third Gaze" says that Seetanath is the suppressed self of Sharad (73). Even I will say Seetanath dwells inside everyman, it is matter of discovery of the suppressed self. Sharad knows that all were nothing but stories, but his irritation to reach at some definite conclusion shows that Seetanath is deep inside him. Seetanath's ghost takes Sharad to the knowledge of human existence beyond his routine existence. When Sharad asks Seetanath why he had committed suicide, Seetanath takes out a scrap book full of images. The images show that the human history is the history unspeakable cruelty, beastly extortion and bloodbath. The images range from the Joan of Arc to the Vietnam War, from Bhima's Revenge to Hitler's concentration camps. Seetanath says that in the ancient Egypt, the wonderful pyramids were built on the frozen blood glued with sweat of the thousand labour, and in the ancient Rome, people laughed at the sight of lion tearing human heart with sharp claws. The scrap book is full of images of tragedy of humankind in Alabama cotton filed, Spanish Civil War and Pearl Harbour. Seetanath holds the view that every man is responsible for everything happening around him and every human should take the collective responsibility of the guilt. Sartre nourished the same concept of responsibility which he called 'objective responsibility'. He says in *Being and Nothingness* "There is no innocent victim of war", "we have the war we deserve" (709) and "man is responsible for everything which happens to man" (708). In his play *Loser Wins*, Sartre through Franz's tape recorder addressed the whole humanity to take the responsibility of what has happened, what is happening and what will happen. In *Tringsha Shatabdi* (Thirtieth Century) similar philosophy of 'objective responsibility' can be found. Here Sharat arranges a trial of those who were responsible for the World War II. Almost the entire world is held responsible including the victims of the war. At the end Sharat accuses himself for the war too. Here Sharat like Franz also used the tape recorder to spread the message of responsibility of the human being.

In *That Other History*, Seetanath realized that human history is either the visage of endless cruelty of one over another or the conglomeration of passive gestures commanded by existence; and to him living in this absurd world is an act of passivity too, thus he has committed suicide. He pursuades Sharad to accept his logic and to take the responsibility of every human act. He repeatedly asks Sharad "Why he lives" but Sharad has no answer. Then Seetanath shows that Sharad is living an inauthentic life dipped in world of daily routine. Sharad like Amal Vimal and Kamal in *Evam Indrajit* is imprisoned in the countless self-deceiving gestures like passing the exam, job, marriage, family and children. Seetanath sums up the life of Sharad in the following ways, "There was only one meaning to become man. Study, learn, pass the exam. To stand on one's own feet which means get a job. Which in other words meant that by regularly selling a big chunk of one's self, establish a timely boarding and lodging arrangement" (Act III, 20). Seetanath narrated how he had continued living in the world of "being for others" and "being in itself" (Sartre's term for the states of unconscious being), till the day when he decided to put an end of the absurd of life, Seetanath shows that there is no difference between his own life and Sharad. Here Sircar marvelously shifts the dialogues which Sharad and Vasanti has shared early in the play to Kanak and Seetanath's conversation emphasizing how Sharad was engaged in his meaningless existence like Seetanath. The audiences realize that Seetanath is the alter ego of Sharad. Both are in the deadly vortex of absurdity. While Seetanath revolted against the absurd living by voluntary death, Sharad goes on living in the world of mechanical gestures. Then Seetanath leaves Sharad to realize the other history of human existence. As Seetanath's ghost had faded away, Sharad too decided to commit suicide like Seetanath; but the chance appearance of Vasudev with news of Sharad's promotion saved him. He returns from the valley of the dead with a dreadful knowledge.

> Vasudev: ...Hey, are you OK? You are not going mad or anything are you?
>
> Sharad: Mad? Yes. Vasudev, I will have to be mad. For my job—my promotion. I will have to become mad—there is no other way for me to live. (Act III, 23)

Seetanath gives him the "Tree of Knowledge" which drives him mad like Indrajit. But he realizes that while Seetanath escapes the absurdity of life, he has to fight the nightmare every day from now on.

Here the play explains two different kinds of rebellion—one who escapes the absurdity by suicide and other who believes in futile struggle without having any hope of redemption. In *The Myth of Sisyphus,* Camus has discussed about those two attitudes towards absurdity—first is an emotional response and other is an intellectual rebellion. In *The Myth* Camus says about the first kind,

> You continue making the gestures commanded by existence for many reasons, the first of which is habit. Dying voluntarily implies that you have recognized, even instinctively the ridiculous character of that habit, the absence of any profound reason for living, insane characters of that daily agitation and useless suffering. (13)

Recognizing the evil of human existence Seetanath decides to ridicule absurdity by voluntary death. Frustrated by his desire Seetanath is consumed in the vortex of despair. The terrible stasis of the existence fatigues Seetanath. He wants to escape into the world of oblivion. In the course Seetanath like Caligula, enters into the realm of self-destructive nihilism. Camus calls Caligula and Kirilov's suicide as 'superior- suicide'. Kirilov in *the Possessed* too realized that life is bad dream and by suicide he wants a full control of his own life. He thinks that by suicide he can assert his liberty. By killing himself he wants to be God. But to Camus and Sartre, suicide is the annihilation of all the freedom. Camus has denied the status of metaphysical rebellion to those who destroy the other and destroys self. In *The Rebel* he says,

> Hatred for the creator can turn to hatred of creation or to exclusive and defiant love of what exists. But in both cases it ends in murder and loses the right to be called rebellion.... Apparently there are rebels who want to die and those who want to cause death. But they are identical, consumed with the desire for life, frustrated by their desire and therefore preferring generalized injustice to mutilate justice. (73)

To Camus metaphysical rebellion is not an emotional reaction to absurd but it is an intellectual gesture. Suicide or death is the end of all our suffering and our freedom; it is a submission to life and death to dominate over the individual. Like Camus, Sartre too considers death as a limit to our freedom and death removes all meaning from life and it is the negative side of the nihilism. And suicide is an act of cowardice. To Sartre "Suicide is an absurdity which causes my life to be submerged in absurd" (B&N, 690). For existentialist, death in the form of suicide is the temptation of an illusionary freedom from nihilism. Actually, suicide is an escape from the battle. The redemption lies in the futile struggle with a conscious dissatisfaction and simultaneous rejection. Thus, Sisyphus who is embodiment of metaphysical rebellion never commits suicide.

Here Seetanath like Kirilov wants to escape by rejecting the life. And Camus has criticized Kirilov for this rejection. For him living with awareness and accepting the absurdity is the hallmark of the metaphysical rebellion. Sharad here redeems at the cost of Seetanath. He accidentally escapes death but Sharad's accident implies his positivity which dwells inside himself. He always strives towards life force. In the battle of life and death he continually strives for meaning, value and preciousness of life; he says, "...the history of death cannot become the history of life" (Act III, 20-21). On the other hand, Seetanath aims at Kirilov's instinct, "If living becomes impossible. Die!" (Act III, 20). Seetanath dies but he explains to Sharad the essential contradiction of being alive. Seetanath's logic involves the instinct, while Sharad's accident implies intellect.

Thus *That Other History* is a play of revelation of the other side of the history of human existence. Like Maurice Maeterlinck's *The Blue Bird,* the whole play *That Other History* happens in "the land of memory" of both Sharad and Badal Sircar and in the process both realize the presence of the bullfighter of *Death in the Afternoon* in life and in art.

WORKS CITED

Camus, Albert. *Caligula and Three Other Plays*. Trans. Stuart Gilbert. New York: Vintage Books, 1958.

——. *The Myth of Sisyphus*. Trans. Justine O'Brien. London: Penguin Books, 1975.

——. *The Rebel.* Trans. Anthony Bower. London: Penguin Books, 2000.

Chakraborty, Biplab. *Pessimism and Contemporary Bengali Literature.* Calcutta: Firm KLM, 1985.

Prasad, G.J.V. "The Third Gaze: The Theatre of Badal Sircar". Ed. Lakshmi Subramaniam *Muffled Voices: Women in Modern Indian Theatre*. New Delhi: Har-Anand, 2002.

Sartre, Jean Paul. *Being and Nothingness: A Phenomenological Essay on Ontology*. Trans. Hazel E. Barnes. Washington Square Press: New York, 1972.

Sircar, Badal. *Evam Indrajit*. Trans. Girish Karnad. *Three Modern Indian Plays*. New Delhi: OUP, 1989.

——. *Prabaser Hijibiji* [Scribbling from Abroad]. Kolkata: Lekhani, 2006.

——. *That Other History*, Trans. Vinod L. Doshi. *Enact*. 123-24 (1977): 1-23.

Rashomon. Dir. Akira Kurosawa. Perf. Toshiro Mifune, Machiko Kyo, Takashi Shimura. Janus Films, 1950. Film.

18 Realistic and Expressionistic Techniques in Mahesh Dattani's *Dance Like a Man*

N. Ankanna

I am practicing theatre in an extremely imperfect world where the politics of doing theatre in English looms large over anything else one does. Where writing about the middle class is seen as unfashionable.... I am certain that my plays are a true reflection of my time, place and socio-economic background... in a country that has a myriad challenges to face politically socially, artistically and culturally (Dattani, xiv).

Theatre is not a mute and mechanical representation of social dynamics but it is a lively representation of social dynamics and the voices resounding in context of totality of human experience that consciously or unconsciously affect the existing dynamics of human sensibility. Mahesh Dattani, one of the exponents of modern Indian drama, thematically shows about the areas where the individual feels exhausted. Dattani in the process of engineering the current of Indian drama by bringing it closer to the real life experiences tried to articulate the voice of the oppressed sections of the society whose identity is shrouded in the cover of myths and social prejudices. They have been dragged in darkness, doomed to survive in perpetual silence bearing the oppressive burden of the hegemony of the elitist class.

Drama is the most wide-ranging, the most polyphonic of all the arts: it both represents life and is also a way of seeing it. It can never become a 'private' statement—in the way a novel or a poem can—without ceasing to be meaningful theatre. As a play is staged, a multitude of signs are unleashed for the audience to react to, requiring considerable agility on their part. The performance is forever in flight, and in the wealth of signs and the perceptive capacities of the spectator. Dattani within the framework of dramatic structure tries to investigate the identities of those who occupy no space in social order. The social awareness, social discrimination in the name of religion, humiliation of humanity in the aroma of social pride, irrational acceptance of prejudices, sacrificing the ethical code based on human love, are brought to the stage through the dramatic vision of Dattani. The social conventions often hamper the growth of individual and do not acknowledge the call of human love. The perpetual clash of the commitments of an individual for social order and the force of personal derives makes life intolerable. Dattani with the fine balance of stage and performance imparts an exceptional vehemence to such situations. In the traditional society of India, the identity of gays, lesbians, hijjras and homosexuals has not yet been organized. Dattani dramatizes the crisis of those relationships that are not rigidly demarcated in terms of socially accepted gender constructions. All his works so far—plays, films, screenplays, focus on the marginalized entity. Mahesh Dattani is responsible for successfully launching the Indian theatre in English. The plays of Mahesh Dattani emerged as 'fresh arrival' in the domain of Indian English drama in the last decade of the twentieth century.

Dattani here maps the context of his work. The setting for all of Dattani's plays then is necessarily embedded within the mechanisms of the middle class Indian family, and this is the context from which he operates. Working within his own time and place, and not an alien and distant westernised world, removed from the everyday ground realities with which the urban Indian audience could easily identify, Dattani was already set on a path very different from earlier attempts at staging Indian drama in English. Dattani enunciates, "In drama, one explores the distortions of everyday speech, the weight and flow of everyday movement, and endeavours to bring to them a sense of music" (Dattani, xv). And this reverberates in the everyday, normally spoken English idiom that comes so naturally to him.

Dattani's early plays especially concern themselves with the apparatus of the family that is entrenched within the middle class milieu-of which the playwright self-admittedly is a part and would attempt to 'connect' with audiences drawn from similar backgrounds. His characters situate themselves firmly within the family (and the society) in specific milieus and probe into the nature of their settings. Dattani unambiguously chooses his location within the dynamics of a pre-existing structure of the contemporary urban Indian family which then turns into the site of the ensuing conflict within his narrative. With newer realities piling on the older, 'acceptable' realities, his plots and subplots often work to destroy the very edifice in which they situate themselves, blasting the given stereotypes that shape the structures. He makes use of the available stage space to reveal these structures in concrete terms, and once again, achieves the sense of fractured reality by splitting up his performance spaces in practically all his plays into multi-level, multi-dimensional spaces. His characters move and speak in these spaces with voices that echo and reverberate, to sometimes consolidate and sometimes parody the narrative structures.

Often the issues are veiled or masked, placed behind facades that need to be penetrated, but these are nonetheless issues deep-rooted in a definite space and time and within a stimulating societal context not merely an exercise in self-questioning. Most of his plays are constructed around social issues, though not on any specific 'message'. Dattani maintains the stance of a non-judgmental observer, and never intrudes into the plays he writes nor attempt to sermonize. Instead he invokes that very difficult art and craft of humour. Commenting on his craft, Dattani once said that theatre is a reflection of what you observe. To go beyond that would be to sermonize and would cease to be theatre. However, giving this reflection a clever twist, a slight distortion to get your point across is well in order: "The function of drama, in my opinion, is not merely to reflect the malfunction of society, but to act like freak mirrors in a carnival and to project grotesque images of all that passes for normal in our world. It is ugly, but funny" (Roy, *The Hindu*).

As he says, the audiences must arrive at their own answers, as also together, in terms of a community response, because unlike TV or cinema where the viewer does not have to contribute, theatre is a shared experience:

> Audiences need to make the effort...[in] a moment of truth...people who don't know each other join in from all corners of the darkened hall to applaud and declare their appreciation of that important moment. And that's when you know a play works. (Nair, *The Gentleman*)

Again, Dattani dispenses with the notion that the viewer can treat a play like a 'roller coaster ride', which, even at its most terrifying moment one knows will rapidly and happily end on safe grounds. "It's only when you are left hanging in air you start to question your own personality, perceptions...the theatre is a collective experience and the audience have to finish in their own heads what the playwright began" (Nair, *The Gentleman*). His plays and his ideology fit beautifully into Aristotle's six-point formula—Dattani feels that music and dance are integral parts of a play. He himself has trained in ballet, which introduced him to Western Classical music. He has also learnt bharatanatyam and the story line, the mood, the mythos of *Dance Like a Man* derives from this. This play was written and first performed in Bangalore, in September 1989 to date there have been more than 200 performances of this play all over the country and abroad, many directed by Lillette Dubey, who is one of the directors Dattani trusts. The play was published in 2000.

In the play *Dance Like a Man*, Dattani uses the family home as the setting. The home, its tangible, physical presence becomes crucial to the very existence of three generations of its occupants, often dictating its own terms to their habitation. The meaning of this space however, alters with each generation. Amritlal carries the baggage of his own times and tries to manipulate the next generation—Jairaj and Ratna—to carry it forward. Jairaj and Ratna, ironically, do the same with their own progeny, and try to pass on their preferences to Lata. In this handing down of cultural context, a number of revelations are made and several 'hidden' stories are told that begin to reveal the fissures in these spaces, cracks that widen enough to crumble the entire structure. The structure that Amritlal passes on conditionally to his son causes irreparable harm to him and his marriage to Ratna. They, in their turn, try to transfer their own ambitions to Lata, who, however, proves to be a very different kettle of fish altogether; she is a talented dancer, but is quite happy to marry Vishwas, the rich mithaiwala's son, who for his part is suave and comfortable with his complete ignorance of Bharatanatyam—the passion of the preceding generation.

The narrative looks into the life of Ratna and Jairaj, dancers based in Bangalore, now past their prime, reflecting on the past and the way the past affects their present, and is to affect the future. Dattani here explores two key aspects—the general inhibitions of a man taking up dance, which is usually and 'traditionally' performed by women, as a career and the relationship between a husband and wife who have grown apart and have done enough harm to each other, and their daughter Lata on whom they have thrust their frustrated ambitions. Lata, meanwhile, would marry Vishwas, a man who wants nothing to do with their art and whose father owns half the buildings on Commercial Street and makes mithai. Dattani creates a range of layers in this play, in a language close to everyday speech, and humor that is easily accessible to any viewer, as the human predicament is explored subtly. Music, melos, is integral to this play is about Bharatanatyam. The play functions at two levels, the realistic and the expressionistic.

Moving effortlessly between the past, the present and the future (as past), synchronically dissolving the different time shifts, the play travels back and forth between several generations. Innovatively using Lata and Viswas to play the young Ratna and Jairaj during these shifts and the old Jairaj taking on the role of his father, Amritlal, Dattani displays the sophistication that he has by now acquired as a playwright. Jairaj with his passion for dance is all set to undo the stereotypes that his imperious father, Amritlal, who claims to be a social reformer, carries. An old devdasi teaches Ratna the ancient secrets of her art, further infuriating Amritlal. Contradictions are torturous for Amritlal—the prostitute as an artiste, a man as a dancer, and a long-haired guru with a womanly walk—all of which he counters with money. He makes a pact with Ratna. He will consent to her career in dance only if she helps him pull Jairaj out of his obsession and makes him a 'manly' man. The two can then enjoy the security of his riches. The play focuses on the merits of multiplicity, transcending mere 'tolerance' to recognition and empathy, while situating itself historically within the context of the materialistic, acquisitive society of the 1990s. Typically, Dattani poses a few uncomfortable questions —the sexual construct that a man is, and the pigeonholing of masculinity within a Hindu undivided family—are set against the idea of the creative artist searching for artistic fulfillment within the claustrophobic constraints of the world that he inhabits.

The preoccupation with 'fringe' issues forms an important element in Dattani's work—issues that remain latent and suppressed, or are pushed to the periphery, come to occupy centre stage—quite literally. With Dattani, this becomes the only way to actually push these 'invisible' issues forward, to create at least an acknowledgement of their existence.

> ...you can talk about feminism, because in a way that is accepted. But you can't talk about gay issues because that's not Indian, [that] doesn't happen here. You can't talk about a middle-class housewife fantasizing about having sex with a cook or actually having a sex life—that isn't Indian either—that's confrontational even if it is Indian. (Mee, 24-25)

Much of 'mainstream' society, Dattani believes, lives in a state of 'forced harmony', out of a sense of helplessness, or out of a lack of alternatives. Simply for lack of choice, they conform to stereotypes like 'homosexuals' that in some sense leads to a kind of ghettoisation within society, little spaces to which the marginalized are pushed. The way in which this is tackled, the struggle to be heard and seen are the stuff of the plays. In terms of gender, Dattani's focus somewhat shifts its perspective:

> Gender is a major part of it [...] it has to do with my own comfort with both the feminine and the masculine

> self in me [...] the masculine self is very content; it doesn't need to express itself. But the feminine self seems to seek expression [...]. (Katyal, *Seagull Theatre Quarterly*)

Only the marginalized that are actually affected can even begin to question the state of affairs. Hence many of Dattani's characters push forward this agenda, touching upon a host of taboo topics and placing it at the forefront for public discussion. But the playwright himself declines the tag of an activist/reformer and instead chooses to top off even the contentious issues in the plays with heavy doses of humour. Having studied in missionary schools with emphasis on the 'canonical' literary texts, Dattani makes a significant joke:

> All the great writers were English or at least Anglo Irish. Shakespeare, Yeats, Whitman (I don't think it occurred to any of my teachers that the great writers they eulogized with missionary zeal were either gay or bisexual or considered completely immoral in their times! (Ayyar, *Gay Today*)

Dance Like a Man is a play that deals with one of Dattani's pet concerns—gender—through one of his principal passions, dance. The automatic assumption, when one refers to gender as a principal concern, is that the exploration would be of women's issues. He wrote of this play: "I wrote the play when I was learning Bharatanatyam in my mid twenties [...] a play about a young man wanting to be a dancer, growing up in a world that believes dance is for women..." (Ayyar, *Gay Today*). Characteristically, Dattani raises a few unlikely questions about the sexual construct that a man is. The stereotypes of gender roles are pitted against the idea of the artist in search of creativity within the restrictive constriction of the world that he is forced to inhabit. Jairaj with his obsession for dance is all set to demolish these stereotypes. This is the twist that the playwright gives to the stereotypes associated with 'gender' issues that view solely women at the receiving end of the oppressive power structures of patriarchal society. The play dispels this notion and explores the nature of the tyranny that even men might be subject to within such structures. Jairaj and Ratna live within such a structure: the domain of the patriarch Amritlal, Jairaj's father. His antipathy to a great many things that concern the activities of his son and daughter-in-law draws the boundary lines for their behaviour within his sphere of influence. Dance for him is the prostitute's profession, improper for his daughter-in-law, and absolutely unimaginable for his son. He forbids Ratna from visiting the old devdasi who teaches her the intricacies of Bharatanatyam; he cannot tolerate the sounds of the dancing bells that ring through their practice sessions; is aghast at the long-haired guru with an effeminate walk and cannot, most of all, stomach the idea of his son—a man—becoming a professional dancer. The underlying fear is obviously that dance would make him 'womanly'—an effeminate man—the suggestion of homosexuality hovers near, although never explicitly mentioned. And hence Amritlal must oppose, tooth and nail, Jairaj's passion for dance. He makes a pact with Ratna. He will consent to her career in dance only if she helps him pull Jairaj out of his obsession and make him a 'manly' man. The two can then enjoy the security of his riches.

Through the seamless movement in time and space, Dattani weaves in the intricate web of gender relationships and the givens of societal norm spanning three generations: The minimal use of characters maximizes the staged impact of the stereotypes through time. Amritlal and the old Jairaj; Vishwas and the young Jairaj; Lata and the young Ratna are to be played by the same actor. As they shed/put on different characters, the resonating sense of time and change illuminate and give newer meanings to the issues that Dattani raises. Amritlal, the frustrated patriarch changes into the equally frustrated and alcoholic Jairaj who interviews Vishwas, the prospective groom for his daughter. Meanwhile, Vishwas, the son of a rich mithaiwala, an alien to the world of dance, transforms into the young Jairaj who is consumed by his love for the art form. Lata, the most pragmatic and level-headed of the characters also plays the insecure, calculating and scheming young Ratna who has to survive despite the few choices that are offered to her. She will be haunted as the older Ratna by the ghosts of the past that nonetheless do not daunt her determination to realize her own unfulfilled ambitions through Lata, her daughter (and, as the audience would identify-herself). Like the characters, the stage iconography too helps to consolidate and reinforce these strong reverberations. Amritlal's house moves through time, changes character along with its owner. The old cupboard, the shawl, the rose garden and the rest of the stage set all leave their impact in the juxtaposition of the stereotypes.

The tragedy for Jairaj is that he has chosen to pursue a career that is considered 'right' only for women. That is why Amritlal is willing to have Ratna as the dancer and not Jairaj. Amidst these resonances is played out the angst of Jairaj and Ratna who are obviously holding back a deep, dark secret, which will be revealed towards the end of the play. Like in all battles, a completely innocent individual becomes the victim: the baby son of the dancing couple. Dattani refuses to assign the blame or the status of the 'wronged' party to any one: "I refuse to have protagonists in a fixed role as victim. If you have a victim, it implies that there is a persecutor and it also implies that you will eventually have a rescuer" (Ayyar, *Gay Today*). Ratna is not, as many would suggest, depending upon the interpretation of the production, the negative presence in the play. Dattani has often been taken to task (mostly by Indian critics) for being a 'woman hater' of sorts because,

> [My] women protagonists fight, scheme and get a piece of the action albeit at great personal cost. These are seen as 'negative' qualities, sadly by some women too [...] but really we have yet to see feminism find expression in Indian society. (Ayyar, *Gay Today*)

Jairaj, being present in the house when the double dose of opium is inadvertently administered to the baby is equally culpable and shares the onus of the blame, something Dattani never tries to shift to Ratna. However, it is perhaps this death that binds the two together in shared tragedy. The last lines of the play reverberate—"We were only human. We lacked the grace. We lacked the brilliance. We lacked the magic to dance like God" (Dattani, 447). The basic premise with which one would go to see English language theatre in India would be that this theatre is necessarily exclusivist, with a tendency towards 'elitism'. This was the case, until Dattani's foray into the scene changed the entire situation, homogenizing the audience with his theatre, and his theatre with the tastes of his audience. Like his repeated assertion that despite the fact that he is himself rooted in the Gujarati milieu, where his own familial context is concerned, because the family itself was displaced and resettled in Bangalore, he had to constantly search, as it were, for this sense of identity in a place where the linguistic community was alien to his own. English education, and the constant need to use this third language as the vehicle of communication, then somehow made itself an integral part of his own identity. Hence, the 'natural' ease born out of necessity and the sheer habit with which Dattani uses his chosen tongue, being comfortable in no other. In creating and locating the self and constructing the identities of the characters who people his theatre, Dattani seems to contribute to the matrix of the processes that Erin Mee refers to as "a way of decolonizing the theatre" without, however, resorting to "a politically driven search for an indigenous aesthetic and dramaturgy" (Mee, i), that motivated the writers of the Theatre of Roots movement. Using the dramatic tools left over from the colonial era such as the proscenium stage and other paraphernalia along with the language itself, which, he declares is an English developed in India, a "hybrid language that is spoken in a unique, uninhibited manner" (Vardhan), Dattani begins to simultaneously subvert the borrowed structures with his almost subconscious use of accents, clothes, music, cultural moorings and beliefs specific to the context of his plays. The emerging drama is rooted profoundly in the location where the playwright chooses to implant it. And it is from this location that the issues are explored.

> I really feel that people have to come to terms with the fact that English is an Indian language. Just as it is American or Canadian or Australian. We should celebrate the fact that India has this enormous capacity to absorb from all sources. (Nair, *The Gentleman*)

This was the mechanism that helped the Indians survive colonisation, unlike the American Indians. "We may claim to be rigid and pure, but we are the most flexible and impure of all races! The sooner we come to terms with that, we can get on with the rest" (Nair, *The Gentleman*). As Dattani chooses to deal with themes relating to the complex workings of the modern/urban Indian family, his protagonists search for their identities within the often oppressive structures of custom, tradition, gender, and sexuality within this location. In a dramaturgical sense, these structures and identities often become enmeshed in Dattani's use of the split stage, with the interior movement of the plays collapsing with the exterior, fragmented locations.

Much of his work is built around a social issue that in a sense helps to locate the moorings of his characters within the religious/national identities embedded within the individual/familial identities, "I am not interested in characters asking existential questions in a limbo. My characters exist in a definite space and time, in a social context that's what stimulates me. I don't focus on a message but the context is important" (Santhanam). It this context that is enmeshed throughout his work that evokes a distinctive sense of place, of location and identity, that is nonetheless never a fixed or rigid concept, but is forever making and unmaking itself. But while history and cultural components are important in the construction of identity in his plays, equally important are the underlying, often repressed parts of the self that are allowed out of the closet to add the hitherto peripheral dimensions to his characters, as also to the context which reshapes itself. His plays reinforce the experiences and narratives of the marginalized in a society where stereotypes always hold center stage; ridden with prejudice, guilt, and dishonesty, survival is not easy for the 'misfits'. These are some concerns that go into the exposition, exploration and refashioning of the self and the society in Dattani's works.

'Postcolonial India, having undergone a long-drawn-out period of linguistic bewilderment and cultural recoil after independence, remained undecided on whether to revert to the vernacular or continue to develop anglophonic literature and theatre, but with a different focus and indeed, a new identity. Dealing with a colonial hangover, it was some time before local accents could become amalgamated into stage productions but not without a measure of self-conscious embarrassment. It required some truly confident and self-assured playwrights and directors to make this phenomenon a workable reality in terms of the English language theatre in India, reflecting local realities. This sense of local colour in *Dance Like a Man* predominates in the numerous productions of the play, thus, becoming an important subtext. The strong flavour of a Bharatanatyam household, the opulent saris, the sounds in the background often accompanied by background Carnatic music together build up the intense sense of space that is integral to the shaping of the characters.

Exploring and juxtaposing the contemporaneous and the early history of India in personal terms, the play probes into three generations of conflict. Pitted against the background of classical dance and drawing upon centuries—old traditions, to stage such a play in English is hardly a mean achievement. Having done that, Dattani goes a few steps further to work out a critique of the social mores and attitudes within which his characters evolve and situate themselves. In the materialistic society of contemporary India, Dattani in his typical style, raises important questions on the very constituents of a man's identity —in terms of sexuality, as the head of the family and as an artist. The play reflects on the self and the significance of the other, through the frameworks of gender and gender roles: the prostitute as a dancer and an artist; the man as a dancer; the guru who sports long hair and has an 'effeminate' walk—categories that the older generation, fed on its perception of the self cannot come to terms with. This clash brings about the play of property and money in deciding and manipulating the construction of identities that would conform, but the result is tragic. Perhaps, the resolution is suggested in the third generation, where the earlier sets of categories collapse and Lata is seen as a successful dancer and a mother, happily married to Vishwas, the son of a rich mithaiwala.

> Dattani once stated, I see myself as a craftsman and not as a writer. To me, being a playwright is about seeing myself as a part of the, process of a production. I write

plays for the sheer pleasure of communicating through this dynamic medium. (Nair, *The Gentleman*)

This is the whole point in the distinction between a playwright and a 'writer' using any other mode. The entire exercise of putting on paper the script of a play is only one of the many necessary ingredients in the genesis of a play, in the birth of drama. It is, perhaps, the beginning, but merely one element in the complete theatrical experience. Two distinct phenomena, though inter-related, can be seen here: the written text and the performance, the concepts of the stage and the page. The genre of dramatic literature has certain embodied peculiarities. The texts of plays can be read, as distinct from being seen and heard in performance. The term dramatic literature implies a contradiction in that 'literature' originally meant something written and 'drama' meant something performed. Many of the problems in the study of dramatic literature stem from this paradox. Even though a play may be appreciated solely for its qualities as writing, one must remain alert to the volatility of the play as a whole. From the inception of a play in the mind of its author to the image of it that an audience takes away from the theatre, many hands and many physical elements help to bring it to life. It is this phenomenological 'livedness' that seems to lie at the core of the problem that we presently struggle with.

Theatre is perhaps not essentially a *literary* art, though it is mostly taught thus in universities and schools. It is often assumed that reading the text of a play can assimilate the theatrical experience. In part, this is a result of the influence of theatrical critics, who, as writers, tend to have a literary orientation. While reviewers in the popular papers may give greater credence to such elements as acting and dancing, critics in the more serious journals are interested in textual/thematic/structural values. Then is drama a literary type at all? Various theorists have often called this to question, because without the necessary reference to the extra-literary institution of the theatre, it would be seen to lack the very vehicle of its reception.

Since drama is such a complex process of communication, its study and evaluation is as uncertain as it is mercurial. All plays depend upon a general agreement by all participants—author, actors, and audience—to accept the operation of theatre and the conventions associated with it, just as players and spectators accept the rules of a game. The script of a play is the basic element of theatrical performance. In the case of many 'masterpieces' it is the most important element. But even these dramatic masterpieces demand the creative co-operation of artists other than the author. The dramatic script, like an operatic score or the scenario of a ballet, is no more than the raw material from which the performance is created. The actors, rather than merely reflecting a creation that has already been fully expressed in the script, give body, voice, and imagination to what was only a shadowy indication in the text. The text of a play is as vague and incomplete in relation to a fully realized performance as is a musical score to a concert. It is in a performance that the text reveals its meanings and intentions through skillful acting in an environment designed with the appropriate measure of visual drama. It is only when the script of a play assumes a disciplinary control over the dramatic experience itself that the student of drama gains measurable evidence of what was intended to constitute the play and dramatic literature is discussed as such. In fact, the distinctive factor in Dattani's case was that he started out as an actor and dancer, but went on to become a writer because there were no plays in English on contemporary Indian issues. "I'm a reluctant playwright. I would choose to direct first before I write. But I wanted more plays written primarily in the English language for Indian audiences" (Katyal, *Seagull Theatre Quarterly*). It is interesting to note that there are hardly any playwrights who have actually begun with roots in the theatre or have come into play writing from acting and directing. As Dattani says, "I think that's the tragedy. I think that's what they lose out on. They have to have a theatre background. ...you should begin by getting involved in a production. Because there's nothing like that experience" (Katyal, *Seagull Theatre Quarterly*). And the notion of group work is vital in theatre for the director who is putting together the show. Then where does the playwright come in? "If you look at my plays, you would find that each character, every character has, you know, his or her space in the play, which an actor can develop." He explains that the playwright has to realize that he is not writing to be read and that the actors are going to take away the script and do other things with it. Beginning precisely from basic entries and exits, to the justification of a character's presence on stage, these are things that may be found wanting in the work of playwrights who do not have a background in theatre. In another interview (parts of which I have already quoted in another context), Dattani responds to a few important questions—Does the actor in him battle with the playwright who battles with the director? Does he find himself making compromises torn between the three roles? The actor, the playwright and the director, he says, are all necessary for each other in a production as in the process of gardening; where a whole is made of many parts and affected equally by the conditions that would determine a garden's verdure and beauty. Rather than write to pander to what he calls 'vanity actors', Dattani would write for an actor in 'the true sense of the word'. No theatre is possible without an actor or without an audience.

> Everything is geared towards 'rasa'. Which is why I always direct the first production of any play I write. That enables me to put in more stage instructions, which go on to become a kind of blue print for other directors. That way, there is no conflict. (Nair, *The Gentleman*)

Having quickly traversed some of the stage/page problematics, and also how Dattani himself deals with them would be in order to look at a few of his plays that actually take into account the art and the craft of writing a play, and of staging it. The fact that Dattani is intrinsically a theatre person, rather than a writer, is evident in the way he is able to structure the stage mechanism effectively and how he, at times, allows the texts to speak for themselves, and look at their own workings and methodology. He employs a language that is often pungent, clear and sharp, pushing the spoken word to its limits, and interspersing them with pregnant silences that only someone with an intimate inwardness with theatre can. Dattani, from his years of being a "reluctant" playwright to a highly successful (and celebrated) one, has carried on the business, as he says, "of holding a mirror up to society" (Dattani, xv) through an art that is both entertaining as well as issue-based; self-aware and rooted in its milieu.

From the time he began his career on the stage in Bangalore the city where he had grown up, enjoying, as a child the spectacle of the Gujarati theatre that sometimes travelled there—to doing English theatre that was mostly derivative in nature, and finally to becoming one of the leading and most performed playwrights of the country, actor-director Mahesh Dattani has come a long way. While he admits to being a 'reluctant' playwright, perhaps the seeds of his success lay in this very reluctance: he needed English plays to perform, and they were unavailable. So he wrote them not as a writer writing a self-consciously 'literary' work like a novel or a poem—but as a performer amalgamating the 'extra-literary' polyphony of the stage in his writing and keeping audience reception in his mind. That has perhaps made all the difference to the manner in which Dattani has managed so fluently to communicate with such audiences as well as the reason, ultimately, for the 'literary' quality of his output.

Dance Like a Man also begins with a directly personal relevance (Dattani's career in dance) and goes on to become a resonant work on contemporary society as it moves back and forth in time, spanning three generations. The important aspect in this play, as in all of his plays, is the emphatic 'staginess'—the self-conscious theatricality that is deliberately worked into the writing. It would never be enough to read the playtext—its peculiarities may only be realized through the mechanism of the stage. As Michael Walling points out, "His plays fuse the physical and spatial awareness of the Indian theatre with the textual rigour of Western models like Ibsen and Tennessee Williams. It's a potent combination, which shocks and disturbs through its accuracy and its ability to approach a subject from multiple perspectives" (Walling, 229). The play ends with these words, words from the heart, words bound to stir the soul of the audience,

> We are only human. We lacked grace. We lacked the brilliance. We lacked the magic to dance like God. (Dattani, 340)

In terms of pedagogy there has hardly been much interest in the work of Indians who write drama in English, and few universities that include a paper on Indian writing in English in mainstream 'English literature' courses would also include in its ambit, 'Indian English Drama' as they would the genres of poetry and fiction. Although things are changing, as they stand, there is a lot of room for change and indeed, universities must open up to the idea of an English theatre based in India as a *bona fide* literary genre. This is an imperfect world for these purposes, and to quote Dattani again, a world,

> Where if I wrote about the working classes, I am told, I would gain international recognition (but if I were, in fact a working class person, no middle-class critic or theatre practitioner would give me the time of day.... Where there is no real professional theatre.... Where I am met with open hostility in parochial Universities. Where in literary circles, I am seen as inferior because I am a playwright.... (Dattani, xiv-xv)

It is against such a backdrop that one is to evaluate the achievements of Mahesh Dattani. Man of multiple roles, he has always managed to make his audiences sit up and listen, and listen with such involvement that they even begin to forget that they are in fact, watching a play in an 'alien' tongue. He could, in a sense be seen as one of the strands that carry forward the traditions of Indian theatre through the necessary dynamic of change and innovation. Not having to repeatedly revisit his roots, he works instinctively and meticulously, anchored to the contemporaneous urban realities, collaborating with artists to put up his shows, pushing the frontiers of his art, and nudging his audiences into acknowledging it.

WORKS CITED

Ayyar, Raj. "Mahesh Dattani: India's Gay Cinema Comes of Age". *Gay Today*. 8. 48, 2004. http://gaytoday.com.

Dattani, Mahesh. *Collected Plays*, New Delhi: Penguin Books, 2000.

Katyal, Anjum. "Of Page and Stage: An Interview with Mahesh Dattani". *Seagull Theatre Quarterly*. 24. January 2000. http://www.seagullindia.com.

Mee, Erin B. *Drama Contemporary: India*, New Delhi: OUP, 2002.

Nair, Anita. "An Unvieling of a playwright in three Acts". *The Gentleman*. May 2001. http://www.anitanair.net.

Roy, Elizabeth. "Freak Mirrors and Grotesque Images". *The Hindu*. 15 March 2002. http://www.hinduonnet.com.

Santhanam, Anitha. "It's the silence that affects me most". 2001. http://www.maheshdattani.com.

Vardhan, Manisha. "I'm No Crusader: I'm a Theatre Person: Mahesh Dattani". June 2004. http://www.3to6.com.

Walling, Michael. "A Note on the Play" in Mahesh Dattani, *Collected Plays*, New Delhi: Penguin Books, 2000.

19

Family Facades and Mocking Marriages: A Reading of Dattani's Plays

Dibyabibha Roy

Mahesh Dattani's workmanship puts an end to the social stereotypes of patriarchy and consumerist attitude towards women. Sexuality has always been the focal point of study in his plays. However one can read between the lines of his plays and decipher the issues of family and marriage, the two sociological structures which are the basis of a civilized society. Dattani makes and breaks the social stigmas of conventional Indian families and marriages, attacking the hypermasculinist rhetoric of Indian society. Let me begin with an observation of John McRae, who writes about the play *On A Muggy Night in Mumbai*:

> The intrusive wedding music [in the play] becomes the accompaniment to a dance of death indoors—and the audience must go through the classic cathartic emotions of terror and pity as the characters' masks fall, their emotions unravel, and their lives disintegrate. For the fault is not just the characters'—it is everyone's, in a society which not only condones but encourages hypocrisy, which demands deceit and negation, rather than allowing self-expression, responsibility and dignity. (McRae, 46)

It is clear by now that Dattani writes about a society 'which ...encourages hypocrisy' and curbs the freedom of the individual by not allowing self-expression. Hence, he starts his job by choosing the very foundation of the society where socialization occurs from childhood: the family. His characters belong to the family and within the family they disrupt the norms and voice out the alternative ways, the ways which have never been brought into the light and he leaves the audience to arrive at their own answers as they share a common experience together. He says, "Audiences need to make the effort...[in] a moment of truth...people who don't know each other join in from all corners of the darkened hall to applaud and declare their appreciation of that important moment. And that's when you know a play works" (Nair). It is the grotesque picture of the hidden truth that Dattani brings out in his plays and that is the reason for the success of his plays as well as a triumph of Indian English drama.

Dattani chooses his location within the dynamics of a pre-existing structure of the contemporary urban Indian family which then turns into the site of the ensuing conflict. It is this family where lies the locus of his narrative. His plays "concern themselves with the apparatus of the family that is entrenched within the middle class milieu—of which the playwright self-admittedly is a part—and would attempt to 'connect' with audiences drawn from similar backgrounds" (Chaudhari, 24-25). Gitanjali Prasad observes on Indian family:

> If we look at the family in India a little more closely, however, it is clear that making generalizations about the family in our country is perhaps more difficult than it is elsewhere. We do not have a uniform civil code with regard to family-related legislation such as marriage, divorce, inheritance and adoption...indeed, if we look at the country as a geographical entity, we see both matriarchal systems and patriarchal systems. In addition, attitudes and practices vary in cities and rural areas, amongst the rich and the poor and also amongst the English-speaking elite and those from a more traditional milieu. (Prasad, 9)

Thus Indian family is a matrix of tradition and modernity and Dattani's concern is undoubtedly with the 'English-speaking' urban middle-class family which is his known forte. The values that a family generates are thought to be the foundation of a state as well as nation. The picture of a traditional joint family has always been projected as the source of pleasure and perfection. Even today, when we look at the television serials we are given a prolific view of a joint family, of course with its vices too, but the central idea remains that one can implement one's full potential only in such a family. Dattani remains non-judgmental in his assertion of any particular order. Instead, what he does is to achieve a mean: his families have a patriarchal head, his children and their wives or husbands. Therefore, on the one hand he takes up few strands of the traditional family and on the other, makes them come in conflict with the modern sensibilities. What gains significance in the ensuing discourse therefore, is the obvious question of marriages and the social stigmas attached to the institution of marriage.

In the Rig Vedic age the family was the source and the foundation of the political and social structure. The members of the house lived together in one house and the home provided for the all-round development of the individual. The family was patrilineal, with a few exceptions, and the master of the house, *grihapati* or *dampati*, was a benevolent, kind and affectionate man. A man usually married one wife and the wedding that took place in the bride's home was accompanied by prayers of the relatives who wished for "an abundance of sons, but daughters were treated kindly" (Prasad, 5). The point I'm trying to make here is that the family has always been under the control of the eldest male member and the women had to be subservient to the needs of the men in the family to an extent as can be seen below:

> A girl, a young woman, or even an old woman should not do anything independently, even in (her own) house. In childhood a woman should be under her father's control, in youth under her husband's, and when her husband is dead, under her son's. She should not have independence. A woman should not try to separate herself from her father, her husband, or her sons, for her separation from them would make both (her own and her husband's) families temptible. She should always be cheerful, and clever at household affairs;... When her father, or brother with her father's permission, gives her to someone, she should obey that man when he is alive and not violate her vow to him when he is dead. (Doniger and Smith, 115)

But Arpa Ghosh observes a different reason for the subservience of the women. She says that all housewives are not the victims of male torture but "economic dependence of the wife on husband and addiction to the soft life that a rich husband's money provides are definitely tools of oppression that women hand over to men" (Ghosh, 190). However the paradox here is that a society which expects women to be at the beck and call of the men in their lives, have to be 'cheerful and clever at household affairs' for the smooth functioning of the family. Dattani's plays apparently conform to this stereotypical idea of the men at the helm of familial power and in the plays like *Bravely Fought the Queen*, *Do the Needful*, *Seven Steps Around the Fire*, *Dance Like a Man, Where There is a Will* and *Tara*, we find the patriarchal voices at their gendered best.

Dattani concerns himself with the projection of a traditional joint family scenario in the 'lavish house' of Hasmukh Mehta in *Where There is a Will.* The play begins with the three main characters, Hasmukh Patel, Sonal, his wife and Ajit, their son. A little later his wife Preeti, who is pregnant, enters into the living room making it a family portrait that shows that everything is in its place. But as the plot develops, the picture-perfect family of the self-made industrialist Hasmukh Mehta shatters down bringing out the "humour of the play [which] is sheathed in layers of Ibsenesque black comedy with asphyxiated overtones that are Dattani's main tools" (Chaudhari, 28). In this play, as in *Dance Like a Man*, the 'traditional' family values "clash with the unexpected twists in the tale that completely subvert existing stereotypes" (Chaudhari, 28). The ways in which a man's desire to make everyone in the family subservient to his whims and wishes comes true when we come across Mehta's attitude and behaviour toward his family members in *Where There is a Will*, to an extent that he can say: "Please let him (Ajit) drop dead" (*CP*, 455), he despises everyone in his family yet they must all stay yoked together for sailing smoothly. The fact however remains that the wife remains a slave to her husband in a monogamous marriage whereas the husband can seek pleasures outside. Engels finds marriages to be conditioned by the class positions of the parties becoming an instrument of convenience, and observes:

> ...marriage of convenience turns often enough into crassest prostitution—sometimes of both partners, but far more commonly of the woman, who only differs from the ordinary courtesan in that she does not let out her body on piece-work as a wage-worker, but sells it once and for all into slavery. (Engels)

He goes on to explain the cause of the supremacy of the males in the family:

> In the great majority of cases today, at least in the possessing classes, the husband is obliged to earn a living and support his family, and that in itself gives him a position of supremacy, without any need for special legal titles and privileges. Within the family he is the bourgeois and the wife represents the proletariat. (Engels)

Here lies the basic role of the *grihapati* or *dampati* in the family, as Hasmukh Mehta represents in the play as does Amritlal in *Dance Like a Man* or Nitin and Jiten in *Bravely Fought the Queen*. Hasmukh tries his best to keep his family under control, but as Ajit vehemently opposes his father, Hasmukh finds it difficult to tolerate his own son because he could never make him in his own image for the "child is a continuation of man's ego, and his [the father's] affection for the child is a form of egoism" (Russell, 24). Whereas, Jiten who had inflicted physical pains on his wife Dolly bears resemblance to his deceased father's nature who had victimized Baa (his mother) in the past, and in her state of agony she says to him, "Jitu is just like his father. Just like him" (*CP*, 284). Family values in these plays are continuously subverted and if Baa is the matriarch in the absence of her husband, she has long imbibed the staunch vigour of a patriarch, to an extent that she can tell her son to beat his wife: "Jitu, hit her [Dolly] on the face but not on the.... On the face, only on the face!" (*CP*, 311), and the true faces of the characters are unmasked to the readers/audience who have to realize that happy families today are utopian. Hasmukh and Sonal, Ajit and Preeti, Jiten and

Dolly, Nitin and Alka, Jairaj and Ratna, Suresh and Uma and Deepali and Kamlesh, the couples in Dattani's plays are victims of family that have chained their development as individuals. Commenting on Hasmukh and Sonal, Chaudhari writes:

> The colourless relationships between the two couples that comprise the family are developed in elaborate vignettes; portraying two singularly unexciting generations of couples, sexually insipid and loveless, who remain in a typically materialistic and money-oriented upper middle-class milieu. (Chaudhari, 30)

The families that we see in these plays are thus dysfunctional ones. The husbands and the wives are 'separated by some dark secrets' which are slowly untied in the progress of the plays. Dattani's choice regarding the marriages is significant. In *Tara*, he brings into the foray the diversity of Indian marriages by making Bharati a Kannadiga and Patel a Gujrati. On the one hand where he celebrates the unity in diversity, on the other, he draws upon the fissures that Indian society has always ignored.

Dattani enters the arena of another sociological structure, perhaps one of the most significant aspects in his plays, is his handling of the marriage issues. *Seven Steps Around the Fire* looks at the hijra community, the eunuchs, who have always led a marginalized existence in the society. They have always been looked down upon as they fail to belong to either of the biological sexes. However, the society steeped in prejudices and superstitions grace their presence on the significant occasions. Uma, in her voice over in the play says,

> The two events in mainstream Hindu culture where their [the eunuchs] presence is acceptable—marriage and birth—ironically are the very same privileges denied to them by man and nature. Not for them the seven rounds witnessed by the fire god, eternally binding man and woman in matrimony, or the blessings of 'May you be the mother of a hundred sons.' (*CP*, 11)

The play is a murder mystery where as the truth unfolds, we come in a direct conflict with our stereotyped ideologies and find how the playwright makes a mockery of the societal institutions that are regarded highly in our culture. Uma, the daughter of the vice chancellor of Bangalore University is married to Chief Superintendent Suresh Rao. Uma is a postgraduate student of Sociology and in her search for her research materials she gets entangled in a mesh in the world of the hijras, and slowly uncovers one of the bitterest truths of the society, which have been suppressed by those in power. In the play Dattani has tried to articulate the voice of the oppressed sections of the society whose identity is shrouded in the cover of myths and social prejudices. They have been dragged in darkness, doomed to survive in perpetual silence bearing the oppressive burden of hegemony of the elitist class. Uma, the educated protagonist comes face to face with the hypocrisy of the political family in power and in the process we, the readers come face to face with another stark reality of the society. In the play, Dattani deviates from the current of feminism or masculinism and he ventures to explore the marginalized sections of society striving against the irresistible forces of social apathy. The plot focuses around the act of murder of Kamala, a eunuch. Her absence in the play, like Kanhaiya's in *Bravely Fought the Queen*, lurks out large on the minds of the readers, as Arpa Ghosh observes, almost akin to the ghost of Banquo in *Macbeth*. Uma is motivated to investigate into the murder case and in the process unveils the mystery that actually wears off the hidden masks of the society regarding marriages. Interestingly, the play begins with the chanting of wedding mantras that mimic the entire institution called marriage: "Sanskrit mantras fade in, the ones chanted during a Hindu wedding. Fire. The sound of the fire grows louder, drowning the mantras. A scream. The flames engulf the scream" (*CP*, 7). Uma enters the police station and meets Munuswamy, the man in charge and seek out to interrogate Anarkali, another eunuch and the chief suspect of the murder. Munuswamy exercises his absolute authority over Anarkali, who is deliberately addressed with the neuter gender third person pronoun "it" by him. In the process, Uma gets close with Anarkali, who confides in her and declares that she had not killed Kamala. The antipathy of Munuswamy towards Anarkali is the voice of the social system that refuses to acknowledge the third sex, which does not conform to the normative genders. Although the play slowly opens up a new discourse on the 'voice' of the hijra community as the subalterns, but the dénouement which is an astute pessimistic one, asserts that perhaps the marginalized third sex, can never have a healthy life of their own in the play. Leela Gandhi observes,

> 'subaltern studies' defined itself as an attempt to allow the 'people' finally to speak within the jealous pages of elitist historiography and, in doing so, to speak for, or to sound the muted voice of, the truly oppressed. (Gandhi, 2)

Dattani makes the oppression significant by revealing that Kamala, the eunuch was married to Subbu, the son of the politician and therefore the entire incident of murder was contrived by Subbu's powerful father who could never acknowledge the union of the two. Written for the radio, the play is perhaps the shortest play in Dattani's oeuvre, but it places two basic arguments and in doing so the playwright succeeds in his attempt to denounce societal reservations. The play therefore demonstrates the inability of the society to go beyond the sex defined roles of the eunuch community and also their incapability to share human emotions and build relationships. Dattani brings out a mockery of the heterosexual marriage in the union of Kamala and Subbu, but Subbu's suicide in the end, is an implied acceptance by the playwright who is not able to break free from the shackles of societal chains. In the process, he too becomes a victim of the normative rules which he himself has tried to break. The play ends with an emphatic address by Uma:

> They knew. Anarkali, Champa and all the hijra people knew who was behind the killing of Kamala. They have no voice. The case was hushed up and not even reported to the newspapers. Champa was right. The police made no arrests. Subbu's suicide was written off as an accident. The photograph was destroyed. So were the lives of the two young people. (*CP*, 42)

The play thus undermines the sanctity of the sacred institution of marriage. In the background of the Sanskrit mantras and the fire signifying the man-woman bonding with the seven steps around among the Hindus, lay bare the fault-lines that legalize the custom of marriage. Dattani not only questions the validity of such an institution but also shows how the marginalized transgender people are the victims of the Repressive State Apparatus. Miruana George thus concludes:

> The postmodern art breaks through the stereotypes, questioning the refusal to recognize the differences and the unrepresented. Norms and rules are challenged, as irregularities are exposed. The anomaly with regard to what is projected as ideal and the disruption in practice points at a fragmented cultural setup. This failure is addressed to foreground the subaltern to voice the suppressed facts and sidelined communities. (*George*, 149)

Marriages in ancient India were classified into eight divisions by historians and we also find a detailed analysis of the marriages in *Manusmriti*. These eight forms of marriages are: *Brahma*, *Daiva*, *Arsha*, *Prajaptya*, *Gandharva*, *Asura*, *Rakshasa* and *Paishacha*. The literary history of India provides numerous examples of the various forms of marriages in Hinduism and although the myth that homosexuality was imported from medieval West Asia or from modern Euro-America still resides but the modern literary history of India still remains silent on the handling of such issues. It is here that Dattani brings out the marriages of the same sex in light and opulently discards the heterosexual marriages. Marriages are mainly due to the process of procreation and it is needless to mention that the males were always under the supervision of the family heads to marry with or without knowing their consent and while women bear heavier burden in marriages because of their subordination, men are equally weighed down by these burdens. Ruth Vanita mentions,

> Married off early, often against their will, Indian men, in traditional families even today, are expected to provide not only for wife and children but also for their parents, younger siblings and dependent relatives, including

> widowed, orphaned, and disabled aunts, uncles, cousins, nephews, and nieces. This kind of household is the one described in many medieval texts. The ideal man is supposed to uncomplainingly sacrifice his own interests to the upkeep of his entire extended family. (Vanita, 73)

Thus, we find Kamlesh, Sharad, Bunny, Ranjeet and Deepali, all homosexuals in the play *On a Muggy Night in Mumbai,* in their own way setting up their lifestyles, either visible to or invisible from the eyes of the society but carving out a private domain for themselves. Dattani is a master craftsman and he does not make these characters married couples but in bringing out their sexual orientations, he subverts the heterosexual marriage systems prevalent in the Indian society. Kamlesh has had a relationship with Prakash, a man whom we later see as Ed, fiancé of Kiran, Kamlesh's sister. To forget the pangs of separation from Prakash, Kamlesh had revived a relationship with Sharad, but in vain. Kamlesh, a fashion designer in Mumbai, had "left my [his] parents and my sister to come here [in Mumbai], all because of him [Prakash]" (*CP*, 69). It is clear that Kamlesh lives alone so do most of the characters in the play. It is attributed to the modern culture of living a solitary life distanced from the family, which offers a different discourse. Sarah Lamb observes, "Many who live alone have become very creative working purposefully to construct a sense of self, life, social relations and activity *outside of the family*" (Lamb, 89). In an evening in his flat the friends meet up to discuss Kamlesh's psychological turmoil and reflect that they "have all been through the pangs of separation.... As gay men and women, we [they] have all been through that..." (*CP*, 68). Sharad, the more rational and rooted to reality, inflicts pain on Kamlesh for having 'used' him for his own pleasure and confesses "I have ruined a year of my life being a housewife for you and all I get is a kick on the ass!" (*CP*, 56). And we come to know how Sharad had decorated the kitchen of Kamlesh's flat and had put everything in place when he was living with him. They might not have led a sanctioned married life but the trials and tribulations that they have gone through are similar to any heterosexual couple.

Bunny, a television anchor, however plays a dual life. He is married to a woman and has a kid, but behind his family man image is a closet homosexual. Dattani chooses every frame of his background carefully, and when Kiran is delighted to see the anchor in flesh and blood, she says, "I don't watch much TV but I have seen some episodes of *Yeh Hamara Parivar*" (*CP*, 76), and it is here again that the playwright subtly subverts the notion of a happy family life, making a closet homosexual the ideal anchor of a family programme because, as Bunny admits he had the quintessential image of a family man who could reach to the viewers easily. But we realize what masked life he leads and although he confesses that he loves his wife, "...I give her so much more. More than a heterosexual man" (*CP*, 85), he adds "she is content". It is this particular word that gets problematized in the play. The homosexuals need to be 'contented' with their closed claustrophobic environment as they do not get a social sanction and it is here that there is a continuous mockery of the heterosexual marriage that runs as an undercurrent in the play. Bunny's position can therefore be examined, as David Glover and Cora Kaplan state:

> Mad for men, yet preferring women: this figure of passion that is aberrant precisely because it is uncontainable and uncontrollable, carries over into queer's latest incarnation; a phase in which queer becomes a signifier of attitude, of a refusal to accept conventional sexual and gendered categories of a defiant desire *beyond* the regular confines of 'heteronormativity'. (Glover and Kaplan, 106)

Sharad vehemently says that the "world acknowledges two people who enter a union pact, so they have to stick by that" (*CP*, 72), hereby suggesting ways that homosexuals have a fluidity which cannot be denied. They might be scorned or disapproved in the society but Dattani's concern is to create a room of their own. In an article by Ruth Vanita, "Homosexuality and Hinduism", she quotes Hindu philosopher Jiddu Krishnamurty who said, "every individual has both male and female in them. Sometimes one dominates, sometimes other, it is all fluid" (Vanita, website), while mathematician Shakuntala Devi in her book *The World of Homosexuals*, observed, "Marriage is the union of spirits, and spirit is not male or female" (Vanita, website). Dattani's humour in presenting the discourse on alternate sexuality and marriages is noteworthy. In a dialogue between Ranjit, Ed and Kiran, we find how the playwright makes a statement yet in the garb of stark humour:

> Ed (directly to Ranjit): You have something against weddings.
>
> Ranjit: No, not at all. If that's what people really want.
>
> Ed: Of course they want it.
>
> Ranjit: Right. Of course they want it.
>
> Kiran: I really wish they would allow gay people to marry.
>
> Ranjit: Oh, they do. Only not to the same sex. (*CP*, 98)

The marriage between people of the same sex finds mention in the ancient scriptures as well. The term 'homosexual' may be a coinage of the late nineteenth century psychiatry, there are references to the third sex in the Vedic literature. Identified as *kliba* (gay men) and *svarini* (lesbians), the ancient literature provides numerous examples proving that they had an existence of their own and they were allowed to remain united. In fact the social treatises like the *Arthashastra* and *Manusmriti* record that the punishments and penances for the same-sex people were lighter compared to heterosexual people. In *The Laws of Manu*, we find, "If a twice-born man unites sexually with a man or a woman in a cart pulled by a cow, or in water, or by day, he should bathe with his clothes on" (Doniger and Smith, 268). Even the *Arthashastra* imposes a minor fine on the one who indulges in *ayoni* (non-vaginal) sex. Ruth Vanita, observes,

> The sacred epics and the *Puranas* (fourth to fourteenth-century compendia of devotional stories) contradict the law books; they depict gods, sages, and heroes springing from *ayoni* sex. Unlike sodomy, *ayoni* sex never became a major topic of debate or an unspeakable crime. There is no evidence of anyone in India ever having been executed for same-sex relations. (Vanita, website)

And perhaps it is here that Dattani dehistoricizes the history of a country that is apparently steeped in traditions and rituals but fails to look at the past and construct a present for the deprived. It is here that the agony of the characters become clear as Ranjit admits, "Yes, I am sometimes regretful of being an Indian, because I can't seem to be both Indian and gay" (*CP*, 88). Dattani parodies the rituals and rites associated with marriage and the fireworks or the music which act as the background score of the play, as also in *Seven Steps Around the Fire* and we realize the sham and the hollowness that the society celebrates. It is perhaps in the words of Bunny that the significant truth comes to light: "...we should forget about categorizing people as gay or straight or bi or whatever, and let them do what they want to do!" (*CP*, 88), echoing Judith Butler's much discussed gender roles as performative. Vikram Seth's poem "Dubious" sums it up all:

> Some men like Jack
> and some like Jill;
> I'm glad I like
> them both but still.
>
> I wonder if
> this freewheeling
> really is an
> enlightened thing-
> or is it greater
> scope or sign
> or deviance from
> some party line?
>
> In the strict ranks
> of Gay and Straight
> what is my status?
> Stray? Or Great? (Seth, 377)

Dattani's concern with the depiction of the tabooed relationships and marriage is also the theme of his romantic comedy *Do the Needful*. The play is set around the concept of arranged marriages in Indian families. It begins with two set of families, one Gujrathi (the Patels) and the other Kannadigas (the Gowdas), who are busy negotiating on the marriage prospects. Alpesh, the son of Mr. and Mrs. Patel is described as 'thirty plus and divorced' while Lata, the daughter of the Gowda couple is 'twenty-four and notorious'. Dattani, not only situates the play as a discourse on inter-caste marriages as he has done in *Tara*, but also reveals the real motives behind such negotiations. Chandrakant Patel leaves no stone unturned to demonstrate how worthy his son was as far as marriage was concerned. He informs the Gowdas that "Today he is earning very well. He is the sole supporter of the family" (*CP*, 129), and Devraj Gowda has his own thoughts too, "He [Alpesh] is richer than we are" (*CP*, 121). But in an aside later we come to know the façade of hollowness and hypocrisy that the Patels wear on their faces. Alpesh confesses:

> What could I say to them? Daddy had his colleague approve the loan. We paid enough bribes to get the damn thing off. We hired the underworld to have Grandpa's tenants evicted...I hate lying and liars.... In case you think I am rich...I am just the caretaker. It's all his. I can't walk on him without living it all. (*CP*, 136)

It is therefore all about finding 'a suitable match' for the Patels to hide their gruesome realities. The scene is also not very different for the Gowdas. Prema Gowda, Lata's mother regards marriage as the ritual in which the considerations of the caste, social status and regional diversities are more significant than the choice of their daughter. Alpesh tries to resist his parents, "You know what happened with my last marriage..." but in vain and when Lata states that her parents are 'ruining my [her] life', she is resisted by her parents too. The mental spectrum of Lata and Alpesh, seems to have no harmony with the ideal of parents. The parents may have their figments of imagination and desires, but the reality is somewhat alarming.

Alpesh is yet another homosexual character in Dattani's works. Although we do not find his lover as a physical presence in the play, but his confessions are always directed towards Trilok. Like Kamlesh in *On A Muggy Night in Mumbai*, he too finds his passion for Trilok, out of his control: "Oh! Trilok, Trilok, Trilok" and makes a confession "It was not in my control" (*CP*, 126). On the other hand, Lata is in love with Salim, a terrorist and she too finds herself caught in the web of arranged marriages: "Salim, I know you are allowed four wives —what's the point in thinking of all that now? I will have to be content keeping you as a lover. How are we going to work this out?" (*CP*, 126). The families therefore come to a hasty decision to avoid such unnatural relationships to set them 'straight'. Dattani points at the shared spaces between women and gay men, who are "both under the tremendous hegemony of 'mainstream' patriarchal society that forces them to conform and live lives that are alien to their nature" (Chaudhari, 69). He has carefully set the play in the form of exteriors and interiors, significantly portraying the 'manifestations of the social spaces controlled by the idealism of the parents' and the 'invisible mental spaces of Lata and Alpesh' respectively. It is when Lata acknowledges to Alpesh, "Look. I don't want to marry you. I am in love with someone else" (*CP*, 149), that Alpesh too admits his confession, "Good. I am glad you don't want to marry me. Because I don't want to marry you either" (*CP*, 149). Therefore when she finds Alpesh involved physically with the Mali, she finds a consolation. His homosexuality is a retreat for her. Both of them finally decide to marry and to keep the mutual agreement in order to share the spaces of their own. By doing this, they not only can keep the families happy but avoid being the subversives. The agreement comes in the form of a Hindi phrase that Dattani strategically chooses: "*Teri bhi chup, meri bhi chup*" ("Your silence and mine as well") (*CP*, 142), to "enmesh the dominant issues of homosexuality and gender, arriving at an ingenious solution that finds liberation in the teaming up of two subversives (Lata/Alpesh) with different agendas (Salim/Trilok) against the hegemony of a common oppressor—the family/society" (Chaudhari, 62). While in *On A Muggy Night in Mumbai*, he has deliberately denied the hypocrisy and sham of the family and the society with a radical stand, in *Do the Needful*, he makes a conscious effort to come to a compromise in order to maintain peace and status quo. In the marriage of Lata and Alpesh, what comes out is the shared spaces that the marginalized now come to share together and in this sense he calls for a liberation rather than guilt, as Chaudhari has observed too. Dattani thus demonstrates, what Joe Rollins has observed:

> With a minimum of effort and expense, one man and one woman can enter into a relationship with the state that brings about numerous legal benefits, obligations, and privileges. Despite some advances, marriage thus stands as one of the last clearly exclusive, forcefully bounded brightly illuminated enclaves where gays and lesbians may not tread; it remains for heterosexuals only (or at least, for those who want to appear that way). (Rollins, 458)

The stereotypes that Indian families have always considered are that the woman comes from a different family and therefore she can always be subjugated while the males can reign supreme making their bodies the site for sexual politics. Child rearing has been considered the ulterior goal of a woman maintaining the private sphere while the men could be the monarchs of the outer sphere. The plays discussed in this paper deny identifying the rigid binaries and defeats patriarchal views on marriages and control. The likes of Deepali, Uma, Lalitha, Dolly, Alka and Lata are no more "the essential burden that society has to bear for its collective sustenance, women in families are now able to sustain themselves through their professional skills and therefore the educated women remaining dependent on male members of the family has become a matter of choice rather than compulsion" (Dasgupta and Lal, 15-16). Deepali projects Adrienne Rich's challenge against 'compulsory heterosexuality' and reveals that women need not be dependent on men for financial or economic supports, as well as adult sexuality and psychological completion. And men are no more the sole providers for the family. There has been a disruption in the joint families today and what these characters in the play depict is the new trend of living a solitary life, choosing the partners according to their wishes and do not abide by the normative rules that have always put them in a caged dynamics. From a 'perverted matrishakti' as seen in Baa to the lesbian Deepali, from married gay men Nitin and Bunny to the intelligent and conniving Alpesh, Dattani's characters are in search of an 'alternative' from the traditional sociological key concepts of families and marriages.

WORKS CITED

Chaudhari, Asha Kuthari. "The Setting: The Constructed/Deconstructed Family", *Mahesh Dattani: An Introduction.* Delhi: Foundation Books, 2005.

——. "The 'Invisible' Issues: Sexuality, Alternate Sexualities and Gender". *Mahesh Dattani: An Introduction.* Delhi: Foundation Books, 2005.

Dasgupta, Sanjukta and Malashri Lal. "Introduction". *The Indian Family in Transition: Reading Literary and Cultural Texts.* Sanjukta Dasgupta and Malashri Lal, eds. New Delhi: Sage Publications, 2007.

Dattani, Mahesh. *Collected Plays.* (Vol. I) New Delhi: Penguin, 2000.

Doniger, Wendy and Brian K. Smith, trans. *The Laws of Manu,* chapter 5. New Delhi: Penguin, 2000.

Engels, Friedrich. Chapter 2, "The Family", Section IV. *The Origin of the Family, Private Property and the State.* Marx/Engels Internet Archive (Marxists.org) 1993, 1999, 2000. 4th December, 2011. <http://www.marxists.org>

Gandhi, Leela. "After Colonialism". *Postcolonial Theory: A Critical Introduction.* New Delhi: OUP, 1998.

George, Miruana. "Constructing the Self and the Other: *Seven Steps Around the Fire* and *Bravely Fought the Queen*". *Mahesh Dattani's Plays: Critical Perspectives.* Angelie Multani, ed. New Delhi: Pencraft International, 2007.

Ghosh, Arpa. "Hypocrisy and Hollowness in the Indian Joint Family System". *The Indian Family in Transition: Reading Literary and Cultural Texts.* Sanjukta Dasgupta and Malashri Lal, eds. New Delhi: Sage Publications, 2007.

Glover, David and Cora Kaplan, "Queering the Pitch". *Genders,* New York: Routledge, 2000.

Lamb, Sarah. "Modern Families and Independent Living". *The Indian Family in Transition: Reading Literary and Cultural Texts.* Sanjukta Dasgupta and Malashri Lal, eds. New Delhi: Sage Publications, 2007.

McRae, John. "A Note on the Play: *On A Muggy Night in Mumbai*", *Collected Plays.* New Delhi: Penguin, 2000.

Nair, Anita. "Mahesh Dattani: The Invisible Observer." 20th November, 2011. <http://www.anitanair.net/profiles/profile-mahesh-dattani.html>

Prasad, Gitanjali. "Introduction: Changing Perceptions", *The Great Indian Family: New Roles, Old Responsibilities.* New Delhi: Penguin, 2006.

Rollins, Joe. "Review Essay: Same-Sex Unions and the Spectacles of Recognition". *Law and Society Review*. Vol. 39, No. 2. June, 2005. 22nd November, 2011. (Blackwell Publishing) <http://www.jstor.org/stable/3557622>

Russell, Bertrand. "Patriarchal Systems." *Marriage and Morals*. London and New York: Routledge, 2009. <http://books.google.co.in/books>

Seth, Vikram. "Dubious", "Vikram Seth: Poems (English)". *Same-Sex Love in India: A Literary History,* Ruth Vanita and Saleem Kidwai, eds. New Delhi: Penguin, 2008.

Vanita, Ruth. "Introduction: Medieval Materials in the Sanskritic Tradition". *Same-Sex Love in India: A Literary History,* Ruth Vanita and Saleem Kidwai, eds. New Delhi: Penguin, 2008.

——. "Homosexuality and Hinduism". 22nd November, 2011. <http://www.galva108.org/hinduism.html>

20

The Problem of Identity and Existence in Tendulkar's *A Friend's Story*

Shukla Chatterjee and *Sukla Basu (Sen)*

Theoretical debate from the late twentieth century has centered on identity and function of the subject or self. The self maybe treated as a given, as something inner and unique or as a combination of the given and social where the self is determined by its origins and social attributes leading on to a concept of the evolving self which becomes itself through particular acts or the various subject positions one occupies through the various stages of life. Again, debates on identity highlights that identities are not fixed, neither can they be categorized and labeled. This is because identities consist of varied components and that to categorize by one characteristic is wrong. Yet when we talk about identity and self or subject, we tend to focus on our gendered self in terms of sexuality—male and female and also try to locate our self/subject in terms of gendered identity—masculine and feminine. Keeping this debate in mind, Queer theory proposes that we deliberately challenge all notions of fixed identity in varied and non-predictable ways. Therefore in the line of Sedgwick and Butler, Queer theory argues that the heterosexual subject is constructed through the repression of the possibility of homosexuality and confirms that fundamental categories of identity are cultural and social productions rather as a result of political cooperation than the condition of possibility to be a subject at all. This is to follow a norm, something that few of us can carry out according to expectation, as we never can appropriate the gender norms we are supposed to inhabit which leads to existential problems.

It seems ironic in the context of a gradual opening up of the debate on gendered identities, Indian intellectuals should find themselves in a quandary as to the politically correct stance they should take on the issue. The theatre has always been a platform for a protest, reform or reformulation of collective opinion. As in the West, so in post-independence India, the public stage has more often than not given direction to nascent thought and judgement about societal concerns that the Indian legal system took long to take cognizance of. For example, the freedom to follow one's sexual orientation has found poor representation in dramatic texts and even when a fearless expositor of anomalies like Vijay Tendulkar made it the central problem in one of his plays, he was queasy about acknowledging his responsibility in performing so path breaking a role.

Mitrachi Gostha or *A Friend's Story* (1981) by Vijay Tendulkar serves as a good case-study for the examination of gender norms in the Indian theatre, one that is a significant marker of accepted socio-cultural practices in the public sphere of entertainment. It was first performed in Mumbai by Bhumika with Rohini Hattangadi in the lead role of Mitra, who exhibits and lives lesbian tendencies. Although Tendulkar denied that it was a discourse on Indian homosexuality, the contemporary audience rejected the play and presentation stopped after 25 performances. The play and its stage history is an important documentation of post Independence India's take on homoeroticism both in life and in fiction. This paper, therefore primarily tries to find out why Vijay Tendulkar denies that it is a discourse on Indian homosexuality. This question would lead us further to examine the socio-cultural milieu that goes into the making of the play which is both a reason for and the result of the evolving of the gendered identity or the self.

Before we analyze the sexo-political ideologies configuring the cultural structurisation in the play, we must have a clear outline of the plot of *A Friend's Story*. It is a coming-out story of Sumitra Dev—a fictional character based on a real woman. As she realizes that she is a lesbian, she also feels strong and adamant in her decision to like and love Nama. Mitra's frustrated desire for Nama feels like a slow suffocation for her which she cannot overcome. On the other hand she finds in Bapu, the narrator, a true friend and reveals her ailment to him openly. Meanwhile, Pande, Bapu's roommate falls in love with Mitra's boldness. But when he comes to know about the abnormal trait of Mitra, unable to withstand the shock, he joins the military. Again, as Nama's boyfriend comes to know about the relation between Mitra and Nama, he tries to take revenge on Mitra by exposing her in college and rusticating her to ruin her career. Amidst all these developments, Bapu and Mitra's friendship succeeds with Bapu's immense effort to correct Mitra and restore her tendencies to accept straight relationships whereas Pande and Dalvi, not knowing what to do with their simultaneous desire and fear for an independent, strong woman like Mitra, actually indulge in torturing Mitra and demonize her. Unable to withstand the mental torture imposed on her by society, Mitra struggles with her own self but ultimately leads herself to self destructive acts.

This basic structure of the play confirms that it deals with and documents the life-changing moments of a lesbian—Mitra and therefore is definitely a play on lesbianism. However, Tendulkar in most of his interviews and comments emphasized that

> It is not a play about Mitra's character. It's about her boyfriend of one who has just entered into her life. He is in such an adolescent state of mind to understand something strange that is happening in his life. It comes to him as a shock. And before he can do anything, it is all over. So the play actually deals with Mitra's boyfriend rather than Mitra herself. One should relate her to him in the circumstance. (47-48)

Such a contention on the part of Vijay Tendulkar is really difficult to accept. If we take into consideration only the stage history and the making of the play, we come to know that in 1940 when Tendulkar was in his teens and lived in Pune, he became acquainted with 'Mitra' who had a craving for a girl. Thus a rare, unusual and confusing issue of lesbianism entered Tendulkar's mind to shock and confuse him a lot. In the mid 1950s he wrote about the lesbian Mitra for the first time in the form of a short story titled 'Mitra'. This story appeared in one of Diwali annuals in Marathi and was much appreciated.

About thirty years later, when Tendulkar moved from Pune to Mumbai, Mitra was again in his mind. By then he had seen her living as a spinster in Pune. So in 1981, when Tendulkar finally wrote *Mitrachi Gostha* or *A Friend's Story*, he was an adult then with enough knowledge of the same-sex world. Moreover, he was also well aware by then of the outcome of the life of a real life lesbian living as a spinster and the subtle and overt violence that she suffered in terms of sexo-political ideologies. These experiences and knowledge together definitely make *A Friend's Story* a theatrical representation of individual and social protest against lesbians and homosexuality.

Homosexuality is generally considered a taboo subject by both Indian civil society and the government. Though in recent years, the attitudes towards homosexuality has shifted slightly, it was not so in the 1980s. Guided by Section 377 of the Indian Penal Code, homosexuality was then strictly considered to be an unnatural act and thus illegal. The law treated homosexuality as a criminal offense punishable up to life imprisonment. Under such strict and rigid jurisdiction, to write and produce a play on the life of a lesbian was near impossible. Yet the play materialized. The show is said to have been sneered at by men and hated by the women. Perhaps this is also one of the reasons why the straight forward playwright Vijay Tendulkar, who dared to write about the lesbian Mitra, actually deviated from his position when questioned. It is strange to note such a stand of Tendulkar, who in most of his other plays actually tears apart various aspects of heterosexuality and the sexual, psychological violence embedded within the discourse for an open analysis. There are evidences of severe controversies faced by *Sakharam Binder*, another of Tendulkar's plays that openly displayed sex and violence on stage. In spite of the severe controversies that extended even to the banning of the play, Tendulkar always supported the depiction of open violence and all aspects of heterosexuality through his unique portrayal of man-woman relationship in the play. If such are the notions of Tendulkar for *Sakharam Binder*, why does he not take a similar stand for his *A Friend's Story*? Why, in spite of writing about a lesbian, Tendulkar withdraws from his position?

Any theory or cultural/political creation treats heterosexuality as the norm as opposed to homosexuality. Compulsory heterosexuality is always examined as an institution that powerfully affects mothering, sex-roles, relationships and societal prescriptions for women. On the other hand homosexuality among women or lesbian existence is usually treated as a marginal or less "natural" phenomenon, as mere sexual preference or as the mirror image of heterosexual or male homosexual relations. In fact, in almost every country and every culture, homosexuality and more specifically lesbianism is ostracized and hounded by law. They are inhumanly branded as 'queers' and 'aberrations'—precisely what they are not. In actuality, homosexuals, whether male or female are normal human beings. Just because they love their own kind, they are marginalized. According to psychiatrists, "Relationships should be defined by comfort levels and not societal sanctions. Like heterosexuality, homosexuality is an orientation which is not unnatural." Medically speaking, there are even evidences that point to homosexuality being a function of biology. In spite of the naturalness of homosexuals, such demarcations continue in the name of tradition, culture and biasness of heterosexuality.

We need not go far to literally investigate the authenticity of the fact. Since our dealing of the discourse is related to the Indian context, a deep look into the social history of India reveals that such relationships which are today termed abnormal did exist in the past as well. Indian literature drawn from Hindu, Buddhist and Muslim fiction testify to the presence of same-sex love in various forms. Even ancient texts such as *Manusmriti*, *Arthashastra*, *Kamasutra*, *Upanishads* and *Puranas* refer to homosexuality. Not only were there texts that represented same sex relations but there were many that even constituted a continuity of the discourse. From these ancient texts of literature and history, it is found that same-sex love and romantic friendship have flourished in India in various forms, without any extended history of overt persecution. Evidence of existence of complex discourses around same-sex love and male homoerotic subcultures flourished also from the erotic temple sculptures at Khajurao and Konark. These irrefutable evidences only prove that Indian concept about same-sex love was much open and liberal in the past than in the present. However, during the 19th century, British administrators and educationists imported their generally anti-sex and specifically homophobic attitudes into India. Under the colonial rule, what used to be minority puritanical and homophobic voice in India became mainstream. The new homophobia was manifested in India by the British law of 1860 through Section 377 of the Indian Penal Code. This law though was decriminalized in England in 1967, continued to remain in action in India since 1860 until in 2009, the Delhi High Court decriminalized homosexual intercourse between consenting adults throughout India. Thus in spite of having such a strong ancient historical support, India for the past hundred and fifty years has persistently followed the tradition of the new homophobia of which probably Vijay Tendulkar is also a victim.

Tendulkar too might have been aware of the ancient history of the country. But owing to the present social scenario and the condition that laws are supposed to represent socially acceptable do's and don'ts, he withdraws from his position. Tendulkar's *A Friend's Story* in spite of his denial, therefore becomes

(a) representation and representation of society's embarrassments towards homosexuality,

(b) a stark commentary on the nature of romantic love—both heterosexual and homosexual and finally,

(c) a critique of heterosexuality although a man-woman friendship is found to be relatively stable though not sufficiently stabilizing.

In *A Friend's Story,* Mitra is portrayed as 'different'. Her body lacks feminine curves and her attitude too, bears masculine traits, having a stubborn nature like a boy. Though by appearance she is a woman, she inherits the nature of a man. Tendulkar clearly sketches a picture of Mitra's costume as "a white saree, a plain borderless blouse with a collar, and white tennis shoes...never any colour." This points evidently to the fact that Mitra wanted to stand out in the crowd, almost in male white attire. So in the close intimacy with men, she is rather comfortable, whereas the thrill, the passion that is natural between a woman and a man, is felt by Mitra when she encounters Nama, her co-actor and a woman. This is where the problem of the play arises. When Bapu, comes to know about the truth of Mitra, he is shocked and dazed. Bapu even questions the unusual traits of Mitra to his audience saying,

> Do such women exist? Are they born like that or do they get conditioned as they grow to what they are? Is it an ailment or a human trait of a particular kind? What would happen to Mitra? (*A Friend's Story*, 18)

As these questions plague the adolescent mind of Bapu, he feels detached from and repulsed by Mitra but ultimately gets involved with her, trying to help her in being a true companion and guide her life through the right path. The other male characters of the play also react violently and repulsively towards her. Pande's reaction reveals the deep hypocrisy embedded in a religious system that at once worships women deities and also cultivates same-sex (male) bonding and platonic love. Again Manya Dalvi, resolves to spread the news of her unusual trait to rusticate her from the college and "wreck all her chances". Such reactions reveal that our male-dominated society not only fails to feel for such different human beings on the grounds of humanity but also fear the independent and strong stance of women like Mitra. The treatment that Mitra receives from her family too is immoral and inhuman. Because she is born a woman, she is taught to fear men and act as a girl rather than as a boy. All these instances throughout the play clearly reveal society's uncontrolled rages, hesitations and humiliations that are extended in various ways towards homosexuals. As society around Mitra violently assault and demonize her in order to keep their position intact, the play becomes in all a representation and re-presentation of patriarchal society's embarrassments towards homosexuality.

According to Tendulkar, *A Friend's Story* is a love story—Mitra's love story, which was a romantic homosexual love. The play reveals at various moments how Mitra strongly opposed heterosexual coupling and romantic love between a man and a woman. The essence of romantic love that Mitra feels as she comes close to Nama is revealed as she out of excitement confesses before Bapu—"I've fallen in love—with a girl" she justifies her strange feelings saying,

> Never felt anything so powerful before this. In school I might have felt a tug now and then, but never understood what it was. During the rehearsals I felt the same way, but always dismissed it. That night, while the love scene was on, things came to a head. I lost control. Her touch...her very desirable body in my arms...she moved away as if she sensed it. That night, I saw myself in a flash of lightening. I knew I didn't want a man. I need a woman. I'm different, different. (24)

It is the desire to have Nama as her partner that reveals the romantic homosexual love and at the same time challenges heterosexual love.

By portraying the reactions of Mitra, Nama and Dalvi prominently, Tendulkar not only represents romantic love both heterosexual and homosexual but also starkly comments on it. In the world of Mitra, love has no redeeming qualities. Rather it is a game of power that reduces players to bestial levels. Aggressiveness is noticed in both Mitra and Dalvi's character as they both yearn for Nama. So when it comes to expressions of romantic love, whether it is heterosexual or homosexual, the reactions are all same. From his analysis of the three characters, Tendulkar comments that the expression of romantic love, the sexual act is no more than a sordid transaction. Thus both heterosexual and homosexual nature is part of the natural laws of God.

The man-woman friendship in the form of Nama-Dalvi couple and more specifically Mitra-Bapu couple is found to be relatively stable rather than sufficiently stabilizing. Though Nama blatantly followed Dalvi and his possessiveness Nama and Dalvi relation was actually not stable. That is why when society failed to accept Mitra and Nama's relation, Nama did not return to Dalvi. Rather she moved to Calcutta to get married to a stranger. Similarly the friendship between Bapu and Mitra is also very strange. This friendship goes through a succession of quick, dramatic growth spurts that reveal the complexity of friendship and show that which Bapu ultimately comes to represent a homophobic society. Through these two man-woman friendships what Tendulkar actually aims at is a critique of heterosexuality. While Nama and Dalvi finally cannot unite with each other, the friendship between Bapu and Mitra too often feels forced. Though Bapu clearly stands in the play for that part of society that is more willing to understand women like Mitra, the audience is never sure why he really sibes around her. The friendship between Bapu and Mitra, and also to some extent the Nama-Dalvi relationship, try to show dramatically Mitra's plight that no one in this world, not even the person who is faithful as a friend, will understand a woman like Mitra. As Tendulkar portrays society's adverse reaction towards Mitra, he doesn't necessarily protect Mitra's position. Theoretically therefore, through Mitra's character this play works to denaturalize heterosexuality and explore heterosexuality's roots against patriarchy.

It is usually seen that men by their instincts try to keep women suppressed under their will and enforce compulsory heterosexual orientation on women. In order to maintain a higher position patriarchal social norms are designed in such a way that heterosexuality and to some extent male homosexuality is given preference whereas a lesbian existence is resisted and marginalized. Thus in *A Friend's Story*, though Mitra's love for Nama does not develop into a fruitful lesbian relationship, it actually measures the limits of a heterosexual relationship clearly pointing to the fact that if homosexuality cannot be stabilized, heterosexuality too can be unstable.

Another interesting instance to be noted here is that since the appearance of cross dressing male actors in Patanjali's *Mahabhasya*, India's dramatic productions have been characterized by a fluid role playing of gender. Tendulkar harps on this fact as he tries to develop a suitable situation for the meeting of Mitra and Nama to develop their homosexual coupling. Tendulkar tries to emphasise through the words of Pande,

> The principal says no more plays with a mixed cast of boys and girls. It makes us immoral, it seems!

That while having all women and/or all men performances was intended to prevent transgressive heterosexual couplings, this very norm itself became a space where same-sex desire and couplings could flourish. So in a way Tendulkar tries to critique the hypocrisy of patriarchal society that at one place gives scope for same-sex desire to flourish while on the other imposes resistance for such preferences to develop.

In the context of multi-variant Indian sexuality, if we think of heterosexuality as the "natural" emotional and sensual inclination for women, lives such as Mitra's are seen as deviant, as pathological, or as emotional and sensually deprived. But Tendulkar crucially turns the lens of our vision to consider the degree to which and the methods whereby heterosexual preference has actually been imposed on women to differently understand the meaning of individual lives and work and recognize a central fact of women's history that women have always resisted male tyranny. This is what makes Tendulkar's disavowal of his political position on homoeroticism all the more problematic. Mitra's own identity formation is so very dependent on society's sensitization to it. In a sense Tendulkar's 'fear' of public censure is representative of a collective national response to the central question of an acceptable sexual identity. The playwright's intention to have it translated at the beginning of this century is perhaps an indication of how this collective attitude had changed substantially in the quarter century between its first production and its all India projection through translation. The picture on the cover of the English translation published in 2001 which shows Mitra and Nama in a very affectionate pose, stands as a visual reminder that such relationships are no longer considered despicable in 21st century, post-modern India. The demonization of homoeroticism no longer troubles Vijay Tendulkar in 2001 perhaps because theory and practice in the West had legitimized an English rendition of the subject. So even though he denies to have written about homosexuality, *A Friend's Story* stands widely acknowledged as the first Marathi play and perhaps even the first Indian play in contemporary Indian theatre on same-sex relations defining in clear terms issues of identity and problems of existence through Mitra's question

> Who makes us the way we are and sends us here? Why are we what we are? (8)

WORKS CITED

Art and Entertainment. "Mitrachi Goshta, an Excellent Production." Review. Bombay: *Evening News*, 1981.

Ramnarayan, Gowri. "Vijay Tendulkar's Mitrachi Gostha." n.d. *Humanities Retooled*. <http://www.humanitiesretooledorg.htm>

Tendulkar, Vijay. *Mitrachi Goshta: A Friend's Story*. Trans. Gowri Ramnarayan. Delhi: Oxford University Press, 2001.

Vanita, Ruth and Saleem Kidwai. *Same-Sex Love in India: Readings from Literature and History*. Palgrave Macmillan, 2001.

Vanita, Ruth. *Queering India: Same-Sex Love and Eroticism in Indian Culture and Society*. Routlege, 2002.

Wadikar, Shailaja B. *Vijay Tendulkar: A Pioneer Playwright*. New Delhi: Atlantic Publishers and Distributers, 2008.

21

The Comic and the Surreal: An Analysis of Death and Destruction in Satish Alekar's *The Terrorist* and Mahesh Dattani's *Brief Candle*

Alpna Saini

Mahesh Dattani writes in the introduction to his play *Brief Candle*, that he must write serious literature in order to portray the seriousness inherent in life (3), but he goes on to achieve a comic undercurrent in a supposedly morose theme like death. The farcical undertone in the play is not used for relief from a serious heavy scene but is interwoven in the very fabric of the theme, as if attempting a mockery of death as an event of consequence.

Set in a cancer hospital full of dying terminally ill patients, fighting death in their own distinctive ways, *Brief Candle* showcases a farcical comedy, that the residents are rehearsing to be played in the memory of the dead writer, Vikas who is not so dead and keeps on coming back to intervene. Deepika, the doctor who was Vikas's sweetheart once, Amar, the prostate cancer patient lamenting over the loss of his maleness, Shanti, the breast cancer patient and Amol who dies before the play—are all defined by their singular cases of illness and Vikas has written slapstick roles for them that blow their distinct peculiar orientations out of proportion to produce farcical effects. Comic and serious, thus, intertwine dissolving the boundaries that separate them. Even a joke could result in a long philosophical soliloquy about the meaning of life and death.

Satish Alekar too in his inimitable style, attempts an amalgamation of the comic and the subtle in his play *The Terrorist. The Terrorist* was originally written in 1989 and is probably inspired by the insurgency in Punjab in that period. There are oblique references to the north as the center of organised terrorism. Bapurao, the protagonist of the play, therefore, wants to take his son, Babu to the north, so as to make him a successful terrorist. The unrest in the south needs to be manipulated, Bapurao tells his son, "We are going north to observe unrest and to learn the art of manipulating it" (176).

There is, thus, an indirect theory of the southern religious fanaticism having been inspired by the Khalistan terrorism of the north. Alekar depicts the northern terrorist organisation as being extremely professional and business-like. In fact, he clearly differentiates between the peaceful fanaticism of the southern Hindus and the militant tendency of the northern Sikhs. In the words of Bapurao,

> There is no professionalism like yours in our part of the country. That is why, sahib, this peace is killing us. Indeed, our peace is so frightening that we don't know what to do with it. (195)

Terrorism is seen in this play as an industry, an entrepreneurship, that would put to use the unemployed, insignificant, good for nothing youth of the country, as Bapurao tells the head of the terrorist organization:

> Then I read about your line of business in the newspapers and was relieved. Sahib, we want to offer this child of ours to you. Invincible Master of the north, take care of this child and make him into an excellent terrorist. Transform this shapeless hunk of meat into a human being! (195)

He wants his son to be given the gift of "pure, boundless violence", as if that were the only trait that would define a human being. Through violence, he wants his son to achieve confidence, pride and power which Khalistani terrorism is aptly believed to bestow. So, power and money is what it is all about, even in Alekar's play. It is the dream of power and authority that drives the protagonist of the play, Bapurao to push his son, Babu on the path of ethno-religious insurgency to burn in the fire of religious fundamentalism. Bapurao remarks, "once the fire is lit, we will quickly have progress, power and wealth" (181).

His wife, Bhavna when asked whether Babu is going to start a business, explains that sending Babu to train for a terrorist is a "business investment" and that, "Babu is not going to start a business. There'll be business because of Babu" (200). Alekar thus locates the terror-politics within the commerce of the nation.

This is the reason why a terrorist is the darling of the media. Alekar explores how the discourse of a ruthless, all-powerful terrorist is constructed by the media and how it returns to influence and shape the persona of a terrorist in the eyes of the people. The over-hype surrounding terrorist activities in media has gone on to create an omnipotent fourth world on the globe, which is the center of power. We must always live in a shadow of fear, under a cloud of violence, at their mercy. Bapurao defines the role of media, when he addresses the chief of the terrorist organisation in these words:

> The headlines of the TV news bulletins always mention your name first.... In fact, thanks to you, we know that blood can be spilt in countless ways. We know that grief can be expressed in a variety of ways. (195)

The depiction of violence and bloodshed in media and the over-sensationalisation of the terror-issues is one of the ways how the discourse of a blood-thirsty, power-wielding terrorist is constructed.

Alekar presents an inverted, dystopian scheme of things in his play, in which a terrorist receives an enviable reception in the society. He becomes as desirable as a political/religious leader would be. People want to be associated with him, know him, be close to him and even offer him their daughters in matrimony. He becomes an invisible center of power and money. Earlier in the play, when Babu is still an aimless and jobless youth, he is in love with Malvika whose parents disagree to the match. Her father Madhavrao says, "My daughter is not such a burden on me that I'd marry her to Babu" (186) and he tells Malvika to have nothing to do with Babu as he is a brainless boy.

But later in the play when Babu returns as a terrorist, Madhavrao himself visits him with a proposal of Malvika's hand. He tells his wife, Manda, "You know what their son has become. Otherwise do you think anyone would agree to marry his daughter into such a family?" (209). Manda too feels elated about having a terrorist for a son-in-law, "No one else has a terrorist for a son-in-law. Only we have" (209).

The "three pillars of society" in the play that is, Halogenwala, the municipal corporator, Vastu, the builder and Vihang, the researching intellectual too indulge in cheap sycophancy at Babu's wedding and are even ready to take orders from Babu. Bapurao's Boss also behaves timidly and abjectly with him after his son has returned as a terrorist. He is even ready to carry Bapurao's lunchbox and goes on to offer his daughter's hand to Babu in matrimony.

Through this inversion of the stigmatization of a terrorist in society, Alekar deconstructs the clean, respectable image of religio-political organisations, leaders and other lackeys in state machinery that wield this kind of power in society. Through this reversal, Alekar tries to draw a parallel between a terrorist organisation and such state-protected politico-religious groups, implying that ultimately, every powerful organisation works through terror and violence—be it physical or psychological. The play suggests that such socially acceptable groups are as good as any extremist terrorist organisation. Bandopadhyay interprets this inversion as follows:

> ...the legitimization of the daily terror in the political domain and the power it represents that gives terror a value of its own—a value that the powerless would cherish and strive after. (10)

This reversal of antisociality of terror-structures exposes the sham that our society indulges in—that is, it legitimizes those terrorist groups that wear a religious/political mask and condemns those that operate barehanded. It is this legitimacy and power that provokes the youth to embrace chaos, defiance and violence as a way of life. Through this inversion of the status of a terrorist in society, Alekar succeeds in providing a hypothetical, surreal dimension to his world which is full of comic and fantastic elements.

The comic stance of these two playwrights deconstructs the imagined purposefulness of life. It attempts an existential mockery of the enforced seriousness in the otherwise banal sequence of our lives. The exalted ideals of love, life, war, power and nationalism merge into the farcical, fantastical, aporic purposelessness. Samik Bandopadhyay remarks in the introduction to *The Terrorist*, that the farcical element in the play is used to disrupt the realism of the movement of the play (12). It is probably a reaction against the obsessive realism of their contemporaries. For example, when Tendulkar creates a Sakharam Binder, or when Karnad conjures up a Tughlaq, we find this Miltonic high seriousness which is, probably, a technique to focus single-mindedly on the issue in hand. But Dattani asks, "Why do we lead such heavy lives?" He tries to lighten this "unbearable heaviness of being" by acknowledging it head-on, albeit comically in his plays (3).

The farcical attitude of these plays also works towards achieving a distance in order to look at the issue objectively. It is not possible to view serious issues like death and terrorism through a lachrymosal tear-blurred vision and it is difficult to analyse them with an emotionally charged unanalytical brain. Therefore, Dattani takes recourse to comedy as an alternative exercise to explore the mystery of death and Alekar analyses a terrorist and the society he lives in through their follies and foibles exaggerated to the point of slapstick humour. Bandopadhyay sees "ruthless political logic running underneath the appearance of the comic book absurdity" and "comic strip characterisation" (11-12). In other words, the absurd is only a mask to delineate the real in different, unexplored terms. It is a means to objectify and place the crux of the matter under the comic microscope, hoping to find unexpected results.

Moreover, Alekar believes that theatre is non-realistic and false where everything has to be made up. Therefore, he has chosen a form which is full of fantastical situations and dream sequences, with no reverence or lament for passing of things. Alekar suggests the uselessness of theatre as a means of escape in *Begum Barve* and breaks into the "facade of fantasy" for escape (287). Bandopadhyay remarks, "It is Alekar's mode to let the fantasies flow till they overlay reality" (285). Therefore he imbues the critical moments of the play with comic surrealism, be it Bapurao's decision to take Babu to the north, or the final assassination of Gadkari at the hands of Babu as his first mission. The conversation during the journey carries a comic undertone without being obvious about it as when Babu explains the reason of his restlessness, he says:

> When I go to a restaurant, my favourite dish is always unavailable, if I have a headache and I take a pill, I don't get any relief. It is as if the plate of rice served before me has no rice—or a woman with a mangalsutra has no bindi! (175)

And during the assassination of Gadkari, a comic situation is created when Babu's whole family gets ready to accompany him to be witnesses of his first mission in the guise of beggars. When Babu kills Gadkari, his final words are:

> You messed up everything. Listen to me carefully. You shot me before the time. I, Gadkari...am the author of this play. You shot me before I could write the end of this play. Don't tell anyone.... Because of religion however ...the characters in the play...have stopped recognizing the producer.... (228)

Similarly, Dattani resorts to the farcical and the fantastical to escape the existential tension in *Brief Candle*. For example, when Amar is presented to be a desperate sex-maniac in Vikas's play, the playwright probably intends to relieve the immediacy of longing that has come to be somehow associated to Amar due to his illness. His character in Vikas's play seeks the help of receptionist Deepika to get into Shanti's room, he tells Deepika, "And once I am in her room, could you have some wine sent to the room, but don't take too long. But not if the 'Do Not Disturb' sign is turned on" (9). He is confident of his skill in satisfying a woman which speaks largely of his fear and insecurities after being afflicted with prostate cancer. Amol also remarks about laughter being a means of escape:

> Each one of us laughing and fighting when together but holding back some little secret...some fear, laughing louder so our secret will go unnoticed. (37)

Besides the comic element, another important feature of these two playwrights' surrealistic world is a general kind of aporia linking it to the realm of the Real, by which Lacan understands that area which neither culture nor language can penetrate or represent. This Real can only be explored through fantasy and the aporic exclamations of the speaker. In *Brief Candle*, the long monologues of Vikas, Amol, Shanti, and Amarinder are examples of this. Vikas tells Deepika about a dream of his in these words:

> I woke up with the vision of your face. I knew then what my destination was. But I looked into the mirror, and saw myself. I realized that it will soon be me who will move away by staying still. (40)

His incomprehensible monologue suggests some deep layers of meaning which probably language cannot penetrate. Similarly in *The Terrorist*, when Bhavna, Bapurao's wife tells Malvika about her dream that red flowers are turning into blood and then back into flowers, she replies:

> It is a very strange dream. But why do those things happen? How did I know that you were going to describe your dream. Sometimes, I feel that I think too much—about the future, the past—like the wind, my thoughts flow everywhere. I feel that my shadow falls over the entire world; and that my harmless shadow stoically faces every calamity. (208)

Both Bhavna and Malvika talk in a world beyond language's reach, forming a part of the surreal experience that theatre has come to be in Alekar and Dattani. It is arguable whether it is a means of escape from the existential burden or a novel instrument to take the bull by the horns.

We can definitely conclude that the farcical/surreal/ fantastical stance in Alekar's *The Terrorist* and Dattani's *Brief Candle* is not a device to provide comic relief as in Shakespeare and Marlowe who first broke from the Greek tradition of keeping the comic and the tragic separate and introduced comic interludes in their plays. But in Alekar and Dattani, this attitude is the very heart of these plays. It does not attempt to relieve the misery of death and destruction, but to analyse this misery in a new light and to come to terms with it in whichever way possible, although it may strike as bizarre to some.

WORKS CITED

Alekar, Satish. *The Terrorist*. Trans. Alok Bhalla and Jayant Dhupkar. *Collected Plays of Satish Alekar*. New Delhi: Oxford University Press, 2009.

——. Interview with Satish Alekar by Samik Bandopadhyay. *Collected Plays of Satish Alekar*. By Satish Alekar. New Delhi: Oxford University Press, 2009.

Bandopadhyay, Samik. Introduction. *Collected Plays of Satish Alekar*. By Satish Alekar. New Delhi: Oxford University Press, 2009.

Dattani, Mahesh. *Brief Candle: Collected Plays*. New Delhi: Penguin Books, 2010.

Lacan, Jacques. *Four Fundamental Concepts of Psychoanalysis*. Trans. Alan Sheridan. New York: W.W. Norton & Co., 1978.

22 *Dramatic Chronicle*: A Very Brief Review of the Growth of Indian English Plays

Pinaki Roy

Students and researchers dealing with Commonwealth writings in general and Indian English Literature in particular are aware of the rather 'recent' emanation and development of this South-Asian genre of English literature. While Indian literature began approximately in 2000 B.C. (Indian Literature xi), and that in English around A.D. 1150 (Albert 9), Indian English Literature was conceived only two hundred and nineteen years before in England. The Bengali traveller and surgeon Sheikh Din Muhammad (1795-1851) inaugurated the trend of Indian English writing by publishing in 1793 his travelogue Travels of Dean Mahomet. Beginning with prose, Indian English Literature, by the beginning of the 20th century, had clearly distinguished itself in fields of poetry, novels, drama, and prose. As Nand Kumar writes, "Of all the four genres of literature—poetry, prose, fiction, and drama—the last, being an audio-visual medium of expression, is supposed to have been the most effective means of representing man's acts and feeling on the stage" (v). It should, therefore, follow that Indian English drama, whose history started approximately in A.D. 1831, is among the more influential subgenres of Indian English Literature. However, Iyengar states, "Modern English dramatic writing in English is neither rich in quantity nor, on the whole, of high quality. Enterprising Indians have for nearly a century occasionally attempted drama in English—but seldom for actual stage production" (226). Iyengar's criticism notwithstanding, Deshpande prioritises Indian English drama for being an efficient confluence of ancient Indian traditions and modern

European innovations (Modern xi). In the following sections of this essay, an attempt has been made to very briefly trace the history of Indian English drama, with references to its colonial and postcolonial phases. The postcolonial phase—not only of Indian English drama but of any literature in general—is most important because it "thematis[es] the problems of colonialism [...] [,] [and is] interested in the ways in which native societies respon[d] to Western cultural presence. [...] [It is] about history, with many [postcolonial] authors suggesting that native cultures should understand their history [...] better" (Nayar, 36).

It is pertinent to ask at the beginning whether Indian English Literature, especially Indian English drama, is postcolonial in its very existence? If, according to Sheobhushan and Anu Shukla, postcoloniality existed "in India even before independence" (Indian English, 5), Indian English drama, in extension, can be said to have assumed an anti-imperial identity by the time of its conception. Aparna and Vijay Dharwadker attest to this idea by observing that the 19th century Indian English literature, when Indian English drama matured, was marked by a complex "cultural exchange between [the] English and [the] India[ns]" (English, 91), which in itself was a postcolonial phenomenon. The postcoloniality of Indian English drama therefore becomes a fact even as the sub-genre starts advancing. This concern became observable as soon as the earliest Indian English play, Krishna Mohan Bandyopadhyay The Persecuted: or, Dramatic Scenes illustrative of the Present State of Hindoo Society in Calcutta, was produced in 1831.

The postcoloniality of Indian English drama could not have been better pronounced than in the identity of the writer of its earliest specimen. Bandyopadhyay (1813-85), who was an educationist, linguist, and Anglican priest, was a prominent member of Henry Louis Vivian Derozio's Young Bengal group and a professor of Bishop's College, Shibpur. Though he himself converted to Christianity in 1832, and later encouraged the conversion of the eminent Indian litterateur Michael Madhusudan Dutt (1824-73), he remained throughout his life a tireless reformer of the 19th-century Hindu society, influencing, indirectly, the gradual strengthening of Indian opinion against English oppressions. His The Persecuted criticises certain practices of the 19th century Indian Hindus that, according to the writer, were resulting in the socio-cultural and moral degradation of the—then Bengalis, enfeebling them to resist the colonisers. The Persecuted is in itself a psychoanalytic drama, focusing on the moral dilemma of a young Bengali gentleman wavering between traditional Hindu beliefs and Eurocentric customs.

With the English colonisers gradually consolidating their grip especially on Bengal, Maharastra, and Tamil Nadu, they funded the construction of theatre-houses in Kolkata, Mumbai, and Chennai, most probably to entertain their own administrative-officials and inculcate their ideologies in Indian intellectuals. However, the history of Indian English drama is more centred in Kolkata than anywhere else because the first globalisation of Indian theatre became apparent in this metropolis in end-18th century, when two plays *The Disguise* (1795) and *Love is the Best Doctor* (1796) were adapted and successfully dramatised in Bengali (and later transliterated into English) by the Russian linguist Gerasim Lebedev (1749-1817), based on the respective compositions of (the English playwright) Richard Jodrell (1745-1831) and (the French dramatist) Jean-Baptiste Poquelin (or 'Molière') (1622-73). While translating the plays, with the help of the Bengali teacher and theatre-activist Goloknath Das, Lebedev used translated lyrics from the oeuvre of the Bengali litterateur Bharat Chandra Roy (1712-60). With assistance from Kolkata-based Bengali scholars, the Russian also founded the first European-style proscenium-drama theatre house in the metropolis, on Ezra Street, in 1795—a time when there were only two theatre houses for the English in the city. Prashanna Kumar Tagore (1801-86) advanced the efforts of Lebedev by establishing The Hindu Theatre in 1831, where portions of *William Shakespeare's The Tragedy of Julius Caesar* (1599) were staged intermittently.

The history of Indian English theatre further advanced in Mumbai where The Bombay Amateur Theatre was established in 1776. As Cody and Sprinchorn note, "The Amateur Theatre's audience in the 1820 was 'society': merchants, the officer of several European regiments, a few barristers, and civilians. The theatre imported to Mumbai in the early 1800s by travelling theatre companies as well as the theatre staged by amateur residents, was intended to provide entertainment and escape for the staff, soldiers, officers, and attendant civilians stationed there. Physically, these theatres (like the ones built in Kolkata) were exact copies of their English counterparts [...]" (The Columbia, 663). By early-19th century, however, performances by visiting European companies in Maharastrian theatre houses, which were already being suspected of covertly practising apartheid (*ibid.*, 664), were slowly replaced by performances of Marathi plays, which were later translated into English and produced to rave reviews. In 1843, Vishnudas Bhave (c. 1819-1901) produced Sita chooses a Husband, which heralded the emergence of Indian drama based on Indian themes in European-style theatres. Bhave's King Gopichand (1853) was at first criticised for its 'crudeness' but was later staged in a 'rectified' version. Vinayak Kirtane (1840-91) produced the nationalistic The Elder Madhavrao Peshwa (1857), which criticised 'people from another isle' for dominating the Indians and alerted the English imperialists, more troubled by the 1861 dramatisation of Dinabandhu Mitra's *The Mirror of Indigo Planters in Bengal*, Upendranath Das's *Surendra and Binodini* (1875), and (the anonymously-written) *The Trial of Gaekwar* (1875). Prior to this advent of nationalistic plays, however, in 1871, students of Pune's Deccan College had performed a translation of Narayana Bhatta's Venisamhar, with Krishnaji Gadgil writing the prologue to the play. Annasaheb Kirloskar's *Shakuntala* (1880) also contributed commendably to the ultimate development of Indian drama in English. In 1853, The Parsi Natak Mandali had been established in Maharastra, followed by The Elphinstone Dramatic Society in 1861. Many other theatrical companies managed by the Parsis were inaugurated in Maharastra between 1853 and 1869, and these included The Zoroastrian Theatrical Club, The Student Amateur Club, The Victoria Natak Mandali, The Empress Victoria Theatrical Company, and The Alfred Natak Mandali. The first recorded play in English from Maharastra was C.S. Nazir's verse-play *The First Parsi Baronet* (1866), based on the life of Jamsetjee Jejeebhoy (1783-1859). Dosabhai Nasarwanji Wadia's *The Indian Heroine* (1877), based on events from the 1857 Indian War of Independence, K.H. Dastur's *The Tragedy of Nero* (1905), Peroz P. Meherjee's *Dolly Persen* (1918), and Jehangir Mody's *Hector, Prince of Troy* (1932) are among the early Indian English dramas from Maharastra.

An important part of early Indian English playwriting was based in the Tamil Nadu-capital city of Chennai ('Madras' until 1996). Here, The Madras Dramatic Society, which encouraged amateur European theatrical productions just like the early Kolkata and Mumbai-based theatrical congregations, was founded in 1875, followed respectively in 1882 and 1895 by The Oriental Drama Club and the amateur Sarasa Vinodini Sabha, the last one founded by Krishnammachary of Bellary. Though Kumar has commented that "modern Indian English drama had no scope for flourishing in Chennai" (13), the Chennai-based theatre-houses saw a number of efficient dramatic productions focussing not only on Indian society but also on Indian history and myths. Some of the early Indian English dramas produced in Tamil Nadu prior to the Indian independence in 1947 included P.V. Ramaswamy Raju's *Urjoon Singh*: or, *The Princess Regained* (1875) and *Lord Likely* (1876), Mangadu Krishnamacharya's *Dasaratha*: or, *The Fatal Promise—A Tragedy* (1901), A. Srinivasacharya's *Harishchandra*: or, *The Martyr to Truth* (1912), T.S. Krishna Aiyar's *Lord Clive: A Drama in Five Acts* (1913), T.B. Krishnaswami's *Nur Jehan: A Play in Five Acts* (1918) and Satya: or, *The Altar of Love* (1919), K.S. Ramaswami Sastri's *Harishchandra: An Allegorical Drama* (1918) and *Draupadi* (1939), Vasudeva Rao's *Nala and Damayanti* (1928), and A.S. Panchapakesa Ayyar's *Sita's Choice and Other Plays* (1935) and *The Slave of Ideas and Other Plays* (1941), among others. Pammal V.S. Mudaliyar (1873-1967), who himself wrote *Pushpavalli* (1893) in order to protest against the segregating mentality of the English audience, designed the ethics of The Amateur Theatre in 1891. The most prolific of the pre-independence Indian English playwrights was Venbakkam V. Srinivasa Aiyangar (b. 1871), whose dramatic productions included *Vichu's Wife: A Little Comic Play in Two Scenes* (1911), Blessed in a *Wife: An Indian Society Drama in English in Three Acts* (1911), *The Surgeon-general's Prescription: A Play in One Scene* (1913), *The Point of View: A Drama in Three Acts* (1915), *The Bricks Between* (1918), and *At Any Cost* (1921). Irene Joshi of the University of Washington Libraries has compiled a list of many other eminent pre-independence Indo-Anglian dramatists and their plays in her webpage "South Asian Literatures in English, Pre-Independence Era" (1998). (http://www.lib.washington.edu/subject/southasia/pre1947.html).

Peter Barry, while writing about postcolonial literatures in general, has divided the publications and productions into Adopt, Adapt, and Adept phases based respectively on the overt dependence of the subaltern writers on their colonial counterparts, their decision for partial independence, and their ultimate declaration of full cultural independence (196). The first phase for Indian English dramas rather quickly paved the way for the second as soon as Michael Madhusudan Dutt began producing and translating his superior plays. A talented litterateur and linguist who was responsible for the maturing of blank verse in Bengali writings, Dutt the dramatist wrote the verse drama *Rizia: Empress of Inde* (1860) based on the life of Razia al-Din (1205-40), the Sultan of Delhi from 1236 to 1240. Prior to this, he had adapted *Ratnavali* (1858), supposed to have been originally written in Sanskrit by Harshavardana (c. A.D. 590-647), into English and the play, focussing on the love affair between Udayana, King of Kaushambi, and Ratnavali, the daughter of King Vikramabahu of Simhala, was spontaneously applauded by its European spectators. In 1859, Sermista was translated from Dutt's original Bengali version. Based on an ancient Aryan legend, the drama explores the problematic relationship between the friends Debjani, the daughter of Sage Shukracharya and Sermista, the daughter of the demon-king Vrishparva, and their relationship to King Yayati of Yadav dynasty. Other than anonymously translating

Mitra's *The Mirror of the Indigo Planters* in 1861, Dutt also produced the critically-acclaimed *Is This Called Civilisation*? in 1871. The Anglophile litterateur's plays demonstrate their author's desire to be directed by the metrical standards of English drama and yet explore areas and aspects that are typically Indian. Reviewing his plays, Kshetra Gupta has drawn readers' attention to the efficiency of their metrical aspects, their decorativeness, and their unparalleled emotiveness (Dutt, 80). Other than Dutt, R.N. Rai mentions only Ram Kinoo Dutt's Manipur Tragedy (1893) as among the 'very few Indian English plays' produced in 19th century Bengal (Perspectives, 13).

Before moving on to discuss the dramatic oeuvre of Aurobindo Ghosh (1872-1950), Naik comments, "Owing to the lack of a firm dramatic tradition nourished on actual performance in live theatre, early Indian English drama in Bengal, as elsewhere in India, grew sporadically as mostly closet drama; and even later, only Sri Aurobindo, Rabindranath Tagore, and Harindranath Chattopadhyay produced a substantial corpus of dramatic writing" (98). A nationalist and later a great Indian philosopher, Ghosh was tried and acquitted at the Alipore Bomb Case of 1908. Prior to this, between 1891 and 1916, he wrote five complete and six incomplete verse plays. *The Witch of Ilni: A Dream of the Woodlands* (1891) and *Achab and Esar* were written before Ghosh left England for India in February 1893. His other plays in English include Perseus the Deliverer, *The Viziers of Bassora: A Dramatic Romance*, *Rodogune*, *Eric: A Dramatic Romance*, and *Vasavadutta*, all identifiably written between 1893 and 1916. While *The Viziers of Bassora* is based on the 12th century The One Thousand and One Arabian Nights, Perseus the Deliverer focuses on the Greek legend of Perseus and Andromeda, the tragic Rodogune is located in Syria, and Vasavadutta "shows how Vvtsa Udayan, the king of Cowsambie, caputured throiugh treachery by Chunda Mahasegn, the king of Avunthie, neatly turns the tables on his captor by capturing the heart of Vasavadutta, Chunda Mahasegn's daughter" (*ibid.*, 100).

The influence of Rabindranath Tagore (1861-1941) on the subgenre of Indo-Anglian drama has been mentioned by different literary historians, and in his Indian Writing in English, Iyengar dedicates a separate chapter of twenty-two pages, entitled "Tagore the Playwright" towards commemorating the litterateur's dramatic contributions. While a number of plays, including *Chitra* (1913), *The Cycle of Spring* (1917), *Sacrifice and Other Plays* (1917), *Red Oleanders* (1924) and *Natir Puja —The Court Dancer's Worship* (1927), have been translated by Tagore himself, his other plays like *The Post Office* (1914), *The Curse at Farewell* (1924), *Three Plays—Mukta-Dhara, Natir Puja, and Chandalika* (1950), and *Devouring Love* (1961) have been respectively translated by Debabrata Mukhopadhyay, Edward Thompson, Marjorie Sykes, and Shakuntala Rao Sastri. Either an exhortation on human beings to accept death as a reality of life (*The Cycle of Spring*), celebration of humanistic values over mammonism (*Red Oleanders*), or focus on love (*Chitra*) or religious fanaticism (*Natir Puja*), Tagore's Indo-Anglian plays easily achieve universal contexts.

Among the other more efficient Indo-Anglian dramatists writing in pre-independence India were Harindranath Chattopadhyay (1898-1990), Thyagaraja Paramasiva Kailasam (1884-1946), Joseph Mathias Lobo Prabhu (1906-99), and Bharati Sarabhai (b. 1912). The younger brother of the Indian freedom fighter and poet Sarojini Naidu (1879-1949), Chattopadhyay was a left-leaning M.P. of the Vijayawada constituency between 1952 and 1957. Known primarily as a poet, Chattopadhyay began his drama-writing career with the fantasy-based *Abu Hassan* (1918), and included in his *Poems and Plays* (1925) the seven plays on lives of Indian ascetics—*Pundalik, Saku Bai, Jayadeva, Chokha Mela, Eknath, Raidas,* and *Tukaram*. He also wrote a few social plays—*The Window, The Parrot, The Sentry's Lantern, The Coffin,* and *The Evening Lamp*, and compiled them in *Five Plays* (1929). While *The Window* and *The Parrot* are focuses respectively on Indian's impoverished proletariat and bondage of customs, *The Sentry's Lantern* depicts the mental states of a merchant, a bourgeois poet, and a poor worker who are about to be hanged, while bourgeois artists and romantically-bent individuals are lampooned respectively in *The Coffin* and *The Evening Lamp*.

Besides these, other than the non-dated *The Sleeper Awakened*, an allegorical attack on the evils of modern civilisation Chattopadhyay's dramatic works consist of *The Saint: A Farce* (1946), criticising the corruptions of Indian holy-men, *Kannappan*: or, *The Hunter of Kalahasti* (1950), on untouchability, and the Buddha's-life-based *Siddhartha*: or, *The Man of Peace* (1956).

Other than the reformative plays—for example, In the *Clutch of the Devil* (1926) and *The Trial of Science for the Murder of Humanity* (1942)—of A.S. Panchapakesa Ayyar (1899-1963), Sarat Kumar Ghosh's *The Prince of Destiny* (1910), Kedarnath Dasgupta's *Calif for a Day* (1916) and *Bharata* (1918), and Dhangopal Mukhopadhyay's *Layla-Majnu* (1916), pre-independence Indo-Anglian playwriting received a huge boost in the productions of Kailasam. The acknowledged Kannada 'king of farces', Kailasam, who had spent several years in England, freely mixed Kannada and English in his plays, most of which are based on different episodes of the Indian epics, *The Ramayana* (c. 500 B.C.) and *The Mahabharata* (c. 400 B.C.). During his lifetime, the humour-writing Kailasam produced only one full-length Indo-Anglian play *Karna*: or, *The Brahmin's Curse* (1946). His other productions include *The Burden* (1933), *Fulfilment* (1933), *A Monologue: Don't Cry* (1933), and *Keechaka* (1947). Lobo Prabhu contributed to the sub-genre of Indo-Anglian drama more than a dozen melodramatic plays, including *Mother of New India* (1944), *Death Abdicates* (1945), and the post-independence *Collected Plays: Apes in the Parlour The Family Cage, Flags of the Heart, Winding Days, Love becomes Light,* and *Dog's Ghost* (1956). Bharati Sarabhai, inspired by the philosophy and socio-political activism of Mohandas Karamchand Gandhi (1869-1948), produced respectively in 1943 and 1952 two Indian plays in English—*The Well of the People* and *Two Women*. While the first suggests an unconventional solution to the rampant practise of untouchability, the second play, while depicting the lifestyles of Anuradha and the devotional singer Urvashi, suggests that to gain spiritual peace and fulfilment, an individual needs not abjure his or her worldly belongings and society.

With India becoming independent from the English colonial rule in August 1947, the Indo-Anglian drama began to demonstrate more mellifluousness than ever and also became more daring. On Indian playwriting at this juncture, G.P. Deshpande thus comments at length: "By the time independence came to India in 1947, modern drama, as we knew then, was deeply aware of the west and also of modernity. Inasmuch as it was a response to colonialism and imperialism, it was also a response to modernity, for colonialism and imperialism were 'modern phenomena'. With the arrival of political independence, we do not quite have postcolonial theatre. In fact, the phenomenon of the 'postcolonial' is more than doubtful and debatable. It was not even a phenomenon. It is the usage of the post-ideological world looking at the emergence of a political independence in the third world. To brand it 'postcolonial' made a lot of sense at least superficially. At another level, it helped the thinking processes which wanted to announce the end of imperialism. [...]. 'Postcolonial' was and is a post-political category" (Modern, xiv).

Among the important post-independence Indian English dramatists are Govindas Vishnoodas Desani (1909-2000), Habib Tanvir (1923-2009), Nissim Ezekiel (1924-2004), Asif Currimbhoy (b. 1928), Dina Mehta (b. 1928), Vijay Tendulkar (1928-2008), Girish Karnad (b. 1938), Pratap Sharma (1939-2011), Gurcharan Das (b. 1943), Manjula Padmanabhan (b. 1953), Cyrus Mistry (b. 1956), Aamir Raza Husain (b. 1957), and Mahesh Dattani (b. 1958). Some of the dramatists mentioned above are not 'Indo-Anglian dramatists' in the strict sense of the term, but their oeuvres have been translated into English and they are usually considered to exert considerable influence on Indian populace. One may also mention here the internationally-recognised Bengali leftist-dramatists Badal Sircar (1925-2011) and Utpal Dutt (1929-93) and the English translations of their diverse social plays. The transliterated and dramatised versions of the novels of Mahasweta Devi (b. 1926), especially that of her 1975 novel *The Mother of 1084*, have also contributed to her becoming a major figure in the filed of Indo-Anglian drama. It may be mentioned here that for a better understanding of the history of post-independence Indian English playwriting, Aparna Bhargava Dharwadker's Theatres of Independence: Drama, Theory, and Urban Performance in India since 1947 (Iowa City: The University of Iowa Press, 2005), is quite helpful.

Often reverently grouped among the early post-independence Indo-Anglian dramatists, Desani was born in Kenya, educated in England, and wrote in India. A Buddhist philosopher who gained eminence through his novel *All About H. Hatterr* (1948), Desani's lone but influential contribution to the ever-expanding sub-genre of Indian English drama was the abstract play *Hali* (1950), an allegory about everyman's quest. With the name of a Muslim saint and wearing long hair, bangles, and anklets, the protagonist of Desani's play represents general humanity. The 1950 play is introduced by Edward Morgan Forster (1879-1970) and Thomas Stearns Eliot (1888-1965) who respectively mention that the play "keeps evoking heights above the summitcity of normal achievement" and contains "often terrifyingly effective" imagery.

Originally a leftist Urdu dramatist, Tanvir trained in acting at England's Royal Academy of Dramatic Arts and in direction at Bristol Old Vic Theatre School. His *Charandas Chor* (1975), translated into English by Anjum Katyal and abridged by Sally Jones, may be identified as the Indian version of the Theatre of the Absurd where a petty thief's insistence on following honest paths of life ultimately leads to his execution. Tanvir's drama-writing began in 1954 with *Agra Bazar* and concluded in 2006 with *The King's Blood*. *The Broken Bridge* (1995) is another commendable production from Tanvir.

The Indian Jewish litterateur Ezekiel, who won the Sahitya Akademi Award in 1983 for his poetry-collection, published *The Damn Plays* in 1969. Ezekiel, who taught English at Mumbai, Leeds, and Puducherry, contributed to the sub-genre of Indo-Anglian drama a few social and personal plays like *Marriage Poem: A Tragi-Comedy* (1969), *Nalini: A Comedy* (1969), *The Sleepwalkers: An Indo-American Farce* (1969), *Song of Deprivation* (1969), and *Don't Call it Suicide* (1994).

Almost always a controversial figure, Asif Currimbhoy's dramatic oeuvre consists of socio-political plays like *The Clock* (1959), a psychological play; *The Tourist Mecca* (1959), which like the 1965 *The Hungry Ones* and the 1971 *Darjeeling Tea*, focuses on the West-East cultural encounters; *The Doldrummers* (1960), on the Maharastrian 'hippie-culture'; *The Dumb Dancer* (1961), another psychological play; *The Captives* (1963), on the 1962 Sino-Indian border conflict; *Goa* (1964), about the liberation of Goa by the Indians; *Monsoon* (1965), about imperialism; *An Experiment with Truth* (1969), on India's struggle for independence and the assassination of M.K.Gandhi; *Inquilab* (1970), about the Naxalite Revolution; *The Refugee* (1971) and *Sonar Bangla* (1972), about the India-Pakistan-Bangladesh conflict and war of 1971; *Om Mane Padme Hum* (1972), about the Chinese aggression against the Tibetans; *Angkor* (1973), on politics in south-east Asia; *The Miracle Seed* (1973), on Maharastra famine; and *The Dissident M.L.A.* (1974), on students' agitations in Gujarat. Currimbhoy, as Iyengar writes, "can contrive interesting situations, his dialogues are arresting, and he has a sense of atmosphere; and his plays are actable" (245).

The female Parsi litterateur Dina Mehta's *The Mythmakers* (1969) is an important Indo-Anglian play focusing on the violet anti-immigrant demonstrations in Mumbai. The open-ended play criticises the Indian politicians for indulging in dirty machinations, regionalism, and provincialism. Her *The Brides are not for Burning* (1993) criticises the Indians' burning of their wives or relatives to death over the issue of dowry. Nilufer E. Bharucha credits Mehta for not 'moving to the West' in her writings though she belongs to the diaspora (Shifting, 80).

Vijay Tendulkar wrote 27 full-length plays and 25 one-act plays all throughout his dramatic career. A consistent critic of the excesses of Indian society, Tendulkar's oeuvre, written mostly in Marathi, consists of plays of the absurd and cruelty. Some of his more famous plays are available in English: *Silence! The Court is in Session!* (translated by Priya Adarkar in 1979), *Ghashiram Kotwal* (1984), *The Churning* (1985), *The Threshold* (1985), *The Last Days of Sardar Patel* and *The Mime Players*:

Two Screen Plays (2001), Mitrachi Goshta—A Friend's Story: A Play in Three Acts (translated by Gowri Ramnarayan in 2001), Kanyadan (2002), and *The Cyclist* and *His Fifth Woman*: Two Plays by Vijay Tendulkar (translated by Balwant Bhaneja in 2006). *Silence! The Court is in Session!* and *Ghashiram Kotwal* are Tendulkar's most famous Indo-Anglian plays, and are appropriate and powerful critiques of the cruelties and corruptions of the Indian society.

Karnad, a Kannada playwright, often takes the help of history and mythology to compose superior plays, some of which have been translated into English by Karnad himself. Originally a philosopher and economist who studied at Oxford, Karnad briefly taught at the University of Chicago before dedicating himself to fulltime writing. His English plays include *Yayati* (1961), based on a Mahabharata-king, *Tughlaq* (1964), focussing on the mental turmoil of the 1325-51 Turkish Sultan of Delhi, Muhammad bin Tughluq (c. 1300-51), *Hayavadana* (1971) based on Thomas Mann's *The Transposed Heads* (1940) which draws from the 11th century Indian collection of folktales, *Kathasaritsagara*, and *Naga-Mandala* (1988), drawn on an Indian folktale. He also acted as the screenwriter for *Samskara* (1970) based on a social novel by Udupi Rajagopalacharya Ananthamurthy (b. 1932).

Pratap Sharma, who studied in Sri Lanka, and later at India's Shimla, associated himself with Mumbai's Indian National Theatre in 1961. Also a writer for children, Sharma produced two famous Indo-Anglian plays respectively in 1968 and 1970 —*A Touch of Brightness* and *The Professor has a War-cry*. Banned for sometime in Maharastra like Currimbhoy's *The Doldrummers*, Sharma's *A Tough of Brightness* focuses on Mumbai's brothels and slums. Later, in the 1970 play, the protagonist Virendra, after learning that he has had been born after a Hindu professor deserted his mother who was sexually-assaulted by a Muslim and a European, dies at the end while killing his mother's deserter. In *The Professor has a War-cry*, Sharma innovatively uses the demon from the traditional Kathakali dance to demonstrate the internal turmoil of Virendra.

Gurcharan Das, easily an Adept-phase dramatist like most of his post-independence fellow-writers, criticises the English colonising mentality in his *Larins Sahib* (1970), later included in his *Three English Plays* (2003), the other two being Mira and 9 Jakhoo Hill. In his anti-imperial 1970 play, Das, who studied at Harvard, delineates the life of the English imperial-representative Henry Lawrence, who attended the court of King Dalip Singh (1838-93) of Punjab between 1846 and 1847, and who passed from being a progressively-minded Englishman into a segregating dominator.

Manjula Padmanabhan, a Delhi-based diplomat's daughter who grew up in boarding schools, is originally the author of several children's books and a comic-strip artist. Her dramatic oeuvre includes *Lights Out*! (1984), *Hidden Fires*: *The Artist's Model* (1995), *Sextet* (1996), and *Harvest* (1996). Lights Out! explores the sentiments of Leela who has had been molested outside her house and whose husband Bhaskar is unready to protest the victimisation of women. Surinder, the exasperated husband of Leela's friend Naina, plans to kill the molesters of women but ultimately, like Bhaskar, he is non-performative. Durgesh Ravande offers a fine review of Padmanabhan's 1984 play in "Manjula Padmanabhan's Lights Out!: A Critique of Urban Hypocrisy", a 2007 Triveni article: http://yabaluri.org/TRIVENI/manjulapadmanabhanslightsoutoct2007.html. Her other critically-acclaimed drama *Harvest*, which was selected for the Onassis Prize in 1997, is a futuristic play about the sale of body parts and exploitative relations between developed and developing countries, and is identifiably of postcolonial nature.

While Cyrus Mistry's *Doongaji House* (written in 1978 and produced as late as 1990) depicts the decline of a Maharastra-based Parsi family in postmodern India where the members of diasporic Parsi communities are shown as confused over reacting to changing situations, Aamir Raza Husain, an Awadhi aristocrat who studied history at New Delhi's Saint Stephen's College, probably criticises the traditional Hindu-Muslim division in Indian societies by dramatising an episode from *The Ramayana* and naming it *The Legend of Ram* (2004). His *The Fifty Day War* (2000) commemorates the Kargil War of May-

July 1999 between India and Pakistan in which both the countries lost approximately four thousand and six hundred soldiers and civilians.

The list of post-independence Indian dramatists writing in English would be an ever-expanding one, but the shortage of space calls for the conclusion of this essay with a reference to the oeuvre of Dattani. The first Indo-Anglian playwright to win the Sahitya Akademi Award, Dattani studied and matured in Bangalore, and post-graduated in marketing and advertising management. The Indian dramatist has nine Indian English plays to his credit, including the 1998 B.B.C. radio-play *Seven Circles Round the Fire: Where There's a Will* (1986) (on the deceased businessman Hasmukh Mehta's will that installs his former mistress in his house where Mehta 'lives on' as an apparition), *Dance Like a Man* (1989) (on the importance of choosing the right vocation in a family of Bharatnatyam dancers consisting of the father Amritlal, his son Jairaj, Jairaj's wife Ratna and her daughter Lata), *Tara* (1990) (a feministic focus on the deprivation of women in Indian families), *Bravely Fought the Queen* (1991) (positing the legend of Lakshmi Bai (1835-58), the freedom-fighting ruler of Jhansi, against suburbian boredom), *Final Solutions* (1993) (on Hindu-Muslim riots, their antagonism and hypocrisy), *Night Queen* (1996) (on homosexuality), *On a Muggy Night in Mumbai* (1998) (on closeted homosexuality), *Seven Circles Round the Fire* (on Indian eunuchs), *Thirty Days in September* (2001), and *Brief Candle* (2009). It needs to be mentioned at the end that Dattani is being consciously followed by a number of young Indian dramatists writing in English especially in Kolkata and Mumbai, and it would only be a matter of a few months that a number of new and efficient Indo-Anglian dramatic productions would be added to the sub-genre of Indian English drama. It may be remembered that Deshpande has already had applauded the post-1960 playwrights' 'awareness of the theatre and the multiplicity of form' in his introduction to *Modern Drama: An Anthology* (xvi), and they are expected to perform and deliver.

WORKS CITED

Albert, Edward. *History of English Literature*. 5th ed. New Delhi: Oxford University Press, 1979. Rpt. 2003.

Barry, Peter. *Beginning Theory: An Introduction to Literary and Cultural Theory*. 2nd ed. New Delhi: Viva Books Pvt. Ltd., 2008.

Dutt, Michael Madhusudan. *Madhusudan's Complete Works*. Kolkata: Sahitya Samsad, 1965. Rpt. 1990.

English Postcoloniality: Literatures from around the World. Eds. Mohanram, Radhika, and Gita Rajan. Westport: Greenwood Press, 1996.

Indian English Novel in the Nineties: Studies in Contemporary Literature. Eds. Shukla, Sheobhushan, and Anu Shukla. New Delhi: Sarup and Sons, 2002.

Indian Literature: An Introduction. Eds. Dev, A.N., B.B. Tiwari, and S. Khanna. New Delhi: Pearson-Longman, 2006.

Iyengar, K.R. Srinivasa. *Indian Writing in English*. New Delhi: Sterling Publishers Pvt. Ltd., 1962. 5th ed. Rpt. 2001.

Kumar, Nand. *Indian English Drama: A Study in Myths*. New Delhi: Sarup and Sons, 2003.

Modern Indian Drama: An Anthology. Ed. Deshpande, G.P. New Delhi: Sahitya Akademi, 2000. Rpt. 2004.

Naik, M.K. *A History of Indian English Literature*. New Delhi: Sahitya Akademi, 1982. Rpt. 2005.

Nayar, Pramod K. *Postcolonial Literature: An Introduction*. New Delhi: Pearson Longman, 2008.

Perspectives and Challenges in Indian English Drama. Ed. Tandon, Neeru. New Delhi: Atlantic Publishers and Distributors Pvt. Ltd., 2006.

Shifting Continents/Colliding Cultures: Diaspora Writing of the Indian Subcontinent. Eds. Crane, Ralph J. and Radhika Mohanram. Amsterdam: Rodopi, 2000.

The Columbia Encyclopaedia of Modern Drama. Eds. Cody, Gabrielle and Evert Sprinchorn. New York: Columbia University Press, 2007.

23 Tara: The Lonely Star

Sanchita Das

All the world's a stage,
And all the men and women merely players:
They have their exits and their entrances;
And one man in his time plays many parts.
(Shakespeare—*As You Like It*, 266)

Mahesh Dattani takes on what he calls the 'invisible issues' of Indian society in his plays. By pulling out taboo subjects from under the rug and placing them on stage for public discussion, Dattani challenges the constructions of 'India' and 'Indian' as they have traditionally been defined in modern theatre. He is known for bringing into the open those issues which the Indian society and culture tends to brush into the garbage pail, because they are uncomfortable, has written and produced the play *Tara*, which has several entry points.

The play can be approached through the issue of simple man-woman relationship, or it can be responded to in terms of the disabled children's struggle against a variety of odds, which have been put in their way by nature, or chance, or accident of their birth. Or one can respond to the text through the positioning of the girl-child in Indian culture and society.

The man-woman relationship is dramatized through the interactions between Mr. Patel and his wife Bharati. He is shown to be often rude and authoritarian, when it comes to dealing with her and taking decisions. He turns out to be a caring husband, too, in his looking after Bharati during her bouts of depression. His words about Bharati reveal his concern: "May be I'm expecting the worst. It may never happen—no. Things are getting out of hand. I must worry about her. Yes. I am worried—about my wife" (Dattani, 330). But at the same time, he exhibits a streak of harshness, even heartlessness towards her. His admonition to Bharati not to give one of her kidneys to Tara who needs a kidney transplant, is not the result of his concern for his wife's health, but is the product of his cruel attitude towards her. When questioned by Bharati why he is against it, his answer is in keeping with his overall treatment of his wife: "Because I do not want you to have the satisfaction of doing it" (Dattani, 344). This quite negates his professed concern which he talks about when Bharati is in the throes of depression. Similarly, he deprives Bharati of the chance to confess her sin to Tara which she has committed towards her (Tara). That would have relieved her guilt and possibly her malady, but it seems that he does not want relief for her. His words sound heartless: "No. I don't want to give her the satisfaction of confessing" (Dattani, 377). His summary dismissal of Bharati's opinions as inconsequential and not paying heed to her expostulations on behalf of Tara represents him as a typical overriding patriarchal husband. It is another matter that we come to know later why Bharati was rapidly trying to champion Tara's case—it is not for the sake of Tara that she does it. However, with Bharati's underlying motive for her effusions of love towards Tara becoming clear, the play does not linger on intensively on the unequal relationship between the husband and wife. This, therefore, is not the central strand, determining the progress of the plot.

The theme of odds faced by the physically challenged children in society no doubt comes through. Tara's artificial leg, the ridicule she is subjected to by her peers at school and in the neighbourhood (by Roopa, Prema and Nalini—the last two do not appear on the stage) and the limp caused by the artificial leg which symbolically serves as the marker of a disadvantage compared to others are indicative of the playwright's interest in this issue. Roopa's words about Tara are representative of the attitude of Prema and Nalini, and possibly of the society at large: "She is a real freak of nature all right" (Dattani, 342). But in this case, too, we find that this disability does not pose an insurmountable challenge to Tara, who has the capacity to laugh at it herself, and laugh at the imbecility of those who consider it great deprivation and a subject of pity or ridicule. She is very much capable of holding her own and making the best of her life, with all its givens. This, too, therefore, does not frame the whole of the play, demanding detailed attention.

I would, therefore, like to use the last prism, that is, the positioning of the girl-child in Indian society to enter the text and raise the following questions: Who has killed Tara? And why? I would like to argue in the course of the essay that it is not one individual who has killed Tara. It is the socio-cultural system which is responsible for her death. The beliefs, the attitudes, and the prejudices that are deep-rooted in the collective Indian cultural psyche become instrumental in taking Tara's life. It is a complex play. Issues of class and community interplay to weave the plot of the play and bring about the climactic moment of reversal of expectations. This reversal of expectations in the matter of Bharati, Tara's mother, who sympathized with Tara, actually is not the central point the play makes.

Coming to the question who has killed Tara, it is proper to know who Tara is, what her background is, in what sort of family, neighbourhood and society she is born and lives and dies. She is a Siamese twin, born to the Patels—Mr. Patel and Bharati, his wife. Born conjoined as one body with her brother Chandan, she is separated by a complicated, technologically advanced surgical operation by Dr. Thakkar who is visiting India from London. The discrimination against her begins right from the process of surgery. I would revert to it later, but I would like to mention in passing the three levels on which Tara is deprived of what is her due: (i) At the hands of Nature, which makes her weaker and reduces the chances of her survival. In Dr. Thakkar's words: "Our greatest challenge would be to keep the girl alive. Nature wanted to kill her. We couldn't allow it." (Dattani, 376), (ii) At the level of society whose attitude is reflected through her peers—her classmate in class nine, Roopa and her friends Prema and Nalini, who find amusement in her wooden leg, (iii) At the level of family, especially at the hands of her mother and maternal grandfather—they deprive her of one of the two healthy legs. Briefly going over the three levels of discrimination, we find that it is the last which would need detailed consideration:

1. Discrimination against her by nature is accidental. Generally, born as single children, girls have better chances of survival than boys. But in this case, Tara happens to be the weaker of the two twins.
2. As far as discrimination by the society is concerned, Tara is not overly disturbed what others think of her infirmity. Therefore, it is almost insignificant.
3. Discrimination by the family is a serious matter, as it is conscious and is the result of a conspiracy against her. At the time of surgical separation from her brother, a conspiracy is hatched against her by none else than her very own mother, Bharati, who has conceived and produced her, her grandfather (maternal) and Dr. Thakkar. She gets deprived of one of the two healthy legs. The Siamese twins had three healthy legs. One of the healthy legs had greater chances of survival on the girl child as the blood supply to it came from the girl's body. But Tara was not given her due. She was deprived of what was hers because Bharati wanted to have a healthy and able son. So, Chandan was given the two healthy legs. This conspiracy needs to be commented upon in the light of what happens to the girl child in Indian society. There is no specific and clear answer because there cannot be one. No one individual is responsible for what happens to her, because this has to do with the positioning of the girl-child in the Indian society.

The point I am trying to make is that all types of discrimination Tara faces at the hands of her family members are the consequence of their being prisoners in the hands of collective unconscious that constitutes their psyches. The sources of this collective unconscious are the cultural/religious texts which determine Indians' attitude towards women.What happens to the girl child in the Indian society? She faces infanticide and if by chance she is born, she is abandoned either to die, or to be picked up by an orphanage or by a needy couple and or compassionate couple who just want a child. More often than not, the abandoned girl child dies. Ironically, this happens in a society, which has a mythology, with goddesses being worshipped as Kali and Durga (shakti), Saraswati (as wisdom) and Lakshmi (as wealth). Indian society which seeks to occupy high moral ground through its belief in the concept of 'vasudhev kutumbkam' does not hesitate in exterminating its daughters by short-term or long-term means.

There are two pointers in the play which make me believe that Dattani also wants us to interpret it along the lines of the social system being the culprit in the matter of cruelty to girl children. The following conversation between Chandan and Roopa serve as one pointer:

> Chandan: What would you do if you had to choose between a boy and a girl? Who would you choose?
>
> Roopa: I think it's more civilized to drown her (girl) in milk. (Dattani, 365)

Chandan and Tara's maternal grandfather was a wealthy man. He was in politics and came very close to becoming the Chief Minister. His will is a testament of the kind of treatment that is meted out to girls in Indian society. Mr. Patel and Chauhan are talking:

> Patel: He [grandfather] left you a lot of money.
>
> Chandan: And Tara?
>
> Patel: Nothing.
>
> Chandan: Why?
>
> Patel: It was his money. He could do what he wanted with it. (Dattani, 360)

The worst part is that this conversation takes place in the presence of Tara. No consideration whatsoever for her feelings! Tara is the victim of this collective social system.

Having been successfully separated from her twin broher, her ordeal continues. We have talked about the conspiracy of her own mother against her. Her father, Mr. Patel, is not much different from his wife, though Bharati is guilty of a more serious crime/sin against Tara. He continuously and doggedly favours Chandan when it comes to giving him higher education abroad, and a career. Tara is discouraged openly, not with standing her feelings in the matter, even though she is more intelligent, sharp and witty and would perform well if given opportunities in life. It is only when Chandan refuses to go to College without her, Patel thinks of sending Tara, too, to college. Bharati supports Tara in the matter of higher education and in some other cases, but her support is tainted. It is the product of the guilt and cannot be interpreted as fighting the systemic odds in Tara's way.

Economic and religious/cultural factors have been responsible for the antipathy against and inferiorization of the girl child. A boy helps in contributing to the famiy income, whether by working in the field, or elsewhere. It is through him that the *vansh* (clan) continues, because of the patriarchal system which requires the members of the family to carry caste names, coming from the father (male side). Parents can attain *moksha* only if a son does the *kapaal kriya* (breaking of the skull while being cremated). So, either girls are killed at birth, or abandoned. The medical and technological advances have made it possible to detect the sex of the fetus. This has given an impetus to the killing of the girls. All this factors combine to create the social system in which the girl child has to live and die.

Tara is killed by the social system, which controls the minds and actions of people. The trauma of coming to know the role her mother had played in her life, and the discrimination she faces at the hands of her father and grandfather becomes too much for her. And why is she killed? Tara is not wanted. Girls are not wanted. They are irrelevant from the points of view of religion and economics. They are dispensable.

It is noteworthy that discrimination against Tara continues even after her death. Chandan, who was always interested in writing, and who has come to England for higher studies, has transformed into Dan. He turns the story he writes into his own tragedy. It is only incidentally that he has to tell Tara's story, too. Dan apologizes to Tara for doing this: "Forgive me, Tara. Forgive me for making it my tragedy" (Dattani, 380). It is quite another matter that it becomes Tara's tragic story also. But that is only incidental.

The play presents a mirror to the Indian society to see its true face. It tries to shock the society out of its grooved thinking. Through racy dialogue and bare minimum stage-setting (by just picking out the characters through cross fadings of light) the playwright effectively portrays the interactions among the characters. The authenticity of the play is established by making Chandan (Chandu at home and later called Dan after his arrival in England) as the narrator/writer of the play. He is one of the Siamese twins (the other twin being Tara, his sister) and nobody could know better than he does.

WORKS CITED

Dattani, Mahesh. *Tara* in *Collected Plays*. New Delhi: Penguin, 2000.

Katyal, Anjum. "Of Page and Stage: An Interview with Mahesh Dattani." *Seagull Theatre Quarterly*. (December 1999).

Shakespeare, William. *The Complete Works*. Oxford & BH Publishing Co. Pvt. Ltd.: New Delhi, 1980.

24 Vijay Tendulkar's Journey Towards Self-discovery: Some Reflections

Ashok K. Saini

A writer is born in a society which has got certain traditions. The lifestyle of the people in that social setup is decided by the prevalent religious ideas, rituals, philosophy, modes of thinking and behaviour, its manners and etiquettes, etc. These form the raw material of the writers in their creative efforts and the writers support them, appreciate them or attack them in their works of art (Vandna Pathak and Urmila Dabir, 2009, 101).

Tain in his dominant *History of English Literature* reveals race, moment, and milieu as the three issues that mould literature. It is certainly the amassing of all past experiences, however as critics such as Rané Wellek say, it is more prominently the circumstances of a meticulous time of the history of a country or a race, the Zeitgeist. Tain relates his feelings regarding civilization to literature. For him a work of literature is a transcript of contemporary manners, a representation of a certain kind of mind. Behind each document there is a "man". One studies the document in order to know the man. But Tain is not a biographer; when he writes "man", not the individual author but the author as a representative of his race, surroundings, and epoch (www.netscape.com, 2006). The contemporary dramatists elucidate on the existent issues that get overlooked in the flash of recent ways of living. Tendulkar in an interview says:

> What is reality? The coexistence of the observer and the happening makes the reality. Reality becomes reality only when it is seen. There is nothing like absolute reality. Your perception of what is happening combined with the happening makes the picture of reality complete. Don't

> get frustrated, write what you see (http://passionfor cinema.com).

In his plays, we in general find contemporary socio-political issues. He has concentrated on the alienation of the modern individual. He has tried his best to satirize contemporary politics and depicted social and individual tensions in his plays as well. The evil too in the world has been nicely portrayed by him at large in his dramas. He always has been controversial, because he has always been contemporary in his concerns, social, political and theatrical. All his plays compact with the oppression of the weak by the powerful.

> Tendulkar is one of the dramatists who have picturized the contemporary age he lives in.... What distinguishes him from his fellow dramatists is the fact that he not only picturizes but also dramatize and not only raises issues but also rises to provide remedies to the riddles recurring from time to time. (Binod Mishra, 2008: 39)

Vijay Tendulkar has been the leading playwright of Marathi for more than fifty years. He started his career as a dramatist with his play, 'Shreemant' (The Rich Man) in 1955. He was born on 6th January 1928. In 1948 he worked as Sub-Editor in 'Navbharat'. He also worked for 'Maratha' and 'Loksatta'. He was the Executive Editor of 'Vasudha' and 'Deepawali'. He wrote columns for 'Manus' and 'Maharashtra Times'. His album of one-act plays *Ajagar Ani Gandharva* (The Python and the Gandharva) won Maharashtra State Government Award. Tendulkar has to his credit a number of Marathi plays which have been translated not only to English but also in some other languages. His well-known plays are *Ghashiram Kotwal, Silence! The Court is in Session, The Vultures, Sukharam Binder, Safar* (Journey), etc.

Tendulkar play *Silence! The Court is in Session* was awarded the Kamaladevi Chattopadhyay Award in 1970 and in 1978 he became the member of General Council, Sahitya Academi, New Delhi. He worked as a guest lecturer at Tata Institute of Social Sciences, Bombay from 1979 to 1981 and in the year 1979 he became the Vice-Chairman of the National School of

Drama. The film 'Akrosh' won Filmfare Award for the best screenplay in 1983 and in 1984 he was awarded 'Padma Bhushan'. Drama festival of his plays was organized by Amol Palekar at Pune in 2005 and in 2004, 'The Tendulkar Festival' sponsored by the Indo-American Arts Council was organized at New York.

In the middle of Marathi playwrights, Tendulkar remained in burning dialogue because of his controversial plays. His play *Ghashiram Kotwal* is variously appraised and enjoyed by the audience in India and overseas. Initially it was written in Marathi with the Marathi folk dance, music and culture. The play symbolizes the chronological incident of Nana Phadnavis's approach. In the prologue of the play he writes:

> This is not historical play. It is a story, in prose, verse, music and dance set in a historical era. Ghashirams are creations of socio-political forces which know no barriers of time and place. Although based on a historical legend, I have no intention of commentary on the morals, or lack of them, of the Peshwa, Nana Phadnavis or Ghashiram. The moral of this story, if any, may be looked for elsewhere. (*Ghashiram Kotwal,* 1986: iv)

Therefore, he acknowledges the legend from the history. He has presented the verity that Ghashirams are shaped by the social-political compels too. Ghashiram Kotwal is not a new theme for the Marathi literature. Moroba Kanhoba Vijaikar's novel *Ghashiram Kotwal* appeared in 1873 (*The History and Culture of the Indian People, The British Paramount and Indian Renaissance,* 1991: 187).

Tendulkar's *Ghashiram Kotwal* was performed in 1972 in Pune. The play begins with the dance and song of Hindu God Ganapati and Goddesses Saraswati. In this play the dramatist presents the Brahman from Shingeri, Tanjore, Rameshwar, Kumbhakonam, Banaras and Poona. This drama is a bitter satire on the so-called corrupted priests of the contemporary society. But what matter most in his play is the technique or the proper symbols at the proper places which makes this scathing and sarcastic presentation lively and humorous. Thus, the dramatist has presented the existent portrait of Indian society.

Tendulkar's *Silence! The Court is in Session* (23rd impression, 2008) has a well-knit plot and the dramatic techniques employed here are extremely pertinent and exemplary. The central theme of this play is the plight and predicament of a woman whose bodily wealth is plundered by a gang of selfish men. It is the story of the Miss Leela Benare, a dutiful and punctual school teacher, who becomes the victim of the carnal desire of some men who seldom take care of her modesty and position in society. The humiliations faced by Miss Leela Benare were unbearable to a forsaken woman who is in the constant search of an identity of a married woman.

The play was initially written in Marathi under the name *Shanta! Court Chalu Ahe,* which was afterward translated in to numerous languages. The anecdote of the play is concerning the members of a theatre coterie in exploration of a topic that could become further interesting to the audience. The title of the drama itself is somewhat humorous. It brings to light the authoritative attitude prevalent in the majority of the law courts. The title reveals how the legal system while warning people to listen also intimidates the accused by the mere exclamation of the word *Silence!* We come across this authoritative and manly voice many times when in the mock play. Accordingly the play *Silence! The Court is in Session* is by all accounts a satire on judiciary.

The issues of power and violence find place in all his plays in English translation. His plays are not written for the purpose of pure amusement. He portrays in his plays, the vicious stages of man in our society nowadays. In *The Vultures,* Tendulkar exhibits on the stage, the complete bloodshed arising from greed and immorality. It portrays the domestic violence caused by ravenousness. The selfishness and greed of human being are the central issues of the play. The characters in the play are eveready to deceive one another to acquire extra wealth.

The internal battle between good and evil feature strongly in all his plays. Evil people in his plays are selfish, self-centered and incapable of worship. The vulturine nature dominates the relations of middle class family in 'Vultures'. The play is an exceptionally dominant anecdote of cruel violence and terrible greed. The play was essentially written 14 years before it was produced (1970) and published in 1971. The play shocked the conservative sections of the society then, as Tendulkar used the language which was not normally used on the stage.

The play *Kanyadan* is possibly the most contentious of Tendulkar's plays. It deals with psychological study of the social tensions caused by the casteism in India side by side with the development of Jyoti's character from a soft-spoken and highly cultured Brahmin girl into a hardened spouse of her Dalit husband. The difference among upper castes and Dalits is a tremendously insightful question which features in Tendulkar's *Kanyadan*.

Jyoti, the daughter of a Brahmin family, makes a decision to marry a Dalit writer, Aran. Even after more then sixty years of sovereignty, Dalits continue to undergo desolation and ill-treatment at the hands of the upper castes. Jyoti comes from a politically and socially dynamic family. Nath Devlanikar, her father, is an MLA. Her mother, Seva is a social worker. This play presents the accurate portrait of the public. It can't be termed as anti-Dalit or anti-Brahmin. The play shows how our romantic idealism fails miserably. The disparity in the society and the sufferings of the people are the major concerns of Tendulkar. He believes in the common man. The basic question 'Why does innocent suffer?' remains unanswered. The question like 'Why should the dishonest thrive?' troubles him (Amarnath Prasad and Satish Barbuddhe, 2008: xiii).

Therefore, *Kanyadan* is not the story of triumph; it is the permit of trounce and logical perplexity. It presents expression to a profound rooted malaise and its pains. Tendulkar appears pragmatic and he raised the burning communal problem of untouchability through intellectual confusion. Arundhati Banerjee writes:

> Tendulkar is highly realistic not only in the delineation of characters and human relationships but in the depiction

> of the setting in which these characters enact the drama of their lives. (*Five Plays*, 2005: xv)

Tendulkar in *Kamala* makes use satire to scoff at the hypocrisy of the urban upper middle class. At the centre of the play is a self-seeking journalist, Jaisingh Jadhav, who treats the women he has purchased from the flesh market as an object that can buy him a promotion in his job and a reputation in his professional life. Sarita, his wife, is well educated and hails from a village called Phaltan. Kamalabai is Sarita's servant and she too hails from Phaltan. Though highly educated, Sarita lets herself be reduced to the status of a slavish, docile wife. Tendulkar explores the position women in contemporary Indian society. Through Sarita, Jadhav's wife, who is in her own way as exploited as Kamala, Tendulkar exposes the chauvinism intrinsic in the modern Indian male who believes himself to be liberal indeed.

In *Kamala,* Tendulkar's vision of the family becomes more violent. He demonstrates the bestiality and atrocity of people in a family living in a nauseatingly consumerist world. Like in most of his plays, in *Kamala* too, Tendulkar projects women as victim. The play highlights the gender stereotyping that is forced upon the women. In this play the theme is borrowed from a real-life incident.

Contrary to his other plays, *His Fifth Woman* was written in English and graphically portrays the discriminations and disproportions suffered by women in this male-dominated mundane world and explores the life after death. It visualizes a picture of the next world based on the egalitarianism where there is no distinction between the rich and the poor and between the man and the woman. In this play Tendulkar advocates the cause of the economic independence of woman, which will ensure that their wishes and body may not be trampled down under manly vanity. Dr. Balwant Bhaneja writes:

> His plays show how complex the responses of the human heart and soul are leaving us with no option but to engage with his protagonists and the emotional world they inhabit. (Bhaneja, Balwant, 2006: xiii)

The Cyclist (Safar, 1991) is intended to be Vijay Tendulkar's final play and perhaps his eventual comment on himself and the reality surrounding him. Tendulkar in his early sixties in 1991 had written 28 full-length plays, his works singularly recognized for intellectual integrity, innovative form and content. Despite its numerous productions, *The Cyclist* has continued to confound its directors and audience. It is a skillfully crafted, uninterrupted piece about the adventure of life told through a cyclist's journey. As an experimental playwright, his each play, in its form and structure, is different from the previous one. The play is not about one but three journeys: geographical, an historical journey of the bicycle, and a psychological exploration. In the play, unlike most of Tendulkar's other plays, there is no strong female character.

Vijay Tendulkar doesn't pursue verbosity and contemptible sentimentalism of Marathi Theater or contemplates only on a superior story. This of course doesn't mean that he does not tell an excellent account but that he is also interested in efficient presentation. His interest in form and technique has facilitated him to remain 'experimental' persistently. The most important contribution of Vijay Tendulkar as a playwright is his circumspectly crafted forms and designs.

Modes of narration, story telling, metaphoric composition and an apt presentation of music make the writer grand in the field of dramatic art. He dives deep into the psyche of middle class life, takes his materials from myths and legends of our golden past and tries his best to make these characters of legends the vehicle of his new vision of life. His works demonstrate the absurdity of contemporary life and his vigorous and perpetual struggle to gain excellence even amidst of the tribulations of the world.

WORKS CITED

Bhaneja, Balwant, Introduction, *Two Plays: The Cyclist and His Fifth Woman* by Vijay Tendulkar, New Delhi: OUP, 2006, xiii.

Binod Mishra, "Vijay Tendulkar's SILENCE! THE COURT IS IN SESSION: A Satire on Judiciary", in *Creative Writing and Criticism*, Bulandshahr, Vol. VI, No. 1, Oct. 2008, 39.

Deepak Ghare, *Ghashiram: Ek Wadal,* Granthali, 2nd Edn. 2005. http://passionforcinema.com/a-conversation-with-sir-vijay Tendulkar/ on 17th Dec. 06.

Jaydip Singh Dodia, K.V. Surendran (ed.), *Indian English Drama: Critical Perspectives*, New Delhi: Sarup & Sons, 2000.

Kushwaha, M.S. (ed.), *Dramatic Theory and Practice: Indian and Western*, New Delhi: Creative Books, 2000.

Prasad, Amarnath and S. Yadav (eds.). *Studies in Indian Drama in English*, Bareilly: Prakash Book Depot, 2003.

——. *The Plays of Vijay Tendulkar: Critical Explorations*, New Delhi: Sarup & Sons, 2008.

Prasad, Amarnath and Satish Barbuddhe (eds.). *The Plays of Vijay Tendulkar: Critical Explorations*, New Delhi: Sarup & Sons, 2008, xiii.

Priya Adarkar (Tr.), *Five Plays*, New Delhi: OUP.

Samik Bandhopadhyay, *Collected Plays in Translation: Vijay Tendulkar*, New Delhi: OUP, 2004.

Sturges Warner, *Director's Note Two Plays by Vijay Tendulkar*, New Delhi: OUP, 2006.

Tendulkar, Vijay, *Ghashiram Kotwal,* Translated from Maratha by Jayant Karve and Eleanor Zelliot, Calcutta: Seagull Books, 1986.

——. *Silence! The Court is in Session,* Tans. Priya Adarkar. New Delhi: OUP, 23rd Impression, 2008.

——. *Five Plays*, New Delhi: OUP, 2005, xv.

The History and Culture of the Indian People, The British Paramount and Indian Renaissance, Part II, Bhartiya Vidya Bhawan Bombay, 1991, 187.

Vandna Pathak and Urmila Dabir, "Crooning of a Different Drummer: Valmiki's 'Joothan'", in *The Indian Journal of English Studies,* New Delhi. Vol. XLVI 2009, 101. www.netscape.com, Tuesday, 21 March, 2006.

25 The Traditional and the Contemporary: A Study of Technique in Girish Karnad's *Naga-Mandala*

Shahewar Syed and *Apara Tiwari*

A.K. Sinha from "Girish Karnad: Thematic Concerns and Technical Features" in *New Directions in Indian Drama* comments on the playwright's technical skills:

> In all his plays—be the theme mythical, historical or legendary, Karnad's approach is modern, and he uses the conventions and motifs of folk art, like masks and curtains to project a world of intensities, uncertainties and unpredictable denouements. He rightly believes that the energy of folk theatre comes from the fact that although it seems to uphold traditional values, it also has the means of questioning these values. The various conventions the chorus, the music, the apparently unrelated comic interludes, the mixing of the human and the non-human worlds—permit a simultaneous presentation of alternative points of view. Like Bertolt Brecht, Karnad strives to break the 'illusion' of the theatre by which the spectators become so engrossed in a play that they forget, for the time being, what they are. Therefore, like Brecht, Karnad leaves the stage apparatus visible, presents synoptic announcements, has narrators directly talking to the audience. (105)

Girish Karnad a noted stage actor, playwright, film actor, television artist and a creative figure, was born at Matheran, near Bombay in 1938. It is true that Karnad was initiated into the writing of drama by chance, but there were several influences that went a long way into shaping his dramatic taste and genius. The earliest influence was that of the company Natak that was in vogue in Sirsi. The "Yakshagana" plays which he used to see with the servants also appealed to him due to their buffoonery and horseplay. But the greater influence came from the naturalistic drama of Henrik Ibsen and through him that of G.B. Shaw. Karnad was also influenced by Shakespeare considerably. But the influence of the Kannada drama was quite profound and deep on him. Karnad represents the best traditions of the Kannada drama which was quite rich with romantic plays, tragedies, comedies, poetic and blank verse plays. Karnad took keen interest in all of these; *Yayati* (1961), *Tughlag* (1964), *Ma Nishad* (1964), *Hayavadana* (1971), *Aujumallige* (1977), *Hattina Hunja* (1982), *Tale-Danda* (1988), *Naga-Mandala* (1988). Karnad bases this play, *Naga-Mandala*, on two folk-tales from Karnataka, which he acknowledges to have heard several years ago from Professor A.K. Ramanujan. Divided in two parts and beginning with a prologue with numerous characters, the play represents Karnad's unique dramatic technique with the employment of supernatural elements, dance, music, flames, folktales in dealing with the Prologue and the second part of the play (story's story). This second part is divided into Act I and Act II which deals with the story of Rani.

In the Prologue, the identification of the flames with young, sprightly and vocal women and the stories that they tell each other is a brilliant device used by Karnad for creating a particularly female context and content in the man-oriented folk tale. Each flame is a female, a storyteller. A Stranger, a writer himself, enters into their conversation, and listens to a new tale. The dramatization of the tale now begins outside his house. Appanna comes home simply for his meals. He keeps Rani locked up at home and visits a concubine. The subsequent pain and loneliness of Rani, who is still very attached to her parents, are emphasized by the narrator.

Appanna treats both Rani and the prostitute in an unfair manner. Neither of the relationships is complete. He reprimands the old lady Kurudavva and her son Kappana when they attempt to become friendly with Rani. Providentially, mischief is done, with which a happy turn of events takes place with the snake-lover's entry.

Complications build up when Rani becomes pregnant. Appanna is aghast forcing his wife face public trial. Rani has been faithful to her husband. This conviction is now at stake. The nervous and frightened young girl finds within herself a new courage and confidence and gains social respectability. She emerges triumphant from the public trial, as the snake does not bite her. The husband and wife turn towards each other, with a greater sense of relationship. The girl-bride now becomes the mother to be and as such receives a new social recognition. The double ending of the play *Naga-Mandala* presents duality through the structural device. In the first one, the Naga enters Rani's bedroom and dies for the sake of Rani and her family. In the second one, the snake does not die. He is allowed by Rani to live in her tresses. The lover is always present; he lives with her, within the family. The ironic element in the play becomes insightful when Appanna is left holding the child of another entity in public and asked to respect his wife as a "goddess".

Kurudavva, the blind woman, plays a significant part in *Naga-Mandala* though the only way she is connected with the plot of the play is that the Cobra falls in love with Rani because of the magical power of the root given by Kurudavva to Rani. *Naga-Mandala* is a play about narrativity or the truth of fiction.

Karnad has depicted a mythological legend in a very interesting and humorous style using the old conventions and motifs of folk tales and folk theatre; masks, curtains, dolls, the story within a story, to create a bizarre world. Ideas from Indian myths and legends become a vehicle of a new vision. By the use of myths, he tries to show the absurdity of life and man's eternal struggle to achieve perfection. According to Seema Suneel from "Girish Karnad's *Yayati* Reconsidered" in *New Directions in Indian Drama*:

> In plays like *Yayati* and *Hayavadana* Karnad has taken traditional puranic themes but has given a fresh interpretation to these. His plays have pioneered a style

> which unites the elements of traditional Indian theatre, such as "Yakshagana" and strikingly modern sensibility for contemporary socio-political realities. (125)

Naga-Mandala is a mythical play which attracts the reader's attention on the ignorance of society towards the pain and suffering of women. The story is based on two Kannada folk tales where supernatural elements are used. He mixes the two worlds; natural and supernatural. The word "Naga" is non-human; a snake associated with Lord Shiva. It holds the earth on its hoods. It is worshipped on the day of Naga-Panchami in the month of Sravan. There are several stories and superstitions associated with the cobra. It is a fertility symbol. In *Naga-Mandala*, there are human characters like Rani, Appanna, Kurudavva, Kappanna and the villagers; similarly there are animal characters like cobra, dog, mongoose and abstract characters like Flames and Story. It is a strange mixture of non-human and human characters, myth and folk tales, past and present. As C.L. Khatri says:

> In this play he [Karnad] makes use of the non-naturalistic techniques of the traditional Indian drama-myth and folk tales—to explore the contemporary realities and personal anguish. The popular folk tale of Naga is used to undertake a discussion on moral order. It is also used as a kind of cultural anesthesia to eliminate from our racial unconscious cultural pathogens such as caste and gender distinctions and religious fanaticism. (58)

The snake-lover's story has been treated as a "Vrat-katha". A story told during the festival of cobra worship where women pray to the cobra for blessing them with safety, and progress of their family. As Santosh Gupta from "*Naga-Mandala*: A Story of Marriage and Love" in *The Plays of Girish Karnad* A.K. Ramanujan says that, "ritual tale itself is a public event told during the cobra festival to propitiate the snake, to ensure safety and fertility within marriage" (12). Snakes are the symbols of human maleness and strength. Nagas are sometimes portrayed as handsome men, or as half-man and half-snake, the top half using the torso of a man, the lower half a coiled snake. The folk element of *Naga-Mandala* and the magical power which the cobra possesses remind us that we are watching a play.

Karnad's plays are particularly concerned with psychological problems, dilemmas and conflicts experienced by modern Indian men and women in their different social situations. The greatness of his drama is attested by the tone and expression of transforming any situation into an aesthetic experience. Employing humour and irony as tools and making ingenious use of myths and folk forms in his plays to exorcise socio-cultural evils, he presents a comprehensive picture of human life.

Appanna, the main male character of the play means 'anyone' in Kannada. This kills his individuality. With nobody to take care and with enough money to spend and spare, Appanna is an unguided and wayward youth who regularly visits a concubine. Indian society does not take responsibility of such youths so Appanna is not responsible for his lapses too. The character of Rani is however, a portrayal of sufferings due to societal traditions, a conservative society, which believes marriage is not a bond but bondage; to live according to one's husband's life and demands. A Hindu husband can enjoy any liberty. Hindu wives have no voice in anything. The old Indians traditions still continue where the parents fix a match for their daughters with a rich boy with status and marry them off without the consent of the bride and bridegroom. If the boy is found poor in morality, it's the girl's destiny and Rani is the victim of such a concept. The question of Rani's chastity in the play is raised as she is believed to have got her child from the lover-snake. The society elders are ready to examine the chastity of Rani but no one questions Appanna's immoral behaviour. Karnad exposes male chauvinism here. But when Rani's chastity is proven by the snake-ordeal, the attitude of elders suddenly changes, insisting Rani to be a goddess. Her husband too accepts her child but Rani becomes the victim of societal injustice. Besides raising the painful condition of woman in Indian society the author also gives a deep psychological message that in a love triangle none of the persons can be happy. It is another matter that no love exists between Appanna and Rani. The lover-snake is upset to find his lady-love in the arms of somebody else,

"Rani! My queen! The fragrance of my nights! The blossom of my dreams! In another man's arms? In another man's bed?" (42). Strangely, the Naga accepts the situation and withdraws from the contention and it is here that Karnad shows double standards of the society.

The plays of Girish Karnad mirror the contemporary social and political life of his country in a mild satirical style. It is his choice to deal with themes both in his dramas and other literary compositions where social and political ills of the day are satirized, but in a mild way, affording much pleasure for his readers and spectators. He was so effectively inspired by his study of the prevalent English dramas of eminent men-of-letters in England at the Oxford University that he translated his ideas into his own dramas which brought him much popularity.

The subject of *Naga-Mandala* like his other plays reflects the problems and challenges of contemporary life. With the gift of a creative intellectual Karnad views the subjects of his plays from his own imagination and personal experiences. Employing folklore and mythology as a medium to communicate his own independent and original feelings, thoughts, and interpretations, he then forges a link between the past and the present.

Shape-shifting is another device which is very cleverly and effectively used by Karnad as a central structural strategy. *Naga-Mandala* has several examples of shape-shifting. Shape-shifting is the term cultural anthropologists and folklorists use to describe the transformations that are so common in the myths and folklore of most cultures. The result is a confusion of identities which reveals the ambiguous nature of human responsibility. In *Hayavadana*, Padmini seeks a boon from Goddess Kali in order to transpose the heads. In *Tughlaq*, king Tughlaq uses the incredible concentration of power in his hands to effect a change in the capital.

Karnad is a gifted dramatic craftsman whose *Naga-Mandala* is noticeable for consummate excellence of dramatic technique. The flawless plot deals precisely with suspense and surprise to help in its logical development. The characters are correlated and promote the unity of effect. Karnad's English is simple and he has successfully moulded it to express the typical Indian ethos. Commenting on the characteristics of a good plot Henry Arthur Jones says:

> Story and incident and situation in theatrical work are, unless related to character, comparatively childish and unintellectual. This should indeed be only another phase of the development of character.... A mere story, a mere succession of incidents, if these do not embody and display character and human nature, only give you something in raw melodrama, pretty much equivalent to the adventures of our old friend, Mr. Richard Turpin. (186)

Karnad's dramatic technique also includes his use of eloquent language presented with a unique mixture of symbols, idioms and phrases without sacrificing grace. The typical Indian straightforwardness in his style however, showcases rich vocabulary, where an appropriate word for every situation and every character is used. Together with his refined, lucid and precise language Karnad is unsurpassable as a humorist and satirist in modern Indian English drama. He weaves subtle irony in the plot of his plays and skillfully reveals the ludicrous, the grotesque and fantastic inhuman existence. His characters are living characters displaying rich and complex symbolism. Different motifs of an interesting story, an intricate plot, scope for spectacle and dramatic conventions are all interwoven with subtle care in his plays. The dramatic technique in *Naga-Mandala* is an aesthetic experience giving a new lease of life. About this effect on his plays Kirtinath Kurtkoti writes:

> With this new theatre going around them, new playwrights like Girish Karnad have been able to bring to drama a first hand knowledge of the practical demands of the stage and a better understanding of dramatic style and technique. (5)

The function of dramatic art according to Karnad is twofold. It is a means of entertainment as well as a serious work of art with the purpose to explore the duality and complexity of human characters. It focuses on the problems of society especially those that are faced by women. His *Naga-Mandala* leaves his audience thinking and with a sense of satisfaction while coming out after watching his plays. The most sparkling quality of his *Naga-Mandala* is that he does not take his ideas from Western playwrights; his ideas are taken from traditional values and especially from the problems of living men and women in Indian society. It is based on the vision of reality. In this play the presentation is traditional but he presents it with modern dramatic techniques, as R.N. Rai from "Brecht's Non-Aristotelian Theory of Drama and Dramatic Art of Girish Karnad" in *Girish Karnad Naga-Mandala: A Critique* mentions:

> Sometimes he uses chorus or song in order to suspend the flow of dramatic action and provide multiplicity of themes. Music, mime and exotic imagery create vast opportunities for colourful improvisation. He is aware of the importance of stage lighting which has a style and character of its own. Light paints, multiple pictures ebbs and flows with the action in the drama. The use of dimmers, gently fading the lights in or out, provides immense scope for magical possibilities. (133)

The inference to this appraisal draws a beautiful fusion of the traditional and the contemporary; visible in both the content and the form. Aligned together in the play is Karnad's technique of presenting the treatment of plot and theme.

With this play, *Naga-Mandala* Karnad has sought to unfold the mysteries of a woman's heart and the double ending of the play has been admitted with tongue in cheek. Through the ironical ending the dramatist has ventured to awaken the deadened spirits of the male chauvinistic society coupled with communicating the sensitivity of a woman's heart. The emotional-individualistic-self of a woman is usually crushed under heavy synonyms like, goddess, mother, sati, durga, shakti, savitri, sita, idolizing the image of a woman of Indian society, which is ironically a far cry from reality. Left with no other alternative she is left to accept her socially formulated destiny succumbing to the pressures of the male dominated world.

In so far as the play and its assessment are concerned, Karnad has evocatively conveyed the application of traditional to the contemporary times like an astute technical craftsman. But the question is still left to be answered as to how far the Indian woman been able to liberate herself from the clutches of 'man-made' social-taboos and her so called destiny in this contemporary world.

WORKS CITED

Gupta, Santosh. "Naga-Mandala: A Story of Marriage and Love". Ed. Jaydipsinh Dodiya. *The Plays of Girish Karnad: Critical Perspectives*. New Delhi: Sangam Books Limited, 1999.

Hudson, W.H. *An Introduction to the Study of Literature*. New Delhi: Kalyani Publishers Ludhiana, 1978.

Khatri, C.L. *Girish Karnad Naga-Mandala: A Critique*. Bareilly: Prakash Book Depot, 2002.

Karnad, Girish. *Hayavadana*. Madras: Oxford University Press, 1996.

——. *Naga-Mandala: Play With A Cobra*. New Delhi: Oxford University Press, 2002.

Sinha, A.K. "Girish Karnad: Thematic Concerns and Technical Features". Ed. R.K. Dhawan. *New Directions in Indian Drama*. New Delhi: Prestige Books Limited, 2000.

Suneel, Seema. "Girish Karnad's Yayati Reconsidered". Ed. R.K. Dhawan. *New Directions in Indian Drama*. New Delhi: Prestige Books Limited, 2000.

26

Complexities of Human Relationships in Vijay Tendulkar's Play

R. Manjushree

> Vijay Tendulkar is a prolific playwright of Marathi language. He has to his credit twenty-eight full-length plays, twenty-four one-act plays and eleven children's dramas. Most of his plays have been translated into English and in some other languages of India. They are being taught in most of the universities of India. His play *Ghashiram Kotwal* made him a writer of International fame in the mid seventies. *Silence! The Court is in Session* is also a well-known play which earned many laurels not only in India but also in the world. Though some of the plays of Vijay Tendulkar are controversial in theme, yet they are read and enjoyed as they containing a very rich and beautiful literary projection. The beauty in most of his plays lies in lies in Tendulkar's art of dramaturgy, his connotative and metaphoric structure suffused with the colour of some suggestive images and symbol, words and phrases, his extraordinary portrayal of some bitter and harsh truth of life through music and metaphor. (Prasad, 221)

In this background Vijay Tendulkar's *Kamala* is a play which is based on a real life incident. But here Kamala cannot rebel against her condition as we observe in other dramas most often as the suppressed women characters will rise against patriarchal society or against the system. Jaisingh Jadav who has bought Kamala for ₹ 250 at an auction in the market is a journalist. As a journalist he wanted to exhibit Kamala in the press conference and tried to prove that still such a slave system is present in the democratic India. So it's clear that 'Vijay

Tendulkar is known for his concern for burning social problems and anomalies of Indian society and mindset' as said by Shubha Tiwari.

> In most of his plays, Vijay Tendulkar presents women in pairs. They are quite different from each other. He portrays them as loyal, docile, religious, hard working, self-effacing and tender-hearted, the other type of woman is more selfish, wily vicious and assertive. Even then they resemble other in the ultimate truth of being commanded by men, for their pleasure and under their Laws. (Chandra, 2006)

Kamala is a drama with two contrasting characters named Sarita and Kamala, where Sarita is a well educated and self assured woman, wife of Jaisingh Jadav and is childless. While Kamala is illiterate and understands man-woman relationship and says to Sarita:

> Memsahib, if you won't misunderstand, I'll tell you. The master bought you; he bought me, too. He spent a lot of money on the two of us. Didn't he? It isn't easy to earn money. A man has to labour like an ox to do it. So, memsahib, both of us must stay here together like sisters. We'll keep the master happy.... (Adarkar, 35)

After this Sarita started to feel that, she is also a slave in her own house and then decided to leave her husband but when Jadav is betrayed by his editor, she gives him moral support. This shows a compassionate human being in her. In most of Tendulkar's works he deals with different aspect of the human character. In an interview he said, "The history of human culture has taken very complex twists and turns. Yet even today, my inspirational strength lies in the hope with which I look forward to tomorrow. I have consistently depicted the indomitability and grit of the human spirit in my writings. But I have never allowed that to lead me into drawing unreal, comforting conclusions" (Interview with Shirish, 188).

> This statement explains his themes with social and aesthetic ideas of Tendulkar's playwriting. Exploration of woman relationship, Social-individual tensions of the

> society, alienation of the modern individual to contemporary politics as the themes of his plays. His sense of humor and intense compassion are two other hall marks of his creative self. He continues to experiment and explore the potentials of the dramatic genre his primary area of creation. (Chandra, 2006)

Then the question rises about the way in which we look at the issue of tribal identity and the simultaneous construction of an educated humanist subject. Kamala Critiques how these discourses of identity suppress difference, heterogeneity and multiplicity in an effort to maintain hegemonic relations of power. Power works in constructing identities and subjectivities and redefines the culture within the multiplicities of relations of difference. How human beings treat each other and how they try to utilize the opportunity?

> *Sakharam Binder* is Tendulkar's most intensely naturalistic play. According to crititcs, "for many decades no play has created such a sensation in the theatre world of Maharastra as Vijay Tendulkar's Marathi play *Sakharam Binder*. It explores the complication of human nature and the manifestation of physical lust and violence in a human being. After sproduction of *Sakharam Binder* Tendulkar was accused of deliberately choosing sensational themes to get cheap publicity. He says, "Every play is not for everybody," "A play is a work of art when it reveals its theme and essence exclusively through its mode attendant detailing rather than through statement and speech." Sakharam Binder fulfils these criteria and is therefore an artistic play. (Tandon, 158, 2006)

Sakharam Binder is a character in the play *Sakharam Binder* who always tries to criticize the religion and traditional norms which are bounded with everybody's life. Sakharam is against the institution marriage and he says that he gives freedom for women. He gives shelter for women who leave their husbands or women who will be thrown out of the houses by their husbands. By taking up such modern thoughts and realities of life Vijay Tendulkar focuses on the major aspects of human life how human beings create their relationships with each other.

> The play revolves around Sakharam, a binder by profession and a Brahmin by caste. Sakharam ridicules the institution of marriage: the fake respectability of married men and their double standards as they cheat on their wives. He is unmarried and frankly admits that he is a whoremonger and a drunkard. But he is honest and his logic is simple: a man needs sex and housekeeping, a woman needs security. Marriage legitimizes these needs, but it creates gutless men who cheat on their wives. There is no chance for a man to be honest in marriage. So Sakharam rejects marriage in favor of a system of contractual cohabitation with single deserted women. He expects his women to be subservient to him as the owner of the house, to live with him as a wife, and to provide him with every service, including sex—an expectation disturbingly similar to the advice a Hindu bride would get. There is no emotional involvement whatsoever. His expectations are, in fact, no different from traditional Hindu husbands. But unlike a Hindu husband, he does not impose anything on the women. (Cody, 1181)

Vijay Tendulkar brings out these male characters in different ways Jaisingh in *Kamala* and Sakharama in *Sakharam Binder* plays. Both acts as if they give freedom to woman but indirectly they exploit women in the name of liberty.

> …'*Sakharam Binder*' who leave an indelible impression on our mind. These are not just fictional characters but clearly prove Tendulkar's competence in probing and portraying the intricacies of the female mind. (Tandon, 229, 2008)

> His *Sakharam Binder*, first performed in 1972, exploded on the stage like a bomb, its protagonist was the eponymous Sakharam, who debunks all the sacred traditions of the self-righteous Hindu middle class to the point of sacrilege. (Kasbekar, 57)

Sakharam Binder is a person who loves physical pleasure and treats women as without any sentiments or humanity. He behaves very materialistic and thinks only the benefit of keeping those women who are shelter less. It is clear he encashes women's helplessness and their economical weaknesses.

> *Sakharam Binder* (1972), and *Kamala* (1981) are Tendulkar's such plays which deal with sex and violence. The impact of the twin human instincts on social fabric has been the prime concern of the playwright. (Sharma, 50)

Initially in the play *Sakharam Binder*, Sakharam acts as a protagonist. But the play is completely taken over by Laxmi who is very mild and sacrifices herself for everything and acts as the typical religious woman by doing pooja and being honest to her husband and obedient to her master as 'The Angel of the House' termed by Virginia Woolf in her work *A Room of One's Own*. In which a woman is picturised as unselfish, sacrificing and sympathizing. But at the end of the play Laxmi controls the entire situation and rises Sakharam's feelings against Champa saying that Champa has got an affair with Sakharam's friend Dawood. Sakharam who feels aggressive kills Champa and he will be shocked by his own act of killing. Laxmi takes over the entire scene and tries to manage to hide the dead body of Champa.

> The play Sakharam Binder explores the plight of women in all helplessness along with the depiction of complexity of human nature. Sakharam is the protagonist of the play, but the action of the play revolves round the character of Laxmi. (Wadikar, 51)

So the play *Kamala* was inspired by a real life incident—the Indian Express expose by Ashwin Sarin, who actually bought a girl from a rural flesh market and presented at a press conference. Vijay Tendulkar made use of this concept and showed how human beings have already left human values in the name of humanity itself. Though the central character of the play, a self-seeking journalist, Jaisingh Jadav, who treats the woman he has purchased from the flesh market as an object that can procure from him a promotion in his job and a reputation in his professional life. Jaisingh buys, Kamala, an Adivasi woman, at the flesh market for rupees 250. Jaisingh one who wanted to give sensational news to the reporters through Kamala and then he planned to send Kamala to send her to orphanage and wash his hands off her safety. So Jaisingh not only exploits Kamala but also Sarita his wife. Modern men who think that they are liberal minded indirectly exploit women. It can be seen where he puts restrictions on Sarita for each and every thing. Tendulkar is a creative writer with a fine sensibility. He has made a mark in the field of literature and drama, he has given the post-independence Marathi drama a new idiom by doing this he has put Marathi drama on the national and even international map. Tendulkar is one of those dramatists who use their medium in the service of their favourite socio-political ideology. He is not out to propagate any particular philosophy of life. In *Sakharam Binder* play Champa and Laxmi, suffer sexually, physically and psychologically from Sakharam. As it is clear that these two pairs of female characters are depicted in such a way that they are exploited Sarita and Champa whom we feel that they are strong enough to resist but they fail, Kamala and Laxmi who looks innocents but reveals the truth of human life and relationships.

WORKS CITED

Cody, Gabrielle. H, Evert Sprinchorn. *The Columbia, Encyclopedia of Modern Drama*. Volume 2. New York: Columbia University Press, 2007.

Chandra, Anusheel. "Perspectives and Challenges in Indian-English Drama". Neeru Tandon (ed.). *Vijay Tendulkar: A Critical Survey of his Dramatic World*. Delhi: Atlantic Publishers, 2006.

Jain, Sonali. "Muffled voices women in modern Indian literature". Elit Lakshmi Subramanyam (ed.). *Kamala: Within and Beyond*. New Delhi: Har-Anand Publication, 2002.

Kasbekar, Asha. *Pop Culture India: Media, Arts, and Lifestyle*. California: Library of Congress Cataloging-in-press, 2006.

Natak Ani mee, Vijay Tendulkar. *Interview with Shirish Pai, Priya Tendulkar*. Thane: Dimple Publication, 1997, 188.

Prasad, Amarnath. "Indian Literature in English: Critical Assessments". Ajay Kumar Srivastava (ed.). *The Plays of Vijay Tendulkar: A Brief Study*. Vol. I. New Delhi: Sarup and Sons, 2007.

Sharma, Ashok Kumar. "Ghashiram Kotwal: A Study in the Politics of Power and Revenge". Shubha Tiwari (ed.). *Contemporary Indian Dramatists*. New Delhi: Atlantic, 2007.

Tandon, Neeru. *Feminine Psyche—A Post Modern Critique*. New Delhi: Atlantic, 2008.

Tendulkar, Vijay. *'Kamala'*, translated by Priya Adarkar, *Five Plays*. New Delhi: Oxford University Press, 2002.

——. *'Sakharam Binder'*, translated by Kumud Mehta and Shanta Gokhale, *Five Plays*. New Delhi: Oxford University Press, 2002.

Wadikar, Shailaja B. *Vijay Tendulkar: A Pioneer Playwright*. New Delhi: Atlantic, 2008.

27

Indian Theatre of the Roots: *God-Demon* and *Hayavadana*

Lipipuspa Nayak

This paper collates two modern plays: *God-Demon* (2007) by Hrusikesh Panda, a senior playwright and fiction writer from Odisha, and *Hayavadana* (1975), the celebrated Kannada play by Girish Karnad as representative of what the post-colonial literary discourse labels 'the Indian Theatre of the Roots (Crow, Brian and Bansfield, 1996). It amazes me no end that, the plays, separated by a good quarter century, and a spatial and linguistic dislocation that is rather conceited, should have such uncanny parallels in theme and structure. And eventually lure me into this article—an objective evaluation of the plays from a common perspective of the post-colonial dramatic discourse.

The 'Theatre of the Roots' is a genre of plays, that have post-colonial dates of creation, where the playwrights attempt a return to their roots along with a quest for a national and racial identity. This is a form of protest as well as revenge on part of the artist. Return to one's roots, through nostalgic use of historically documented past, nuances of Indian civilization, myths, racial stories, legends, ancient literary sources, local performing arts techniques, indigenous aesthetic principals and structures is a post-colonial syndrome, a base of resistance and recovery of self of the writer against the reality of cultural disruption of colonialism. The plays here are classic representatives of this sub-world of post-independent Indian drama, but this recovery of self, structured in these plays, is not against the cultural disruption of a particular time warp. The plays are dated in the post-colonial times, but transcend the time-warp to understand universal human predicaments and absurdities and make timeless statements on them.

Both the plays are thematically indebted to an early Sanskrit romance: *Kathasaritasagara* by Somadev, a masterpiece that, in my view, also doubles up a critique of the ancient Indian storytelling art. This indebtedness is partial though, for both the playwrights have transcended their original source and made their respective works eternal statements on human predicaments. The section of the source text, here, is *Vetalapanchavimshatika*—a series of stories where a brave, wise, just and adventurous king is fated to answer questions on the incongruities and absurdities of the world—delineated through intricate and absorbing anecdotes—from a ghoul. *God-Demon* (original Odia *Brahmarakshas*, 1997) is sourced after one such story with an ascetic *brahmarakshas*—a god-demon—as the protagonist. A newlywed vainglorious royal couple provokes the wrath of the eponymous demon, Brahmarakshas as they desecrate his abode, a banyan tree, while spending their first nuptial night under it. A *brahmarakshas* is an accursed entity haunted by his sense of unrequited salvation, and is therefore entitled to his demon's brutal might and disposition. But he is also an ascetic as he has a Brahmin's soul and is cursed by Braham, he too is bound by ethics, morality and justness. By performing carnal acts under his abode the royal couple also tamper with his abnegation and austerity and therefore must atone for their sin with the king's life. The queen, a hermit's daughter, borrows from sanctified customs and tradition and pleads for a substitute sacrifice. *Brahmarakshas* agrees, with some gruesome conditions: the substitute sacrifice must be a seventeen-year-old sagacious Brahmin youth who must embrace his status of the sacrifice; the parents must clasp his limbs at the time of sacrifice, the minister must fan him, the queen must embrace him and collect the spurting blood in a skull-bowl after the king beheads the boy. The minister is efficient, and within seven days —the relief granted by Brahmarakshas—Pragalbha, the sacrifice-to-be, is ushered in under the banyan tree and the royal priest performs the propitiatory rites. At the end of it when the king raises his sword Pragalbha, hitherto fearless, composed, cooperating and detached from worldly ties bursts into uproarious, protracted spells of laughter. His laughter weakens

Brahmarakshas, his appetite and his sense of revenge, and the youth is spared.

The original story ends here, with accentuation of the aberrant behaviour of Pragalbha: in the face of ultimate injustice, when incongruities and absurdities sadly fail an innocent person, he can only laugh the laughter of the insane—as he has already tried, without success, the defenses of depression, withdrawal, anger, rebellion, compromise, assimilation. Hrusikesh in *God-Demon* lifts his story beyond this immediate theme of behavioural dynamics of mankind, and expands the possibilities of such a drama and its actors a millennium later. Alongside, the plot also unfolds with a lot of original drama. With some very singular creative strains, the playwright makes a complex contemporary metaphor of the episode in terms of intrigues of politics, loneliness and the resultant sense of resignation of people at the top, the eternal issue of displacement and the subsequent tilted balance in man-nature cohabitation. Pragalbha explains that his uproarious laughter was a natural outcome of his observation of the illusory world and its ways he had been inhabiting so far: the irrational behaviour of his parents who decide to exchange him for a fortune; the newly married who falls in love with him; the selfishness of the king who agrees to sacrifice an innocent youth like him in favour of his life; the royal priest who religiously and unabashedly performs the rituals of sacrifice of an innocent boy like him; the intrigues of the curt where the minister conspires to be the king; Brahmarakshas, immensely powerful with the purity, intellect, abnegation, asceticism and knowledge of a Brahmin is also conscienceless as he is empowered with the might of a demon; and so on. He delivers a long, powerful monologue: "...When an ordinary man, an ordinary man like me faces injustice, what does he do? He becomes sad, depressed, and out of frustration, may become an escapist. He may abandon the battleground. May banish himself. He may commit suicide. When a person like me can maintain a philosophical distance from such injustice, then, he may cogitate with dispassionate intellect: why do things happen the way they do? He chooses a logical step to solve the problem and proceeds along the step. But when the injustice and perversion increases, he becomes anxious and amazed. After suffering one layer of injustice and perversion, he becomes angry, and resorts to violence. His actions are no more logical; they are destructive. With endless sad tears he sails away his sorrows, blaming his fate and the gods. He is acclaimed and made a hero if he succeeds in the rebellion. Perhaps he brings in some changes in the social system. Or in course of time, he too, joins the perpetrators of injustice. If he is defeated, a tragic story comes to an end. But beyond all this, when the social injustice and perversion of judicial systems exceed all realms of logic, cross all limits of reason, then what does a poor simple person like him do? When he fids that the injustice is so absurd that it is beyond all comprehension, then what does he do? Appropriate response, frustration, anger, rebellion—when injustice goes beyond all these reactions, then what does a wretched man do? Except for laughing? This laughter is not a smirk; it is not an abandoned laughter, not the laughter of happiness. It is not a pretended simper, it is not a spontaneous amused laughter, it is not a giggle, it is not a violent or perverse laughter. It is yet another laughter —the spontaneous laughter of a person who is utterly and ultimately helpless, an uproarious laughter [*Pragalbha bursts into roaring laughter*] (59-60).

Brahmarakshas, the violent demon-protagonist of the original is granted a complete cycle of reason in *God-Demon*. The playwright dissects deep into the psyche of the character who must epitomize that kind of violence, which in real may be just a façade. The demon explains why he prefixes the sacrifice and those gory conditions—to teach the participants the distance between political roles and emotional exuberance, as "governance means sin, that does not surrender its conscience completely before the evil spirit; it motivates and compels each and every citizen in the kingdom to surrender his or her conscience," (p. 60) so much so that the parents of a pearl-like boy can trade his life for wealth and prosperity. One of the eternal statements of the play thus comes from a highly resigned, skeptical and near-devastated Brahmarakshas who educates the audience about the way nations and civilizations eventually acquire their fate: "...The world can bear, with difficulty, one or two sinners. But how will the world go on under the rule of a king, who tempts and exhorts the entire citizenry of the entire kingdom along the path of universal sin?" (70-71).

He also champions the cause of environment. A *Brahmaraksbas*, cursed by Brahma, the creator, hangs between the heaven and the earth, and is in a perpetual limbo. He chooses a self-exile away from the worldly life but would hardly find a wood left to inhabit. He, the native, is displaced from his abode and finds his food and dwelling lost to the fancy of the king, the colonizer who hunts and fells trees to create more landmass—to satisfy his monarchical arrogance. This happens alongside a violation of the demon's peace, abnegation and distance from the political and economic society. He becomes a metaphor of the archetypal aborigine who gets displaced by colonial exploitation, but who also 'speaks back as the subaltern': "Ha, ha! You can argue, I see. Very good. Excellent! This suits royalty. Ethics of all kinds of warfare is defeated here. We dark-skinned people, honored you like a guest, and you snatched away governance from us through conspiracy! When we gathered to greet you, you had already conspired and taken away our lands. When we became independent again and asked for our lands, you taught us your religion and rules...you have exploited us a lot..." (19-20).

In the process we are exposed to his sad predicament: he is a sad loner in a world of utter insensitivity; a world wrapped up in rhetoric and semantic expostulation, rites and rituals. He is distanced from the society, is powerless, like the intellectuals and opinion makers of a society and eventually ends up a man at the top. Even his relapse into subaltern savagery and violence, in the execution of the sacrifice, too fails as Pragalbha, the sacrifice, outshines him in both wisdom and a sense of detachment from worldly matters and ties rather unusual for his age. His hurt moves the audience: "Yes Pragalbha! I am ashen with the smoke of remorse and repentance. I wish I could have been reduced to ashes.... This world will not change much. May be, there will be small changes. A minister may be killed by a kotwal. You intelligentsia and elites, you banished me.

Because I was such a storm in your world that it would have upstaged your existence. I am not surprised. Nor am I very sad. I have crossed the age of being surprised or sad" (p. 66).

And his loneliness is poignant, real and infectious: "Of what use will be the elucidation of my life, someone unknown, a sylvan demon like me, and for whom, in this modern and civilized world—I cannot understand. Aloneness is about absence, about something not being there, about deprivation. If anything fills up this vacuousness, even if meagerly, it is my life. How lonesome is my life! Even a bird does not talk to me, because I am a demon...how will this long and helpless life of darkness drag along, bearing the heavy burden of the wisdom of an ascetic and the might of a demon? I am alone in the branches and leaves in this terrifying darkness of night. If only I could be afraid, time would elapse! But whom can I fear, I the god-demon? No, my intense, ruthless, endless days and nights go unspent. A boat can cross a river, but can a boat hop from one leaf to another?... Damp and soggy clouds and fog are my only guests. Even the most ominous beasts and birds are frightened to come near me. I have been banished by Brahma. Silence is my only rosary that I count endlessly. The only burden on my back is the sin of others [*Points to all with his hands. Everyone hangs his/her head. Except Pragalbha.*]" (pp. 67-68).

The play owes a lot of its power to these lofty and poignant monologues, that leave the audience with a haunting sense of melancholy. Yet, Hrusikesh leaves a scope for hope in the play even when he transposes an ancient, picaresque story to the current, turbulent times. He develops the character of Pragalbha to that height where he both complements and outgrows Brahmarakshas. Pragalbha spells hope against the ineluctable tragic helplessness of Brahmarakshas; with his youth, courage, wisdom, uprightness, perseverance, righteousness, even a quaint sense of humor he makes the world a little liveable and provides the audience with the much required catharsis and purgation through his prolonged monologues on social justice and the ways of the world: "Fearlessness! Again! And you grant it to me? I didn't have fear, so why do I need fearlessness? What is its relevance? And you give it away as a grant? How can you,

O Brahmarakshas, grant something that you don't own? Leave it. [*Pause*] many questions have been posed to me. I will try to answer them with the little knowledge I have. Please forgive me if I commit any mistake, learned assembly!" (p. 55).

Hayavadana is an extended metaphor of complexities in human relationships and the primordial psychic-existential dilemma of one-upmanship of intellect over body. The play explores the possibilities to present this dilemma, with powerfully delineated details of human behaviour and action when a man is haunted by a crisis of identity: what should identify his persona—his body or his head that houses the intellect, and which eventually will endear him to a woman? The thematic content is portrayed through the absurd situation of the behaviour of two different persons when their heads get swapped. The original source—a depiction of a love triangle among three characters: Devadatta, Kapila and Padmini—underscores the triumph of the head over the body; the head, the nest to the intellect, and not the body, must identify a person. Two close friends, Kapila, an ironsmith with the body of the perfect male and Devadatta, the scholar and poet with the perfect head of intellect, Scriptural knowledge and wisdom are the best of friends—'one mind one soul' as Bhagavata, the omniscient narrator in the play swears repeatedly. The friends, we are told, can die for each other. This friendship somehow obscures after Devadatta marries Padmini, a ravishing beauty from the lane of the merchants, because with time Kapila and Padmini develop intimacy. Padmini is drawn towards the macho body of Kapila, and Kapila as the matchmaker for Devadatta has been smitten with Padmini's beauty from the beginning. Devadatta had pledged his head and arms to lord Rudra and goddess Kali in the woods as a precondition to his successful betrothal of Padmini, a pledge that remains overshadowed and unanswered in the immediate excitement and bliss of marriage. It comes alive to him in a state of acute mental agony, spawned out of the inevitable bouts of jealousy for Kapila as well as in understanding of the inescapability of the desires of the body. Along a journey to Ujjain by the trio he remembers his pledge to the deities, visits the goddess alone and offers her his head.

Kapila in search of his closest friend too reaches the venue, is inconsolable about his friend's plight and beheads himself. Padmini goes looking for the men, finds their trunks and severed heads and decides to hack her head, when the goddess manifests and in a feminist bonhomie grants her the boon of the lives of the men. She asks her to attach the heads to the trunks, a task Padmini botches up by swapping the heads and the bodies—Kapila's head on the trunk of Devadatta and Devadatta's head on Kapila's. Both men stir back to life, and to the bizarre reality of their disjointed existential predicament; the crux of which eventually tells on Padmini—with whom will she go home now? Both the men claim her; go to a sage for a verdict and the sage divines: Devadatta is the person who carries Devadatta's head and rightfully deserves Padmini as wife, since head is the ultimate identity of a person's persona and it outweighs the body's stake to the same always.

The source of Hayavadana, Karnad's play, exhausts at this point probably, the sage's verdict mirrors the original expostulation the king had extended the ghoul. The absurd dilemma the friends have been thrown into for no fault of theirs. Karnad, however, extends the plot along a logical unfolding of flux: what bodily and behavioural possibilities those swapped personalities may experience and exhibit till their last breaths? The feeling of incompletion acts as a corollary to the issue of identity; will the bodies, with the other's head on each, behave like their person? Kapila (the head of Kapila on Devadatta's trunk) goes away into the forest, an act of self-exile, as he loses to Devadatta his claim for Padmini. Devadatta (the head of Devadatta on Kapila's trunk) is decreed to escort Padmini back home. Padmini is benefitted, with the best bargain—the best head on the best body—a neo-feminist stand protractedly evident in the play.

Initially the bodies experience their genetic disposition; Devadatta (with Kapila's body) indulges in physical maneuverings—wrestling, swimming—like Kapila and Kapila tries his hand at writing verses, carrying along a delicate body: "When this body came to me, it was like a corpse hanging by my head. It was a Brahmin's body after all—not made for the woods. I could not lift an axe without my elbows moaning. Could not run a length without my knee howling. I had no use for it. The moment it came to me, a war started between us..." (p. 55).

Karnad presents this complex theme powerfully, with a look for the minutest of details of human action and behaviour in such abstract eventuality. With time, the behaviour of the person has change, the force of the body weakens and the head begins to overtake. Kapila with the burden of Devadatta's sensitive body, is finally acted upon by the dictates of his head, and avows that the head must always win: "Now I can run ten miles and not stop for breath. I can swim through the monsoon floods and fell a banyan. The stomach used to rebel once—now it digests what I give. If I don't, it doesn't complain" (p. 56).

And with this gradual confounding of what had appeared to be an answer to the dilemma, that the head always triumphs over the body, the audience is led along another maze of events. The plot thickens further. Padmini is no more enamored with Devadatta, as the force of his body is slowly giving in, and goes and finds out Kapila. In a run up to another crescendo, Kapila asks Padmini why she has come to him again when he has been trying to uproot the memories of his body: "Why should one tolerate this mad dance of incompleteness? One beats the body into shape, but one can't beat away the memories in it. Isn't it surprising? That the body should have its own hosts—its own memories? Memories of touch—memories of *a* touch—memories of a body swaying in these arms..." of a warm skin against this palm—memories which one cannot recognize, cannot understand, cannot even name because this head wasn't there when they happened..." (pp. 57-58).

So the original dilemma returns to where it had begun—the friends slowly are dictated upon by the memories of their bodies, resume their race for Padmini, get into a duel and die. Padmini witnesses the macabre event, leaves her son with Bhagavata, with the request to reach him to his grandfather's house five years down and embraces self-immolation as a married, chaste woman. Her act may be a parody of the once prevalent social custom (her speech to the goddess at page 63 is enough evidence of it), which provides the play a theatrical element; but she has no alternative in any case, like earlier. Only this time she does not evoke the life-instilling power of the goddess. Before she rides into the pyre, she makes a dying statement—the final statement of the play, on the complex absurdities of the body-head duel, the subsequent haunting sense of incompleteness and human behaviour: "They burned, lived, fought, embraced and died. I stood silent. If I'd said, 'yes, I'll live with you both', perhaps they would have been alive yet. But I couldn't say it...I know it in my blood you couldn't have lived together. You would've had to share not only me but your bodies as well..." (p. 62).

However, *Hayavadana*—the best of Karnad's plays in terms of dramaturgy as I consider it—owes its brilliance largely to its powerful prologue where this narrative of incompletion has been transplanted to the existential predicament of a horse-headed man. This is a parallel plot in the play, which the playwright has invented independent of the source text and has blended into the fabric of the play, and is not a sub-plot as critics point out. As Bhagavata prepares to relate the tale of the swapped heads after the customary invocation to lord Ganesha, Hayavadana, the eponymous protagonist with a man's body and a horse's head enters the stage and shares with the actors his embarrassing, sad and absurd existential quandary and pleads for a reprieve. He also shares, in a mixed surreal and neo-real dramatic setup, his birth details, his unsuccessful trysts with the religious shrines to overcome his tragedy, and his subsequent recourse into causes of national values, such as patriotism, ecology, and so on. The Bhagavata empathizes with his condition, and directs him to the temple of goddess Kali with one of the actors as his escort. In fact the creation of his character, abrupt and with the air of a passing theatrical material, does not impinge into the central plot in the beginning and with his departure obliterates. It is only when the play appears to be ending, after the cathartic act of *sati* by Padmini, he resurfaces, and the audience awakes to another climax. This time he is a complete horse, though still haunted by his inborn burden of deficiency with his human voice. In an environ of reversals where the stage exhibits lighthearted dramatics and Hayavadana upsets his values and beliefs, he blares aloud the national anthem so that it may ruin his voice and get that closer to a horse's. To all this farcical events on stage, is entwined the presence of Padmini's boy, silent, sulky and serious. Finally the boy speaks and laughs when Hayavadana shares the completeness of his form with the actors and bursts into guffaws. They strike a bond and as he obliges the repeated demands from the boy to laugh, his laughter metamorphose to a horse's neigh. Perhaps the child is predisposed with the wisdom of his father, and with the intriguing history of his birth is disinterested in the world in the beginning. Perhaps, again, he identifies a flash of his own birth history with Hayavadana's exotic yet sad account of birth and befriends him. Or, as a child he merely finds a laughing horse too tempting to hold back his power of articulation or emotion.

The plays engage powerful dramaturgy where genres of theatrical modes blend to present reality on stage: surreal, neo-real, non-naturalistic, real, melodrama, high drama, parody, mime, archetypes.... The ancient literary archetypes, particularly in matters of christening characters or religious practices, make a comeback. The king in *God-Demon* is named Chandrabaloka; Devadatta in *Hayavadana* is a Brahmin youth of unassailable wisdom; an ancient, humble kingdom ought to be named Dharmapura, the *brahmarakshas* is named Jwalamukha, a sagacious Brahmin youth who can defeat everyone in reasoning is called Pragalbha, and so on.... But of course Padmini, who causes her husband and her lover to die twice each, and commits a *sati*, brilliantly crowns this cycle of parody—'Padmini' is the supreme category of women as described in the Indian treatises on amatory. The cast is a mix of human, non-human, and divine entities. It is a whole huge world of make-believe, where a *brahmarakshas* materializes on stage, not with a mask on, but with a massively-built dark form, loud archetypal make-up and macabre jewelry of skull-head garland (I was among the audience on several performances). A royal couple walks the stage in a neo-real ambience. In the same vein, a horse-headed man, and later a complete horse appear and perform on the stage. Rites and rituals of a real sacrifice are performed. The stagecraft crescendo to conduct a real beheading, which of course does not take place, but which does build up a high decibel tension among the audience. Beheadings do take place in *Hayavadana*, where the playwright resorts to an assorted theatrical devise of local performing arts and folk elements: curtains, masks, mime, the Bhagavata—the omniscient narrator as a crucial character. But he impedes neither the neo-real nor the surreal theatricalities of the stage and is seamlessly woven into the structural ambience. *God-Demon* with a number of issues—ethics, morality, governance, civilizational mores, errors of history, loneliness of people at the top—to address, enacts them in a neo-realistic manner through high gripping drama in several crescendos. Not once the play loses its grip on the audience. With an ostensibly classical structure and theme, the play uses *hastamudra*s, songs based on Indian classical *raga*s, lofty and long dialogues and a chaste idiom. Only Gopalia, the ordinary citizen who does not belong in the scheme of grandness of the play, speaks a colloquial tongue and pulls away the audience from the world of make-believe. He, though small in stature in the play, does have a counterpart in the Bhagavata in this particular context. Both are real characters.

Extreme care goes into the development and evolution of the characters in the plays. Even minor characters, despite their appearance as fillers, are treated with dramatic aesthetics of very high quality. They are assigned dialogues and songs essential to the plot and its unfolding. Padmini's state of disillusionment and handicap to manage life with Devadatta, after the swapping of the heads, has been presented through the symbolic choric songs of the stagehands and musicians. Gopalia, the simpleton who is the only ordinary citizen in the game of governance, raises the most sensitive question: "Alas! If only this Sudarshan Chakra were destroying the sinners!" (p. 4) in the beginning to —"You smile and keep smiling like Lord Krishna in Puri paintings. Why don't you say anything lord?" (p. 65) towards the end. He and the royal priest, who executes the act of the sacrifice, are the only characters who do not contribute to the process of transgression. The concept of the substitute sacrifice

—the crux of the plot—comes from Indibaraprabha, a hermit's daughter who has married the king only the previous day. The irony heightens when she finds the gory conditions of the demon of no particular cruelty. Her character further transforms when she is attracted to the sacrifice within a week of her marriage and queen-hood. Her behaviour baffles even Pragalbha, the wisehead who has a sage like detachment for worldly ties and bonds: "...The God-Demon did not ask you to fall in love with me. You had no political compulsion to fall in love with me. Yet you fell in love with me...I was amazed to think—why does an adolescent girl, married seven days back, fall in love with a man, who is about to die? And you vowed to collect the blood from my severed neck and offer it to the god-demon! What kind of love did you love Indibaraprabha? Why were you so attracted towards me? [*Slowly, uttering every word clearly*] The way a dying man enamours?" (pp. 57-58).

Or perhaps, with her upbringing in a world of austerity and rites and rituals, she is expected to have knowledge of sanctified customs and Scriptural practices, and her offering the idea just provides structural coherence to the plot. I would however grant her action the extreme possibility: she is avenging the insatiable royal lust. As Pragalbha tells her: "No, no, don't bow down your head. I am not talking of chastity or sin. This king has seen many a woman; he will see many more women in future, he will enjoy many more women..." (p. 65). Padmini in *Hayavadana* is developed along the same neo-feminist vein. She is unabashed in her avowal of Kapila's body of muscles: "[*Watching him, to herself*] How he climbs—like an ape. Before I could even say 'yes', he had taken off his shirt, pulled his dhoti up and swung up the branch. And what an ethereal shape! Such a broad back—like an ocean with muscles rippling across it—He is like a Celestial Being reborn as a hunter.... How his body sways, his limbs curve—it's a dance almost. No woman could resist him...and then that small feminine waist which looks so helpless (the last one is a reference to Devadatta)" (p. 25).

Her character becomes more convincing as the play juxtaposes her flamboyance with Devadatta's increasing sense of insecurity towards their relationship. He, "comely in appearance, fair in colour, unrivalled in intelligence, the only son of the revered Brahmin Vidyasagara, the apple of every eye in Dharmapura..." (p. 2) in the beginning of the play, almost falls from grace, rather steadily, as he fights his bouts of jealousy over Padmini's proximity to Kapila. At one point he reduces to a bundle of pathetic sentimentalism and becomes laughable. The decimation of his character is not due to his jealousy of Kapila's body—he is entitled to a normal human emotion— but because he nullifies his reason with which he once "had failed the mightiest pundits of the kingdom in debates on logic and love" (p. 20). Padmini must not be repentant of her behaviour and action because Devadatta, whom she had married for his erudition, can no more stake claim to that. He had always lost his body to Kapila now he has lost his reason and mind while Kapila has not faltered in his character.

The neo-feminist viewpoint in the plot comes a full circle when in a quasi-farcical dramatic denouement leading up to another climax; Goddess Kali salvages her of her apparent sense of guilt. Padmini's guilt is more fear and anxiety driven: "...How can I go home? Home? And what shall I say happened? And who'll believe me? They will say the two fought and died for this whore. They are bound to say it. Then what will happen to me? No, Mother Kali, no,—it's too horrible to think of. No! Kapila's gone—Devadatta's gone. Let me go with them [*Picks up the sword.*]" (p. 31). Yet the goddess materializes at her plight, and in a feminine solidarity even ignores her selfishness and puts life back into the bodies, but not before grudging them their falsehood, hypocrisy and chauvinism: "The rascals! They were lying to their last breaths. That fellow Devadatta—he had once promised his head to Rudra and his arms to me! Think of it—head to him and arms to me! Then because you insisted on going to the Rudra temple, he comes here and offers his head. Nobly too—wants to keep his word, he says—no other reason!

"Then this Kapila. Died right in front of me—but 'for his friend'. Mind you! Didn't even have the courtesy to refer to me. And what lies! Says he is dying for friendship. He must have known perfectly well he would be accused of killing Devadatta for you. Do you think he wouldn't have grabbed you if it hadn't been for that fear? But till his last breath—'Oh my friend! My dear brother!'

"Only you spoke the truth...because you're selfish—that's all..." (p. 33). Padmini delivers the final celebratory statement of her triumph: "Fabulous body—fabulous brain-fabulous Devadatta." Even with her act of *sati*—self-immolation of a married woman dedicated to her husband after the husband's death, later in the play she does not descend to a pathetic character. In the still prevailing mock-heroic ambience, and in the absence of any tragic sentimentalism, she has not been treated as the victim of a once cruel practice of a patriarchal social set-up; she dies on her own self—a woman who epitomized frankness and honesty in the matter of her sexuality and eventually is immortalized in the sensuous full-blossomed tree of the Fortunate Lady in the woods.

The readers may find a miniscule speck of Brahmarakshas in Goddess Kali—her very brief appearance notwithstanding—particularly in the context of their decimation. Brahmarakshas, banished from the civilized society has opted a self-exile, but finds his life has become insufferable and is futilely in search of a wilderness. Kali is a marginalized goddess in the Hindu pantheon and is often portrayed in a negative light, with her propensity for bloodshed and violence. In a rare flash of brilliance, and with brevity, Karnad upsets this archetype; he not only makes her a life-giver, but lends the goddess an undiscerning sense of benevolence: "Thousands used to flock her temple once. No one goes now, though...she used to give anything anyone asked for. As the people became aware of this they stopped going" (p. 100). And yet she is indifferent to the decline in her status and ends up a savior. Interestingly, both the characters relapse to deep and prolonged spells of slumber in the plays, as if to fight their existential angst.

As a creative work of art, *God-Demon,* with its massive thematic and dramatic possibilities and explorations, is a metaphor in grandness. The thematic scope of *Hayavadana* is rather restricted. Yet, with its powerfully sustained storyline of multiple climaxes, complex dramaturgy, attention to details in treatment of the content, non-naturalistic stagecraft of folk ingredients and practices, songs that are metaphors to the episodes on stage, humour, comicality and mock-heroic characters, I will rate this classic among the best of Indian plays, alongside *God-Demon*. My opinion is that the excellence of *Hayavadana* lies more in its parallel plot of the horse-headed man, which is the creative invention of the playwright. Meant to heighten the metaphor of incompletion of the central plot, it cannot, obviously, have an autobiographical overtone about it, but its protagonist is unambiguously the instrument both to trumpet and carry out at various levels Karnad's ideology as an artist. Throughout the play the playwright makes furtive references to plays that make audience doze off during performances. A character like a horse-headed man and a complete horse with a human's voice, despite the obvious limitations in their stageability, will definitely ensure the attention and participation of the audience. And the parallel plot has been designed such that it ensconces the central plot, so as to disprove the apprehension of the Bhagavata: "And there is our large-hearted audience, it may be that they fall asleep during a play sometimes" (pp. 3, 7). At another level Hayavadana steps out of the limited scope of his character he had been conceived with and critiques the notions on arts, literature and national prosperity hitherto held sanctified. In the last major dialogue, almost a parting one, he objects to the absurd experience a child is exposed to with the burden of memory of a depressing song as a lullaby. His resentment is downplayed by Bhagavata, the symbol of institutions of society and perhaps their infallibility: "What is their in a song, Hayavadana? The real beauty lies in the child's laughter—in the innocent joy of that laughter. No tragedy can touch it" (p. 70). To which Hayavadana responds stoically—perhaps a veiled laconic protest of the playwright: "To be honest, Mr Bhagavata Sir, I have my doubts about this theory. I believe—in fact I may go so far as to say I firmly believe—that it's this sort of sentimentality which has been the bane of our literature and national life. It has kept us of accepting Reality and encouraged escapism. Still, if you say so, I won't argue. Come, child, let's have another song" (p. 70).

And this consolidates my opinion further.

WORKS CITED

Crow, Brian and Chris Bansfield. '*Girish Karnad and an Indian Theatre of Roots*' in an *Introduction to Postcolonial Theatre*, New York: CUP, 1996. 136-60.

Karnad, Girish. *Hayavadana* (Eng. Tr. Girish Karnad) Calcutta: Oxford University Press, 1975.

Panda, Hrusikesh. *Brahmarakshas* (Eng. Tr. *God-Demon*, Lipipuspa Nayak). New Delhi: Sahitya Academi, 2007.